FOUNDATIONS
OF MODERN
EDUCATION

STUDY THE PA

FOUNDATIONS OF MODERN EDUCATION

RYLAND W. CRARY and
LOUIS A. PETRONE

 Alfred A. Knopf New York

ACKNOWL-
EDGMENTS

We wish to express our appreciation for permission to quote:

From *Classroom Management* by William Bagley. Copyright © 1922 by The Macmillan Company. Reprinted by permission of William C. Bagley, Jr.

From OLD FAVORITES FROM THE MC-GUFFEY READERS by H. C. Minnich. Copyright © 1936 by American Book Company. Reprinted by permission.

From TMI-Grolier Programmed Textbook *General Science, Biology, and Chemistry* by Schaefer, Jeffries, Harakas and Glaser. Copyright © 1967 by Grolier Inc. Reprinted by permission of Grolier Inc.

From OLD FAVORITES FROM THE MC-chine, *Course TM-101, Modern English: Spelling,* by Lyn Sandow. Copyright © 1968 by Grolier Inc. Reprinted by permission of Grolier Inc.

From HUMANIZING THE SCHOOL, by Ryland Crary. Copyright © 1969 by Alfred A. Knopf, Inc. Reprinted by permission of the publisher.

From ARITHMETIC OF COMPUTERS by Norman A. Crowder and Grace C. Martin. Copyright © 1960 by U.S. Industries, Inc. (Tutor Text Series). Reprinted by permission of Doubleday & Company, Inc.

From pp. 85–86 in PHILOSOPHY OF EDUCATION: Learning and Schooling, by Donald Arnstine.
Copyright © 1967 by Donald Arnstine

Reprinted by permission of Harper & Row, Publishers, Inc.

From "Attitudes Towards Labor" by Robert E. Doherty, published in *The School Review,* vol. 71 (Spring, 1963). Reprinted by permission of *The School Review* and The University of Chicago Press.

For the interview excerpts appearing here on pages 363–364, 1971. Columbia Broadcasting System, Inc. All Rights Reserved.

Published with the permission of Columbia Broadcasting System, Inc. From an interview conducted by Mike Wallace on the television program CBS EVENING NEWS WITH WALTER CRONKITE broadcast on November 24, 1969.

Tables:
Table 1: Adapted from estimated figures from 1968 NEA Research *Bulletin,* p. 12. Reprinted by permission of the National Education Association.

Table 5: "State Income and Educational Expenditures" adapted from the 1968 publication *What Everyone Should Know About School Financing* by the National Education Association. Reprinted by permission of the National Education Association.

Table 6: "Percent of Revenue for Public Elementary and Secondary Schools from State Governments, 1967–1968" from page 47 of the 1968 publication *What Everyone Should Know About School Financing* by the National Education Association. Reprinted by permission of the National Education Association.

Table 7: "Percentage of Superintendents and Board Members Exposed to Specific Pressures" adapted from *Who Runs Our Schools?* by Neal Gross. Copyright © 1958 by John Wiley and Sons. Reprinted by permission of the author.

Table 8: "Percentage of Superintendents and Board Members Pressured by Specified Sources" adapted from *Who Runs Our Schools?* by Neal Gross. Copyright © 1958 by John Wiley and Sons. Reprinted by permission of the author.

Table 9: "Responses (in percents) of Two Groups of Students to Items on a Labor-Management Scale" from "Attitudes Towards Labor" by Robert E. Doherty. Published in *The School Review,* vol. 71 (Spring, 1963). Reprinted by permission of *The School Review* and The University of Chicago Press.

Table 10: "Major Problems" from the NEA Research *Bulletin* 46:4 (December, 1968). Reprinted by permission of the National Education Association.

Figures:
Figure 1: "Major Foundation Grants" from *The Chronicle of Higher Education,* November 3, 1969. Reprinted by permission of *The Chronicle of Higher Education.*

Figure 2: "Status of Major Legislation" from *The Chronicle of Higher Education,* November 3, 1969. Reprinted by permission of *The Chronicle of Higher Education.*

Figure 3: "What States Spend, per Capita, for Higher Education" from *The Chronicle of Higher Education,* October 27, 1969. Reprinted by permission of *The Chronicle of Higher Education.*

Photo credits:
Chapters 1, 2, 3, 5, 7, 8, 10, 12, 13, 14, 15: reprinted by permission of *The Point,* Charles Robb, Editor-in-Chief.

Chapter 4: photo courtesy *Schoolhouse,* produced by the Joint Research Project: Aluminum Company of America; Eggers and Higgins, architects; and Walter McQuade.

Cover and Chapter 6: by George Gardner.

Chapter 9: reprinted by permission of the University of Pittsburgh, Office of Information Services.

Title page, Introduction and Chapter 11: by Charles Gatewood.

PREFACE

This book is intended for use in basic courses, perhaps the first course, in a teacher education program. It does not presume to be an "introduction to education." We were all introduced to education in the formal sense, probably about the age of five or six, and to human learning with the very dawn of consciousness. Neither is it a "principles of education" text. For one thing that sounds pretty didactic. It sounds as though the principles of education were fully known and agreed upon, and that we knew them thoroughly and could convey them intact to the reader. But that is really not the case.

Most of the principles of education are in dispute and have been throughout the ages. To give the student a neat set of established dicta is to do him a dual disservice. It diminishes the scene, obscures the totality, censors out much that is real, and it denies him a preview of the aspect of education most attractive to lively people, the fact that the view of the schools, its ways and its purposes, is at the very center of the most vital social and philosophical controversy of our time.

So we choose to call the work *foundational*. It is groundwork for knowing and entering a lively profession. We also call it *modern*, for we have tried to address it to the real issues, to place its emphasis not only where the action is, but where it appears likely to be. Being modern does not in our view mean standing naked in the contemporary scene. Modern man is cloaked in culture. Culture has its origins which bear upon the pres-

ent human condition. Thus to be foundational means to bring
history and philosophy to bear. But this work is not a history and
philosophy of education. It is not intended as an effete cultural excursion into the lore of education as an end in itself. Rather it attempts to draw upon these studies to illuminate the contemporary
and to give depth and pertinence to present issues.

The work is necessarily interdisciplinary. Beyond history and
philosophy, the writers have drawn upon sociology, economics, psychology, anthropology, and political science. This is not to demonstrate that the social sciences can be useful, which needs no proof, but
simply to use them. But the subject is education, and the focus is on
the school.

In a sense all matters human bear upon education. The authors
would, therefore, be grateful to be possessed of a universally encompassing erudition. This would, indeed, be useful, but it is not claimed.
Hence, we have given scrupulous attention to the phrasing of unanswered questions and to the selection of our reading lists. These are
intended to be guides to inquiry, not academic window dressing. The
work is intended to be, perhaps most of all, *foundational* to inquiry
about education. If it serves our purpose well, it will be useful
throughout the student's teacher education; if it arrives where our
fondest hopes would have it, it will serve him throughout his career in
education.

In a word, though our aim is to be readable and sensible, we do not
blush at our effort to put an intellectual press on the student. We
have written, wishing at every turn that we knew much more. It will
do no harm if reading the book induces some of the same feeling in
the student.

We know we do not start from scratch with students in examining
issues relevant to education. That is where the students live these
days. Bureaucracy, dehumanization, Vietnam, student power, teacher
power, black power—these are already words with rich emotional con-
notations to students. Our observation causes us to place our bet
with confidence that we are truly dealing with a new breed of prospective teachers.

This new breed, to survive in the schools and to help remake them
into true institutions of education, must have more than high morale,
an evocative vocabulary, good will, and a bag of tricks. The ills besetting the society and the school are profound. The worker in the
school will either be victim to these ills or contributor to them, unless
he most profoundly understands the nature of the institution and the
roots of its troubles.

Therefore, this work tries to go beyond analysis and diagnosis. It
attempts to help the student discover the ways to new effective institutional attitudes and behaviors. It seeks to build foundations for a
more effective social process within the school. It assumes that persons bent on teaching are today very aware of what they are up

against.   We assume serious-mindedness and try to respond to it; we do not patronize by presuming to teach it.   The prospects in education are exciting, even when realistically assessed, for those who will do a man-sized job in the schools.   Education is on the verge of becoming a true profession.   If a realistic appraisal of conditions and prospects discourages some, we think that likely to have been a service both to those persons and to the schools.

The writers, in company with all sensible men, are troubled by the times in which we write.   Troubled, but not dismayed.   We write in confidence that the school can become much more than it is; it is a sober judgment to say that it will have to.

So, in the final sense of the matter, this book is *foundational* in one more way: it tries to build foundations of competence for entering the school with a profound understanding of what it means to be a professional in education.

CONTENTS

FOUNDATIONS
OF MODERN
EDUCATION

INTRO-
DUCTION:
WHERE THE
ACTION IS

the accomplishment: an introduction

Our schools have kept us free. This is the seasoned judgment of the great historian and social critic Henry Steele Commager. This accomplishment is proof of the soundness of the view that an intimate relationship exists between democracy and education. It was the view of the "founding fathers," and it was the twentieth-century view of John Dewey, greatest of American educator-philosophers, who gave an outstanding work that very title—*Democracy and Education.*

Education in America has other, though not unrelated, goals; one of the prime aims being to help people "get ahead in the world." The universal school has constituted a veritable ladder of success, a basic instrument of social mobility, as it were. Thus, when equality of opportunity is stressed, a first emphasis is likely to be placed on equality of educational opportunity. Conversely, when limitations upon equal opportunity are noted, critics generally focus their attention first upon the failures or derelictions of the schools. Such criticism is fair and justifiable, for in a society committed to practical democratic values good schools for *all* the children are a basic requirement.

In the year of this writing it would be ludicrous to assert that all is well with the schools. In reality, education is in crisis, and its future is not assured. All is not well with the world. You and we, the authors, are well aware of that fact. No matter how well the schools have performed, they will have to do better, much better. Quite possibly to do better they

will have to do less of certain things than they are now doing and, perhaps, to cease doing some things altogether. Furthermore, some
critics and a considerable body of evidence suggest that the schools
are not doing some things that they ought to do, and even claim to do,
well at all. None of these realities will be glossed over in this volume.

The introductory emphasis upon accomplishment, therefore,
should be taken as a fair acknowledgment of achievement within a
very sobering context.

Nonetheless, a most dramatic and significant achievement of the
American educational enterprise has been that *it has made excellence
commonplace.* This assertion flies in the face of charges by critics
that the very universality of American education necessarily causes a
general debasement of standards. These critics sometimes moderate
their view by admitting a general *quantitative* uplift, but they continue
to press their contention of a pervasive *qualitative* deterioration effect.

But the evidence does not bear out this view. For example, in
recent years many prestige institutions of higher learning (such as
Michigan, Harvard, California, Stanford, Pittsburgh, and Columbia)
have substantially raised their entrance requirements (usually expressed in terms of S. A. T. scores). If the lower schools had indeed
been guilty of a general leveling downward, this demand for excellence
(expressed in academic achievement terms) could have resulted in
but one outcome—a reduced enrollment in freshman classes at these
institutions. Such was not the case. These same institutions were
able to raise standards, yet increase the size of their entering classes,
and still be forced by press of numbers to turn away thousands of
qualified applicants. The latter, in turn, by seeking other collegiate
residence could leaven other campuses with the now abundant yeast
of high qualification.

Harvard University may be fairly taken as a symbol for high academic standards. Yet, an official of Educational Testing Services asserts from test evidence that the nation's schools turn up 50,000 boys
annually capable of meeting the rigid entrance requirements of that
university.

A homelier illustration may lend weight to our argument. In the
early 1920s Charley Paddock enjoyed the designation of the World's
Fastest Human. Indeed he was, and he seldom found himself in close
company when he broke the tape at the end of the 100-yard dash in
9.6 seconds. This was excellence, and it was rare. A 9.6-second "hundred" is still fast running. It is excellent, but it is by no means the
record—nor unique, nor even particularly rare. In fact, today in a
state *high school* meet two or three boys may break the tape in a
photo finish at a faster time. The clock runs no slower than in the
twenties; the standard of excellence has been raised, not debased, and
many more meet or exceed it. Thus, extended educational opportunity
(in this case, physical education) indeed, makes excellence not merely
commonplace but more excellent still. So much for the contention of

the elitist critic that universal, democratic education necessarily degrades standards, shortens yardsticks, and conduces to a common mediocrity

Just what is the process involved in universal education? Thomas Gray in his *Elegy in a Country Churchyard* (1750) spoke of the phenomenon of wasted, unrecognized talent in these terms:

Full many a gem of purest ray serene
The dark unfathomed caves of ocean bear:
Full many a flower is born to blush unseen,
And waste its sweetness on the desert air.

Universal education—disdaining elitist notions that talent is both sacred and confined to a few families, classes, places, and races—casts its nets ever more broadly. It reaches out, furnishes nurture to the very broadly distributed human talent. Its defect lies not in its universal reach, but in its inability to reach certain neglected segments of the community. Even when its search does extend to this segment, it is only a "feeler." The corollary may then be stated: *the larger the democratic outreach of education, the larger will be the discovery of excellence.*

The question for society is not one of scarcity of human quality. It is a question of knowing what to do with, how to use, the quality that abounds It is a question of finding something better to do with discovered and nurtured excellence than to frustrate it, or to set it to work on trivial and even destructive enterprises.

Students preparing to enter the schools in professional roles, as never before, are getting "where the action is." H. G. Wells' phrase that civilization is "a race between education and catastrophe" has become a cliché, but it does state an ever more pressing reality. For so many men and women of our organized and bureaucratized society, life is very much, as Thoreau put it, a time of "quiet desperation." They might well describe the structured, comfortable, but empty patterns of their days by reciting the lines of Macbeth:

Tomorrow, and tomorrow, and tomorrow,
Creeps in this petty pace from day to day
To the last syllable of recorded time. . . .

But though this can be and often has been the mood of teachers and students in the ritualized school, it need not be and must not be the mood for the school of the future. Man may truly be approaching the next to last syllable of his existence. If he would delay the final punctuation of his history, he must find the concepts to extend the sentence and prolong his existence indefinitely. He must find the words and meanings that will do this, he must teach them in school, and he must make the sustaining understandings universal.

By joining the educational force, you are most certainly placing yourself where the most essential, the most sustaining, the most exciting action is.

toward the key questions

Readers of this book have chosen education as their profession. For many, not all, this choice has been very seriously arrived at. For some, it probably represents, more or less by default, something to do. For many, not all, the schools will be their life work. For some, it may be a way station en route perhaps to matrimony, or graduate school, or military service, or more lucrative employment. Regardless of your reasons for selecting education as your field and regardless of the length of your sojourn in an educational institution, you must know what you are doing when you elect education.

This book seeks to let you know what you are in for in electing education as a profession, whether for a short term or for a long, long time. Certain questions, involving the fate of the individual, the nation, and of all mankind, are inescapable wherever you live, whatever you do. They are the questions under which every citizen of this century lives, whether or not he would choose to acknowledge them. But these questions, which we have spelled out below, come home with special force to anyone who enters the doors of a school in any responsible position.

1. Can the individual be rendered so strong and so responsible that he will accept and endure the tremendous burden of freedom?
2. Can a nation of tremendous diversity, terribly torn by bitter divisiveness, find and use the disciplines of intelligence and good will that will strengthen its common denominators and its problem-solving abilities so that for the first time in our history "unity amid diversity" will be a reality and not simply a hopeful phrase?
3. Can mankind subdue its aggressive impulses, its power madnesses, its nationalistic lusts and fears and make itself capable of survival in an age when it has the capacity and the all too evident disposition to destroy itself?

This is where the action is, right with these questions. We assume that by choosing education you want to be with the action—and that is where we intend to put you.

If you teach for but one year, you will affect, for better and for worse, some persons. It will be a good year, or a bad one, for you. It is presumed when you are hired that you will be doing a job that you can do, and on that presumption you will be getting paid for it.

As a matter of fact, you may be getting paid quite well. As a beginning teacher in Englewood, New Jersey, in 1970 you were paid $8400 a year, which was the top of the scale for beginners that year. In all probability, this figure will be exceeded by the time you read this. If a beginning teacher is paid at a scale approaching this, the question is *not*, "Is he getting paid enough?" It is, "Will he be worth his pay?" In fact, in 1970, if the starting pay was $8000, it meant that the new teacher, often single and usually quite young, received as much annual income as *half* the families in the nation—and that nation the most affluent in human history. True, this could not compare, nor can it still today, to what an O. J. Simpson will make fresh out of college or a Willie Mays without finishing high school, but if you play ball as well as these men you will not be teaching for a while at least. Nor will it approach the income of some adolescent rock singers or even disk jockeys.

It is true that the material rewards of education used to be terrible, just awful. But the young person entering the profession today benefits from a twofold legacy: one, a by-product of American affluence, and the other, the direct result of organized teacher militancy, which you may first enjoy the fruits of and which, if you choose to be a responsible rather than a hitch-hiking professional, you may further by your efforts. However, be under no illusion that you will become rich pursuing a career in the teaching profession.

If in this volume we do not talk about some subjects, we will not be talking about education at all. If this book, which is supposed to be a basic text for new teachers, reads as though the authors had never left the isolated countryside or skirts the real questions that you know are the important ones, it will deserve nothing but your scorn. However, do not come to such a conclusion too early. Here are a sample of some of the passing realities that we will relate to the job of the school and your job in it: (1) *a nation at war*—war consumed a huge bite of our national income for years, cost tens of thousands of lives, bitterly divided the nation, and deeply alienated many of the youth (and at this writing that war continues); (2) *space research*—space adventures absorb billions upon billions, while on earth the poor go hungry, unhoused, and naked to the elements. An ill-fated monkey has returned from a $92 million sojourn in space, but cancer research cannot scare up half that support. At the time that simian joy ride would have built 4,600 houses of $20,000 quality—which would have made quite a change in the lives of 20,000 inhabitants of whatever urban ghetto had been its beneficiary; (3) *racial discrimination*—black Americans have run out of patience with being victims of a generalized bias and discrimination. They have found identity and meaning, and they demand recognition of their equality and their right to justice— NOW.

professionalism versus trivia

The outstanding characteristic of the new breed of teachers that the authors address themselves to should be a better set of priorities. A new professionalism is needed in education.

New teachers, more than a little idealistic and purposeful, are often subject to a form of culture shock when they report for active duty. They remember school; so they enter a relatively familiar environment. They are prepared for a certain degree of confusion, noisy corridors at passing time, student rambunctiousness, academic routines, the vulgar necessities of roll-taking, and the keeping of rosters and records. They are in a new role, to be sure, but it is a role to which they have all responded, and have observed and practiced to some extent during their teacher preparation.

But now they view teaching from the inside looking out. They are dwelling among teachers as teachers. And what gives them the largest surprise, even to a traumatic extent, is the *schoolteacherishness* that abounds.

What is this? As we define it, the *schoolteacherish* is the disposition of teachers to be fussy over the insignificant, to elevate trivia to matters of great significance, and to shun matters of importance and value.

To say that there is a general disposition toward the schoolteacherish among faculties is no slander. It allows for the significant minority who are true teachers, which is a praiseworthy condition. However, the culture of the school throughout the nation is bogged down in trivia. We are not speaking of the burden of detail and petty chores (some necessary, but far from all) that the busy administrative and supervisory staff unloads upon the teachers' desks. We are speaking of the *chosen* triviality of mind so general among the practioners of what should be a profound profession.

To be sure, the schoolteacherish are a serious group. The things that induce the frowning concern and the sources of worry and fret are what are astonishing. The new teacher spending her first free periods in the "faculty room" might anticipate sharing in lively discussions like those that had so enlivened the klatches and bull sessions of college days: talk of good books and films, of great issues, of profound concern for life and the children.

But what really goes on is quite another thing: Chitchat about the price of this and that—but never a speculation worthy of the name about the causes of inflation; some angry argument or silly banter about politics—but never a serious discussion of a political issue; superficial talk about children: gossip, vindictive personalization— even slander.

In teaching teachers it is not always easy to excite a discussion of a real issue in education. In a graduate class in education one of the authors, after eliciting barely a ripple of response on the matter of race relations in the school, brought up "gum chewing." How the discussion came alive! Assertion versus counterassertion, anecdote followed anecdote. The class responded. There was involvement, participation, cognitive and affective expression—all the attributes of full-dimensioned learning, except for one small flaw: the content was silly. The discussion proceeded for a full half-hour; then the author called time and made a few pertinent observations. You can perhaps imagine what they were.

The authors do not believe, or choose to act upon, the proposition that such behavior is typical of today's teachers. Call it rather a conditioned behavior of an outmoded school-teacherishness. Teachers are among those who are crying for relevance and significance in education. The students are everywhere calling for these things. Thus, as never before, education is very clearly 'where the action is.'

1

PROGRESSIVE VERSUS TRADITIONAL EDUCATION

It is now our purpose to introduce for initial consideration the set of educational theories and practices commonly called *progressive education*. This movement has been largely responsible for the special character of American education. Without it, American schools would have been just schools. Much that progressive education advocated was never widely adopted. But all that it proposed was widely discussed. The entire educational scene was, and still is, in active ferment of controversy over the thrust of progressivism's central views and practices.

Alternate and opposing theories of education have been proposed. Historically, in the 1950s and 1960s educational practice moved in directions quite contrary to the progressive trend. But recent problems and issues have come home hard to the school. Education has had to restudy its formulations, to seek new solutions. Part of the restudy has led to rediscovery. The educational scene is beginning again to find practical utility in what the progressives had learned.

the traditional base

Progressive education may be somewhat understood as *a reaction against* certain views of education and educational practices. Among the premises of traditional and conventional schooling that progressivism attacked were the five considered below.

1. *The main function of education is to transmit the culture.* In other words, the school is a place where the student is systematically inducted into possession of the knowledge that has been accumu-

lated and sorted and that the school (representing society) asserts
that all members of the society should hold in common.

2. *Learning is best achieved in a formal context.* Formalism in
education has two major meanings: (a) the learning situation—the
classroom itself—should be formally structured, and (b) learning
could be defined and made easier within a formal setting.

The orderliness of the environment is both conducive to achievement and an end desirable in itself. Therefore, the formal classroom
was marked by efforts to preserve neatness of individual desks, seats
in straight lines and rows (which was not left either to virtue or to
chance as they were fastened securely to the floor), upright postures
of students, window shades drawn to precisely equal levels, and fixed
marching order at dismissal time. This was the more extrinsic, and
in a sense the more visible, aspect of formalism, and much time and
energy was directed to its preservation.

Since "true" learning could only take place in formal structures,
the most strenuous efforts of course construction and curriculum were
directed to the problems of *scope and sequence*—how much shall be
undertaken and in what order. The outlines thus prepared (and
now and then repaired) tended to become glorified beyond whatever
real purposes they served as conveniences to learning. Studied and
formalized organization of material acquired an idealized, almost
mystical quality: they became "the structures of knowledge," "the
disciplines." Formalism made of its discipline not merely an instrument for learning, but an obstruction to it. Reaching "outside"
or beyond the assignment or "working ahead" became matters for
verbal reproof, active discouragement, and even academic penalty.

3. *The teacher is the authority, and his role as authority is consistent, desirable, and justifiable.* The very classroom arrangement
symbolized this attribute. The neat ranks of desks facing one way,
toward the seat of wisdom and power, were the cue to the philosophy.
Even the teacher's desk conveyed the atmosphere of authority. It
was heavier and was often kept between the teacher and class as a
visible sign of the barrier between them. Occasionally, of course, the
teacher might enter the aisles of desks—not infrequently stepping
down from a raised platform to do so—to give an admonition, inter-
cept a note, or administer a rap on the knuckles, or a box on an offender's ear. The appeal in reason for justification ranged from the
abstract "to teach respect for authority," to the practical "to teach
them the way the world is and to know what the boss expects when
you go to work." The basic philosophical assumption was more profound. The mature, it was asserted with the force of an axiom, must
assume responsibility for the instruction of the immature. The
teacher, by definition, equaled the mature; the students, the immature. The assumption, not altogether senseless, was interpreted so
restrictively that it allowed no room for entertaining such heresies as
maturity is not solely a matter of chronological age or grade in school;

some students are much more mature than others; not all teachers are mature; some teachers are less mature than some of their students These arguments were not encouraged. Basically, the relation of teacher to student rested on a position once solid in the common culture: grownups have certain rights and prerogatives in relating to children, including the right to give them directions without any explanation or justification other than that it is a demand coming from adult to child and must therefore be heeded unquestioningly.

4. *Certain subjects hold a very central worth for education.* These tended to be the subjects with the more ancient sanctions, though the languages, especially the modern ones, had a more recent favor. Actually the better subjects, in the estimate of the formalists, had two main qualities: (1) they possessed long academic histories, preferably traceable to the classic *trivium* and *quadrivium;* and (2) they were peculiarly suited to a break down into orderly lessons, step-by-step procedures, grade-to-grade sequences. There were also two secondary qualities by which the formalist evaluated the relative worth of a subject: (1) that it possess no immediate or direct practicality, no vocational utility in the workaday sense; and (2) that it hardly be capable of being learned or it was unlikely to be learned outside of the school. This lack of either practical application or likelihood of being learned by the unschooled (possibly because no uncoerced intelligence could convince itself of the sense of learning it) led to an important and marked distinction between the attributes of *the educated* and the *uneducated man.*

The net consequence of the use of such criteria as the four previously stated was to bulwark such subjects as Latin and Greek, algebra and geometry, and grammar. These all qualified, both in the eyes of formalist and critic (who argued mainly over the virtue of the qualification) in each of the four particulars:

1. They had genealogies traceable to antiquity.
2. They were intrinsically easy to reduce to structured patterns.
3. They were free of vocational taint in most practical realms (except of teaching).
4. Few would embark on their study unless mobilized by the school to do so.

In the day of dominant formalism the educated had all sorts of instruments for one-upmanship over the unlettered. "All Gaul," he could say, "is divided into three parts": which would not exactly bowl over the learned, but would be sufficient to excite wonderment among the untutored at the witless wisdom of the educated man. Only a person who had gone to school could intone, "A straight line is the shortest distance between two points," without feeling silly. Thus, an education bred self-confidence. An illiterate blacksmith, who only knew a good deal of practical physics, would blush to tell a child, "It will be shorter for you to take the path to the privy than if you walk around yonder tree."

5. Finally, *the formalist held confidently to the view that the utility of education could be largely defended in deferred terms. Education is preparation for life.* On close examination this statement seemed to diminish to preparation for the next test, or the next year of school, or for the then remote goal of college study. "What good is this?" the presumptuous student inquired even in the formalist school. He might be inquiring it of Latin, or algebra, or grammar. The answers usually revealed the deferred quality of the *why*: "Because it will help you in your English (or when you become a doctor!)"; "Because it is necessary before you take geometry"; "Because I am putting a lot of questions on this in my next test." Or more generally—"Because it will discipline your mind (someday, somehow)"; or "Because you never know when you will need to know it and it will come in handy when you do."

the progressive challenge

Progressive education not only distrusted the foregoing assumptions but also actively challenged all of them. Although the progressive movement was not defined and did not become an active force until the twentieth century, its challenge to formalism had deep roots in Western civilization. The progressive made use of tradition, but his use was based upon a better appraisal and selection of ideas and sources from the past.

True, the progressive movement was the beneficiary of new knowledge and insights that had either matured or come into being in the twentieth century. Among these sources were:

1. A broadened conception of the implications of democracy in social, cultural, and educational terms.
2. An enhanced knowledge of the world through the discoveries of science and an increasing disposition to trust the method of science, even to defining it as the exclusive method of intelligence.
3. An enhanced knowledge of society and culture and institutions, largely the product of the newer social sciences, which themselves adapted and considerably applied scientific method to their inquiries.
4. A more sophisticated view of the human person, largely drawn from two sources: (1) the extension of psychological insights from many complex sources, especially the Freudians; and (2) the systematic observations of child growth and development (in the manner of the naturalist at work observing the behavior and growth of animal species), which was particularly productive for progressive educators.

The impact of progressivism on American education was great. It was always a complex movement with many facets and differing emphases. We shall attempt to analyze and make some sense of its central tenets, but these never constituted a defined creed that all progressives believed and acted upon. It is important to note at the outset that progressivism never became the majority mode for American education. Its principal fountainhead became Teachers College of Columbia University, where John Dewey, its philosopher, taught and where William Heard Kilpatrick served as its evangelist. At Teachers College John Childs explored its philosophical underpinnings, and such unlike men as George S. Counts and Harold Rugg sought in varied ways its social implications. But pure (rather broadly applied) progressive education never spread far from a few teachers colleges and schools of education and their demonstration and laboratory schools. The general impact upon education was never that of a revolution; it was merely one of *modification* in varying degrees. The schools in the main remained, and remain, methodologically, conservative, teacher-dominated, formalistic in organization and expectation, schoolteacherish and conventional in their view of adult-child relationships.

This fact should be remembered when critics of whatever qualification or motivation ascribe any ills of society, politics, or general behavior to "progressive education." Progressive education never had the chance to qualify either as the redeemer or the subverter of American civilization. Education does have a bearing on the quality of a culture; in general terms whatever is ascribed to education in terms of virtue or fault must be credited to a relatively conservative kind of school and classroom practice, for that is the kind of education that has been and remains dominant in the United States.

Progressive education broadly applied affected a small minority of schools. However, it modified behavior in specific matters in many. That progressive education did not sweep the country was not because it was tried and found wanting. It was obstructed by the strongly entrenched academic and social forces that were threatened by the dynamics of change. No movement in education was so research based and research proven. In the *Eight Year Study*,[1] the most formidable piece of longitudinal research on education yet conducted, progressive education met conventional education and bested it in the latter's chosen field of primary emphasis, college preparation. The study found that *progressive schools, giving no special emphasis to college preparation, did a better job of actually preparing for college in terms of student success at college than conventional schools, which placed a primary emphasis on college preparation.* (The full report on this study will be reviewed in Chapter 9.)

The central distinctions between progressive and conventional edu-

---

[1] *Adventure in American Education* (New York: Harper, 1942). Vols. I–V.

cation lay in the view of the child and of the adult-child relationship
and the role of the child in the learning situation. The differences
seem basically to be derived from a difference in the view of human
quality.   One view holds all humans (regardless of age level) as
worthy of trust and respect; the other views all persons with suspicion
and apprehension. It is, of course, not only a differing view of others,
but of *self* that is fundamentally involved. The roots of greater respect for the child run deep into antiquity. Socrates taught by directing himself to the perceptions of his pupil. He put no barriers of
formal order between philosopher and seeker. He established what
Martin Buber came to call an "I-Thou" relationship with his pupils.
Jesus, confronted with conventional adult impatience at the intrusion
of the young said simply, "Suffer the little children to come unto me,
and forbid them not, for of such is the kingdom of Heaven." The
record of ordinary schoolroom and social practice is full of evidence
of disdain and distrust and even abuse of the child. Children through
the years have been denied communication—"Little children should
be seen and not heard"; have been branded by outrageous clichés—
"Spare the rod and spoil the child"; have been put to work in street
and mine and mill and field. And even today, when the crueler devices
of exploitation have been curbed, children are used in one of the
meanest forms of psychological servitude: to act out and to fulfill the
frustrated ambitions of their parents.

Most schools were ever hateful to the child. But history does record that there always was a challenge from the best schoolmasters,
the educators who give modern education its seminal insights and
continuing inspiration. Ancient Rome's greatest teacher and master
of oratory, the Spaniard Quintillian, asserted the need for kindness
and concern as instruments of effective teaching. Renaissance teacher
Vittorino di Feltre broke with the confines of classroom and roamed
with his students in pleasant gardens in true companionship. Comenius in the seventeenth century developed methodologies that showed
respect both for learner and for learning. He invited student interest
with illustrated texts to appeal to broader sensory involvement. Rousseau asserted a radical turn-around in the common view of man:
against the common view of man's innate depravity, he posed the
thesis of the natural goodness of man. Froebel in nineteenth-century
Germany laid much of the groundwork for a humanized study of
child growth and development. Pestalozzi in Switzerland demonstrated how love and concern and escape from academic walls could
change the child's distrust of learning to vibrant interest. Bronson
Alcott, father of the author of *Little Women*, kept for a while a truly
progressive school in New England before the Civil War. Maria
Montessori and John Dewey, differing in cultural origins and methodologies, were at one in their view of the necessity for respect for the
child and the prime importance of allowing him to seek his own moti-

vations and interests. Thus, progressive education is both modern and deeply rooted historically.

effects of progressivism

The effects of progressive education, as earlier asserted, were mainly in terms of modifications of attitudes and procedures. The following may be taken as a useful checklist for attempting to assess the impact of progressive education on a given school or classroom.

1. Interest in acquiring knowledge about the child's family and social origins with a view to using this information for the child's educational advantage.
2. Planning activities and projects that are meaningful and rewarding to the child at the time he is engaged in them.
3. Consultation with the child with respect to his interests in planning learning.
4. Student-teacher cooperative planning.
5. Minimizing of grade-threat and test-scare motivations.
6. Use of the child's perceptions and experience in the classroom.
7. Discussion tending to replace question and answer recitations.
8. Encouragement of questions, inquiry, dissent.
9. Respect for individual differences as an asset to learning instead of studying them with an eye to erasing them.
10. Studies chosen for real life consequence to the child in terms of personal and societal needs.
11. More emphasis on the contemporary scene.
12. A problem-solving rather than a didactic approach to learning.
13. Flexible classroom arrangements responsive to the function of the learning situation.
14. Authority seen in the evidences found, not in the text or the teacher's say-so.
15. Shared respect among all learners, including the teacher, as the base for discipline.
16. Discipline perceived as a requirement for learning rather than as a moral exercise teaching respect for authority.
17. Disciplinary requirements that are flexible according to the needs of the given enterprise.
18. Full-dimensioned learning, involving action as well as talk and study.
19. Experimentation.
20. Escape from academic confines: field trips, outside learning, outside visitors welcomed and utilized.
21. Open-house activities that show the school functioning—students learning, instead of rigged exhibitions of students' productions.

~~22.~~ A broadened choice within curriculum.

23. An extended cocurricular program well integrated with the curriculum and defensible in educational terms.

~~24.~~ A general atmosphere of relaxation, happiness, and friendliness about the school.

~~25.~~ Light and color in abundance.

In whatever measure these twenty-five items are found in a school or classroom, it is evidence of modification in the direction of progressive education. Not one of them is held in high esteem or broadly practiced in traditional or formalistic education. Not many schools exemplify in practice the majority of these items. The writers of this text advocate the implementation of all of them.

analysis of progressivism

Progressive education was so complex a movement that a brief analysis runs the risk of oversimplification. However, for the purposes of this chapter, we shall attempt such an analysis. Progressives were active in three major areas: (1) the humanization of the view of the child; (2) methodological reform; (3) development of new approaches to curriculum. Overall, their abiding goals may be characterized as humanitarian, democratic, and scientific. Of course, not all progressives labored in all three vineyards. In the active arena of education, it was probably not possible to find one truly *complete progressive*. Nevertheless, there was a common drive toward reform in all the areas, and there was consistency and communication and interaction. There was also, as in all movements, a range of intensity and commitment: there were, indeed, both moderate and radical progressives. A common tie, however, united the movement: *a willingness to experiment and to accept change*.

The Humanization of the View of the Child

The progressive sought to liberate the child from being held to an academic lock-step. It rejected the notion that the child came to school as an empty vessel to be filled systematically with the knowledge that the school in its wisdom held to be good for him. It rescued *experience* from its damaged reputation and made it the central instrument for learning. The child's own experience was acknowledged, called upon, and utilized in the classroom. The child was reckoned to have a life outside the school. The effort of the new approach was to relate the experience, the life of the child outside the school with the experience of the child within the school. In consequence, both realms of experience would tend to enrich the other, enhance meaning, and produce a continuing motivation for further inquiries.

By this process it was believed that a greater integration of the child's personality and a more consistent self-knowledge would be achieved. It was a part of the standard vocabulary of the movement to speak of "educating the whole child." For those who question the validity of this concept, the burden of proof ought to be on them; for, in all logic, the alternative would seem to be to educate *a part* of the child. Just how could you manage to do that when the entire child is sent to school, never a mere portion of him?

The child's own questions and problems were held in a new regard by the progressives. "Felt needs" were to be sought out and capitalized upon in the classroom. Overall, the classroom was given a new characteristic of "child-centeredness." It was by no means a surrender of emphasis on learning. Instead, it was a reaction against the subject-centeredness of traditional education. Emphasis was placed to a new degree upon the learner rather than exclusively on what was to be learned.

To be sure, practioners could stumble onto error in working out such concepts as felt needs and child-centeredness. There may have been teachers so bemused by phrases that they came into the classroom and simply asked, "Well, class, what shall we do today?" There were cases where child centered came to be equated with child dominated. In these instances children's tyranny, which is at least as bad as any other, was sure to emerge. But such was not in any sense consistent with basic progressive philosophy, and there were plenty of better models for inept practitioners to learn from.

The progressive held the child in respect. As a consequence of that respect, he was confident of certain outcomes: The child is a natural learner and will take to learning readily—if it is related to his maturity level, the real problems within his experience (his felt needs), and his capacities. The child is a resource; he has knowledge and experience that can be mobilized to extend both. The child is somewhat responsible. If trusted, he can assume responsibilities, and thereby—and perhaps only thereby—he may become more responsible.

Progressive education originated in child study and was profoundly respectful toward it. It sought substantially to make child study a basic element in teacher education and to minimize emphasis on such courses as classroom management and methods, which amounted to indoctrination in techniques of manipulating students as standardized *objects*. Thus, teachers and parents, too, began to acquire a new sophistication in childhood education and child rearing. It is quite probable, indeed, that progressive education spread more widely through kindergarten and the primary grades than in any other level of the school. If so, the causes would seem to be that it was more conventionally acceptable to pay direct attention to the child at that age, and also that the subject centeredness of the school was not so acute at that stage.

Certainly, insofar as they were affected by the child study movement, both home and school in the 1920s and 1930s began to operate tentatively on new insights, new premises, and, no doubt, some new biases. Norms of expectations for child behavior tended to be less arbitrarily imposed by adult fiat and more likely to be derived from observation of typical behavior at a given age, stage, or phase of development. In matters as diverse as potty-training and learning to read, the gauging of the correct moment tended to shift from "when he ought to" toward "when he is ready to."

Permissiveness tended to acquire an enhanced virtue as a directive in dealing with the child in home and school. It had a broad range of applied meaning from the sensible to the absurd. To some, it meant a liberation from arbitrary restraints and the seeking to allow both what was constructive and what would do no particular harm. To others, it seemed to mean to allow little Joe or Shirley to do anything they pleased. The latter interpretation did little to enlarge the general repute of permissiveness. In general though, the child study movement helped (1) to educate adults to try to look at a child's behavior from the point of view of the child; (2) to diminish confidence in mere punishment—corporal or otherwise—as the most trustworthy means of developing desirable behavior; and, (3) to render illegitimate the view that an absolute domination of the child's life by an imposed adult (and presumed mature) authority is morally, educationally, or socially sound.

Methodological reform

The traditional, conventional classroom was not so much a place for learning as a place for *checking up on learning*. It was a place for *recitation*, and the principal method to elicit recitation was question and answer. The questioning was by no means Socratic, which attempts to get at the perceptions, experience, and insights of the pupil. Socratic questioning leads the student to probe for the answers so that inconsistencies, illogic, and errors of perception are revealed and thus lead the pupil to enhanced meaning and better conclusions on the basis of a process in which he has participated fully. In a one-to-one relationship under a masterful teacher, as in a tutorial session, it is a most stimulating and gratifying technique, one to which the conventional question-answer method bears little resemblance. The questions of the conventional teacher tend to be petty, directed to a random selection of facts with little evidence of attention to a scale of importance. They also tend to be numerous. Studies have shown teachers to average from forty to eighty questions within a forty-minute class period. Rapid-fire questioning is the only fitting term for this.

In the conventional classroom situation learning necessarily must take place elsewhere. Recitation is not learning. Some spillover of learning may take place, in a none too meaningful setting, for those students who pay sufficient attention to pick up some answers that they had not known before. Some good "games" have been part of the recitation. Students have studied the teacher's behavior closely, particularly his reactions. When unprepared, it has often been a useful dodge to show a bright eagerness, a rapt attentiveness, or a frantically assertive hand in the air. A question whose answer is known might be skillfully invited by a student's feigning inattention, fussing with something in his desk, or staring vacantly into space. This is all good clean fun, but it is learning only as it develops a "con" man's skills.

Learning was assigned, ordinarily in more or less perfunctory terms: "Read pages 44 to 51 in your text (and be ready to recite on them tomorrow)"; or "Work the even-numbered problems on page 111" (this left the odd-numbered ones available for *homework* or for punitive purposes). Assignment sometimes allowed for attention to individual differences; extra work might be imposed on pupils who disrupted class or had been unable to complete the day's assignment. Most ingenious were adaptations for quicker students who could readily read the assigned pages or "do the problems" in a fourth to a tenth the time that the teacher thought desirable. These he could reward with the opportunity to answer "on paper" questions at the end of the chapter or to work some more problems (of the sort already mastered). Not more learning, just more work. Except for the overeager and compulsives, this was excellent inducement to keep your light hidden under a bushel.

Learning then was relegated, or assigned, to be done in study hall or in homework. *Homework* is not to be construed as the kind of consequence to real learning in school that follows into life elsewhere. Homework is not the voracious reading that some children do because an exciting school experience has got them "hooked" on books. Homework is not the eager, self-motivated following of news media because a good social studies course has enlivened awareness to the world and its doings. Homework is not the listening to good music because somewhere—perhaps in school—the child's aesthetic potential has been activated. Nor is the voluntary pursuit of a hobby in astronomy, physics, or chemistry spurred by an awakening to the meaning of science in some good classroom. No, these things are not homework; they are worthwhile and satisfying things done at home, partly because learning has taken place at school. The school can claim the responsibility only when the school itself is a place for learning and a place where *learning is made truly an aspect of living*. The latter words constitute a key concept of progressive education.

Homework is the drudgery that the school that neglects learning imposes upon the children. It is an evidence of default of responsibility. It puts learning in a setting devoid of professional direction or assistance. It puts children at the mercy of parents—and vice versa, for that matter—in learning situations that parents have every right to expect the schools to handle. Since the schools cannot defend homework as learning, they argue its merit in character building. If

imposed drudgery be the best form of character building, well, hooray
for the sweatshop, hooray for slavery, hooray for homework! (Each
of these institutions has been defended in such terms in the historical
past.) But the evidences are clear: in unsupervised homework students learn what they could learn without the school, or they re-
hearse and strengthen their errors; they learn for later display, not
for intrinsic satisfaction; they learn through drudgery a disdain for
learning; they learn, because it is a basic truth underlying homework,
that the school is incompetent and irresponsible, unable and unwilling
to give the pupil a life of learning within the school. As for character
building, the only students who stay home to do homework already
have an abundance of props to character.

As far as parents who support homework are concerned, pertinent
observations should be made. They may simply not understand that
the homework they help to enforce is proof that the school does not
know what it is doing. They may themselves be so apprehensive of
their children's use of free time that they welcome any disciplinary
props. This would seem to imply that some parents are a little impoverished for moral resources, including communication. As for
cultural and intellectual resources, it is a poor home or community
that has nothing better for its children to grow on than homework.

Now, let us establish our perspective again. The case against homework is not the central point. The basic indictment is of the conventional classroom with its recitation method that drives learning out
of the school. It takes place elsewhere; the school merely collects its
scraps of evidence that learning has taken place somewhere. In the
main, it takes place nowhere.

But when the school itself becomes a place of learning, where
learning is living and living is learning, then things begin to happen
at home and in the community that show that learning has become
part of the students' lives. *Educational consequences* are what parents have a right to expect of the school, not homework.

The foregoing appraisal is the authors'. It is also exactly the kind
of analysis that led to the methodological revolution that was a part
of the progressive education movement. The main shift of emphasis
was to make the classroom itself the place where learning was effected, not the place where proofs were given that it had taken place.
The classroom, therefore, became a workshop, a laboratory, a functional library, a forum—all these and more too. It became a complex institution with forms flexible enough to fit changing functions.

Physical environments changed. Desks and chairs were unscrewed
from the floor. Circles of chairs tended to supplant neat rows. Face-
to-face interaction in a guided discussion meant communication that
necessitated that all participants see each other. In the old classroom
setting it was only essential that each student see the teacher and, of
course, that the teacher keep an eye on all his pupils.

When the classroom became a primary focus for learning, the time schedule came under scrutiny. The short class period, interspersed with study halls, seemed inefficient. A longer class could give time for study, for learning. *Supervised study* became a legitimate use of class time. It had obvious advantages. It legitimatized study. By giving it prime time, as it were, the school seemed to say it regarded study as a matter of prime importance. It put study where professional assistance was ready. It gave a chance for attention to individual differences.

Suppose, for example, a basic assignment in a text were given. In ten minutes, perhaps in twenty, some students have read the chapter that many will spend the entire hour reading. The teacher will be ready to suggest other reading, not more of the same, to those who did not require the full period, but it will be related material that rewards rather than punishes fast readers. Or the teacher may collect four of five of these early finishers and talk with them about the problems that they may raise. He will be alert to the class, stopping at a signal to give the meaning of a word, or explain a troublesome concept, or at the sign of frustration or dismay finding an alternate easier account of the subject for a student whose reading ability is laggard. Thus, even for conventional study—reading or working problems—*supervised study* affords radical improvement over the traditional classroom.

In the classroom where recitation is minimized, the line between studying and learning is erased. Discussion now focuses upon meaning—upon the why's and wherefore's. Textbooks are at hand, neither forbidden nor worshiped. In the course of discussion they may be turned to freely as a resource or to establish an essential fact.

Functional discipline will be the keynote of the progressive classroom. Permissiveness is not its governing principle. Child study did, indeed, in the development of progressive education encourage more *permissiveness* to replace the conventional arbitrary *repressiveness*, so common in the adult relationship with children. It tended to stress "do's" rather than "don'ts," and when the *do not* was an expression of adult responsibility, rather than a ritual response, to garnish it with a brief but sensible reason. Letting the child do as he pleased could amount to laissez-faire, what the most irresponsible parents and even conventional teachers have always condoned. Thoughtful permissiveness should be construed as liberation and encouragement of growth. It speaks with confidence to develop confidence, suppressing its apprehensions to avoid developing fear. Unless the child is courting real and present danger, it responds to the child's inquiry about some new venture, "Can I do it?" with "Go ahead and try."—even if the tongue must be bit to cut off the reflexive caution "better not."

But an error in perception of what was centrally important placed some progressive teachers in a conceptual bind. They mistook the main goal of the progressive classroom. That was to get as effective a learning situation as possible, not as they thought to grant as much permissiveness as possible. When they took the latter as their goal, the learning situation usually deteriorated. General permissiveness reigned too often, and this tended to discredit progressive education. Even the bewildered defensive teacher who felt he was introducing the basic tenet of progressivism (as he misinterpreted it) knew dismay at the consequence.

The progressive classroom tried deliberately to be *democratic*. This stemmed partly from the clear perception by John Dewey of the fundamental contradiction in the school's trying to teach democratic citizenship in a nondemocratic or positively authoritarian climate. It also derived from the fact that democracy is the most effective form of social organization by which groups may seek common purposes while allowing maximum growth and latitude for the individual. Democracy respects human worth, holds the individual high, makes its rules with the consent of the governed, judges all by open and agreed criteria, rewards objectively. These premises applied to the classroom aid and abet learning.

Now in the early days of progressivism, which as you recall was a *reaction against* as well as a *movement toward*, the tendency was to judge the progressivism or democracy of the classroom as simply an absence of restraint or authoritarianism. Absence of restraint, however, led to the predicament of such unhappy teachers as we noted earlier. Absence of authority is not democracy; it is anarchy. These are not even way stations on the road to democracy; quite the contrary, they constitute a vacuum in social organization into which power seekers are sure to move. Anarchy and laissez-faire permissiveness lead to oligarchy, tyranny, and dictatorship. Democracy is not merely the absence of authoritarianism; it is a form of social organization that seeks to help persons and societies achieve their goals with a maximum of satisfaction and a minimum of frustration. Democracy is a positive alternative to authoritarianism.

However, early progressive teachers did often find themselves in the bind of oversimplification. They measured democracy in terms of absence of authoritarianism and wound up with laissez-faire chaos. Sometimes, in despair and profound conceptual error they ascribed the fault to too much democracy; they then did an about-face and became the most terrible authoritarian teachers for miles around. They mistook the alternatives, but it was understandable. Patience, nerves, and self-respect cannot endure the noise, the chaos, and the interpersonal abuses that are part of anarchy.

Kurt Lewin fell briefly into the same conceptual error in his first "climate of learning" experiments. He set up only two alternative situations: the *authoritarian* and the *democratic*. He soon realized that these were not the true alternatives and henceforth designated three models: the authoritarian, the laissez-faire, and the democratic.

In Lewin's experiment, three groups of young boys were assigned a specific learning task: the construction of papier-mâché masks.[2] The project was considered to be intrinsically rewarding and interesting and within the capacities of the boys selected. The "climates" were controlled by leaders (teachers) trained to exercise leadership in carefully studied ways.

The authoritarian leader assigned the task, showed the students the tools, and told them to go to work. He praised on subjective personal grounds. He responded to questions sparingly and grudgingly. He intruded comments and reproofs that had no direct bearing on the task.

The laissez-faire leader simply assigned the task and stood aside. He offered neither praise nor reproof, suggestion nor assistance. Nor did he attempt to discipline the group.

The democratic leader explained the task. He discussed with the group the uses of tools and materials. He responded to questions generously and willingly. His favorable comments were work oriented, not personal. His negative comments were related to functions of the project.

The consequences were illuminating. The democratic group was the happiest. The boys remained friendly and cooperative. There were fewer antagonistic exchanges between students and leader than in the authoritarian group; there were more positive interactions. And they completed the task.

The authoritarian group also completed the task, with the exception of one boy who became the target of aggression within the group. He had been held responsible for most of its errors and had withdrawn from the group (illustrating the classic disposition of authoritarianism to make and persecute scapegoats). Evidences of hostility between leader and group and within the group were found.

The laissez-faire group did not complete its task. It managed a good deal of waste and destruction of materials. It was full of bickering, quarrels, and fighting. When the leader failed to exert any influence, some of the more forceful boys took over the group and dominated it.

About ten years later, one of the authors duplicated, with modifications of age group and subject area, Lewin's basic experiment with three groups in a graduate course in education. There were very similar results.

The basic concept for discipline in a progressive classroom is not merely absence of authoritarianism, it is *more* of democracy. Democracy has authority, but a different base for it. Democracy has organization, but it sees its structures as a means to agreed ends, not ends in themselves. It builds on shared and mutual respect. It utilizes all

[2] Kurt Lewin, Ronald Lipset, and R. K. White, "Patterns of Aggressive Behavior in Experimentally Created Social Climates," *Journal of Social Psychology*, 10, (May, 1939), 271–299.

its resources. It allows majorities to decide all questions but one: they cannot be allowed to persecute minorities. It has a place for leadership, and the place for leadership is to see that these principles are understood and acted upon.

When the conceptual underpinning of democratic discipline in the school is understood, then its functions begin to fall into place. The purpose of the school is to create learning situations. That is the assumption on which the schools are supported, and that is what parents have every right to expect. Children are sent to school to be exposed to learning. To create learning situations is what professional teachers are supposed to be able to do and what they are obligated constantly to be doing. Until the general expectation of the function of the school is drastically and publicly altered there is really no choice about the matter.

The expectation of the role of the school in our society thus makes the definition of functional discipline quite matter of fact. Functional discipline is the motivation and maintenance of behaviors that improve and advance the learning situation and the discouragement and prevention of those that disrupt or impede it. It does not embrace behaviors that are irrelevant in either the positive or negative sense to learning. Authority is not personal; it stems from the definition and obligation of the school. The teacher's crotchets and preferences, unless they chance to bear on the maintenance of learning, have no relevance. His canons for behavior must be professional, not personal.

Functional discipline must necessarily be situational. It varies with time, place, circumstance, and purpose. Recognition of this enlists the good sense of the students. They know that you yell at ball games but not at concerts, generally speaking. They even know something of the pragmatic necessity for company manners now and then. They are only confused by, or resentful of, or turned off and rendered rebellious by rules and restrictions that are senseless or about which no sense has ever been made to them.

In the complex classroom, the scene of many modes of study and learning, the requisite of functional discipline will shift and change with circumstance. When reading of texts or working of problems is the "scene," quiet facilitates study. Quiet is reasonable; it is required; and students will assist in requiring it. When projects are being worked upon, movement, talk, comparison, criticism are in order. To insist upon quiet when noise is functional is to intrude on learning rather than to facilitate it. When small groups are discussing, formal procedures of recognizing speakers are as useless as in a parlor conversation. When the entire group is assembled, signs for recognition by the chair may be useful to distribute contribution and to avoid chaos. However, the skilled discussion leader will welcome rather than discourage an involvement and animation that gets persons vying for the floor and also the spontaneous interaction of persons to persons that does not address itself to the whole group. What of habits of good behavior? That is precisely the subject under discussion. What is desirable is *sensible behavior* according to the sense of varying situations. It is not the habit of warping human behavior into arbitrary patterns without rhyme or reason. No person of sense goes swimming in an overcoat or to church in a bikini.

Progressive methodology reaches its culmination when it involves learners in all aspects of the learning situation. Cooperative, student-teacher planning then becomes a requisite for learning, not a matter of abstract principle. To locate a task or problem, to define it, to factor out its elements, to assess what is already known and what is unknown, to find and assemble resources for its doing, to organize and plan an attack upon it—all these are part of any learning enterprise. As a matter of fact, they are the most significant, most arduous, most rigorous part of it—and also the most rewarding in growth of skills of learning. When these things have been done, a great part of the learning potential in any situation has been exhausted.

Many—in reality, most—teachers do all or most of these things and then bring the students in and direct them to complete the job. Such behavior cheats students. It cuts them out of a large part of the learning process. It renders them culturally deprived in their own classroom. The teacher selects the task, defines it, compiles work sheets and bibliographies, guesses which resources are easy, medium, and difficult, arranges for films, guests, and field trips, and makes assumptions as to what is known and unknown. Then the teacher establishes a schedule for performance and invites the students to complete the task.

This is bad education on several scores. It suppresses discovery and diminishes motivation. It holds participation to a very partial level. It frustrates initiative. It fails to utilize the resources of the class. It expends the teacher's energies, which might be reserved for better purposes. It is at very least inefficient; it ignores basic principles of good administration. But, above all, it is bad education because it cuts the students out of some of the most valuable aspects of the learning situation.

Progressive education, on the other hand, involves the student in planning, not primarily because it teaches the virtue of cooperation (though it does that), but because in the teacher's professional understanding, such involvement is an educational necessity.

Curriculum development and reform

With a new view of child development and a radically changed approach to methodology, the progressive movement could hardly be expected to stop short of attempting to change the curriculum, the program of learning of the school itself. Here the assault was substantive and encountered the most solid and the most bitter opposition. Concerted opposition did not come from parents or teachers. Indeed, parents were quite ready to listen to progressive educators. And since classroom methodology generally was a local, even an individual teacher's, province, opposition to change was splintered. Curriculum change encountered deeply entrenched special interests, academic pressure groups, textbook publishers, and scholarly organizations, among others.

The child-centered movement and the methodological reforms of progressive education gathered momentum in the 1920s. The apex of the drive to alter the curriculum came in the 1930s. In part this was a logical development, a naturally evolving third stage; but even more it was a product of its times. The Great Depression with its profound social and economic pains and problems, and the New Deal with its panoply of social legislation and its giant strides towards the federal government assuming an obligation to promote the general welfare in very real terms—these together brought the nature of the society, the role of government, and the relation of the individual to his basic institutions to the foreground as questions of general public interest and consideration. Strange things had happened in the public arena; in many cases the unthinkable became the reality. Such phenomena as these had to be encountered, appraised, lived with, and made sense of. The booming economy of the 1920s slowed to a lumbering crawl; the Gold Standard was abandoned; 14 million out of a work force of 40 million were numbered as unemployed; banks and business failed by the thousands—and on one stark day all banks were closed by administrative edict. Hundreds joined queues at bread lines and soup kitchens while warehouses and granaries bulged with unsalable surpluses; while millions hungered and many starved, farmers received government subsidies to limit production of food and commodities. These were more than passing strange developments. The old ways of looking at things gave little preparation for sorting them out, let alone making sense of them. To complicate the scene, the winds from abroad brought sounds of portentous events: war in the Orient as a militant Japan invaded provincially divided China, a vicious Fascism warred on Ethiopia, and in Spain a Civil War turned into a dress rehearsal for the looming main event. Ideology became a common word in the vocabulary. "Isms" of several orders were argued, disputed, supported, hated, feared—socialism, communism, fascism, Nazism. A world that had been assumed to be progressing toward a universal democracy was shown to be worshiping new gods and the old deities of tyranny in new raiments. With these troublesome realities and besetting rumors on everyone's mind, it was unlikely that educators would not consider new emphases for the school.

The school's job was to educate. A classic connection between education and democracy had been generally accepted. Now democracy was in travail. What could possibly be more natural and desirable than that the school should look at the trouble, help to factor it out, analyze it, discuss the issues and alternative solutions, and, perhaps, even contribute to their solution.

One educator saw no "perhaps" about it. George S. Counts of Teachers College, Columbia University, published in 1932 a small volume entitled *Dare the Schools Build a New Social Order?*[3] His text sounded a ringing affirmative to his own question.

Counts and those who thought in a similar vein were quickly labeled the *social reconstructionists.* They put themselves in the vanguard of the curriculum movement of progressive education. The main thrust of curriculum reform went nowhere near as far as what they advocated. The general thrust was toward greater contemporaneity (an attention to real social and economic problems to replace classical theoretical approaches) and toward the breakdown of artificial subject matter boundaries—even toward rendering the school more *relevant* (though that word was not "in" in the 1930s).

A great deal of the curriculum thrust dealt with changes in the organization of subjects and content objectives to relate content to the new methodologies. Some of these produced lasting impact; others were transient.

In sum, the progressive education movement attempted to make the school a place of learning. It focused on learning in real terms, the nature of the learner, the learning process, the consequence of learning. It awakened controversy; it aroused opposition; it led to a consideration of other alternatives. The controversy and the opposition and the other options for education are the subject matter for the next chapter.

topics for inquiry

1. Educational Views of the "Founding Fathers"
2. College Admissions Standards
3. Teacher Salaries: Trends Since 1960
4. Educational Statesmen of the New American Nation: Horace Mann and Henry Barnard
5. The Defense of Latin as a School Subject
6. Child Psychology in the Nineteen Twenties
7. The Curriculum Movement of Progressive Education
8. John Dewey's View of *Experience*
9. The Defense of Homework
10. The Distinction Between Permissivism and Laissez Faire

[3] George S. Counts, *Dare the School Build a New Social Order?* (New York: Day, 1932).

subjects for discussion

1. A. S. Neill in his work on his radically different school, *Summerhill*, states:

   > Possibly the greatest discovery we have made in
   > Summerhill is that a child is born a sincere creature.
   > We set out to let children alone so that we might
   > discover what they were like. It is the only possible
   > way of dealing with children. The pioneer school of
   > the future must pursue this way if it is to contribute to
   > child knowledge and, more important, to child
   > happiness.[4]

   a. What is your feeling about Neill's contention?
   b. Do these points reflect governing assumptions in schools as you know them?
   c. If applied, what kind of changes in the school would you foresee?
   d. Is "child happiness" more important to most schools than "child knowledge"? To you?

2. Using the checklist of twenty-five progressive education practices in this chapter, conduct a study of your class' reaction to them on a five-point scale:

5	4	3	2	1
Strongly Agree	*Agree*	*Neutral*	*Disagree*	*Strongly Disagree*

   a. Does your class tend in the main to accept or to reject these practices?
   b. Which practices have the strongest support? Which are most rejected?
   c. To what degree was your high school education characterized by these practices? How about your college education?

3. Lawrence Cremin, the historian of progressive education, states in the concluding paragraph of his work *The Transformation of the School:*

   > The Progressive Education Association had died, and
   > progressive education itself needed drastic reappraisal.
   > Yet the transformation they had wrought in the schools
   > was in many ways as irreversible as the larger industrial
   > transformation of which it has been part. And for all
   > the talk about pedagogical breakthroughs and crash
   > programs, the authentic progressive vision remained
   > strangely pertinent to the problems of midcentury
   > America. Perhaps it only awaited the reformulation
   > and resuscitation that would ultimately derive from a
   > larger resurgence of reform in American life and
   > thought.[5]

[4] A. S. Neill, *Summerhill: A Radical Approach to Child Rearing* (New York: Hart, 1960), p. 111.
[5] Lawrence Cremin, *The Transformation of the School* (New York: Knopf, 1962), p. 353.

      a. How might educational progressivism be related to problems of our time?

      b. What kinds of reform in American life would be supportive to a progressive view of the school?

4. In what order would you rank these as motivations for going into teaching:

      a. Desire to teach a subject

      b. To earn a respectable living

      c. To build character among children

      d. To help build a better society

      e. To change the school

      f. To transmit the culture

      g. To lead the life of a professional person

      h. To make children happy

      i. To shape a satisfying personal career

      j. *Others* (phrase your own)

(Compare notes with your colleagues: What differing patterns of motivations do you find? Have you thought this question over quite carefully, or are you offering a superficial response to the question? Do you think you have searched out a satisfactory basis for your decision to enter education? Do you think this question might be important, i.e., have any bearing on your success, your effect, your happiness as a teacher?) (What do these last words —*success, effect, happiness*—mean to you?)

selected readings

There will be Selected Reading lists at the end of all chapters. But if you should happen to get "hooked" on this one and made it your semester's reading program, in the authors' view, no harm would be done. This might be true of any of the chapter reading selections. Perhaps a sensible alternative would be to pursue one or two in depth and to sample among several others.

BOWERS, C. A. *The Progressive Educator and the Depression: The Radical Years.* New York: Random House, 1969.

    To be read after Lawrence Cremin, below. This historical study is relevant also to the mood and issues of our time.

COUNTS, GEORGE. *Dare the School Build a New Social Order?* New York: John Day, 1932.

    A significant document in educational history and also a radical view on curriculum that, despite the date of its publication, is relevant to current dissatisfaction with the curriculum.

CREMIN, LAWRENCE. *The Transformation of the School.* New York: Alfred A. Knopf, 1962.

    The definitive history of progressive education. This book links

progressive education with basic developments in American society and with the course of social thought. It is so readable and
so literate that it is recommended not only for its important substance, but as evidence to students that educational writing may
be graced by true intellectuality.

DEWEY, JOHN. *Democracy and Education.* New York: Macmillan,
1916.
A modern classic that profoundly relates the purposes of
American education to the major dynamics of American civilization. It is a text rich in conceptualization of both education and
democracy, and it shows the inextricable linkage between the
two. The student will find it rewarding to read from cover to
cover. If this is not possible, at the very least he should familiarize himself with it by intense selective reading.

KELLEY, EARL C. *In Defense of Youth.* Englewood Cliffs, N.J.: Pren-
tice-Hall, 1962.
Exactly what the title states. If parents and teachers really studied and used Kelley's good sense, both the hostility in the school
and the generation gap would be appreciably eased.

MASON, ROBERT E. *Educational Ideals in American Society.* Boston:
Allyn and Bacon, 1960.
A thoroughgoing analysis of the philosophical options for
American education. Readable and informative.

NEILL, A. S. *Summerhill: A Radical Approach to Child Rearing.* New
York: Hart, 1960.
An explanation of the school Summerhill, which is about as far
from the conventional model as you can get. It can both shake
you up and delight you. It furnishes a fresh perspective, and a
vision of just how different education can be. If your fellow students read it, you are sure to argue loud and long over it.

PEDDIWELL, J. ABNER. *The Saber-Tooth Curriculum.* New York: Mc-
Graw-Hill, 1939.
A satire on American education that is both highly comic and dead
serious in its exposé of the witlessness of common educational
practices. Read it! Peddiwell was actually the distinguished educator Harold Benjamin.

34

2
LIVE
OPTIONS
FOR EDUCA-
TIONAL
CHOICE

Education today is alive with controversy. The issues revolve around matters of choice. The concern of this chapter is with theoretical bases for choices, an assessment of consequence of present active choices, and a consideration of a reasonable platform for decision making. The effort has been to make this presentation reality oriented, that is, to deal with potential choices that make some sense and have some chance of being effected. Hence, the term *live options* is used.

Not all theoretically available decisions constitute live options. For example, though some would still be found to argue for it, there seems to be no likelihood of a return to the completely traditional, formalistic school of the past. Neither does it seem probable that the progressive education movement will reappear intact, shouting the old slogans and waving the proud banners of the 1920s and 1930s. But, in the process of decision making for the 1970s, the thrust of progressivism will continue to vie with the restraints of traditionalism, one among other theories bidding for support.

theoretical alternatives

In addition to progressivism, which has already been considered, five theoretical alternatives will be introduced: (1) essentialism, (2) scientistic approaches, (3) institutionalism, (4) innovationism, and (5) existentialism.

essentialism

Essentialism is defined by De-Young and Wynn as "the doctrine that there is an indispensable common core or culture . . . that should be taught systematically to all, with rigorous standards of achievement."[1]

Although the essentialist movement was conceived as a critical response to progressivism, it was largely a reassertion of the traditional view of the school and its purposes. As its spokesmen saw it, essentialism was a defense of education as it had been before it was "corrupted" by progressivism.

The essentialist held progressivism at fault in such presumed errors as:

1. Its emphasis on child-centeredness amounting to subjecting the mature to the dictates of the immature.
2. Its carelessness with respect to discipline, its tolerance for bad work habits and shoddy work, its lack of emphasis on precision and mastery.
3. Its overemphasis in teacher education on methodology at the expense of subject matter competence.
4. Its neglect of the lessons of the past, its overconcern with the contemporary.
5. Its destructiveness toward the structure and sequence of subjects as a result of an overemphasis on individual differences.

Progressivism perceived itself as education peculiarly suited to a democratic society. Essentialism did not choose to attack progressivism by demeaning democracy. Instead, it chose to argue the case in terms of the kind of education most suitable to a democracy.

The great necessity, as essentialists saw it, was for education to induct the new generation into the culture, to locate it within its heritage. The basic subjects—reading, writing and arithmetic—were esteemed by the essentialists. Despite the fact that progressive educators directed much research toward the better teaching of the same three R's, the essentialists seemed to see themselves as the guardians of the three R's in the face of a progressive attack on basic skills.

In their drive to induct children into the culture the essentialists did not trust a child's *interest* as the sole motivating factor. They thought exterior discipline might have to be used to allow interest to develop or to hold students to tasks that were necessary but not necessarily interesting. Even the discipline of failure might be a necessary adjunct to maintaining sound academic standards.

Since the essentialists believed that the education most suited to a democracy was the one that inducted each new generation into the culture, their understanding of the subjects likely to achieve this is

[1] Chris A. DeYoung and D. R. Wynn, *American Education* (New York: McGraw-Hill, 1968), p. 491. The basic positions of essentialism were set forth by William C. Bagley in 1938 in a paper entitled, "An Essentialist's Platform for the Advancement of American Education." Bagley was supported in his views by other theorists including Frederick S. Breed, I. L. Kandel, and William W. Brickman.

vital to our discussion. The traditionalist quality of this group of theorists cannot be overlooked. It is illustrated by their regard for classic languages, algebra, and geometry as pillars of the curriculum. These they chose to think of as "exact and exacting studies." The doctrine of mental discipline, though generally outmoded, had a continuing appeal for the essentialists.

(The essentialist, along with other rhetoricians, often appears to make a virtue of tough talk. Phrases such as "exacting," "demanding," "solid subjects," "rigorous inquiry" abound in the educational dialogue. Students may well examine their content analytically. They may have real substance; on the other hand, the phrases may be simply relics of Puritanism, just a verbal muscle flexing.

In current parlance "solid subjects" is an esteemed phrase. Mathematics still has high esteem as an "exact and exacting" study. However, it should be pointed out that to the student who can work the algebra problems in his head—the student best suited for the subject —mathematics is, in effect, a breeze or a soft touch, not as demanding or rigorous a task for him perhaps as learning to weave a basket or drive a car.)

The essentialists and progressives should be perceived as contending, not as warring, camps. They both held democracy as a desirable goal, but disagreed as to how to educate for it. They both held education as important to society, but disagreed as to the way of making a positive impact on society. Each, perhaps erroneously, suspected the other of being dogmatically authoritarian. Both believed in teaching, but described the teacher's functions quite differently.

scientistic approaches

Basically, scientistic approaches derive from the contention of the philosophical school of logical positivism whose proponents hold that there is no knowledge other than that which may be scientifically verified. To arrive at such knowledge is largely a matter of weighing, counting, and measuring—in a word, *quantification*. Scientism is best expressed by the common generalizations "Whatever exists can be quantified; whatever can be quantified can be measured."

Scientism has something of the nature of science. Although it rejects the old absolutes, "the eternal verities" of which traditionalists often speak, it longs for its own positive proofs. When it operates in an open field of inquiry, it does expand knowledge as far as its methodology will allow. However, when its practitioners create closed systems of a priori assumptions, they share the disposition of all closed minds to reject experience other than their own and automatically to invalidate methodologies other than their own. Hence, they must be designated *scientistic*, not scientific. Withal, the largest consequence of these emphases has been to inflate science and diminish the humanistic in education.

The *educational testing movement* is a prime derivative of this view. Much work of a limited practical value can be attributed to the movement. Intelligence testing (with consequent emphasis on the IQ and sometimes on ability grouping), attitude tests and scales, measures of aptitude, personality inventories, and standardized tests of academic achievement are examples of its influence. That these have been useful to educators is undeniable; that they have been often overused and misused also seems to be a matter of record.

Analytical philosophy, employing the method of language analysis, also stems from the logical positivist bias. Bertrand Russell, mathematician and philosopher, and G. E. Moore were, in a sense, cofounders of this movement. Gilbert Ryle, A. J. Ayer, and Ludwig Wittgenstein are elaborators of the theory. To the analytical philosopher, most problems and confusions of meaning are due to misuse of language. Not only is there an imprecise use of words, but more fundamentally the terms used are not scientifically verified or verifiable. The use of such unproved words and symbols, as though they were proved (known), can only lead to the expression of *nonsense*. For the analytical philosophers, principal culprits in producing confusion and nonsense have been theology and metaphysics. Members of this school also hold considerably suspect terms of sentiment and values.

That language analysts furnish useful tools for rendering language a more precise instrument of communication is as true as the fact that they might induce a horrible literal-mindedness. Bertrand Russell's writings, however, indicate that language analysis is no barrier to literate expression (which one might truly suspect from reading Wittgenstein); they also demonstrate that so lively an intellect must sometimes sally into the unverifiable realm of values and even the existential to assert its fullest being.

Currently, another product of the scientistic view has a very large impact on education—*behavioristic-mechanistic psychology*. To this school of thought, the human organism is governed by the stimulus-response connection. Psychologists in this tradition hold not only that human behavior can be studied scientifically, but that it can be predicted and controlled. That this is to some extent true can be demonstrated. The scientific psychologists, however, are not always precise as to the limits of this extent. Furthermore, the ability to do something, such as to manipulate human behavior, does not answer two questions that are value-laden, even moral, in nature: Should it be done? If so, in what direction or to what purpose should it be done? The fundamental antagonists of the behaviorist movement hold to a more basic contention: The purpose of education is not to manipulate human behavior; it is to nurture and to liberate it.

The most sophisticated practioner of this school is B. F. Skinner, whose refinement of the behaviorist method is termed "operant conditioning." His theories of learning are considerably derived from studies of animal learning. Based on these studies, Skinner has introduced to education the devices of teaching machines and programmed learning to improve academic achievement. However, a fair analysis of the teaching instruments of programmed instruction of Skinner and others brings one to the conclusion that they have as yet failed to produce convincing results, even when measured against conventional classroom procedures, in effecting improved achievement even in the educationally limited sense of academic learning. The research, in a word, fails to support the claims and hopes of the programmers.

institutionalism

The first level on which institutionalism operates is one of organizational defense. That is, the operators of any institution tend to justify not just its intended mission, but every structure, every detail of its day-to-day work. Stock answers to all questions and criticisms are a predictable feature of institutional defense. Of course, as an abstract principle the possibility of institutional error is freely admitted in such terms as: "Nothing is perfect" and "We like to learn from our mistakes." In any specific instance, though, it is rare for the institution or its official spokesman to admit error. The blame for error is always pinned on "outside conditions," or if damning evidence piles too high, then some functionary is publicly sacrificed. A school superintendent or a baseball manager is fired, for example. Such reaction is not a matter of philosophy; it is just the way people in complex organizations defend their status and their jobs.

Institutionalism, however, has a philosophical defense. School administrators, for instance, have tended to see the school as a businesslike organization. The graduated student is seen as the product. The system is judged in terms of efficiency of output; the dropout, in a very real sense, is seen as a factory reject.

Raymond E. Callahan has documented the institutionalism of school administrators in full detail in his work *Education and the Cult of Efficiency*.[2] But Solon Kimball and James McClelland in *Education and the New America*[3] have written the fullest exposition of the institutionalist view. Unlike the great body of observers who see large organizational aggregates as a threat to individual identity and autonomy, they glorify the institution and urge education to help the person to appreciate its worth and to commit himself to it. They express little doubt that the organization man can find meaning and fulfillment in his institutional niche.

Quite apart from the main streams of modern thought, these

[2] Raymond E. Callahan, *Education and the Cult of Efficiency* (Chicago: University of Chicago Press, 1962).
[3] Solon Kimball and James McClelland, *Education and the New America* (New York: Random House, 1962).

authors regard the dilemmas of contemporary man as relatively insignificant. Any confusion that besets him they seem to attribute to his failure to understand the way things are (which to them is basically all right) and to adjust himself to the altogether sensible circumstance in which he finds himself.

innovationism

The approach to educational theory by the innovationist might be characterized as "naked modernism." Substantially, it has no philosophical base. It derives from two primary causes: (1) It is a cultural reflex to the fact that technological advance has produced a warehouse jammed with all sorts of hardware whose salesmen often claim panacea and never less than "breakthrough"; (2) it is a negative reaction to the ideological confusion and stress of the times. Innovationism is an understandable, though witless, weariness with the arduous (and necessary) task of trying to make sense of things.

The innovative view should not be confused with views that support fundamental change. As a matter of fact, innovation is more often than not linked with conservative, even regressive, educational theories—especially of learning, of the learner, of the curriculum, and of the school.

Real change in the quality of eating, for example, must be measured in terms of what is brought to the table and appreciated, to the degree of sophistication of the diner's taste (these corresponding, of course, to curriculum and cultivated self-awareness). No matter what an array of mixers, automatic ranges, and timers the kitchen contains, progress is a matter of new recipes—not of new utensils. Tough mutton and boiled peas are a sorry mess regardless of the panoply of devices that surround their preparation. And if the product of innovation is a TV dinner, the gourmet can only say "Forget it."

If innovation has no philosophers, it has, nonetheless, its prophets. Daniel Bell in his work *The End of Ideology* [4] must be reckoned as one. He sees the resolution of man's problems as a simple matter of devising the instruments by which to solve them. Never mind the disputation as to what the problems are, the priorities of what should be tackled first, or the tangled questions of consequences. These are hard issues, demanding intellectual effort and commitment. These the weary mind quite understandably might choose to shun. But dare we?

Marshall McLuhan is another prophet of innovation. He is a man of such wit and droll disposition that it is often difficult to know when he wishes to be taken seriously and when he is indulging in a colossal "put-on." His prophetic declaration that the age of print has come to a close and an age of new visual media has arrived is obviously not

[4] Daniel Bell, *The End of Ideology*, rev. ed. (New York: Free Press, 1962).

unadulterated hokum, but it is a gross rejection of the basic system of symbolic representation known as language. It is simply nonsense.

Interestingly, McLuhan has through force of necessity turned to the writing of books (very good selling ones at that) in which to foretell the end of the medium of print. His contribution to taking the meaning out of words is best illustrated by his own oft-quoted phrase "The medium is the message." That such a statement has some truth one can readily attest. This work is written in the presence of the ubiquitous television set. I glance across the room; I am aware of its bleak stare as it sits there unactivated. But any character it assumes in my mind, I must invest it with. If it seems ominous to me, it is because of no intent in the medium. It is only in my awareness of its damage to my peace of mind should someone turn it on—and thereby turn me off! If I am conscious of its distractive potential, it is because I know of a counterclaim to my attention—perhaps an old movie or a football game—that awaits my willed action, the turning of a switch. But, after all, it is simply an instrument, thoroughly devoid of intent and feeling, quite neutral. I am altogether its master, not at all at its mercy, a quality that it lacks. If I do activate it, the medium has nothing to say beyond its message; and that will not be a message from the medium but a substance of communication, a message—good, bad, or usually indifferent—that other minds and motivations of men have contrived and intended.

The innovators have certain identifiable characteristics:

1. They accept, without undue recourse to thought, that whatever can be done must be done, that whatever is made must be used.
2. They are dedicated to the primacy of instruments. They mistake the character of message for the characteristics of the instruments which deliver them.
3. Quite often they have something to sell.

Innovation in education, not by the dictionary, but in the current jargon, implies educational hardware: television, teaching machines; computers, language labs; video tapes. The claims of the advocates and salesmen of these are hard and confident. However, the research is far from conclusive about their assertions. No legitimate entrepreneur should be forbidden opportunity to present his wares to the schools. However, since the interests of commerce and of education do not always coincide, it is only sensible that the schools exercise prudent consumership and buy only after a careful study of the research evidence. (See Chapter 9.)

existentialism

The existential camp is rooted in the modern. However, it does not reject dogmatically the past. Therefore, it is inclined to be ecumenical toward many of the disputes between the traditionalist and the progressivist. The existentialist is confident of the decisive character of man; therefore, he does not summarily reject useful tools whether they are presented by language analysts or by the inventor. For developing an educational theory appropriate to American democratic purposes, the existentialist finds it expedient not only to establish a connection with pragmatism, but to extend its seriousness; then he may speak of pragmatic existentialism.

But the existentialist is critical of other theoretical bases for decision-making. He is not against possibilities of social improvement, but he does distrust all utopianism, however, whether of visionary Marxism or of overconfident social reconstructionists. He makes extended sense of pragmatism, but he rejects its sure confidence in good outcomes if only good processes are discovered and used. In addition, he finds that the American pragmatist has dwelt too long in a blissful unawareness of the profound agonies of the human condition. For the existentialist, there is "a tragic sense of life," which the pragmatist ignores.

The existentialist makes little sense of the institutional view of education. As a matter of fact, some existentialists, such as Paul Goodman and Edgar Friedenberg, are unrelenting critics of the Establishment. The existentialist holds that the greatest adversary to human responsibility and personal identity lies in the depersonalized and bureaucratic quality of large institutions.

The existentialist rejects the behavioristic-mechanistic view because he sees its view of man, the universe, and knowledge as inadequate and because he abhors determinism and any suggestion that man is fit for manipulation rather than for liberation. Toward the innovator he has an amused tolerance because of his enthusiasm for his gadgets. In addition, he is amazed at his philosophical naivete.

What does the existentialist bring to school? The first is a wide view of human responsibility. Each person by what he chooses and what he is helps to define the meaning of man. Thus each person, in a sense, is a part of the process of creation. No person (student, teacher, or administrator, for example) can take refuge from responsibility for his acts. The existential staff member cannot say, "I do this because the policy, or the school, or the boss says to," and thus pass on the responsibility for the act. If he chooses to do it, he is the doer and the one responsible for his actions. (The executioners of Auschwitz and Buchenwald thus were not good soldiers, or simply obedient public servants; when they obeyed orders to kill the innocent, they became murderers.) Equally important is that he brings an enhanced view of individual differences. He knows that the purpose of education is to help the student not merely in his process of self-discovery, but also in self-definition. He sees individual differences not as problems to relate to and perhaps to diminish, but as the essence of reality. Thus individual difference is to be authenticated, recognized, and put to work. Thus, *authenticity*, the characteristic of the person knowing and being what he really is, becomes a central concept.

the school as it functions

To proceed to intelligent bases for decision making, it is necessary to analyze the school in terms of its functioning: how does it really operate? The school is a functioning institution. It is, in a sense, a *given*; that is, its nature is defined to many of its functionaries by the going attributes of its day-to-day operation. (Very often one hears that such and such is the philosophy of a school, but philosophy in its true sense is seldom visibly at work. Philosophy seeks the consequences of thought. The examined life is to be lived differently; the examined school would function somewhat differently as a result of that examination. Thus philosophy is brought into active consequence.)

Theoretical considerations are too often matters of concern only to those who write and talk about education. Unless serious thought is to be regarded as mere playful intellectual exercise, it would seem that, philosophy might well be put to work within the school. This is simply a way of saying that educators ought to know what they are doing.

The schools you enter will be widely different in terms of quality of plant and equipment. Modern junior and senior high schools have libraries that many small colleges can scarcely match. Science laboratories are often magnificently equipped, even with planetariums, thanks to funds available under the National Defense Education Act. Language laboratories and closed-circuit television installations are not rareties. Even more impressive, no matter how elaborate the foregoing, are likely to be the signs of preoccupation with athletics: stadiums, gymnasiums, swimming pools, and playing fields. (These are sure signs of concern with competitive sports; they are by no means necessarily evidence of a balanced program of physical education). Many schools are spacious, handsomely designed, and occupy well-landscaped campuses or school grounds.

The fine schools in most aspects of plant and surroundings are mostly found in suburban locations, in small cities, towns, and rural consolidations. The educational plants of the cities, on the other hand, are often in deplorable condition. The urban elementary schools are generally in the worst shape. The cities have sometimes invested in impressive secondary schools while leaving the elementary buildings to literal ruin. In the inner city, where the odds against the school are most formidable, the schools are the worst of all: dingy, overcrowded, firetrappish, rat-infested—a gloomy invitation to the joys of learning.

Thus, we arrive at the very center of the American educational

problem. Where the educational need is greatest, so too is the neglect. Where the children are the heirs of poverty, the educational
opportunities are the worst. This is a terrible contradiction, for this
is a land "dedicated," as Abraham Lincoln put it, "to the proposition
that all men are created equal." This was no less than the initial
commitment of the nation as phrased in the Declaration of Independence. However, Jefferson, though he believed profoundly in
education, did not see the school as the primary instrument of equality
of opportunity. From Thomas Jefferson's perspective, overlooking
the tremendous vistas of the western lands, that instrument was free
land (recall that by his purchase of Louisiana he had literally doubled
the size of the nation).

But by the twentieth century the concept had a new instrument:
free universal compulsory education. In principle this held that no
matter what the child's origin, background, poverty of environment,
give him the school and the school will give him his fair chance—the
knowledge and the skills to compete in the free market of this rather
open society. All other things being equal, the principle should have
worked rather well. But all other things were far from equal. This
brings us back to the present state of the schools of the cities, where
the need for an effective instrument of equality of opportunity is
greatest. Here the schools are the worst and are doing the poorest
job.

What is poverty? Philosophical speculations to the side, let us
simply state our definition in official terms relating purely to income.
Poverty is defined officially as a family of four with an annual income
of $3,553 or less per year. In this richest of nations *one out of five*
families lives in poverty so defined. This is not a particularly inflated
definition of poverty: how many people would feel affluent raising a
family of four, not on $3,000, but say $6,000 a year?

school for the middle class

Basically, with respect to serving as an instrument of equality of
opportunity, the urban school is functioning in reverse as far as the
children of the middle class are concerned. How so? This is a very
broad range. One middle-class child may come from a home supported by an income of $5,000, another from a family income of
$25,000. But each, *if both are white*, will enjoy a reasonably fair
chance as far as the opportunities and attentions of the school are
concerned. Not that the school may do a very profound job in educating the child (which is another question to be dealt with in detail),
but it is an institution that accepts a certain responsibility for him—
namely, to prepare him for a place in society. The middle-class white
student in the American school has certain things "going" for him.
The school is rooted in the culture from which he comes, that is, in
middle-class attitudes and preferences. The places it seeks for its

graduates are chosen in terms of middle-class aspirations. Its teachers and administrators are quite thoroughly imbued with the same culture.

We have carefully avoided the use of the term "middle-class values." *Value* is a term that serves mankind universally. Attitudes, preferences, and notions may be products of a class, ethnic, religious, or nationalistic group. Values are not "notional." They really serve all men well. It is a *value* to be fed, to be nurtured and loved, to have given and to give respect, to feel secure, to know a sense of worth, to possess a sure sense of identity. That these things work well for all persons is substantiated by the fact that nobody seems not to want these things for himself and for those for whom he knows concern. All persons find it *valuable* to have these.

Sometimes the notion develops among a class, or an ethnic group, or a race, or a nation that it has a special qualification for these values, that it somehow deserves more from life than others do. This sort of preference or favoritism toward one's own specially defined group is called *ethnocentrism*, and it is responsible for a devastating amount of divisiveness and hostility in the human community. Ethnocentrism creates *no* values.

This does not say that persons, groups, classes, or nationalities have no right to their special preferences and notions, but that these are not values. If you choose to wear only red neckties, even establish them as official garb for your club or group, the preference is quite legitimate. It only begins to make trouble when the choice begins to assume special merit in the eyes of the wearer beyond simply a preference for red ties. When the wearer begins to feel that his red tie sets him apart and makes him a superior being, then the trouble starts. His conclusion might have taken the course of reasoning that follows: "Well, red is a better color than blue or yellow or green; therefore, I have better judgment than the person who wears a green tie; so, I am probably a better person than he is. If that is so, if I am superior, he is, by pure logic, inferior. If that is so, I deserve somewhat more out of life than he does, for if he is inferior, he cannot truly appreciate the finer things of life. Indeed, if all this be so, why should I not use this other inferior person to get for me what I am so specially fitted for." The potential for trouble is obvious when a simple preference begins to assert itself as a *value*.

Another plus for the middle-class student in school is that the school has a preference for him. It does not have to try to know him individually (and makes no great effort to do so), but on the basis of probabilities, the institution (that is, the teachers and administrators) in a middle-class area is quite sure that it can count on this student to respond quite predictably. In the first place, the institution's expectations are that the overwhelming majority—and in most places, all—of the student body will be *white*. If you are middle class, the odds are twenty-five to one that you will be white. If you are a middle-class black student, the school will be a little embarrassed by your presence, but if you live up to other expectations, the school will begin to forget that you are black. Furthermore, most schools will help you to forget that you are black, by leaving everything about black history and culture out of the curriculum (which is a favor considerably less appreciated by black students than it used to be!).

The school for the most part can assume that the student will *accept the school's concept of its responsibility for him*. The school seeks to turn him out a certified product, custom stamped and inspected. He is not really trained for life because his class and institution frown upon probing deeply into life and raising questions about life (even though it is axiomatic that one cannot educate about anything without raising questions.) The middle-class student is ready when certified—graduated, that is—for one thing: *to go on*. A favorite phrase for class mottoes used to be "Onward and Upward." Actually, though they are still employed, the words are inappropriate, for to "go on" simply means "to go somewhere else." Ironically, where the institution has "prepared" its student to go, though "somewhere else," the "somewhere else" turns out to be not so very different. To paraphrase the French adage about change, "The more one goes on, the more he is in the same place." This leads to the next point.

The student is ready to be institutionalized, and the school is ready to institutionalize him. (Remember, we are not talking about every student, and certainly not *any* student. We are talking about the statistically predictable attributes of the middle-class student in the middle-class school. So, when he goes on, if he goes where he should go—in the institutional sense—he will be in another institution: college, which is so much like high school that he will barely feel a difference; or an office; or the military; or the organization.)

What does it mean to be institutionalized? Two characteristics are the most significant factors: (1) not to think much about life except in its institutional forms, and (2) to conform to the codes. Conformity is the principle institutional virtue. But there are others.

One accepts the institutional virtues without question and acts accordingly. Thus, one always remembers to pass credit upward and blame downward. Actually, this is merely the shrewd corollary of the institutional man's basic rule: always make things as easy and as safe for yourself, as possible. You can see how logically one follows from the other.

The major objective is, of course, *avoid responsibility at any cost*. This is a very primary objective of institutions, which are aggregates of persons so organized that it will be next to impossible to find anyone who can be held responsible for anything.

It is impossible to fit into the institution if you are disposed to such behaviors as saying, "Oh, yes, that is a good idea; it is mine," or "Man, that sure was a blooper, it didn't work at all. It is my fault, I goofed." This may sound like responsible human behavior, but in institutional terms it violates the basic principles of *belonging* to the group. It sets, not so much a bad, as an absurd example. The people who are thoroughly institutionalized simply cannot comprehend anyone who wants to behave like that.

Institutions do have certain tolerance for idiosyncrasies as long as they do not affect behavior in the foregoing matters. For example, in those who basically conform, a school or corporation may accept hair at medium length or dresses way above the knees or to the floor (styles do change), but wearing sandals is, of itself, prima facie evidence of unruly spirit.

The lesser virtues of the institution are, nonetheless, strictly binding. These include punctuality, neatness, precision of speech and performance, careful grooming, acceptable posture, cordiality to all peers (who may someday be your bosses or employees), respectful attention to superiors, and disciplined reserve toward inferiors. Students of psychology will note that these include many of the characteristics of what the Freudians term anality. (This may help to account for the large degree of concern for washrooms in the organizational world.) It is also psychologically interesting to note that a preoccupation with personal ease and safety is likely to induce instant alertness to any threat to these. In many this alertness is sharpened to a generalized suspicion of others—triggered into active anxiety, paradoxically enough, by others either when they come too close or when they stay away. Thus, it seems necessary to conclude that a certain degree of paranoia seems inevitable within the institutionalized person—or conversely and more succinctly, institutions nurture paranoia.

In the functional sense of providing institutionalization, the school does a relatively good job for the middle class, most of whom seem to want their children effectively institutionalized.

This function of education (to institutionalize the students) is not usually so boldly stated by educators. They employ euphemisms for their actions, or state as purposes of the school goals that they often implement only negatively. Or they just run a school without a pretense of stating purposes that make sense.

A few serious educators do defend the school precisely in its capacity to exercise this institutionalizing function. As noted earlier, the only persons who have quite formally attempted the defense in these terms are Solon T. Kimball and James McClelland in their work *Education and the Future of America.*

school for the poor

What of the school and the children of the poor? As far as *values* are concerned, the poor have the same values as all other people. They like to be fed; they hate to be hungry. They enjoy being sheltered from the elements; they hate leaky roofs in wet weather, unheated flats in frigid winter. They detest rat infestations that steal from their larders and bite their babies. They thrive on love and nurture— wither under rejection and neglect. They cherish respect, seek to improve sense of self, demand the right to establish an identity. Since equality of opportunity is a cherished American principle, it would be reasonable then to expect that the school as the most effective vehicle of that principle would be especially tailored to their overwhelming need.

But what do the children of the inner city, of the ghetto, find when they go to school? They find the oldest buldings, the newest teachers, the most remote and inaccessible administrators, the most beat-up texts, and the largest amount of unconcern. They find themselves re- ferred to as the "lower class" or the "culturally deprived." And when they take an interest in their schools (seek change, in other words), they find (or have found until very lately) that there is not one thing that they can do about it.

The schools that so many middle-class children attend are directly controlled by middle-class communities. This does not mean that they are good schools in a profound educational sense, but it does mean that they are tailored to the middle-class image. The school fits the child, in the class if not the human dimension—which is indeed another matter.

But the urban school of our large cities, which in the seventies is becoming more and more the school of the poor, is managed by absentee overloads. The board of education is a citadel of middle- class institutionalization: it runs the schools for all the children according to a set of preferences and practices based on middle-class norms. Look now at the expectation of the school as it greets the student from the inner city, the child of the poor.

The student is rooted in one culture; the school in another. The school has a set of preferences that work directly against him. First, *he is poor, and frequently black.* The middle-class school's ex- pectation is that he at least be white. To atone for his regrettable pigmentation the black student in all decency is expected to show an eagerness to acquire all the earmarks of whiteness, except the one im- possible to achieve. Imagine the culture shock of the white, middle- class oriented school when its black students come to school not eager to be reacculturated, but proclaiming "Black is beautiful," "The curricu- lum must be black relevant." In other words, these students are ques- tioning what the school can do for them as it is presently constituted.

The child of the inner city *is unready to accept the school's concept of its responsibility for him.* He does not trust the school. He knows that the school does not have a good record of preparing him to "go on." Rather he sees that the vast majority of his children never make it to the day of certification. They are called "dropouts," but the dropout has a special perception of the circumstance—he per- ceives himself as a *force-out.*

From the instant a black child first sensed the school's embarrassment, its feeling of betrayal at his coming to school in a black skin, he
acquires an awareness of the basic inhospitality of the school to him
and his kind. He knows that not all schools are as graceless as his
frequently is. He may or may not know that other classrooms are
less crowded. He does not know that the tests he is given are
"culturally biased," but he does know they use a lot of words that
mean nothing to him. He may not know that many of his teachers,
are quite afraid of him and overwhelmed by the feeling that for the
most part they are up against an "impossible job." The inner city
child—black or white—may not know these things, but he suffers the
consequences.

The poor black child is also aware that *the school feels hopeless
about institutionalizing him, and he is not nearly as sure as the middle-
class child that he wants to be institutionalized.*

At this writing, the best that the school can do to "acculturate"
him is follow two inadequate courses of action. It can select a token
few "exceptionally talented" black students and prepare them for the
few places that exist in the institutional world for institutionalized
black persons. To attain one of the "coveted" positions, the black
student will have to overachieve and overconform because of the very
deep skepticism of the school that he really has the quality to make
it. On graduation day, if the black student wins an honor or an award
(which is not uncommon), the pride and self-congratulation of the
Establishment will exceed all bounds. Not only is this a proof to
them of virtue, but a demonstration of consummate educational
achievement. The school, in their minds, has literally proved itself
capable of doing the impossible!

The other course that the school can follow for the children of the
poor, who are so often black, besides forcing them out of school, is to
give them a low-grade vocationalism. Actually, the whole program of
the school as it commonly works is vocational (though that is by no
means the whole purpose of an *education*). To institutionalize really
means to vocationalize. But vocational education means to institutionalize at the lower end of the employment scale. It provides
equality of opportunity in a very limited universe.

from institutionalization to education

It should be clear that in this overview characterization of the school
we are not talking about *education*. If the school attended to total
human development, then it would be educating the youth. Since its
primary and almost total concern is vocational, which is *one* legitimate
aspect of education, the best and the most that can be said of the
school is that it institutionalizes effectively the middle-class segment
of its population.

That this is not enough is evidenced by the growing body of rebellion against and rejection of the school's concept of its responsibility. The school serves, not values, but a fixed set of middle-class notions and preferences. An educational system would—and should —serve humanity by dwelling among the values, the things that serve all men well. To "teach" the values, the school must begin by making the topic that is presently ignored or taboo central to all curriculum. That topic is *life;* life as it actually is. The present ignoring of life by all institutions is dangerously close to acting out the Freudian "death wish." The ancients asserted well "The unexamined life is not worth living." To place a taboo on the examination of life in the curriculum is to put the school in the position of aiding in the creation of conditions that make life not worth living.

All around us there is proof that this is a prevalent and growing conviction. Actual suicides, very high among death causes among adolescents, are the most dramatic evidence. Alcoholism, often traceable to deep-seated loss of esteem for self, is a chosen form of tortured self-destruction. The carelessness for life that results in 50,000 highway deaths cannot be ignored in the evidence. Drug addiction, rampant in our time, is evidence not only of the utter viciousness of profit peddlers, but of a large volume of customers who find life not worth living unless sustained by illusion and artificially induced awareness.

As its most basic aim, education should give men a better hold on life. It cannot do this merely by institutionalizing them. The need is for a school that recognizes the presence of each student on his own personal terms. The expectations for the particular student should not be generalized in terms of social class or by statistical means. It should make no difference to the school where or from what circumstance the student came. Its overriding disciplined attitude toward each student would be: *we are glad you are here.*

The interest in the student's origins and circumstances would be intense, however. But the interest would be personal, objective, and functional. The aim would be to know the student. Today too many schools have two prime objectives in amassing data about a student, neither of them conducive to the student's happiness or growth:

1. To find out what, in the institution's judgment, the student needs to have done to him.
2. To amass a body of evidence that can be used to plead "extenuating circumstances" when the school fails to achieve educational results with the student (often misstated as "when the child has failed").

But the real educational purpose of knowing the student stems from a vital fact of life—the person needs to be known. The human being is the most responsive of organisms; he has a magnificent range of cognitive (intellectual) and affective (emotional) capacities.

Accepted and responded to across the range of his perceptions, the
person thrives, grows, learns. Unconcern and rejection by others
cause lifelessness, apathy, self-distrust. The beginning of the process
by which the life-rejecters, the haters, and the killers are made is in
the holding back of the interest and the concern that makes it possible
for the person to be known.

It is quite intolerable to the human to be *unknown*. The whole
complex apparatus of his sensory, neurological, and physiological
system cries out to be responsive and to be responded to. The key
influences that peer group and family (however structured) have on
individuals are directly related to the fact that in these relationships
persons have the concern to know and to make themselves known.

The school, on the other hand, stands convicted of having very
little influence on the *lives* of its students.

The schoolroom is full of unknowns, its students. The students,
properly conceived are the true *subjects* of education, to be known
and to be nurtured in knowing. Being unknown is ever frustrating.
If the child remains a stranger to the school but enjoys the warm
support of friends and family elsewhere, he may tolerate the strange-
ness of the school while developing increasing cynicism toward it.
His alternative could be to protest. His demand to be recognized
and dealt with is a fruitful source of what the school calls its disciplinary problems. "I will make you acknowledge that I am really here"
is what the disruptive student is often saying. Those who aggressively
call for recognition have at least the ego-strength and the trust to try
to make their presence felt. The most terrible potential is to be found
in the quiescent, the passive *unknowns*. How often the report from the
school is the same when a youth has shot a president or a candidate,
or has taken a high vantage point to demonstrate his marksmanship
on dozens of unknown victims, or goes on a murdering rampage up
and down the countryside. Then when the reporter calls the school
for extended "human interest," it says, "Why how hard this is to believe of that boy. He never made any trouble for us. He was always
such a good, quiet student." To be unknown induces, indeed, a sort
of quiet desperation; but in despair persons may find strange ways
of making their presence felt—strange and destructive.

A corollary of the foregoing is the necessity for the school to be
totally human rather than ethnocentric. The institutional school
serves a class—the middle class—and in that limited sense serves it
well. But class consciousness, class struggle, class warfare are alien
not only to the democratic idea but to the purposes of good education.

The human school, the school that will educate, must serve values,
which are simply everyman's necessities, and among these "are life,
liberty and the pursuit of happiness."

When the school roots itself in institutional preferences and notions, it serves only partially any given person and only a part of the

students who come to it. Thus, our schools are filled with persons
who are only partially fulfilled and with large enclaves of students
who are considerably more frustrated and alienated than fulfilled at
all. The typical school is several schools within one, none of them
profoundly educational. These schools (or tracks) may be designated
as the college preparatory, the vocational-commercial, the general, and
the athletic. All are predominantly *vocational* in either a positive or
negative sense.

The *college preparatory* is the track where the school's strongest
preference lies. It is the most successfully vocational of all. Its immediate vocational goal is to get the student ready to "go on," in this
case to college. The real purpose is to fit the person for the occupational grooves that fit him for social and economic preferment, for
status and position, for the best jobs, for maximum social security.
A case may be made for the proposition that it also begins to train
the person to live "a productive, useful life." This is, after all, where
the doctors, dentists, teachers, and social workers come from.

The college route is also the course taken by the practitioners who
have cheated so extravagantly on medicare, by many lying and graft-
ing politicians, by the con men who devise psychologically sophisticated means of getting people to buy what they neither want nor
need, including lung cancer. The success of college preparation is
mainly vocational, its failure humanistic and ethical.

We are not trying to write the school off as a total failure; we are
engaging in professional analysis to find grounds for its reconstruction. But its constructive attainment to date has been severely limited
in the classical purpose of education for demonstrating the merit of
"the good life."

The *vocational-commercial* track pushes upward, even moving—
and quite legitimately so—into narrow paths of college admission.
This track has usually been "terminal" at the high school level. The
advent of wide-scale community college training and the technological
necessity for more sophisticated vocational skills tend to press for
two more years of "college level" preparation. This track is more
candidly, though less effectively and no more exclusively, *vocational*
than the college preparatory. It prepares for jobs, which is both
philosophically and economically desirable. By and large, it trains
for the poorer paying, less status-laden, and upward limited occupations. It tends to perpetuate social class distinctions. Only for the
"lower class" can it be construed as an avenue of upward social mobility. The school misuses this track. First, it abuses the serious
purposes of vocational educators by using it as an academic dumping
ground. These educators deserve their fair share, and no more, of
the unmotivated and relatively incapable students. Second, it tends
to regard vocational education as the panacea for solving the educational ills of the curriculum. The Booker T. Washington notion that

vocational training is an education good enough for some people is a millstone to educational progress.

The size of the *general program* is a good index to the degree of educational unconcern of a school. Where the other tracks are populated with students grouped for certain kinds of special attention, here reside the students who have been segregated for special neglect. Not even a vocational purpose vitalizes its program. It is purely anti-vocational. Its students are comprised of those whom the school actively or casually does not prefer. Whatever races, or social conditions, or ethnic groups are scorned within the community, their children will be overrepresented in the general course. Here will be found the time servers, the unmotivated, the discouraged, the neglected; here, too, the most insipid curriculum, the most crowded classrooms, and the most indifferent students. This is the school's purgatory.

The *athletic course* is seldom acknowledged as a coordinate element in the school. It is both avocational and vocational. It is the direct vocational training ground for the large commercial games, the entertainment world of college, university, and professional arena. For the exceptionally talented and motivated it constitutes an effective by-pass of the somewhat stuffier academic requirements for "going on." The college is, with respect to other special talents, not nearly as flexible in its academic bookkeeping as with athletic prowess. Great ability in basketball, football, or baseball gives the admissions officer deep confidence that the candidate will be able to meet the basic test of the college graduate: to perform satisfactorily in one of the more lucrative occupations.

In its avocational sense the athletic program is perhaps the most truly educational aspect of the school. Its preferences are functional rather than emotional. Give a boy eight inches of stature beyond six feet and a modicum of coordination and he will be preferred regardless of race, religion, or state of "cultural deprivation." Furthermore, on the playing field a good deal more of the person is legitimatized (respected, responded to, and used) than in the classroom. His biological-physical nature is valued and expressed. His feelings are important, even crucial. In the classroom motivation is perceived in cognitive (intellectual terms); here the better half (the affective, the emotional) is stressed. The winner has drive, guts, *desire*. The games of the institutional school are more essential than is often perceived. They offer some escape from the sedentary life imposed on this richly active creature *man*, and they provide an emotional life, scarcely available elsewhere in the school, except in the fantasy life of many daydreamers uncounted in the classrooms.

Would it be well then to abolish these tracks? Since that is unlikely to happen, let us say that in every program the aim of the school should be to develop a *complete education*, an education responsive to the whole person. What are the dimensions of the complete education?

1. The humanistic-ethical
2. The creative-aesthetic
3. The scientific-quantitative
4. The vocational-utilitarian

The four dimensions sum up three things: the sum total of human experience (the resource for knowledge); the dimensions for personal growth and development (the human potential); the possibilities for developing learning (the scope of curricular possibilities).

If the school will accept without preferences all the children of all the people, if it will approach each as a person whom it must get to know, and if it will then attempt to relate its learning experiences to the full potential of the human—then, and only then, can it speak of itself as a place for education.

the concept of total education

In many respects the *total* education of the modern child goes so far beyond the sweep of the school's curriculum that it is erroneous to speak of the child's schooling as his education. Thus if a child's schooling and his education are wide apart, problems are posed for both the child and the school.

A distinction is not being made between *formal* and *informal* education. A distinction may be made between the planned learning activities of the school and what is picked up, and sometimes learned from, outside the school. Formal learning seems to imply defined goals, systematic arrangements, planned procedures, tests, rewards, and penalties. The school builds much of its program upon the structures of formal learning. However, this distinction is *not* what we are dwelling upon in making a difference between a child's schooling and his total education.

The distinction being made is in terms of scope, significance, effectiveness, and relevance. In regard to scope, it appears sensible to state that an adequate education is as broad in scope as the life needs of the learner. Such an education will dwell most upon those things that after careful study and consideration have been concluded to be that which is important in fulfilling the needs of the individual. It will be assumed that these things are well-learned, that they become part of the life equipment of the person, and that they are directly related to the developed interests and experience of the learner. Thus the definition, and subsequent fulfillment of an adequate education, contains scope, significance, effectiveness, and relevance. In this context, the distinction between the schooling and the total education of the person may be developed.

scope

In some respects the scope of the curriculum does indeed *exceed* the scope of the total life demand of any individual. For example, the school attempts to give a large number of its students a competence in a foreign language. Few of these students will ever need a language other than English (which they have learned before they enter school); or if they do come to need another, the odds are very long against it being the one that the school has offered. To be sure, the school will assert quite truly that the student needs the foreign language "to get into college." We are talking, however, of educational need, not of college entrance requirements.

In some areas the scope of the school's intention for its program far exceeds any prospect of achievement; the very vastness of its scope precludes any chance of real learning. The school proposes in history—world history, no less—such a total review of all man's record, his struggles, his achievements, the rise and fall of his civilizations—and all this *in one year*—as would stagger the capacity of an Arnold Toynbee or a Will Durant. In so doing it does more than consign itself to failure. It teaches antihistory: the notion that history is a superficial and pat chronicle of a welter of events, persons, and places. The dangerous conclusion arrived at from such a "survey" is that the meaning of complex events may be summed up in a few definitive phrases, and, probably worst among these well taught delusions, that the text that does all these things is a history book, a book of history.

Vastness of intent leads to no greater absurdities than in literature where the school's anthologies are great bear traps of academic over-ambitiousness. In this field children, many of whom have not yet been taught to read well, and who have a crying necessity to learn better who and where they are (which a personalized use of literature could indeed be responsive to) are invited to relate to, "to appreciate," to learn, even "to master" an aggregate of stuff that many a sophisticated critic or college professor would shrink before—Elizabethan playwrights; seventeenth-century prose and poetry; lyrics, sonnets, epics, odes, ballads, novels, dramas, short stories, tales; romanticism, realism, naturalism; Victorian novelists and even "modern" prose and poetry. Such vastness has its rewards. Some develop a facility for academic name-dropping for whatever cultural value this may have in superficial conversation. More important, English majors aside, a widespread conviction of a general dreariness in literature and a learned distaste for many writers is developed that in most instances is never changed. It is obvious that the current literature course is *not* the way most students get "hooked on books." This is a goal that would be so personally fulfilling and so beneficial to our civilization if broadly achieved that it should warrant serious attention.

Yet, in the main, it can be readily seen that the principal error of the school is not to be overambitious in scope, despite these illustrations of self-defeating vastness of intent that outrun all sense or hope of accomplishment. In many more dimensions the school evades or barely touches upon the matters that affect the student most centrally: who he is, where he is, what he is being and becoming. Under these headings lie most of the questions to which the student wants response and will seek answers. They are both what he wants and needs to know. So, it will be appropriate to shift our emphasis from scope to significance in clarifying and extending this distinction between schooling and total education.

significance

Identity crisis is not an unfamiliar phrase. Modern man is reportedly caught in an identity crisis more profound than any previous generation. It is a refrain we hear from all corners and one that we accept. Modern man shows great signs of failing to know himself. He lacks a sense of self. Lacking this essential starting point, he is at a loss to communicate with others. Often, at least, he is lonely; in the extreme, he is alienated—a stranger wandering alone, frightened and therefore often hostile, among his own kind. He is seeking his identity.

(Surely, there are paradoxes, contradictions, here. Modern man in America is surer of many of his prospects than ever before. He is less in hazard from a multitude of plagues than many anywhere or ever before. Yet he set foot upon the moon before he knew the cure of the common cold, let alone of cancer. He has instruments of immediate, even multisensory, communication at his disposal, including a hot line to Moscow. But instruments are not communicators; only persons are. And what does a person unsure of himself have to communicate? Only the messages that others tell him to relay. Thus he is only an instrument himself, not a communicator. On his own behalf he speaks only his doubts and his fears, his angers and his hostilities. What avail lies in the telephone if it only allows sons in Los Angeles and fathers in Manhattan to continue the angry dialogue of the generation gap, to re-echo the expression of their reciprocal fears and angers, of their self-doubts at long distance? What does it avail that jet travel can bring diplomats from far corners of the earth to sit at a "peace table" when even its shape was a matter of profound dispute? Persons can communicate, even come to agree. But persons who are bound and straitjacketed cannot. A man who serves as an agent, or a representative, limited in his communication to less than his own dimensions of knowledge, trust, and confidence, cannot reach out from his own understanding to find the common denominators of understanding in others on which true communication is based.)

Modern man finds himself in a number of roles and costumes, some of which he inherited, most of which were cast for him by others. He speaks not as a person, but as a representative or a member of a family, of a peer group, of a generation, of a class, of an organization, of a denomination, of a party, or of a nation. There is some necessity in this, for society is comprised of many aggregates of groups, cultures and subcultures, organizations, and nations. These provide certain assurances and conveniences for man. They help him to get some things done, and they exact loyalties.

But somehow the net weight of the organizational world has become too heavy a burden. Participation in common enterprise often has a dual satisfaction in both social and personal terms, but as a member of an institution it is not the individual who is important—it is the institution. Within the institution the individual has no personal identity. As a member, not only other people's purposes, but also *their* doubts, *their* fears, *their* hatreds, *their* enemies—all must become his too. And the demand sometimes becomes ultimate (as in George Orwell's novel *1984*). Black must be seen as white; sense must be perceived as nonsense. When the institutionalization of man procedes so far he has only hard choices. If he rebels at denying himself he stands in the dangerous role of troublemaker, heretic, or even traitor; if he surrenders the testimony of his senses, his judgment, and his experience, he becomes no person at all. In sum, if a person has only an institutional identity, he has no identity at all.

Therefore, it would seem to follow that institutions that would serve man (in our context, the school) must always be checked and scrutinized to make sure that they encompass and accept the totality of purpose of the individual. If the person is free to exert himself freely within the institution—that is, to question authority, name error and absurdity, demand reason, define accountability, to agree and to dissent on the basis of evidence and experience—if he may do these things and remain in good standing and valued, then that institution is in good shape to serve men. If he may not do these things, that institution is not serving him. It is in conspiracy against his identity.

The significance of the school is often negligible—or is positively detrimental in the light of this issue. Large aspects of significance are denied the school.

Take, for example, the matter of sex. In view of the biological nature and the emotional potential of man, and of the large amount of lore and subject matter at hand, would it be extravagant to assert that if a person is born and lives to adult years, he will receive a sex education? He will, indeed. The only question is whether he will have a good or a bad sex education. Perhaps adequate or inadequate would be a better phrasing.

Here is an area of inescapable significance in which the scope of the school's efforts is much narrower than life itself. The most "daring" (if attempts to bring such a significant matter to the school must be so labelled) efforts at sex education in the school still assure that most sex education will take place elsewhere. This may be necessary; some think it altogether desirable. If may also be too bad. For if sex is significant and sex education is inescapable, the school might have certain advantages in assuring that such an education will serve the person well, even enhance his identity as it were. The potential advantages are worth analyzing even more because they reveal fundamental premises of education in a free society than because they apply to the significant proposition.

Education in school does not have to prove itself on an error-free basis. Critics of the school's efforts in sex education often make their case on the basis of "mistakes" the school has made. Such critics often imply that an error-free curriculum in this area does, in fact, exist. Sometimes they have one ready in stock. On close examination the programs are always naive. Often they are dangerous, containing most of the cues that lead direct to the psychiatrist's couch. More often the attempt to censor the school's attempt to be significant in this life area is phrased as "better to leave it to somebody else"— that is, home, family, or church. The unstated presumptions are three—and all untenable—(1) that the source will then itself be error-free; (2) that if "left to," this source will then be the exclusive agent for sex education; and (3) that intelligent efforts of home and/or church will somehow be in conflict with the school.

In matters where life is far from simple (sex is surely one of them), the disposition to assert an error-free position must stem from naivete, a neurosis or "hang-up," or from an authoritarian vested interest. The most neurotic parents will be the most insistent that their instruction in this, or any other area, is error-free. The older boys or girls who are knowingly teaching their younger brothers and sisters and their friends the facts of life are not likely to be motivated to set forth the real limits of their knowledge and insight.

The school, on the other hand, is in a position to be confident of its substance without any pretense of being all knowing. It has at its disposal all of man's accumulated knowledge. It has a sufficient knowledge to be able with some security to set the limits to its knowledge, to be able to say, "This we know because of this evidence, but this we do not know yet." Thus, the very fact that the school knows that it cannot give an error-free education is one of its assets in providing responsible instruction.

The school, insofar as its principal source of content lies in scholarship and science, and not in folklore and prejudice, is disposed to instruct on the basis of evidence. It has confidence that "getting at the facts" is a very essential discipline. Acting upon the facts seems to be a very reasonable goal for the educator. To act in the absence of facts seems ever to be perilous, and to choose to act in opposition to the facts seems only the part of a fool.

So the school by its basic discipline is committed to the facts, at least in those areas where it chooses to instruct or is allowed to do so. If the home, or the church, or the peer group is delivering sex education with a view so responsible toward the facts as this, it will not be contributing foolishness to the scene. Also, it will not then likely see the efforts of the school to teach in the same respect for evidence as a threat either to its influence or to the health and morality of the student. The evidence on any problem respected and heeded tends to bring people together, to create allies—not to foster suspicion, accusation, and enmity.

When people try to rule, or intimidate, or censor the school from teaching in any area of human significance, it is highly probable that they are indisposed toward facts in one or all of the following ways:

1. They are unaware of the range of knowledge available and indisposed to endeavor to extend their range.
2. They are committed to positions that the evidence fails to support or even tends to deny, and they fear to have these positions challenged by evidence.
3. They have some vested interest, some influence, some potential for control that depends on keeping certain facts obscure or unknown.
4. They are, in extreme cases, so completely assured that their utterly subjective view of the world is the fact, and the whole fact, that any other source of evidence beyond their view of things constitutes an attack on their very being.

The way people who fall in the last category see things is the product of a confusion of very human hopes, ideals, fears, frustrations, jealousies, angers, and hatreds that they have increasingly refused to weigh against the perceptions and experience of others. They refuse to set these against the ordinary rules of evidence. To the extremist and the mentally ill alike, the invitation to dialogue is an invitation to self-betrayal. Urging them to accept the discipline of rationality they see as a sure sign of conspiracy against them.

These are characteristics that are likely, one or all, to be present when persons or groups set themselves against the school functioning in an educational manner in any area of human significance.

effectiveness

It is with effectiveness that schooling and total education tend to diverge. The school varies in effectiveness. Our contention is not that the school is completely ineffective, only that it could be *much more* effective than it is. We also believe that other agencies that lack certain advantages and commitments of the school manage to be more

effective. To educators this assertion should be shocking. A series
of questions will serve to make the point:

1. Should the school with all the resources of evidence at its disposal
   graduate millions of students to become or be already victim to
   death-dealing cigarette and drug addiction?
2. Should the school, with its rich investment in science, graduate
   students who in large numbers read horoscopes, patronize astrolo-
   gists and fortune tellers, and otherwise endow or subsidize the
   charlatans and self-deluded?
3. Should the school with all its attention to mathematics and quantification graduate hundreds of thousands who proceed to the marketplace as lambs to the slaughter? Who cannot protect themselves against tricky merchandising and frequent atrocious interest
   rates?
4. Should the school with all its attention to literature turn out a
   reading public that by the testimony of every newsstand prefers
   garbage, pure garbage, for its basic intellectual diet? Should the
   measure of its contribution to general literacy be the elevation of
   trash to every best-seller list?
5. Should the school with all the resources of human civilization at its
   command be content with the well-known reality that its effect
   upon the value system of its students is negligible—often negative
   —in comparison with the effect of the peer group itself?
6. Should the school be content with the generally negative justification offered for its existence? That it prepares for college; that it
   tends to keep a lot of students off the streets, off the job market,
   out of trouble.

The list of questions, all loaded with the assumption that the
school is ineffective where it ought not to be, could be indefinitely extended.

Just why do other agencies succeed where the school fails? They
manage to get somewhere close to where the student lives. They
recognize his real questions at least, then give him the answers that
suit not his needs (the school could, if it would, help him to find and
fill those needs), but their own purposes.

The advertiser, whether he peddles cigarettes, deodorants, skin
cream, or colas, knows his person. He respects that knowledge if
not the person. He knows that each person hungers for recognition,
dreams of being special (being wanted, being loved), yearns for open
country to stroll in with good company, and has sexual fantasies. So
he paints his picture and puts the person in it with his product in his
lips, or draped upon him, or in his hand. It is that simple.

The school with all these and better universal truths at its disposal,
what does it do? Its standard instrument is far too often the put-
down, seldom the build-up. It motivates with the threat of failure,

low esteem, rejection, and few academic medals for prowess. But where are the grand associations of its learnings with the deepest drives and aspirations of its persons? Only in athletics and drama perhaps does the school approach the advertiser's hold on the person (and here the school's success is greatest). Here the student may dream of and even achieve glory. He may be somebody, he may win popularity, he may hear applause. He may stand tall, feel beautiful, attract girls, travel, be esteemed, even adored. Not much like the classroom, is it?

relevance

Perhaps, the primary fault of the school has been to take too much for granted the relevance of its efforts. It may have neglected to ask the critical questions by which it might have assured a greater degree of relevancy, questions such as these:

1. Is this effort, once important, as important as it used to be?
2. Is this effort, quite important though it may be, as important as something we are neglecting to do?
3. Is this effort only important within the school, but quite unrelated to the world outside?
4. Have we consulted with any schedules of relative values or levels of importance in budgeting the time and energy of the school?
5. Have we consulted with the learners as to what is of primary importance to them?
6. Have we consulted with serious literature; have we kept in touch with first-rate representatives of the modern mind in developing our programs?
7. Are we aware of any urgencies in education? Do we know and relate our efforts to the pressing realities, the critical problems that mankind faces in our time? Do we undertake to provide knowledge in life and death matters? Do we inform a student in areas where if we leave him uninformed, his ignorance may kill him?

Relevance is, after all, a matter of degree. The key question is not: "Is it relevant?" It should be phrased: "How relevant is it, and to what?" The teaching of Latin was once held to be relevant to mastering English. But research demonstrated that if mastering English were truly the goal of instruction, then other instruments were more relevant.

"Relevance" can be the slogan for those who would simply place the school exclusively in the center of the contemporary. To admit that this would be to leave man unnecessarily deprived of acquired wisdom only points up the necessity for relevance. Surely it is no fallacy to assert that no matter how far the school reaches into the past, or remote places, for its lessons, they must have some bearing, some direct bearing on central realities for persons living in the here and now and in the uncertain tomorrows.

Further illustrations will not be cited at this point. As a matter of fact, since relevance is a criterion that the authors accept as a discipline, it is their contention that the text is an illustration of relevance in education.

Then, what of total education? Surely, the school may be content to be a little less than life size. It is not the only institution that affects the person. It has the person within its reach for only a few years and on a part-time basis. If the school claims to be educational, however, it should experience great discontent at the broad disparity between its schooling and the potential for a total education. In terms of scope, significance, effectiveness, and relevance, it is a shame that the school reaches for so much less than it might grasp. Surely, the school that enjoys its support on the assumption that it will educate should not be content to be less educational than other institutions that affect the person. If the school cannot grasp a total educational commitment, it might at least extend its reach.

topics for inquiry

 1. The Essentialist View of Education
 2. The Meaning of Operant Conditioning
 3. The Theories of Marshall McLuhan
 4. Existentialism and Education
 5. The Concept of Equality
 6. College Entrance Requirements
 7. Critical Views of the World History Course
 8. Important Issues that the School Neglects
 9. Varied Interpretations of Relevance
10. Sex Education: Attackers and Defenders

subjects for discussion

1. Review your high school education. What educational theories seem to have dominated your school's program? Would other bases for making decisions have improved it? Did your school

develop in its graduates an articulate meaning of a *good educa-tion?*

2. Do you believe that "Whatever exists can be quantified, and whatever can be quantified can be measured"? What are the grounds for your position? Is there any verification of knowledge other than through science? If so, how do you defend your position?

3. It has been said, "Dress codes are a legitimate part of a school's disciplinary program. Decent standards of dress and hair styling are a part of a student's social education. Reasonable codes improve student morale. Sloppy attire leads to bad conduct and lower academic achievement." How do you react to this?

4. List some of the most fundamental and useful learnings that you have acquired to date. What part did school play in your learning these things? Does your experience bear out the authors' contention that the total education of the person far exceeds the school's contribution?

5. Sometimes highly significant events take place in the world around the school. The school has the choice to acknowledge or to avoid considering them.

   With respect to each of the following instances, what should the response of the school be?

   a. The assassination of Martin Luther King, Jr.

   b. Resumption of school after a bitterly contested teachers' strike.

   c. The involvement of the community in a public controversy over air and water pollution.

   d. Participation of the local basketball team in the finals of the state tournament.

6. Your authors seem to feel that putting students down (lowering their morale and self-esteem) is more typical school behavior than building students up (raising their confidence and self-esteem).

   a. Do you agree with their estimate?

   b. Agreed or disagreed, what are some of the techniques commonly used to put down or to build up? In a teacher's repertoire of techniques for relating to students, which do you prefer?

selected readings

CALLAHAN, RAYMOND E. *Education and the Cult of Efficiency.* Chicago: University of Chicago Press, 1962.

Shows the devastating educational effect of modeling the school on business-industrial concepts of efficiency and productivity. Callahan calls the choice of most administrators in adopting this model, "an American Tragedy in Education."

CRARY, RYLAND W. *Humanizing the School.* New York: Knopf, 1969.
Bitter criticism in Chapter XI and XII against the Kimball-McClelland approach and the Skinnerian assumptions and devices. Chapter II is a good summation of existential views on education.

FRIEDENBERG, EDGAR Z. *The Vanishing Adolescent.* Boston: Beacon Press, 1959.
A good companion piece to Paul Goodman's work below. It is particularly good in pointing up the disparity between the schools' purposes for youth and the needs and purposes of youth itslf.

GOODMAN, PAUL. *Growing Up Absurd.* New York: Knopf, 1956.
A standard testament of the student protest movement. The author attributes much human waste to the failure of institutions to establish any sensible bearing on the lives of youth.

KIMBALL, SOLON T. and JAMES C. MCCLELLAND. *Education and the New America.* New York: Random House, 1962.
A very important book because it is the most thorough defense of the role of institutions in relation to education. It should be read because it differs so fundamentally from the views of Goodman, Friedenberg, and others. A class committee might well study this work and review it in detail for the class.

SKINNER, B. F. *Walden Two.* New York: Macmillan, 1948.
Worth reading as a masterpiece of deceptive and beguiling persuasion. We are confident that you will unravel the network of fallacies of which it is woven. An amusing Utopian pipedream, stemming no doubt from good intentions—which are not always the road to Utopia.

Three contemporary works plus a classic furnish a very enlightening short reading list on the strange ways of bureaucracy. They do not all directly pertain to education, but they are relevant to our theme of institutionalization.

PARKINSON, G. NORTHCOTE. *Parkinson's Law and Other Studies in Administration.* Boston: Houghton Mifflin, 1957.

PETER, LAWRENCE J., and RAYMOND HULL. *The Peter Principle.* New York: Morrow, 1968.

WHYTE, JR., WILLIAM H. *The Organization Man.* New York: Simon and Schuster, 1956.

3

INSTI-
TUTIONAL
COMPO-
NENTS OF THE
EDUCATION-
AL SYSTEM

The American educational system in its basic establishment constitutes a continuum that can be considered to range from kindergarten through college. When one takes into account the pushing back of deliberate education to the nursery school and even early infancy, and then the extension of "continuing education" through adulthood and geriatric phases, it may be said that America is involved in education "from the cradle to the grave."

This chapter, however, is concerned with the standard components of the system—kindergarten, elementary school, secondary school, and college and university. The purpose is not to outline administrative or organizational structures; it is to make function apparent. Historical origins are examined only as far as they clarify the institution as it now exists or the problems within which it resides.

All of the components have a few factors in common. All are expanding; all are changing; all have their basic functions in dispute; all are perceived to be, in one dimension or another, in crisis.

The idea of continuum is important. In implication it is quite revolutionary. In the past each component has been for some terminal. Today, even though it is assumed that one will move along through the continuum to at least some stage of the secondary school, the movement to the next institutional level tends to be a crossing of a strange frontier. Educational progress thus tends to be jerky, an encounter with arbitrary, and sometimes irrational hurdles.

Continuity is the reality to be discovered in education. The idea of education from cradle to grave is by no means absurd. For living is learning, and if learning is living, then that is the way it ought to be. The central problem of each component seems to be how to furnish greater connections between its institutional efforts and life itself.

kindergarten

Many view the kindergarten as an appendage to the school rather than an integrated part of it. It is not unusual to hear it referred to as a "preschool level." Nor is it thought of by all as even a necessary "appendage" to the school since fewer than 50 percent of the nation's 21,159 public school systems maintain kindergartens. Of course, in many instances where they are not part of the public school systems they are maintained by private organizations. Still, for about 30 percent of the nation's children school begins at the age of six or seven at the first-grade level. What then, of these children? If the kindergarten is considered an integral part of the total school program it might be argued that children who have no access to it are being denied of perhaps the most important level of education. There is even concern expressed that where there are kindergartens, except in a few cases, they are only one-year programs. The Educational Policies Commission of the NEA in a report entitled "Universal Opportunity for Early Childhood Education" pointed up the importance of kindergarten. The commission not only called for universal acceptance of kindergartens but for two-year programs:

> The development of intellectual ability and of intellectual
> interests is fundamental to the achievement of all the goals of
> American education. Yet these qualities are greatly affected by
> what happens to children before they reach school. A growing
> body of research and experience demonstrates that by the age
> of six most children have already developed a considerable part
> of the intellectual ability they will possess as adults. Six
> is now generally accepted as the normal age of entrance into
> school. We believe that this practice is obsolete. All children
> should have the opportunity to go to school at public expense
> beginning at the age of four.[1]

Some thoughtful objections might be raised against such a suggestion if it were going to mean that children at the age of four would be victims of a rigid curriculum simply pulled down from the elementary school. If this were the case, the children would probably be better off out of school. But the Educational Policies Commission envisions a different program:

[1] National Education Association, Educational Policies Commission, "Universal Opportunity for Early Childhood Education" (Washington, D.C.: NEA, 1966), p. 4.

> We envision a program uniquely adapted to children of ages
> four and five; the program for six-year-olds would be altered to
> take into account the earlier schooling of the children, rather
> than vice versa. . . . One of the main contributions which early
> education can make to a child's intellectual development is the
> enlargement of his span of experience. Under skilled guidance,
> a child's new contacts with the world become new learnings and
> open new possibilities. There are new worlds to discover in
> virtually every situation—the world of nature, the world of play,
> the economic world, the world of oneself, the world of one's
> relations with others.[2]

To a large extent the purposes for early childhood education that
the Educational Policies Commission have stated are basically the same
as those established by the earliest promoters of the kindergarten. Its
purposes from the beginning have been to allow the child to "discover" his world.

historical development

The kindergarten in the United States dates from the mid-nineteenth
century. In Europe, where the kindergarten developed, its origins
can be traced to the eighteenth century. Friedrich Froebel, generally
regarded as the father of the kindergarten movement, founded the
first kindergarten in Blankenburg, Germany, in 1837. His ideas for
early childhood education were largely influenced by the writings of
Jean Jacques Rousseau and the writings and work of Johann Heinrich
Pestalozzi, both of whom advanced ideas that "discovery" should be
the process of education for children. A laissez-faire approach was
not implied. The application of the idea by Froebel took on a deeply
involved program of guidance by the teacher. Perhaps Froebel's ideas
and the subsequent development of the kindergarten can best be seen
against a background of some of Rousseau's and Pestalozzi's ideas.

Jean Jacques Rousseau (1712–1778)
With the publication of his pedagogical novel *Emile*, in 1762, Rousseau offered a radical alternative to the then existing practices not
only of formal education but of child-rearing in general. In place of
rigid adult-prescribed and -directed learning he proposed a permissiveness that would allow for what he felt to be the natural goodness and
intelligence of the child to emerge In the first paragraph of *Emile*
he states:

> Everything is good as it comes from the hands of the Creator
> of Nature; everything deteriorates in the hands of man. God
> makes all things good; man meddles with them and they become
> evil. He forces one soil to yield the products of another, one

[2] *Ibid.*, p. 6.

tree to bear another's fruit. He confuses and confounds time,
place, and natural conditions. He mutilates his dog, his horse,
and his slave. He destroys and defaces all things; he loves all
that is deformed and monstrous; he will have nothing as nature
made it, not even man himself, who must learn his paces like a
saddle-horse, and be shaped to his master's taste like the trees
in his garden.

To Rousseau the worst thing about the school was that it tried to
mold the child, to work against his nature. "Nature provides for the
child's growth in her own way and this should never be thwarted. Do
not make him sit still when he wants to run about, nor run when he
wants to be quiet."

Rousseau's permissivism or "negative education" did not prevent
his stating a positive view of education. He saw the need for a teacher
to direct and guide, but in such a way as to not thwart the natural
development of the child. Rather, he would have the teacher guide
this natural devleopment. Regardless of the paradoxes or inconsistencies on this point that one might find in *Emile*, it is evident that
Rousseau's ideas, especially on the value of play, influenced Pestalozzi
and Froebel. Nor was Rousseau's work to influence only a small
coterie of educators. *Emile* was widely read and had a marked influence on child-rearing practices in Europe in its time.

Johann Heinrich Pestalozzi (1746–1827)

Pestalozzi's influence on the development of educational ideas in
the nineteenth century is unmistakable. Through his writings, especially the novels *Leonard and Gertrude* (1782) and *How Gertrude
Teaches Her Children* (1802), Pestalozzi set forth his general ideas
about education. But perhaps his greatest influence on educational
thought came from his schools at Burgdorf and Yverdon in Switzerland where his theories were put into practice. His work at both
places was highly acclaimed by eminent visitors from Europe and
America. One visiting American educator, Professor John Griscom,
reported on his observations in 1823:

The teacher must be constantly with the child, always talking,
questioning, explaining, and repeating. The pupils, however, by
this process, are brought into very close intimacy with the instructor. Their capacities, all their faculties and propensities,
become laid open to his observation. This gives him an advantage which can not possibly be gained in the ordinary way in
which schools are generally taught. The children look well, appear very contented, and apparently live in great harmony one
with another; which considering the diversity of national character and temper here collected, can be attributed only to the
spirit of love and affection which sways the breast of the princi-

pal of the institution, and extends its benign influence throughout
all the departments.

The success of this mode of instruction greatly depends upon
the personal qualifications of those who undertake to conduct
it. There is nothing of mechanism in it, as in the Lancastrian
plan; no laying down of precise rules for managing classes, etc.
It is all mind and feeling.[3]

Other Americans were to speak highly of Pestalozzi's work either
as seen in his schools at Burgdorf and Yverdon or, in later decades, in
the schools or writings of his disciples. Bronson Alcott, Calvin Stowe,
Horace Mann, and Henry Barnard are only a few of the prominent
names that are associated with Pestalozzi's influence on American
educational thought, though not necessarily practice.

When the Pestalozzian influence was translated into educational
practice in the United States after the Civil War, the translation be-
lied the essential nature of the original idea. This essential nature,
as seen by the early observers of Pestalozzi's work, lay in the absence
of a mechanistic systematization of teaching, the absence of precise
rules, and the like. But systems and rules were to become the nature
of Pestalozzianism in practice.

In 1866 under the direction of E. A. Sheldon the New York State
Normal School at Oswego began a program of teacher education
based on Pestalozzi's ideas. Before long the ideas were formalized
into practical and specific procedures, taking the form but not the
substance of Pestalozzi's ideas. The "object lessons," as they were
called, were finitely detailed procedures that were to serve as models
for teachers. An example of one of these models taken from Sheldon's
manual of instruction appears in Chapter 8 of this book. From the
above it is obvious that Pestalozzi's ideas were to be more directly applicable to the elementary school in America, but they were also to
influence the kindergarten through their application by another European, Friedrich Froebel.

Friedrich Froebel (1782–1852)

Friedrich Froebel and the term kindergarten go naturally together.
The first such school, as we have noted, was begun by Froebel in
Blankenburg, Germany, in 1837. His work was to have a great impact on the kindergarten movement in the United States. Froebel
came under the influence of Pestalozzi during his stay at Yverdon as
teacher and pupil from 1807 to 1810. From his work there he developed his own theories about early childhood education and thus the
kindergarten.

Froebel's faith in the spiritual goodness and eternal unity of man

---

[3] As quoted in E. P. Cubberley, *Readings in the History of Education* (Boston: Houghton
Mifflin, 1948), pp. 443–444.

was the basis of his ideas for the kindergarten. He looked upon
natural development as being the *sine qua non* for a meaningful
existence, thus reflecting Rousseau's philosophy. In his book *The
Education of Man* he stated:

> . . . education in instruction and training, originally and in its
> first principles, should necessarily be *passive, following* (only
> guarding and protecting), *not prescriptive categorical, interfering.*
>
> Indeed, in its very essence, education should have these char-
> acteristics; for the undisturbed operation of the Divine Unity is
> necessarily good—can not be otherwise than good. This neces-
> sity implies that the young human being—as it were, still in the
> process of creation—would seek, although unconsciously, as a
> product of nature, yet decidedly and surely, that which is in it-
> self best; and, moreover, in a form wholly adapted to his condi-
> tion, as well as to his disposition, his powers, and means.

Froebel's views here did not mean that the child could not be aided
by the school. But the kind of education he implied was that which
would be responsive to the natural development of the child. Froebel's mystical interpretation of this natural development and his
notion that it moved toward what he termed Divine Unity led him to
develop a systematic series of playthings and games with directions
as to their use and the insights to be developed therein. It is true
that Froebel approached education in somewhat of a theological sense.
Nevertheless, he provided a great deal of illuminating thought about
the pedagogy of the process. His attempts at establishing a relationship between specifically shaped objects and the natural development
of the mind are still fascinating ideas. More important perhaps to the
subsequent development of the kindergarten were his views on the
meaning of play. Again in *The Education of Man* Froebel stated:

> *Play* is the highest phase of child development—of human de-
> velopment at this period; for *it is self-active representation of
> the inner—representation of the inner from inner necessity and
> impulse.*
>
> Play is the purest, most spiritual activity of man at this stage,
> and at the same time, typical of human life as a whole—of the
> inner hidden natural life in man and all things. It gives, there-
> fore, joy, freedom, contentment, inner and outer rest, peace with
> the world.

Again, Froebel saw play as an activity that could be directed toward certain ends. His viewpoint was to become an essential part of
kindergarten education.

the kindergarten movement in america

Froebel's ideas about education for young children spread not only across Europe but to America as well. The first American kindergarten was established in 1855 in Watertown, Wisconsin, by Mrs. Carl Schurz who had studied under Froebel. Within the next fifteen years ten more German-speaking kindergartens were founded in other parts of the country. In 1860 Elizabeth P. Peabody, whose interest was aroused by Mrs. Shurz's accounts of Froebel's theories, opened the first English-speaking kindergarten in Boston. Though important as beginnings, these private kindergartens were more important in their influence on the public schools' kindergarten movement.

In 1873 William T. Harris, then superintendent of the St. Louis schools, invited Susan E. Blow to establish kindergartens in the St. Louis school system. Initially twelve were started, but the number grew to fifty as soon as enough teachers had been trained. Before long many of the major cities had incorporated kindergartens in their public schools. For the most part they operated under modifications of Froebel's ideas as practiced and written by his disciples. His writings as well as those of Susan Blow and others on Froebelian ideas had a wide audience in this country well before the turn of the century. To some extent the kindergarten has retained some of its original spirit, but the recent trend of increasing formalization in elementary education has begun to press on the kindergarten.

the kindergarten today

The accepted value of the kindergarten as an integrated part of the total school program is borne out by the facts of its growth since the 1920s. From 1923 when the kindergarten enrollment accounted for only 2.5 percent of the total school enrollment, it grew to over 6 percent of the total in 1969. The value of the kindergarten to a child's later educational experiences not only in terms of academic achievement but in terms of social adjustment has been borne out by innumerable research studies. The prospects for the future hold for an expansion in preelementary education not only horizontally to include more school districts, but also vertically to involve a longer period. This expansion has wide support from educational organizations. The general pattern of existing programs is for a one-year program for five-year-olds for five days a week. In 1969, of the 9,766 districts with kindergarten programs 93 percent operated a one-year program for five-year-olds; .4 percent, a two-year program for four- and five-year-olds; and 7 percent a less than one-semester program. Of the total programs 96.3 percent functioned five days a week. The remainder had either two- or three-day programs.[4]

[4] National Education Association Research *Bulletin*, Vol. 47 (March 1969).

Traditionally, the kindergarten curriculum has been unstructured and flexible. Experiences that could be categorized under subject headings are usually provided in a general developmental sense rather than to achieve specified content. The development of skills applicable to all areas is achieved in a more or less relaxed atmosphere through a wide variety of activity experiences. Thus the remark sometimes heard that "real" education ends with kindergarten is in many cases true.

The aims of kindergarten education are those that help children:

1. Become aware of their physical needs; learn healthful habits; build coordination, strength, and physical skills; and develop sound mental and physical health.
2. Gain some understanding of their social world; learn to work and play fairly and happily in it; grow in developing responsibility and independence, yet accept the limits present in living in a democratic society.
3. Acquire interests, attitudes, and values that aid them in becoming secure and positive in their relationships with peers and adults.
4. Grow into an ever deeper sense of accomplishment and self-esteem.
5. Grow in their understanding of their natural environment.
6. Gain some understanding of spatial and number relationships.
7. Enjoy their literary and musical heritage.
8. Express their thoughts and feelings more creatively through language, movement, art, and music.
9. Develop more appropriate behavior, skills, and understandings on which their continuing education builds.
10. Observe, experiment, discover, think, and generalize at their individual levels of experience and development.[5]

It has been well established that in good kindergarten programs children do develop a great many skills and learn a great deal about the world without rigidly structured curricula. Reading, writing, and arithmetic skills are natural outcomes for many children who have been given wide experiences in a flexible program. O. K. Moore has provided evidence of this in his discovery approach, which utilizes a wide variety of materials and experiences. In general, the most valuable experiences are those that promote the natural curiosity and energy that children have rather than discourage such curiosity by a rigidly structured subject matter curriculum.

There is some indication that the press for specific achievement in content areas, especially in reading and arithmetic, has brought structured or formalized programs of learning into the kindergarten. Ta-

[5] Lillian C. Gore and Rose Koury, *Educating Children in Nursery Schools and Kindergartens*, Bulletin No. 11 (Washington, D.C.: U.S. Office of Education, 1964), pp. 21–22.

TABLE 1

Curriculum Experience	Struc- tured	Unstruc- tured	Combi- nation	Not Offered
Number Relationships	52.6%	31.0%	11.7%	2.9%
Reading	41.1	36.5	6.3	14.4
Music	39.1	39.0	5.4	14.8
Art	37.2	48.8	8.5	3.7
Language Arts	31.1	45.3	6.8	15.1
Physical Education	28.1	54.2	5.9	10.1
Health	27.5	56.6	5.4	8.8
Science	15.3	62.6	6.5	13.9
Social Studies	14.1	65.0	5.6	13.5

Source: Adapted from estimated figures of 1968 NEA Research *Bulletin*, p. 12.

ble 1 shows the percentages of kindergartens with either structured or unstructured programs in content areas.

Although it is difficult to define clearly what particular schools might mean by structured or unstructured, it seems clear that in the areas of reading and arithmetic there is a concern for precise achievement. Obviously, if this were to carry over into other areas with the same formality that characterizes so much of the elementary school, the spirit of discovery and enjoyment that is traditionally a part of kindergarten will be simply pressed out. It would be much better if the trend were reversed, with the relaxed atmosphere of the kindergarten pervading the "upper" levels of the school.

One important area of early childhood education that would readily fit here, the Head Start Program, is discussed in Chapter 13.

the elementary school

The elementary school has long been an important part of the American culture. Its development has reflected major changes in the United States not only in social trends, but also in the concept of education itself. This does not imply that one should expect to find a pervasive standardization in the structure and function of elementary schools today. A great deal of variation exists—variation in organization, curriculum, methods, and (in a functional, if not stated, sense) purpose. To some extent the variations reflect enlightened attempts to adapt the school to differing views of societal needs over a background of traditional ideas and practices.

historical development

Although the graded elementary school as we know it today dates back only a little more than a century, its roots go back to the earliest colonial times. The Dame Schools of New England, which afforded, at the very least, reading instruction, were in a sense the forerunners of the primary level of elementary schools today. Their purposes, obviously, were much simpler. For most girls it was the end of formal education. For some boys it was preparation to enter the reading and writing schools. The subsequent developments, such as the monitorial schools, which attempted to extend the rudiments of reading, writing and arithmetic to many of the poor, were equally limited in both purpose and practice. With the establishment and development of public schools and compulsory education laws, came what is now viewed as the elementary school. The increased enrollments made it necessary to organize into graded patterns, the most common of which was the eight-year elementary school.

The establishment of the public elementary school was a result of *social* reform during the latter half of the nineteenth century, but there was also an early movement of *educational* reform within the school that had a significant effect on its development. Much of the present view of the elementary school, if not practice, has evolved from that reform.

The elementary schools of the late nineteenth century for the most part were rigidly formulated both in their curriculum and their methodology. The separate traditional subjects taught by the recitation method was the order of the day for most schools. Discipline, imposed methodically and bulwarked by corporal punishment by the teacher, was considered a necessity. Such ideas had long been given a degree of official sanction as evidenced by an 1874 bulletin of the federal Bureau of Education, "A Statement of the Theory of Education in the United States of America, as Approved by Many Leading Educators":

> In order to compensate for lack of family-nurture, the school is obliged to lay more stress upon discipline and to make far more prominent the moral phase of education. It is obliged to train the pupil into habits of prompt obedience to his teachers and the practice of self-control in its various forms, in order that he may be prepared for a life wherein there is little police-restraint on the part of the constituted authorities.
>
> The commercial tone prevalent in the city tends to develop, in its schools, quick, alert habits and readiness to combine with others in their tasks. Military precision is required in the maneuvering of classes. Great stress is laid upon (1) punctuality, (2) regularity, (3) attention, and (4) silence, as habits necessary through life for successful combination with one's fellow-men in an industrial and commercial civilization.[6]

Although the statement was descriptive of the system, it was at the same time meant to be prescriptive. This is not surprising when one considers that the statement was primarily the work of William Torrey Harris, whose influence on regimentation in education in the nineteenth century is well documented.

[6] As quoted in Daniel Calhoun (ed.), *The Educating of Americans: A Documentary History* (Boston: Houghton Mifflin, 1969), pp. 297–298.

Not only were such habits detailed by the 1874 bulletin to be encouraged by the school organization and methods, but also by at least some of the curriculum material, especially the McGuffey Readers. Examples of some selections from the readers are shown in Chapter 8 of this book.

Nineteen years after the Bureau of Education description was written, a young pediatrician, Joseph M. Rice, reported his descriptions of the schools in the United States in his book *The Public School System of the United States*. About the elementary schools of New York City he declared:

> Now, what is the character of the instruction that will be passed as satisfactory by the superintendents of the public schools of New York city? Surely no one can call me unjust when I answer this question by describing the work of a school whose principal has been marked uniformly "excellent" during the twenty-five years or more that she has held her present position. . . .
>
> The principal of this school has pedagogical views and a maxim peculiarly her own. She believes that when a child enters upon school life his vocabulary is so small that it is practically worthless, and his power to think so feeble that his thoughts are worthless. She is consequently of the opinion that what the child knows and is able to do on coming to school should be entirely disregarded, that he should not be allowed to waste time, either in thinking or in finding his own words to express his thoughts, but that he should be supplied with ready-made thoughts as given in a ready-made vocabulary. She has therefore prepared sets of questions and answers, so that the child may be given in concise form most of the facts prescribed in the course of study for the three years of primary instruction. The instruction throughout the school consists principally of grinding these answers verbatim into the minds of the children. The principal's ideal lies in giving each child the ability to answer without hesitation, upon leaving her school, every one of the questions formulated by her. In order to reach the desired end, the school has been converted into the most dehumanizing institution that I have ever laid eyes upon, each child being treated as if he possessed a memory and the faculty of speech, but no individuality, no sensibilities, no soul.
>
> So much concerning the pedagogical views on which this school is conducted; now as to the maxim. This maxim consists of three short words—"Save the minutes." The spirit of the school is, "Do what you like with the child, immobilize him, automatize him, dehumanize him, but save, save the minutes." In many ways the minutes are saved. By giving the child ready-made thoughts, the minutes required in thinking are saved. By giving the child ready-made definitions, the minutes required in formulating them are saved. Everything is prohibited that is of no measurable advantage to the child, such as the movement of

the head or a limb, when there is no logical reason why it should be moved at the time. . . .

During the recitations many minutes are saved. The principal has indeed solved the problem of how the greatest number of answers may be given in the smallest number of minutes. In the first place, no time is spent in selecting pupils to answer questions, every recitation being started by the first pupil in the class, the children then answering in turn, until all have recited. Secondly, time is economized in the act of rising and sitting during the recitations, the children being so drilled that the child who recites begins to fall back into his seat while uttering the last word of a definition, the next succeeding child beginning his ascent while the one before him is in the act of descending. Indeed, things appear as if the two children occupying adjoining seats were sitting upon the opposite poles of an invisible see-saw, so that the descending child necessarily raises the pupil next to him to his feet. Then, again, the minutes are saved by compelling the children to unload their answers as rapidly as possible, distinctness of utterance being sacrificed to speed, and to scream their answers at the tops of their voices, so that no time may be wasted in repeating words inaudibly uttered.

Nor, according to Rice, were the schools of St. Louis any better:

When the aim of the supervision is limited to securing results, though the children be rendered motionless and the room as silent as a grave, the school is entirely lawless, because the only laws which the school should obey—the laws of mental development—are entirely ignored. The superintendent here reigns supreme; his rulings are arbitrary; his word is law. But in exercising his license he deprives the child of his liberty. The child is twisted and turned or made immobile to suit the pleasure of the teacher, and the fact that the child is a frail and tender human being is entirely disregarded. The innocent child is thrust into bondage, the years of childhood are converted into years of slavery. . . .

In one regard the treatment of the children cannot be considered otherwise than barbarous. During several daily recitation periods, each of which is from twenty to twenty-five minutes in duration, the children are obliged to stand on the line, perfectly motionless, their bodies erect, their knees and feet together, the tips of their shoes touching the edge of a board in the floor. The slightest movement on the part of a child attracts the attention of the teacher. The recitation is repeatedly interrupted with cries of "Stand straight," "Don't bend the knees," "Don't lean against the wall," and so on. I heard one teacher ask a little boy: "How can you learn anything with your knees and toes out of order?" The toes appear to play a more important part than the reasoning faculties. The teacher never forgets the toes; every few moments she casts her eyes "toe-ward." [7]

Although perhaps not what was called for by W. T. Harris, the elementary school as Rice saw it exemplified the school at the turn of the century. His reports were corroborated by others.

The reform movement in education begun by Francis W. Parker in the 1870s, and carried on by John Dewey and others in the 1900s, did not have wide acceptance even by the 1920s. To many educators the elementary schools were still viewed as institutions wherein pupils were to be "trained" and disciplined. For example, William Bagley in his textbook for teachers, *Classroom Management*, saw the aim of education thus:

> Fundamentally, the task of the school is to fit the child for life in civilized society. The child, when he comes into the world, is not, like the young of most animals, adapted by nature to the life that he must lead. During the plastic period of immaturity he must be trained and instructed in order to enter, at maturity, upon the life that is represented by the social world into which he is born. [8]

And if the child should for any reason balk at the "training" Bagley had this advice:

> If a pupil can be stimulated to effort in no other way, it is far better that his tasks be performed, even inadequately, through the stimulus of physical pain than that he be permitted to grow up in ignorance. [9]

Even the inflicting of physical pain was given in methodological formulas for teachers by Bagley. Just one of his many directions on corporal punishment, a topic to which he addressed several chapters, is offered here:

> There should be a "standard" method of inflicting corporal punishment. Blows upon the head, in the neighborhood of the spinal column, or near any vital organ should be rigidly prohibited. Just what cutaneous area can be most effectively stimulated is a matter of differing opinion, as is also the particular instrument to be used. Many good teachers advise "spanking" for young children, and there is much to recommend this traditional means of discipline. Upon those who have grown callous to the palm of the hand, a shingle may be profitably employed,

[7] As quoted in David B. Tyack (ed.), *Turning Points in American Educational History* (Waltham, Mass.: Blaisdell, 1967), pp. 328–332.
[8] William Bagley, *Classroom Management* (New York: Macmillan, 1922), p. 7.
[9] *Ibid.*, p. 15.

although it should be noted that some authorities object to any
blows upon the buttocks as unhygienic—maintaining that they
tend to cause congestion of the capillaries in the neighborhood
of the genital organs. . . . St. Louis prescribes that corporal
punishment "shall not be inflicted otherwise than by using a
thin rattan upon the fleshy part of the back." LaCrosse, Wisconsin, rules that corporal punishment "shall be restricted to
the use of a leather strap, preferably on the palm of the hand."
A light "switch" (such as the birch of our grandfathers) applied
around the legs is sometimes effective. Unyielding rods should
not be used in any case, and it is always well to avoid anything
that will leave a "welt," which, although it may look far more
dangerous than it really is, is apt to cause troublesome investigations.[10]

In further deference to "troublesome investigations," Bagley, in a
tone that implies that the school and its pupils are natural enemies,
asserts:

In view of the natural tendency of the child's mind to exag-
gerate or, at least, to distort actual occurrences, it is well always
to have an adult witness when punishment is inflicted. . . . Also,
every precaution should be taken to eliminate any conditions that
might unjustly be turned against the teacher. For example, if a
brittle rod is broken during the act of punishment, the very statement, "The teacher broke a stick over the child," has an ugly
sound, and will surely tell against one in popular opinion, if not
even in a court of law, although the blow itself may be quite
innocuous.[11]

The prevalence of rigid traditionalism in the schools at the time
Bagley wrote his book is attested to by the account of a midwestern
school by Robert and Helen Lynd in their classic, *Middletown*:

Immovable seats in orderly rows fix the sphere of activity of
each child. For all, from the timid six-year old entering for the
first time to the most assured high school senior, the general routine is much the same. Bells divide the day into periods. For the
six-year-olds the periods are short (fifteen to twenty minutes) and
varied; in some they leave their seats, play games, and act out
make-believe stories, although in "recitation periods" all movement is prohibited. As they grow older the taboo upon physical
activity becomes stricter, until by the third or fourth year practically all movement is forbidden except the marching from one set
of seats to another between periods.[12]

[10] *Ibid.*, p. 127.
[11] *Ibid.*, p. 129.
[12] Robert and Helen Lynd, *Middletown* (New York: Harcourt, Brace Jovanovich, 1957),
p. 188.

early reform in education: toward the humane

The schools depicted by Joseph Rice and others or those that Bagley's methods called for did not go unheeded by education reformers. By the 1870s the "child-centered" idea that had influenced the kindergarten movement was also to have its effects in attempted reform of the elementary schools.

As early as 1875 the child-centered approach was to be not only a statement of educational theory but a basis for educational practice in one important instance. Francis Wayland Parker, who became a disciple of Pestalozzi and Froebel, was given an opportunity to put into practice the "new education." Appointed to the superintendency of the Quincy, Massachusetts, schools in 1875, Parker immediately set out to infuse new meaning into elementary education. The conventional rigidity of a set curriculum and rote recitation were replaced by practices intended to develop understanding and meaningful learning. Humane concern for the well-being of the child was to replace the harsh and sometimes brutal discipline of the school in the nineteenth century. The natural curiosity and activities of children were encouraged rather than stifled. Traditional textbooks were replaced or enhanced by newspapers and magazines or by teacher-devised materials. Children were given the opportunity to express themselves through art as well as through content areas where their involvement could be elicited. In short, the child was not looked upon as a passive recipient of precise bits of learning, but as the center of the educative process.

The history of the Quincy program and later the Cook County Normal School in Chicago under Parker reads as an exciting innovation in education, much of which would be pertinent for today's schools. But Parker was not without his conservative critics who charged that the Quincy school children were not learning their three Rs. Their criticisms were answered by the results of an 1879 survey and evaluation of the program by the Massachusetts State Board of Education, which reported that the Quincy students excelled in comparison to other students in the state.

Parker left Quincy in 1880. Until 1883 he was a supervisor in Boston. He then took the principalship of Cook County Normal School in Chicago, where he remained for eighteen years. In charge of its teacher-training program and its laboratory school, Parker was able to further develop and to some degree disseminate his educational theories. Essentially, his purposes were to make the child the center of the educative process and to integrate the content areas of the curriculum into a more meaningful experience for the child. Democracy as a way of life was the approach in the school.

Parker's work stands out as a sharp contrast to what the general picture of education was before the turn of the century. His influence on subsequent developments in educational theory and practice is perhaps best measured by the fact that John Dewey referred to him as the "father of progressive education." Dewey's own children attended Parker's school in Chicago for two years until Dewey established his own lab school at the University of Chicago.

When John Dewey established his school at the University of Chicago in 1896 (he was also head of the departments of philosophy, psychology, and pedagogy), he was to begin a quest for educational meaning that was to carry on for more than a half century. Influenced by the writings of Pestalozzi, Rousseau, and Froebel, as well as by the work of Parker and Jane Addams in Chicago, Dewey was to give progressivism its articulation and advance its meaning to a broader social dimension. His numerous writings through the years were to become the basis for a great many of the significant innovations not only in American schools but also in many other countries. Essentially, the tenets of progressivism discussed in other parts of this book rest on Dewey's writings.

Dewey's direct work with the Chicago Laboratory School is a good example of his reform ideas for education. To a great extent his experiences and writings from those eight years foreshadowed much of his subsequent work in educational philosophy and theory. Basically, the approach taken in the lab school was one that attempted to make learning meaningful by engaging the students in active participation. Newly planned work in the traditional subject areas was enlivened by constructive activities around broad social themes related to the interests of the pupils at various age levels—clearly a radical departure, as had been Parker's work, from the rigid formality of the general schools of that day. The results of this "new education" were impressive. According to Lawrence Cremin:

> By the conclusion of the thirteenth year [age] the children
> had amassed a wide range of knowledge; they had developed a
> multitude of skills and sensitivities, manual and social as well as
> intellectual. They had learned to work both cooperatively and
> independently and could express themselves clearly and concisely.
> They had on countless occasions put new-found knowledge to the
> test, and they had made a clear beginning in all of the major
> fields of knowledge. In short, they were ready for secondary
> education, which Dewey and his colleagues defined as that phase
> of schooling marked by the dominance of distinctively intellectual
> interests organized along logically systematic lines.[13]

There is no doubt that Dewey's work in education stands as one of the important departures from traditional education. The history of American education in the last fifty years is filled with examples of progressive innovation. Many other competent educators, psychologists, and physicians have been influential in the child study

---

[13] Lawrence A. Cremin, *The Transformation of the School* (New York: Knopf, 1961), p. 140.

movement. The work of G. Stanley Hall, at the turn of the century, and later the works of Maria Montessori, Jean Piaget, Arnold Gesell, Benjamin Spock, among others, have provided a great deal of insight about child development and learning.

the elementary school today

As mentioned earlier, a great deal of variation is found in the elementary schools today. Nor is it surprising when one considers the extent of the enterprise. According to estimates from the United States Office of Education for the 1969–1970 school year there are:

      Number of School Districts   —   20,440
      Number of Elementary Schools —   88,556
      Number of Elementary Students—36,900,000
                              (including 4.3 million private)
      Number of Elementary Teachers— 1,251,000
                              (including 152,000 private)

Within this vast system one would obviously find an array of programs—some good, some bad. We might find many that are lifelessly formal and rigid, but we would also find some where exciting things are happening, where children are really enjoying life and learning. We can also find, if we look well enough, some schools where children are punished, either physically or psychologically for simply being children. On the other hand, we can find schools, hopefully in greater proportion, where children are treated with humane respect and dignity, conditions on which they thrive.

To be sure, these are elements that could describe the home or any other level of education as well. But they are undoubtedly the most important elements of description from the viewpoint of the child. His concern is with what goes on in the school rather than with how the school is organized, with what the school will do *to* him rather than with what it might purport to do *for* him. In short, he is concerned with whether the school will do him well or ill. Obviously, these must also be the main concerns of educators. But there are other descriptive dimensions the educator might want to consider, such as the organizational patterns of the elementary school and the curricular structure. These factors in their various forms do not guarantee the level of quality of a school, but certain of their arrangements make more possible the achievement of a school that functions for the good of all its pupils.

graded versus nongraded school

The organizational pattern of the six-year elementary school that has developed since 1930 remains as the general pattern. There are still eight-year schools, but the number is dwindling except in the private sector. The only major organizational change of recent vintage has been the *middle school*, which in some instances has reduced the elementary school to five years. The rationale of the middle school is discussed later in this chapter.

Within the structure of the elementary school, whether five, six, or eight year, there has been an attempt to remove the formal grade labels that to a great extent have forced an unnecessary rigidity on the elementary school. Since about the mid-1950s the nongraded idea has been firmly established as a viable alternative to the graded structure. For the most part, the idea has been incorporated in the primary segment, but some schools have gone through with it to the intermediate segment and a few to the high school. What it means essentially is that children, all of whom have varying backgrounds and rates of learning, are more sensibly treated. It is in the primary years that the nongraded approach has been particularly effective.

To assert that the primary years of schooling are the most important for a child would be to state the obvious. In these earliest years the child is expected to develop some basic skills on which further learning might be built. In particular, he is expected to build a good base of reading skill through which most of his later learning is expected to be gained. Understanding of numbers and skill in working with them are also basic to later school success. Of course, a great deal more makes up the curriculum of the primary years, but reading and number work are the essential needs in terms of ongoing success in school. A child who goes on to the more structured and academically demanding intermediate segment of the elementary school without having gained sufficient reading skill is almost sure to meet with failure in terms of the school's demands. In many instances the failure attitude is developed in children in their first year in school. The "failure" becomes cumulative so that by the time the child has gone through six years of school his most significant conditioned learning has been that he is a "failure." (Under such circumstances one is led to question the beneficence of compulsory attendance laws.)

In the traditionally structured graded system this is what often happens. The only alternative to promoting a child on to a successive grade is to retain him for repetition, which has long been proven to be useless in its purpose and damaging in its consequences. Not that the nongraded arrangement guarantees to avoid such things, but it is precisely to such problems that it is directed. As we have noted, the nongraded approach has as its premise that there are different rates of learning among children. In the nongraded school a child is given the opportunity to develop the necessary skills before moving to levels where these skills are a prerequisite. For some children this might mean three years, for some two, and for others four. Without the press of a lock-step graded system and its lock-step curriculum children would thus be given a better opportunity to develop to their potential.

Although many schools attach the term "nongraded" to their organizational structure, there are, according to reports, few that truly function with the spirit and purposes of the nongraded concept. The others more often make nominal changes and continue with the old practices.

The nongraded plan as proposed by such educators as John I. Goodlad and Robert H. Anderson implies a great deal more than a removal of grade labels. It implies a much broader scope of change that includes the curricular structure, administrative procedures, evaluation and its reporting to parents, teacher attitudes, and such. In stating what would be required of a full-fledged nongraded school Anderson has listed these points among others:

1. Suitable provision is being made in all aspects of the curriculum for each unique child by such means as (a) flexible grouping and subgrouping of pupils, (b) an adaptable, flexible curriculum, (c) a great range of materials and instructional approaches.
2. The successive learning experiences of each pupil are pertinent and appropriate to his needs. . . .
5. Grade labels and the related machinery of promotion and failure are nonexistent.
6. The reporting system reflects the conviction that each child is a unique individual. There are no report cards with A's and F's. . . .
8. For certain purposes, pupils enjoy regular social and intellectual contacts with other pupils of like mind and talent and, for other purposes, with pupils of different minds and talents.
9. The school's horizontal organization pattern allows for flexibility in grouping pupils and in utilizing the school's resources. It is possible to have a nongraded, self-contained classroom pattern, for example, although it is also possible to have a more flexible horizontal arrangement such as the Dual Progress Plan, informal cooperative teaching, in combination with the nongraded arrangement. The author is, of course, deeply committed to the latter (team teaching and nongradedness) as the combination much to be preferred.[14]

Whatever the claims of one arrangement over another might be, they should all be weighed on one factor only—Do they better serve the child? Not the *fast* or *slow* child but *all*! In general, it is apparent that the elementary school has not succeeded in doing well by its pupils. Its *failures* are often explained away by the use of such phrases attached to pupils as levels of ability, lack of background, lack of interest, and so forth. When used as a relinquishing of responsibility or an avoidance of culpability, the school might better attach such phrases to itself rather than to its pupils.

[14] Robert H. Anderson, *Teaching in a World of Change* (New York: Harcourt, Brace Jovanovich, 1966), pp. 68–69.

secondary education

junior high or middle school

When the junior high school appeared on the scene in the 1920s, it served to focus attention on the special educational problems of children passing through the phase of development from childhood to adolescence.   Organizationally, it introduced a new institution into the sequence of common schooling.   The 8–4 division of elementary and secondary education became the 6–3–3, of which the latter two factors constituted the secondary aspect.

The reasons for an institution specially directed toward the pre-adolescent were persuasive. And the times were right. The expectation was that the attractions of achieving a high school diploma would combine with the coercions of higher compulsory age limits on school attendance to hold the mass of students until graduation was beginning to be fulfilled. The increase of population was exerting pressure on the old physical plants; the situation for institutional shuffling was, therefore, fluid. The old four-year high school was bulging at the seams. The eight-year elementary school was likewise over-crowded. The one-room rural school was beginning to be swept up in the first phase of the consolidation movement, thus weakening a bastion of the eight-year elementary block at the grassiest roots. In addition, America was prosperous, optimistic, ambitious, and ready to make a major investment in education. If the reasons were good, the job could be done. The reasons were sound enough. They included these:

1. The transition between the small elementary school with a single teacher for the day's learning to the large departmentalized high school was abrupt and often painful. A transitional institution to bridge the gap could be of service.
2. The incompatability of older students in the elementary school and younger students in the high school with the rest of the student body had often noticeable and sometimes hazardous effects.
3. The special developmental and maturational characteristics of children from eleven to fourteen, expressed in both psychological and biological terms, argued for a school that would be both responsive and sophisticated in respect to their needs.
4. Curricular demands argued for instruction specialization and intellectual challenge that would be more complex and demanding than elementary approaches but more integrated, more personalized, and less structured than the typical high school.
5. Social needs of students included the opportunity for more varied expression and development of interests and talents, a wider range

of activities than was common to the elementary school, but in a context of diminished competition and lowered emotional tone as compared with the high school.

Thus, the junior high school emerged. It became another school inserted between elementary and secondary school, most commonly including the seventh, eighth, and ninth grades, though sometimes consisting of only the seventh and eighth and, more rarely, the sixth, seventh, and eighth grades.

Despite the well-defined high purposes, which if applied made very good sense, the new unit of organization worked no miracles. There was no particular magic in the new name, only opportunity. In the main, as traditionalist administrators and teachers took over their jobs in the new school, which was often the old high school turned over to them secondhand, they simply kept school in the same old way.

The curriculum changed remarkably little. It was still arithmetic in the seventh and eighth grades, and algebra in the ninth. Literature was still studied from seventh and eighth readers. The variable that differentiated education of these youngsters was not in the new organization but in the degree to which any given junior high school was affected by new ideas, by progressivism as it were. The variable was still—good school or bad school.

By the 1960s the junior high school had redefined itself. In the main it had become a little high school, a replica of the senior high conducted for somewhat younger students. Usually, it tended to be something of an educational orphan, somewhat poorer in facilities, conducting somewhat larger classes. Its teachers and administrators frequently spoke of seeking promotion to the high school. True, many teachers expressed special commitment to the institution and special satisfactions in "teaching kids at this age." They served to keep alive in practice some of the initial reasons for the creation of this institutional entity. Teacher education too rarely acknowledged junior high as a special target for preparation.

The school itself seemed to be cut to the academic pattern rather than to the special needs of the preadolescent. Both academia and the common culture were pressing down on the young. The curriculum was changed primarily by pushing the high school subjects downward. Thus biology began to appear in ninth grade; algebra in the eighth to make way for geometry in the ninth; and foreign languages to be taught in seventh-, eighth-, and ninth-grade sequences. Advisers and counselors and parents, too, had mobilized to stimulate achievement in terms of competition for college entrance.

In extracurricular affairs the junior high school operated at the same fever pitch of supercharged competitiveness as the high school. Parties where tuxedos and formal dresses reigned were not uncommon. Preteen-age dating and going steady were customs tacitly acknowledged by the school, and apparently, if not actively encouraged, were at least only nominally resisted by the home. Observation revealed outcomes of what once would have been dubbed unusual social poise in these preteens, and research confirmed that a good deal of precocious sexual activity was not uncommon. Despite warning of such official bodies as the American Association of Health, Physical Education and Recreation (AAHPER) and distinguished educators as James B. Conant, the junior high schools developed full schedules of competitive interscholastic sports, *including football*. Thus, the preteen athlete was regimented into the dreary sequence of recruiting, coaching, and commercial overemphasis that culminates in the Pro-Bowl. (With television for the octogenarian spectator and the pushing down of Little Leagues to Little Little and Pony Leagues, American civilization seems on the verge of achieving a cradle to the grave athleticism, which might be an interesting achievement in the annals of history, approximating we think, the role of Sparta more than of Athens.)

In the 1960s a need for change was recognized. As in the 1920s, conditions were somewhat favorable. Again, the pressure of population had overloaded the school plant; the public was even more ambitious, if not as optimistic as in the 1920s; and a new wave of consolidation, larger school districts, had rendered the situation fluid.

A reconceptualization of the type of education most appropriate to the eleven- to fourteen-year-olds appeared. On the surface, it appeared to reveal much of the educationist disposition to solve problems by inventing new terms. Some new terminology was useful, however. For example, a pioneer reconceptualizer, Donald H. Eichhorn labels the period of preadolescence as "transescence" and defines it as "the period in human development which begins in late childhood prior to the onset of puberty and extends through the early stages of adolescence." [15] The term seems appropriate and convenient. The new name for the institution that serves the "transescent" has become "the middle school."

The Research Division of the NEA estimated that by 1969 over 1,000 middle schools were operating in the nation. Said differently, 1,000 schools dealing with this proximate age range were called middle schools. The Research Division conducted a study of 154 such schools in 51 systems, each enrolling over 12,000 students. The study suggests that a functional definition of the school that tries to relate to the special needs and characteristics of this age group can be set forth. The distinguishing features of the so-called middle school are:

1. A span of at least three grades to allow for the gradual transition from elementary to high school instruction (must include grades 6 and 7 and no grades below 5 or above 8).

---

[15] Donald H. Eichhorn, *The Middle School* (New York: Center for Applied Research in Education, 1966), p. 10.

2. Emerging departmental structure in each higher grade to effect gradual transition from the self-contained classroom to the departmentalized high school.
3. Flexible approaches to instruction—team teaching, flexible scheduling, individualized instruction, independent study, tutorial programs—and other approaches aimed at stimulating children to learn how to learn.
4. *Required* special courses, taught in departmentalized form, such as industrial arts, home economics, foreign language, art, music, typing; frequently an interdisciplinary or multidisciplinary approach is used, e.g., "unified arts," "practical arts," "humanities," "performing arts," "exploratory," "urban living."
5. Guidance program as a distinct entity to fill the special needs of this age group.
6. Faculty with both elementary and secondary education certification, or some teachers with each type (until special training and certification are available for this level).
7. Limited attention to interschool sports and social activities.[16]

Is this particularly new? No, says a comparative reading of the literature on the junior high school. The arbitrarily definable shift, changing the years from seven, eight, nine to six, seven, eight may be read two ways. It is progressive in that it moves to the grade definition used in some schools of the mid-1920s; it is regressive in that it restores the four-year high school of the old 8–4 system, with its relatively young freshman class. No, too, says the research done by Peter S. Constantino.[17] Constantino compared three schools functioning as middle schools with three functioning as junior high schools. Comparisons were made at seventh- and eighth-grade levels. Teacher-pupil relations were assessed on the basis of 148 observations of 48 different teachers.

With respect to curriculum, Constantino found the program of studies in both types was relatively the same. In both the primary sources of curriculum content were either a single textbook or a multitext single-subject selection. Courses of study were used equally and revised similarly in each; curriculum content visible in classroom activities was virtually similar in all respects; content was derived from a single text about 60 percent of the time in both settings; content was derived from subject-matter-centered sources other than texts about 20 percent of the time in both.

As to teacher-pupil behavior, Constantino reported that in both school types "teachers provided for individual differences in the same way." In both, the teacher controlled the class as a single group with

[16] Adapted from National Education Association Research *Bulletin* 47:2 (Washington, D.C.: May 1969), p. 41.
[17] Peter S. Constantino, "A Study of Differences Between Middle School and Junior High School Curricula" (Ed. D. thesis, University of Pittsburgh, 1962).

little or no opportunity for pupil-to-pupil interaction. In both, pupil initiative was demonstrated only as designated by the teacher. Varieties of techniques were similar in both sets of schools. Findings with respect to social-emotional climate were neutral.

What's in a name? Constantino's research cannot be generalized too broadly. Our point is that if a school decides to be significantly different, it can do so, but only by directing its efforts to a fundamental reappraisal of its purposes and practices. The changing of labels and designations is superficial and illusory. At worst, it may conduce to fraud. However, at best, it may generate excitement that goes beyond the semantic into genuine educational inquiry. Renaming the school does nothing. But the school for the "transescent" needs a basic reconstruction. It should have it; the conceptual grounds for the job have been available since the 1920s. They have simply been neglected.

the high school

Attendance in high school is taken for granted today. The attainment of the diploma is not rated as an unusually significant achievement. Yet it was not always so.

Secondary education was not initially intended as part of the common school experience, the common school being the education universally provided at public expense to provide the basic rudiments of enlightenment to assure a civic competence adequate to the needs of democracy. But in the latter nineteenth century as demands of life and society increased, so did educational goals advance. "A good education" implying studies beyond the three Rs was sought by more people.

Soon a struggle emerged over the question: Could the public legitimately provide secondary education, or should this phase of education be supported on the "benefit theory," that is, be paid for as was college tuition by the person receiving the education? The Kalamazoo Case in the highest court of Michigan in 1873 settled the issue and established significant precedent. The court ruled that secondary education was, indeed, a legitimate extension of the state's obligation to establish an educational system and could claim constitutionally public tax support.

By the 1920s high school had become a standard anticipation for most American youth. How far we have come in democratizing educational opportunity is shown by this fact: in 1970 the student finishing eighth grade has a better chance of finishing college than the eighth-grade graduate in 1910 had of finishing high school.

The wide expansion of higher education has changed the institutional position of the high school. In 1900 it was "the people's college." To attain its diploma was a minority achievement. The diploma was not a basic minimum requirement in the job market. It was a convenience in achieving college admission, but it was by no means universally applied. It was not even a requirement for teaching school; most teachers at that time had not gained the diploma.

By 1930 high school graduation was achieved by a majority. It had become, except for unskilled labor, a standard minimum job requirement. It had become an almost universal requirement for college admission. It was a minimum requirement for teaching, and many teachers entered the classroom with this level of academic attainment. It was, for the most, a terminal education. College entrance was effected by a minority, and graduation from college was achieved by a relative few.

In 1970 high school education has ceased for the majority to be terminal. Those who enter the job market at this point come largely from the socioeconomically disadvantaged. And entering the job market at this point puts them at a vocational and economic disadvantage.

Thus, the high school has become not a general terminal point, *but an advanced intermediate phase* on the educational continuum that extends from the nursery school to the graduate seminar. College has become what the high school once was: a standard expectation for most, an increasingly common aspiration and reality, moving toward a universal. The junior college movement, or community college in some states like California, has become a common element of tax-supported universal—though not compulsory—public education. The A.B. degree will presently become a general expectation, as the high school diploma was in 1950.

The compulsions are real, though they are not legal mandates. Emulation is one compulsion; what many parents want and achieve for their children, most parents come to want. They will, at first, seek to achieve it individually, but they are likely to discover, as they have done, that a general public tax-support effort is more sure and more economical. The advance of technology applies a pressure tantamount to compulsion; skills preempted by machines at lower levels of performance drive persons to seek the higher skills that enable them to manage and to program the machines. Competition is a factor. The better jobs go to the better educated, this quality being rudely certified by a quantitative certification of more education received. In the broader sense, life has become so complex that modern man simply cannot find his way around, let alone seek solutions to his problems, with an education that had been reasonably adequate even a decade ago.

The high school is in trouble partly because it has become an intermediate institution that still functions as a terminal one. Because it is obligated to the principle of equal opportunity, it is deeply at fault if it encourages some students to use it as a bridge to further education, while tolerating or encouraging others to accept its program as terminal.

Presently, the faculty and guidance staff would feel that they had betrayed a middle-class student with a "B" average, or an outstanding athlete with perhaps less impressive academic credentials, if they failed to point out the advantages of "going on" and to create aspirations in that direction. But the vocational and commerical programs, because they perceive themselves as terminal in the main, simply conspire to narrow the range of vocational choice and to place ceilings over the careers of their graduates. This is a fault in practice, not a charge against vocational education. All education, if adequate, is in one dimension vocational. College preparatory education is the most completely and successfully vocational of all tracks: it prepares for, and eventually its graduates get, the best jobs. Vocational education needs itself to become geared to the intermediate function of the high school; it must not impose terminal education on its students when the consequence is simply to put them at a disadvantaged position in life.

What of the general students? As in other respects, they are the products of long neglect, the surest evidence of what John Holt calls *The Underachieving School*. Their education terminated at whatever point that their loss of confidence in themselves coincided with the school's forfeit of responsibility for maintaining them within the scheme of learning. The school that tolerates terminal education of this sort to take place is not merely underachieving; it is incompetent.

The American high school in its most distinctive form is *comprehensive*. This means that a variety of curricula serve the varied interest of several subpopulations within one common institution. What actually has occurred sometimes is that several schools for different purposes have been functioning under the same roof, with one or two of them much better than the others. At best, the comprehensive high school is the place where the children of America's cultural diversities come together to learn what they need and want to know, where equality of opportunity becomes real, where they come to know and trust themselves and others. It would seem that the high school must now embrace comprehensiveness in a new dimension. It must accept its role as intermediate education as an obligation to all its students, and to reject termination by default for any.

These words would be brave, but hollow, if we were counting on the likelihood of schools as they now function to make them real. But the content of this text is committed to a reconstruction of education that can enliven and redeem the school by such means as: (1) the development of significant and relevant programs; (2) the use of methodologies that take the student in on learning; (3) respect for and authentication of persons, the acceptance and use of individual differences, not an attack upon them; (4) the criticism of institutional practice and the development of a new political science for the schools; (5) new perceptions of the meaning of *teacher*, along with new conditions of respect for students.

higher education

beginning intentions

For reviewing the beginnings of higher learning in America, let us use the words of the outstanding historian of colleges and universities, because he tells it so well: "This proliferation of colleges—Harvard, William and Mary, Yale, New Jersey, King's, Philadelphia, Rhode Island, Queen's, Dartmouth—all before 1770, this planting of temples of piety and intellect in the wilderness was no accident," asserts Frederick Rudolph.

> Nor was it stubbornness, foolhardiness even the booster spirit of a pioneering people which placed at the disposal of American youth so extraordinary a number of educational institutions. At the beginning, higher education in America would be governed less by accident than by certain purpose, less by impulse than by design.[18]

The first college in the colonies was Harvard, established by act of the Massachusetts legislature in 1636. It opened its doors in 1638 and received its permanent charter in 1650. The first statutes of Harvard (appearing about 1646) contain these among other stipulations:

1. When any Scholar is able to Read Tully or such like classical Latin Author *ex tempore,* and make and speak true Latin in verse and prose *suo (ut aiunt) Marte,* and decline perfectly the paradigms of Nouns and verbs in the Greek tongue, then may he be admitted into the College, nor shall any claim admission before such qualifications. . . .
4. Every one shall so exercise himself in reading the Scriptures twice a day that they be ready to give an account of their proficiency therein, . . .
7. They shall honor as their parents, Magistrates, Elders, tutors and aged persons, by being silent in their presence (except they be called on to answer) not gainsaying showing all those laudable expressions of honor and reverence in their presence, that are in use as bowing before them standing uncovered or the like. . . .
8. They shall be slow to speak, and eschew not only oaths, lies, and uncertain rumors, but likewise all idle, foolish, bitter scoffing, frothy wanton words and offensive gestures.
12. No Scholar shall buy sell or exchange any thing to the value of six-pence without the allowance of his parents, guardians, or tutors. . . .
13. The Scholars shall never use their Mother-tongue except that in public exercises of oratory or such like, they be called to make them in English.
14. If any Scholar being in health shall be absent from prayer or Lec-

[18] Frederick Rudolph, *The American College and University* (New York: Random House 1962), p. 3.

tures, . . . , he shall be liable to admonition . . . if he offend above once a week. . . .

18. Every Scholar that on proof is found able to read the original of the Old and New Testament into the Latin tongue, and to resolve them logically withal being of honest life and conversation and at any public act hath the approbation of the Overseers, and Master of the College may be invested with his first degree.[19]

The purposes of education were implicitly religious, moral, and intellectual. They were intended to discipline both character and social comportment. Purposive was the word for this, a purpose infused with a sense of mission. Rudolph states:

> This sense of mission clearly required more than an ordinary sense of self-confidence. But it did not lack humility, and the sense of pride which strengthened it was a pride that was rigorous in the demands which it placed upon self . . . . Intending to lead lives no less than the purest, aspiring to serve God and their fellow-men in the fullest, they acknowledged a responsibility to the future. They could not afford to leave its shaping to whim, fate, accident, indecision, incompetence, or carelessness. In the future the state would need competent rulers, the church would require a learned clergy, and society itself would need the adornment of cultured men.
> Such men, the Puritans well knew, had to be created from the material at hand. A society that intends to live rigorously, moreover, cannot afford to train its rulers haphazardly. A world that finds the deepest expression of its purposes and goods in the Scriptures cannot afford to ignore the training of its Biblical expositors. A people that expects to have its pretensions taken seriously must recognize its responsibility to the inherited wisdom of the ages, to literature, to science, to learning.[20]

The scope and intent of higher education in America has changed more than a little. It is not our intent to give a short course in its history at this point, rather our intent is to get at some significant insights by a panoramic approach.

the panorama of higher education

If you drive across the country from Maine through New England, among the Middle Atlantic States, and through the Middle West, and into the Prairie States, in hundreds of towns and small cities—many of them off the main traveled roads—you will find the pleasant campuses of the colleges that stand as linear descendents of the earliest institutions of higher education. They are the small liberal arts colleges, sometimes considerably parochial in religious emphasis, more

[19] Richard Hofstadter and Wilson Smith, *American Higher Education*, Vol. 1 (Chicago: University of Chicago Press, 1961), pp. 8–10.
[20] Rudolph, *op. cit.*, p. 6.

often largely emancipated from creedal bias even though still claiming either an active or vestigial denominational affiliation.

New England was the initial home and genesis of these. To a considerable degree, the extension to the West is a consequence of the westward migration of New Englanders, who carried institutional ideas and preferences along with their other baggage.

The student population of each institution will be small in today's terms: 300, 400, 500, perhaps 1,200, 1,500, even 1,800. But if the figure has grown so that it exceeds 2,000, the chances are that history is transforming the respective college into a somewhat different institutional species.

Many of these colleges are known principally within the locality or the region of their residence. The moderately well-informed newspaper reader will have no trouble associating Columbia with New York City, University of California with Berkeley, Harvard with Cambridge, Notre Dame with South Bend. These have several claims to nationwide repute. But what of such as these? Bowdoin, Colby, and Bates in Maine; Hobart and Alfred, in New York; Allegheny, Thiel, and Geneva in Pennsylvania; Wabash in Indiana; Ohio Wesleyan, Illinois Wesleyan, or Iowa Wesleyan; Knox or Monmouth in Illinois; Beloit or Ripon in Wisconsin; or Simpson, Cornell, or Coe in Iowa; Carleton or Gustavus Adolphus in Minnesota? You must be well-traveled or unusually well-informed if you can name the town or city where each of these substantial institutions is located.

The earlier religious impetus in North American higher education was Protestant, its first emphasis the training of an educated clergy. Today these colleges in the main stress a broader appeal: a "good liberal education"; the promise of an emphasis on teaching and concern for students; a wholesome moral environment; and, more rarely, the guarantee of a denominationally oriented program and religious life on campus.

Another variety of church-affiliated education has more recent origins. That is the Roman Catholic college or university. It ranges from small campuses in comparatively isolated settings to great metropolitan surroundings. St. Mary's, St. Vincent's, St. Joseph's— the names of the saints furnish a denominational clue, usually to the smaller type. But Notre Dame University, Fordham University, Catholic University, St. Louis University, and Duquesne University have the characteristics and complexity of other types of large urban universities, as well as a distinctive denominational character of their own. The desire of the Roman Catholic Church to complete an upward extension of its primary and secondary school system has led since 1940 to a large establishment of new, or much expanded, colleges and universities in cities across the land. Often designated simply by name of the city, these are difficult to distinguish as Catholic schools, except by knowing the fact, from other types of institutions similarly named. Thus, the University of Seattle, of San Francisco, of Dayton, and of Fairfield (Conn.) are indeed Catholic-sponsored universities; but New York University and the University of Pittsburgh, are private nondenominational institutions (though the latter is also "state-related"); and the University of Cincinnati and of Kansas City, for example, are secular, and municipally supported.

A journey roundabout American higher education will encounter larger citadels of education. These are the state-supported colleges and universities, which have come to dominate the scene in terms of students served, monetary support, and ordinarily in football prowess (with the conspicuous exception in the latter category of Notre Dame and University of Southern California).

The state university movement began in the South, took roots both there and in the Midwest, migrated to the West, and Far West where it thrived and grew. Until recently, in the East, state-supported education, especially in New England, tended to stand in the shadow of the Ivy League. But the pressure of numbers and the demands for extended higher educational opportunity, spurred perhaps by unfavorable comparison with states as vigorous as Michigan and California, have given impetus to the movement in Connecticut, Massachusetts, and especially in New York State.

The state institutions of the 1920s were usually of three distinct types: universities, which included a liberal-arts-oriented undergraduate program, a graduate school, and a number of professional schools; a state college of agriculture and mechanical arts, owing its origins considerably to the Morrill Acts of 1865 and 1870; and one or more state teachers' colleges. The practical emphasis on agriculture, engineering, veterinary medicine, and home economics in the second category often occasioned a good deal of academic snobbery. The college known as "state" was frequently dubbed "cow college" in more or less good-natured derision. Iowa serves to conveniently illustrate the threefold pattern: The State University of Iowa at Iowa City, Iowa State College at Ames, and Iowa State Teachers College at Cedar Falls—S.U.I., Ames, and Cedar Falls, these were the familiar designations in the 1930s.

But institutions of higher learning have built-in dynamics of ambition and expansion. Each tries to reach the next level of status, either in name or reality. Eventually, it seems, each seeks to assume full university status. This empire-building thrust, while legitimate, occasions professional concern when energies are too early directed to expansion and status seeking, and building solid programs within limited bounds is neglected. Thus colleges seek to become universities; junior colleges, to become four-year institutions.

The genealogy of one institution serves to illustrate the course of development. Macomb, Illinois, in the early years of the century boasted of its State Normal School. In the 1920s it became Western Illinois State Teacher's College. After World War II it was briefly Western Illinois State College, but soon, as a result of expansion in size and somewhat in program, it became Western Illinois State University.

It must be noted that the unholy haste with which former teachers colleges have shed the professional designation has been partly the result of academic snobbery, both from within and without. At professional conclaves professors of academic subjects in particular have been observed visibly to wince when asked their institutional location. The response, "Just a teacher's college," was often forced out with every evidence of pain. No studies have been made to give solid evidence that a change of name has significantly improved the quality of instruction. Research does exist to prove that the primary function of these institutions remains unchanged, whether or not improved by semantic deletion. It is still the preparation of teachers.

The state university has certain general characteristics. It is very expansible, as recent growth has shown. It has, though not universally, a generous admissions policy. As recently as the 1950s it was quite general that any graduate of a certified high school within a state could be admitted to the state university. (Open admission, did not, of course, guarantee his continued residence after the first examination period). Tuitions are low; living costs in dormitories tend to run below comparable private institutions. Reflecting perhaps a closeness to certain vulgar enthusiasms in the common culture, state universities have formidable investments in athletic establishments.

The distinctive characteristic of the state university, educationally speaking, has been a vastly extended concept of the relation of the university to the people, a broadened policy of direct service to the public. This was a natural consequence of its origins, its source of students, and its support. It was also a derivative of the democratic bias applied to higher learning.

It was the University of Wisconsin at the turn of the century that first put into practice the concept of university service to the broader community. In fact, it became known as the Wisconsin Idea. That idea in its full vision was that the university should be of consequence in and have some tangible part in improving the life of every citizen within the state. It is a noble idea. Its best and major consequence has been to shatter the concept of higher education as a refuge from the hurly-burly of life, from the rigors of everyday existence. Its hazards were that it tended to advance the practical at the expense of the theoretical and the applied over the pure and to extend its practicalities in so many directions that energies and resources were dissipated. Trivial concerns gained equal time and budget with significant ones.

Until comparatively recently the Wisconsin Idea was followed more in the agricultural states or in institutions serving rural areas in other states. Universities in cities built psychic walls about themselves, but since the 1960s they have tended to become proudly "urban universities," which implies an acceptance of the fact of where they are. It implies further an acceptance of a willingness to give service and assume responsibility toward the city, the region, and indeed the world.

The boundaries among men tend to become less and less real as time and space are diminished. Thus the purposes and distinctions among educational institutions tend to merge into common purposes. A further excursion among institutions of higher education would reveal many other dimensions of complexity: institutions segregated by race or sex, institutes of technology and theological seminaries, junior colleges, community colleges. And in every category some, by varied criteria, are much better than others. But higher education, though diverse and complex, is linked by circumstance to every reality of the world and to every dilemma of modern man. In a very real sense whether it be a multiversity in a vast metropolis or a little college in a small town in Arkansas, all institutions of higher education dwell among the same problems. Perhaps this is easier for modern man to see from his perspective in space; social science has demonstrated the interdependence of man and society in every particular. But it is no new insight, nor was it new when John Donne so well phrased it: "No man is an island." Nor is any institution.

support of higher education

The primary sources of support for higher education come from varied sources: endowments and gifts, tuition, state or, more rarely, municipal support, denominational support, foundation gifts and grants, and federal grants and other subsidies. No institution depends on a single source of revenue; most draw on several of the foregoing resources in developing their budgets. (It should be added that in some institutions, especially in small liberal arts colleges and in other institutions particularly in the field of the humanities, an indirect source of support is built into the budget—the faculty contribution. Numerous faculty members work for lower pay than the job deserves with schedules heavier than are professionally defensible or educationally sound. This usually unacknowledged contribution of faculty is widespread; it persists because of high-minded dedication and economic naivete. Budget makers in large affluent institutions or in highly competitive fields have learned not to count overmuch on this source of revenue.)

Prestigious private institutions boast the largest endowments; such universities as Harvard, Columbia, Princeton, Rochester, and Yale rank high in this category of support. Even in the most expensive institutions tuition seldom meets half the actual costs of instruction. In low-tuition tax-supported institutions, charges to students represent a very minor fraction of the actual cost of higher education. Foundation grants and federal assistance go in largest amounts to the institutions that are among the most affluent because these have the best-established facilities to conduct the researches and studies contracted for.

The contemporary scene in higher education is illuminated by a sampling of the concerns that foundation grants and federal legislation devote themselves to. Figures 1 and 2 illustrate a number of active interests at a given date, and give in brief some sense of the times.

Since the public sector of higher education now serves the great majority of students, the degree of public support is a key factor determining educational opportunity and the quality of education received. Figure 3 indicates the status for 1969. Significant regional differences are shown. The Far West, the Rocky Mountains, the states of the old Northwest Territory, and the Southwest are predominantly in the upper bracket with respect to public support. The commitment to public education is best established in this area, both in elementary and secondary education and in higher education. The tradition of private education is weakest and its competition for support, therefore, is least in these areas. States in the South, with the exception of Texas, North Carolina, and Florida, fall into the

FIGURE 1 *Major Foundation Grants*

Source: *The Chronicle of Higher Education*, November 3, 1969, p. 6.

THE CLARK FOUNDATION

LIBRARY ACQUISITIONS. To support the purchase of equipment and resource materials for the college library: $12,500 to Cazenovia College

ESSO EDUCATION FOUNDATION

GENERATION GAP. To make comparative studies of the current Syracuse students and those studied by Katz and Allport in 1926. $29,400 to Syracuse U.

MANAGEMENT DECISIONS. To develop and apply a computer-based model for forecasting the consequences of various types of management decisions: $15,000 to Franklin College.

—For continued support of a program to bring about more businesslike methods in the management of predominantly Negro colleges: $40,000 to National Association of College and University Business Officers.

MEDICAL EDUCATION. To support specific projects submitted by various medical schools: $75,000 to National Fund for Medical Education.

MINORITY AID. To provide additional scholarship funds to high-caliber minority students: $12,500 to National Merit Scholarship Corp.

NEGRO STUDIES. To release Louis Lomax from teaching duties so that he may complete his study of the history, sociology, literature, and theology of the American Negro: $15,000 to Hofstra U.

TEACHER EDUCATION. To train public school teachers to work in "free-learning-environment" classrooms: $12,000 to Carnegie-Mellon U. and Chatham College

TECHNICIAN TRAINING. For the planning and coordinating of a project to produce teaching materials in physics for use in two-year institutions: $11,200 to American Institute of Physics.

UNIVERSITY ORGANIZATION. To encourage and facilitate change by reporting reorganizations already effected or taking place, by analyzing and evaluating the reorganizations, and by providing a rationale and recommendations for reorganization: $91,000 over two years to Michigan State U.

VETERANS' EDUCATION To support a pilot project which provides college preparatory programs for servicemen: $15,000 to City U. of New York.

FORD FOUNDATION

EMPLOYMENT PRACTICES. To complete a series of studies on the racial policies and practices of American employers: $145,000 to U. of Pennsylvania.

HUMANITIES PROGRAM. To establish a humanities faculty development program: $25,000 to U. of the South.

INTELLECTUALS. For research on the role of intellectuals in society by S. M. Lipset: $25,000 to Harvard U.

MIGRANT WORKERS AND RURAL POOR. To study the economic factors that influence people in moving from rural to urban areas: $94,000 to Virginia Polytechnic Institute.

PEST MANAGEMENT. To establish an interdepartmental program in the ecology of pest management: $516,000 to Cornell U.

SCIENCE AND SOCIETY. To partially support a student-faculty conference on the social implications of science: $10,000 to U. of Chicago.

SEWAGE TREATMENT. To partially finance the construction of a tertiary sewage treatment plant to process sewage from East Lansing: $450,000 to Michigan State U.

SIMULATION GAMES. For an interdisciplinary workshop on the use of resource management computer simulation games: $75,000 to U. of Washington.

STUDENT-DIRECTED STUDIES. For partial support of a student-directed studies program. $4,000 to U. of California at Los Angeles.

ROCKEFELLER BROTHERS FUND

POSTGRADUATE OPPORTUNITIES. To expand facilities for advising black veterans on the graduate and professional school opportunities available to them: $25,000 to the Graduate Information and Counseling Service for Black Veterans of the Woodrow Wilson National Fellowship Foundation.

	HOUSE	SENATE
HR 13194—GUARANTEED LOANS. Provides interest subsidies to private lenders of up to 3 per cent above the present 7 per cent rate for guaranteed loans to students. (Public Law 91-95, signed Oct. 22.)	Passed Sept. 15 H Rept 455	Passed Aug. 12 S Rept 268
HR 13270—TAX REFORM. Imposes a 7½ per cent tax on income of foundations, limits foundation activities, restricts distribution of foundation income, and reduces tax incentives for charitable contributions.	Passed Aug. 2 H Rept 413	Hearings completed
HR 11959, S 338—VETERANS' BENEFITS. Increases GI Bill benefits by 27 per cent in House bill, 46 per cent in Senate bill.	Passed Aug. 4 H Rept 360	Passed Oct. 23 S Rept 487
HR 11702—MEDICAL LIBRARY ASSISTANCE. House bill extends medical library assistance program 3 years; authorizes $63-million. Senate version extends program 3 years; authorizes $100.5-million.	Passed July 10 H Rept 313	Passed Oct. 20 S Rept 480
HR 11542, S 1563—INSTITUTIONAL GRANTS. Authorizes $400-million in first year for institutional grants for research and science education to colleges and universities.	Reported Sept. 15, H Rept 490	
HR 9010, S 1290—COLLEGE PENSION SYSTEM. Incorporates Teachers Insurance and Annuity Association and College Retirement Equities Fund under College Benefit System of America and protects system from multiple state regulation and taxation.		Hearings completed
S 1242—EDUCATIONAL BROADCASTING. Extends aid for construction of educational broadcasting facilities three years; authorizes $15-million annually. Extends support for Corporation for Public Broadcasting one year; authorizes $20-million. (Sent to the President, Oct. 14.)	Passed Oct. 9 H Rept 466	Passed May 13 S Rept 167
HR 13827, S 2864—COLLEGE HOUSING. House bill authorizes $4.2-million for interest subsidies for college housing construction for fiscal 1971; Senate bill authorizes $1.5-million in 1971, $9-million in 1972.	Passed Oct. 23 H Rept 539	Passed Sept. 23 S Rept 392
HR 14008, S 1—RELOCATION PAYMENTS. House bill provides relocation payments and services to persons displaced by federally supported college construction. Senate bill establishes uniform treatment of persons displaced by federal and federally assisted programs.	Hearings under way	Passed Oct. 27 S Rept 488
HR 14001, S 2843—SELECTIVE SERVICE. To permit the President to establish a random method of inducting young men for military service.	Reported Oct. 16 H Rept 577	
HR 10878, S 1857—NSF AUTHORIZATION. Authorizes $490-million under Senate version, $477.3-million under House bill for the National Science Foundation in fiscal 1970.	Passed Oct. 7 H Rept 288	Passed Sept. 18 S Rept 285
HR 12307—APPROPRIATIONS FOR INDEPENDENT OFFICES. Appropriates $420-million for the National Science Foundation.	Passed June 24 H Rept 316	Hearings completed
HR 13111—APPROPRIATIONS FOR THE DEPARTMENTS OF LABOR AND HEALTH, EDUCATION, AND WELFARE. Appropriates $3.1-billion for Office of Education, $1.45-billion for the National Institutes of Health.	Passed July 31 H Rept 391	Hearings under way

FIGURE 2   *Status of Major Legislation*

Source: *The Chronicle of Higher Education,* November 3, 1969, p. 2.

lowest category of public support. The ten states ranking lowest in public support in 1969 were in descending order: Oklahoma, Ohio, Tennessee, Pennsylvania, Alabama, Mississippi, South Carolina, New Jersey, Massachusetts, and New Hampshire. In the southern states the relatively unfavorable economic position of the region is no doubt a factor; in the northeastern states the long tradition of privately supported higher education contributes to the condition.

the students

The demands of enrollment upon institutions of higher education have become tremendous. For example, college and university offi-

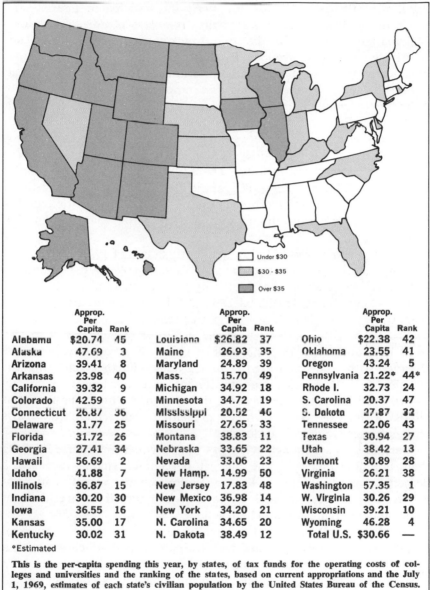

	Approp. Per Capita	Rank		Approp. Per Capita	Rank		Approp. Per Capita	Rank
Alabama	$20.74	45	Louisiana	$26.82	37	Ohio	$22.38	42
Alaska	47.69	3	Maine	26.93	35	Oklahoma	23.55	41
Arizona	39.41	8	Maryland	24.89	39	Oregon	43.24	5
Arkansas	23.98	40	Mass.	15.70	49	Pennsylvania	21.22*	44*
California	39.32	9	Michigan	34.92	18	Rhode I.	32.73	24
Colorado	42.59	6	Minnesota	34.72	19	S. Carolina	20.37	47
Connecticut	26.87	36	Mississippi	20.52	46	S. Dakota	27.87	32
Delaware	31.77	25	Missouri	27.65	33	Tennessee	22.06	43
Florida	31.72	26	Montana	38.83	11	Texas	30.94	27
Georgia	27.41	34	Nebraska	33.65	22	Utah	38.42	13
Hawaii	56.69	2	Nevada	33.06	23	Vermont	30.89	28
Idaho	41.88	7	New Hamp.	14.99	50	Virginia	26.21	38
Illinois	36.87	15	New Jersey	17.83	48	Washington	57.35	1
Indiana	30.20	30	New Mexico	36.98	14	W. Virginia	30.26	29
Iowa	36.55	16	New York	34.20	21	Wisconsin	39.21	10
Kansas	35.00	17	N. Carolina	34.65	20	Wyoming	46.28	4
Kentucky	30.02	31	N. Dakota	38.49	12	Total U.S.	$30.66	—

*Estimated

This is the per-capita spending this year, by states, of tax funds for the operating costs of colleges and universities and the ranking of the states, based on current appropriations and the July 1, 1969, estimates of each state's civilian population by the United States Bureau of the Census.

FIGURE 3 *What States Spend, per Capita, for Higher Education*

Source: *The Chronicle of Higher Education,* October 27, 1969, p. 1.

cials in planning for the academic year 1968 estimated boldly that they had to anticipate a fall enrollment of one and a quarter millions. Yet when registrars had completed their rosters of freshmen, the total enrollment exceeded estimates by more than 225,000.

College going in America has been very largely a middle-class exercise. Table 2 reveals a significant new tendency for children from lower-income families to join the college-bound throngs. The enrollment figures are those for 1968; the anticipated figures were projected in 1966. The largest ratios of excess of enrollments over anticipation occurred in the two brackets representing low- and relatively low-income groups. Enrollments were, on the other hand, practically as planned upon among students from the highest economic category. Junior colleges quite apparently received the major influx of the unanticipated students, especially from the lower-income categories. Private colleges and universities, it will be noted, had a much smaller discrepancy between planned and actual freshman class size, which reflects the higher tuition costs and tighter admissions controls of private institutions. The adverse competitive position of religiously affiliated colleges is graphically illustrated. Among these, the total enrollment of freshmen was 69,000 less than anticipated, a figure reflecting an enrollment only a little better than half of that counted upon.

These freshmen would be the graduating class of 1972. What were the characteristics and attitudes of this new collegiate population? A comprehensive survey conducted by the American Council on Education is revealing.[21] It was based on 243,156 questionnaires returned from freshmen at 358 college-level institutions.

Predictably, three-quarters of the group were eighteen years old as of December 31, 1968. The bulk of them (55 percent) were in the B range with respect to high school grades. Further reflecting the circumstance that collegiate enrollments are no longer primarily drawn predominantly from among the academic elite is the fact that almost a third of these freshmen presented high school transcripts with grades averaging C+ or lower.

Certain high school achievements were frequently reported among their accomplishments. The highest percentage among these (31.5 percent) was varsity sports letter. National honor society had been achieved by 25 percent, and 20 percent had served as president of some student organization in high school.

Ambitions and career plans exhibited a wide range. Approximately two out of five planned to terminate formal education with a bachelor's degree. Almost one-third anticipated taking a master's degree. That graudate schools might anticipate increasing numerical pressures was indicated by the aspiration of one out of ten entering freshmen to achieve the doctorate (Ph. D. or Ed. D.). The long historical distance from the era when educating the clergy was the primary purpose for a college education is evident: only three entering students out of a *thousand* stated plans to seek the Bachelor of Divinity degree (although seven of a thousand named *clergyman* as probable career occupation).

Interesting in view of the fact that presently about half the re-

21 American Council on Education, *National Norms for Entering College* (Washington, D.C.: ACE, Fall 1968).

TABLE 2 *Fall 1968 Freshman Enrollment, by Family Income*

	Less than $4,950		$4,950–7,950		$7,970–11,580		Over $11,580	
	Fall 1968 Enrollment	More or Less than Expected	Fall 1968 Enrollment	More or Less than Expected	Fall 1968 Enrollment	More or Less than Expected	Fall 1968 Enrollment	More or Less than Expected
Public 2-Year Colleges	50,000	+27,000	36,000	−39,000	106,000	+35,000	103,000	+ 5,000
Private 2-Year Colleges	9,000	+ 4,000	21,000	− 6,000	25,000	+ 8,000	34,000	+ 8,000
Public 4-Year Colleges	42,000	+17,000	74,000	−15,000	91,000	+25,000	99,000	+26,000
4-Year Nonsectarian Colleges	9,000	+ 3,000	14,000	− 1,000	22,000	+ 4,000	58,000	+ 4,000
4-Year Sectarian Colleges	15,000	+ 2,000	28,000	−10,000	40,000	−13,000	63,000	−48,000
Public Universities	27,000	+10,000	51,000	− 7,000	101,000	+22,000	159,000	+20,000
Private Universities	4,000	+ 1,000	10,000	0	20,000	+ 3,000	52,000	− 1,000
Technical Institutes	2,000	+ 1,000	6,000	− 1,000	13,000	+ 1,000	19,000	+ 3,000
All Institutions *	159,000	+65,000	311,000	−61,000	420,000	+90,000	583,000	+12,000

* Figures do not add up exactly because of rounding.

Source: U.S. Office of Education, as reprinted in *The Chronicle of Higher Education,* November 10, 1969, p. 1.

cipients of earned doctorates enter college teaching is this circumstance: 10.6 percent of these freshmen state intention of seeking the doctorate, while only 1.1 percent plan to be college teachers. Careers in the schools, however, claim the plans of more students than any other choice. About *one out of four* plan to teach at some level. Thus, the teacher education function seems assured of remaining the first-ranking practical aspect of the undergraduate college.

Some interesting findings are reported under things these students had done in the last year: 71 percent had visited an art gallery or museum; 5.8 percent had taken sleeping pills; over half (52.4 percent) drank beer, but only 15.6 percent smoked cigarettes frequently. Many had attended religious service (91 percent), but not many (4.6 percent) had protested against the Vietnam war or against racial discrimination (7 percent). More of them (43.5 percent) discussed sports frequently than discussed politics (29.9 percent) or religion (29.3 percent) frequently.

Respondents from public universities agreed to a varied extent that:

	Percent
Students should have major role in design of curriculum.	90.4
Individual *cannot* change society.	31.1
College should have the right to regulate student behavior off campus.	19.6
Benefit of college is monetary.	54.4
Marijuana should be legalized.	21.1
Disadvantaged students should get preferential admissions treatment.	38.2
Colleges have been too lax on student protest.	53.1

Diversity of behavior patterns and outlook was obviously characteristic of the class of 1972 taken in aggregate. Yet there seemed to be a yearning toward conformity, for 69 percent of these respondents stated agreement that "my beliefs are similar to others."

the problems of higher education

Higher education in America is a tremendous going concern. It does many things among its vast concert of varied institutions. It does some of them well, and surely does some better than others. It nourishes the intellectual life of the nation. It educates the teachers for the American educational system. It provides centers of cultural and intellectual life in communities scattered broadly across the land. It renders a great deal of practical service to communities. It expands knowledge, conducts research, both pure and applied. It also dwells among many problems.

The student of this text is in all likelihood attending college or university. You are resident, therefore, amid its problems. They are not all, or any perhaps, unknown to you. Higher education is beset by problems, some perennial, some of recent origin. Those that we consider the most important are:

1. Problems of support
2. Allocations of funds
3. Adequate instruction
4. Maintaining quality and quantity

PROBLEMS OF SUPPORT. Increased enrollments and increasing costs put pressure on budgets from all directions. Everything connected with support reads "higher"—tuitions, fees, state support, federal assistance, foundational aid.

ALLOCATIONS OF FUNDS. Within all institutions the problem of raising money is closely followed by that of how to spend it. So many legitimate contenders vie for the operational dollar. Teaching salaries, support of research, administrative staff, instructional materials, pupil personnel services are only a sample of where the funds must go. Every contender could in his view utilize a larger share of the budget, and each contender can make a very good case for his claim.

ADEQUATE INSTRUCTION. At best, instruction in higher education is splendid. Such a state exists when a rare intellect with a profound grasp of his subject and its relationship to other realms of knowledge is combined in a teaching person with consummate skills of communication, and a sensitive responsiveness to learners. A corollary characteristic for the rare individual is a good sense of humor. When such an individual is placed into an appropriate situation for learning among persons characterized as learners by receptivity, awareness, and critical capacity, the ideal conditions exist for true learning. The teaching then must be conducting in scholarship and respect and with a concern not merely that it be attended to and be learned, but that the learning may extend somewhat the meaning of life and being human. In addition, it is hoped that the learning may somehow induce in the learner a greater zest for life and learning, an enhanced tolerance, better appraisals of what is and what ought to be along with an enlightened dread of what could be, and hope and magnanimity, and trust even of self, and a deeper willingness to live within the bounds of love and sense.

If this be a possible definition of excellent teaching, where then is it to be found? Not perhaps in the experience of any of us, but with luck a student may encounter one or two teachers who by approximating the ideal illuminate it.

The problem is at the other end of the continuum. Unfortunately, there is an abundance of mediocre and inept instruction. Two factors are largely responsible for this situation: (1) The preparation of the college teacher is in a discipline whose mastery is guaranteed by the degree of Doctor of Philosophy, the Ph.D. But the rub is that in scarcely any instance does earning the Ph.D., which will serve for many as a certificate to teach in higher education, include any direct instruction or practice in the responsibilities and duties of a faculty man, including teaching. In fact, college and university teaching constitutes just about the only profession one can embark upon without any instruction in method and procedure or supervised practice beforehand. (2) Today the competitive functions of the faculty member tend to push teaching lower and lower on his scale of priorities. Research and publication, consultancies and travel, these are the competing functions. They are the ones rewarded. Good words go to faculty members who place teaching and attention to students ahead of these. Teaching is highly spoken of on every campus. But promotion, salary increases, larger offices and softer chairs, and tenure go to the researchers and the skillful self-aggrandizers. Of course, there is a happy medium; of course, there is a relationship of necessity between scholarship and research and good teaching. But these productive and reasonable balances and relationships are not the issue. Nor are they easy to find in today's academia.

MAINTAINING QUALITY AMID QUANTITY. If the aforementioned is the norm, how does higher education, which serves massive enrollments, maintain a high standard of quality? It does not, and never has. Smaller enrollments once represented selectivity, but the principal selective factors were never simply intelligence, high motivation, and academic aptitude. More active were factors of social class and ability to pay. Today larger enrollments reflect a reduction in the activity of these factors. If the colleges and university are to attain excellence amid great quantity, they will have to study closely, as must the schools, the meaning of *to educate.*

topics for inquiry

1. Piaget and Early Childhood Education
2. Corporal Punishment in Today's Schools: Laws and Practices
3. Departmentalization in the Elementary School
4. Montessori Schools in America Today
5. The Summerhill Society in America
6. The Nongraded High School

7. The University and Defense Projects
8. The Free University Concept
9. ROTC: Status and Issues

subjects for discussion

1. One of the frequent allegations made about the nongraded school
   is that it leads to soft pedagogy, that it lacks fixed standards and
   requirements.
   a. In view of its stated purposes is this a fair charge against non-
      gradedness?
   b. Is there a social-competitive dimension to a graded structure
      that is necessary for motivation?
   c. Is "better" pedagogy the result of either a graded or nongraded
      arrangement?
2. Mark Van Doren, in his book *Liberal Education* states:
   "I continue to believe that the way to produce individual intellects
   is to teach all students the same things and of course the best
   things. They will make their own responses, and discover their
   own ideas; but these will be best when the material for study has
   been the kind of material that is good for everybody." [22]
   a. What are the "best things" to teach?
   b. From your observation, how would this theory work in the
      American comprehensive school?
   c. How would it work in the university?
3. Where do you think it is most desirable to get a college education?
   a. In a small liberal arts college in a sheltered environment?
      Why?
   b. In a major state university in a small city? Why?
   c. In an urban university in a metropolitan city? Why?
4. Since the lottery system has been put into effect for military conscription (1969), some observers have suggested that a lottery
   system also be used for college admission.
   a. Would it not be just as "fair"?
   b. If such a system were used, what might be some of the ex-
      pected outcomes? More colleges? Open admissions?

---

[22] Mark Van Doren, *Liberal Education* (New York: Henry Holt, 1943), p. x.

selected readings

BAYLES, ERNEST E., and BRUCE L. HOOD. *Growth of American Educational Thought and Practice.* New York: Harper & Row, 1966.
> An impressive treatment of the works of Comenius, Locke, Rousseau, Pestalozzi, Herbart, Froebel, Thorndike, and the Progressive educators. It deals with the influence these and others have had on American education.

CREMIN, LAWRENCE A. *The Genius of American Education.* New York: Random House, 1965.
> A positive statement about the purposes of American education as related to the social history of the country.

FROEBEL, FRIEDRICH. *Education of Man.* New York: Appleton-Century, 1887.
> A comprehensive statement of the author's view of life and education.

HERNDON, JAMES. *The Way It Spozed To Be.* New York: Simon and Schuster, 1968.
> A personal response to the real activities that go on in an urban school. The author points up many of the absurdities of the schools today.

JENCKS, CHRISTOPHER, and DAVID RIESMAN. *The Academic Revolution.* Garden City, N.Y.: Doubleday, 1968.
> A solid report on the institutional complexity of higher education that is fascinating in its details and intellectually challenging in its theoretical development.

SANFORD, NEVITT (ed.). *College and Character.* New York: Wiley, 1964.
> An abbreviated version of the major work *The American College.* Among other areas of the college scene, this comprehensive survey deals with the issues of institutionalism, entering support, instruction, student culture, and the effects of college on our culture.

SCHWAB, JOSEPH J. *College Curriculum and Student Protest.* Chicago: University of Chicago Press, 1969.
> A response to student protest without bowing to it. Schwab advocates methods of instruction that include the students in the process of learning. He believes in intellectual fair-mindedness on the part of college teachers.

VAN DOREN, MARK. *Liberal Education.* Boston: Beacon Press, 1943.
> Pressing questions about the meaning of education by a distinguished educator.

VEBLEN, THORSTEIN. *The Higher Learning in America.* New York: Sagamore, 1957.
> Subtitled "A Memorandum on the Conduct of Universities by Business Men." This work is as topical and relevant today as in 1918, the date of its first issue.

4

CONTROL AND SUPPORT OF EDUCA-TION

The public school in America is in legal reality a state-established and state-controlled institution. Its existence is provided for in the various states' constitutions and its organization and management prescribed by state laws. Yet, even within the legal framework of state control, the American public schools have been able to maintain some degree of local autonomy in their management. To be sure, the degree of local involvement varies from state to state in accordance with the various states' statutory provisions. For the most part, however, Americans see their schools as primarily local entities. This varied admixture of state control with local management is one of the unique features of the American educational structure.

The general pattern of state control combined with local management in education has been to a large degree the result of a pragmatic response to social realities in different periods of our history. The involvement of the state was a necessary condition for the establishment of a public school system in a changing society. Even during the early colonial period when local school control was the predominant pattern, there were examples of state involvement. Therefore, in a sense, the historical development of control and support patterns in American education may be viewed not so much as a rapid shift from local to state involvement but more of a progressive shifting of predominance from a local to a state level in accordance with the various political and social presses of the times.

colonial schools

The early colonial concern for education, especially in the New England colonies, is a matter of historical record. Even before the Massachusetts General Court Law of 1642, which required parents and masters to "train up their children in learning and labor," some colonial towns had provided for schools. By 1639 Latin grammar schools had been established in Boston, Ipswich, Salem, Dorchester, and Newbury. Support of such town schools was derived from a variety of sources. Tuition fees, private contributions, and town taxes were all to play a part. An attempt was made to give the early town schools a degree of financial autonomy by establishing some sort of self-perpetuating income. For example, in 1639 Dorchester provided that there should be "a rent of 20 lb. a year for ever imposed upon Tomsons Island . . . toward the mayntinance of a school in Dorchester." [1]

Boston in 1641 provided for a similar plan. Rarely, however, did such plans have any lasting effect. On the whole, the colonial schools were supported by some form of community resources, either general taxes or voluntary contributions, and this pattern of complete local support was to carry through the national period into the middle of the nineteenth century.

Although local support was the pattern of the colonial schools, varying degrees of state involvement did develop in that period but not in terms of financial support. The state made itself felt through compulsory legislation for the establishment of local schools. The 1647 Massachusetts law (see Chapter 6), which required towns of fifty families to establish reading schools and towns of one hundred families to establish Latin grammar schools, was a model for many of the other colonies. For the most part, however, the colonial laws left the tasks of establishing, managing, and funding the schools to local authorities. Therefore, the depth of educational commitment varied in accordance with the individual town's willingness or ability to pay. In general, schooling meant teaching children to read and write and to learn their religion. If the children's parents or masters could not provide for this, they could avail themselves of the town school at a small cost. The colonial laws simply provided that such schools be available; they made no binding stipulation as to how the schools should be structured or operated. Although local autonomy was firmly grounded in practice, the colonial laws at least set a precedent for state involvement in education that was to be followed in the early national period and expanded in the nineteenth-century press for public schools.

[1] As quoted in E. P. Cubberley, *Readings in the History of Education* (Boston: Houghton Mifflin, 1948), p. 362.

early national period

The provisions for education in the early state constitutions to a large degree were replicas of the earlier colonial provisions. The constitutions stated in one form or another that schools should be locally established and locally supported. Education was still thought of as primarily a private matter even though much of the constitutional language put it in a public light by holding it important for the preservation of the peoples' rights and liberties. Certainly, the rhetoric was there, but rhetoric is rarely the prime mover of substantive social change unless it is accompanied by a growing social press. Even so, the framers of the early state constitutions, in speaking about rights and liberties, were not viewing education in the egalitarian sense that was to be the case during the common school movement. They were still part of a society that had maintained a fair degree of hierarchical structure.

During the early national period there was little serious thought about universal public schooling. The central idea in most cases was that the state would supplement private facilities and provide free schools only for the poor. The establishment of pauper schools, it was believed, would provide a minimal education for the lower strata of society, but even this "charitable" plan was ineffectively developed and sparsely funded. There was no press for the ideal of equality of opportunity through education. Even Thomas Jefferson's early proposal for a state system of education in Virginia, which proposed to provide some degree of equal opportunity for the poor, met with defeat in the Virginia legislature. Although Jefferson's proposal, "A Bill for the More General Diffusion of Knowledge," was not in the exact spirit of intent that was to be found in the later common school movement, it was an early attempt to establish a state system of education. Since Jefferson's bill, offered in 1779, is an example of the early concern shown for education in the new country, it is worth examining in some detail.

> This bill proposes to lay off every county into small districts of five or six miles square, called hundreds, and in each of them to establish a school for teaching reading, writing, and arithmetic. The tutor to be supported by the hundred, and every person in it entitled to send their children three years gratis, and as much longer as they please, paying for it. These schools to be under a visitor, who is annually to chuse the boy, of best genius in the school, of those whose parents are too poor to give them further education, and to send him forward to one of the grammar schools, of which twenty are proposed to be erected in different parts of the country, for teaching Greek, Latin, geography, and the higher branches of numerical arithmetic. Of the boys thus sent in any one year, trial is to be made at the grammar schools

one or two years, and the best genius of the whole selected, and
continued six years, and the residue dismissed. By this means
twenty of the best geniuses will be raked from the rubbish
annually, and be instructed, at the public expense, so far as the
grammar schools go. At the end of six years' instruction, one
half are to be discontinued (from among whom the grammar
schools will probably be supplied with future masters); and the
other half, who are to be chosen for the superiority of their parts
and disposition, are to be sent and continued three years in the
study of such sciences as they shall chuse, at William and Mary
college, the plan of which is proposed to be enlarged . . . and
extended to all the useful sciences. The ultimate result of the
whole scheme of education would be the teaching of all the
children of the state reading, writing, and common arithmetic:
turning out ten annually of superior genius, well taught in Greek,
Latin, geography, and the higher branches of arithmetic: turning
out ten others annually, of still superior parts, who, to those
branches of learning, shall have added such of the sciences as
their genius shall have led them to: the furnishing to the wealthier
part of the people convenient schools, at which their children
may be educated, at their own expense. . . . Of all the view of
this law none is safe, as they are the ultimate guardians of their
own liberty. For this purpose the reading in the first stage, where
they will receive their whole education, is proposed, as has been
said, to be chiefly historical. History by apprising them of the
past will enable them to judge of the future.[2]

Although it might be argued that Jefferson's bill implied an intent
to replace the landed aristocracy with an intellectual aristocracy, it
must also be argued that his proposal came at a time when education
was still thought of as a private, not a public, concern. His bill
proposed that education should become a public concern, not only
encouraged by the state, but legally established by the state. To a
large extent, his bill foretold of the pattern that was to develop a half
century later. The essential characteristics of state and local relationships which Jefferson proposed were to become the general pattern in American education. With the obvious modifications through
the years, the pattern is still maintained. But, again it must be noted
that Jefferson's bill was not passed in 1779, and in 1796 when legislative provision for a system of elementary schools was made in
Virginia, it fell far short of Jefferson's proposal. Few men of means
were ready to accept the idea that they should be taxed for the
education of another man's child, except in some small way by providing some meager education for the poor, and even this reluctantly.
The social press that was needed to advance the idea of universal
schooling was still half a century away. And the political shift that

would lead toward a more participatory democracy was not to come until after the 1820s with the growth of the "common man" motif in American politics.

Although by 1800 the states had made some constitutional provisions for education, few of them had followed the provisions with legislative commitments. Even when such commitments were made, the statutes were most often permissive rather than mandatory. The state laws permitted local districts to levy taxes for the support of schools if the constituencies of the districts would approve. Until the 1830s the opponents of general support plans were able to block any significant proposals that would provide for general education. The only accepted programs were those that provided some small support for the children of publicly declared paupers. But the stigma of pauperism and the laxity of standards in the pauper schools rendered such programs most ineffective. Although such programs prevailed until the 1830s, there were at the same time growing forces pressing for educational reforms, especially in the larger cities.

lancasterian monitorial schools

One significant accomplishment of the early educational reformers was the establishment of the monitorial schools in New York, Boston, Philadelphia, and other large cities. At a time when cities were already feeling the problems of rapid growth, with the attendant problems of poverty, the children of the poor were receiving no formal education. The pauper school laws, as mentioned, were most ineffective. There was little support for, and much opposition against, any program that would provide even a minimal education for the poor. Any attempt to tax for the purpose of maintaining schools was bound to meet with opposition. It is in view of this that the monitorial schools might be seen as a wedge into the opposition. Such schools offered the possibility of providing the rudiments of education to large numbers of pupils at a very small cost.

The Lancasterian monitorial schools, named after Joseph Lancaster, a Quaker schoolmaster in England, were promoted in New York in 1806 by the famous Free School Society. The society, along with other humanitarian groups, pressed for any means by which to offer some educational advantages to the growing number of poor children. The monitorial schools were at least able to provide some education to children of the working class at a very small cost. The financial expediency of the program was a particularly persuasive argument in gaining support from those conservative forces who held that education was a private concern, not a public one. Even so, the early monitorial schools of the New York society, and of other cities as well, were supported not by taxes but by contributions. Thus, the establishment of the schools by no means settled the question of tax support for public schools, but it did at least set somewhat of a precedent when the tax-support question became the vital issue in the 1830s.

By any standards the monitorial schools were lacking in educational merits. They were structured so that one teacher could handle from 200 to 500 pupils at one time in one large room. The teacher simply had to teach a "packaged" lesson to selected older pupils who were then the monitors to oversee the learning of the lessons by the younger pupils. The process was unimaginative rote learning, but it did expand significantly the school population in a number of cities. In most places the monitorial schools were the only free schools available until laws during the 1830s and 1840s established public schools. The early monitorial schools were clearly local operations, but they were important in setting a tone for expanding educational interest at a state level, an interest that was to become necessary for the establishment of public schools.

the common school movement

Until the 1830s education in America was primarily a local function. There was some evidence of state interest but little of state involvement in terms of binding statutes or financial assistance. In general, the early district patterns created in some states carried no provisions to either assure that schools be established or that they be supported. The press for public schools, which began in earnest during the 1830s, eventually brought about the patterns of state systems of education that were necessary at the time to achieve any degree of educational base that could provide for a growing population in a period of growing industrialism. The greatest demand for public schools came from the cities, where the problems brought about by industrialism provided a persuasive argument for educational reform.

Increasing urbanization was also a problem of the mid-nineteenth century. With the rapid increase of industrialization after the War of 1812, especially in the northeastern part of the country, and the phenomenal increase of population came accompanying problems.

From 1820 to 1860 the population of the United States increased at the rate of about 35 percent each decade, from about 10 million in 1820 to over 31 million in 1860. No less phenomenal was the rapid increase in industry, having been born of necessity earlier by the War of 1812 and then given nurtured encouragement by the protective tariff of 1828. Just one example of this expansion was the increase in the cotton mills of New England. From only four mills in 1804 the number increased to over 800 in 1831, employing over 70,000 workers. By 1850 the New England mills were employing more than 100,000 workers.

The important aspect of the rapid industrial growth was its effect on society. Of the 100,000 workers in the New England mills in 1850, over 40 percent were children from seven to sixteen years of age. Working hours were fourteen hours a day. Wages were scandalously low, about $1.25 a week for women and children. Nor were laboring men much better off. Canal workers in the 1830s earned at best about $12 a month. Conditions were made worse when the increased immigration of the 1840s simply widened the labor market for exploitive manufacturers.

The backdrop of social conditions in the 1830s provided much fuel for the arguments for educational reform, as well as other social reforms. The rhetoric of egalitarian-minded educational reformers was now accompanied by a social press that carried with it a threat to the security of the social order. Whatever provisions were to be made for public education in the 1830s and 1840s by various state legislatures were to be influenced as much by a concern for maintaining order as by humanitarian zeal. Even the most genuinely humanitarian reformers were keenly aware that many of those who held positions of power and wealth might only be moved by a plea to their propertied concerns. Even Horace Mann, whose reform spirit was unmatched, found it necessary to appeal to the pecuniary concerns of the propertied class in order to assuage their opposition to the common school. In his Fifth Annual Report (1841) he asked:

> Finally, in regard to those who possess the largest shares in the
> stock of worldly goods, could there, in your opinion, be any
> police so vigilant and effective, for the protection of all the rights
> of person, property and character, as such a sound and compre-
> hensive education and training, as our system of Common Schools
> could be made to impart; and would not the payment of a
> sufficient tax to make such education and training universal,
> be the cheapest means of self-protection and insurance? [3]

Others, such as Thaddeus Stevens, also made appeals to the private concerns of the wealthy. In his famous speech before the Pennsylvania Legislature in 1835 Stevens argued that those who opposed the school tax because they felt that it benefited others were mistaken:

> It is for their own benefit, inasmuch as it perpetuates the govern-
> ment and ensures the due administration of the laws under
> which they live, and by which their lives and property are
> protected. . . . He cheerfully pays the tax which is necessary to
> support and punish convicts, but loudly complains of that which
> goes to prevent his fellow being from becoming a criminal, and
> to obviate the necessity of those humiliating instructions. [4]

[3] As quoted in V. T. Thayer, *Formative Ideas in American Education* (New York: Dodd, Mead & Co., 1966), p. 98.
[4] As quoted in George P. Donehoo, *Pennsylvania: A History* (New York: Lewis Historical Publishing Company, 1926), Vol. 3, p. 1344.

Although such practical arguments for the common school were proposed, the major arguments of the educational reformers during the
1830s and 1840s were based on a rhetoric of egalitarianism and
pleaded the need for education to serve the newly acclaimed faith in
democracy.

Throughout the 1830s and 1840s the struggle for the common
school was to meet with continued opposition. Local development of
education by no means answered the needs, nor was it expected to.
The major battles for the schools were on a state level. James Carter
and Horace Mann in Massachusetts, Henry Barnard in Connecticut,
Caleb Mills in Indiana, to mention only a few, continually worked for
expanded state involvement in educational reform. Along with others,
these reformers sought to make the common school a reality at a time
when only a small percentage of children had the opportunity to
attend school and when child labor was a predominant theme in many
cities. In general terms what the reformers wanted were high-quality
schools that would be:

1. Publicly supported by taxation
2. Free and open to all
3. Publicly controlled through elected or appointed officials
4. Nonsectarian in character

The efforts to achieve the common school were supported by
others, notably early labor organizations. They too saw educational
reform as a means by which to promote the egalitarian promise of
Jacksonian democracy. An encompassing example of labor's stand
on educational reform is presented in "The Report of the Workingmen's Committee of Philadelphia, 1830."

> With the exception of this city and county, the city and
> incorporated borough of Lancaster, and the city of Pittsburg,
> erected into "school districts" since 1818, it appears that the
> entire state is destitute of any provisions for public instruction,
> except those furnished by the enactment of 1809. This law
> requires the assessors of the several counties to ascertain and
> return the number of children whose parents are unable, through
> poverty, to educate them; and such children are permitted to be
> instructed at the most convenient schools at the expense of their
> respective counties. . . .
> But the principles on which these "school districts" are
> founded, are yet, in the opinion of the committees, extremely
> defective and inefficient. Their leading feature is pauperism!
> They are confined exclusively, to the children of the poor, while
> there are, perhaps, thousands of children whose parents are
> unable to afford for them a good private education, yet whose
> standing, professions or connexions in society effectually exclude
> them from taking the benefit of a poor law. There are great

numbers, even of the poorest parents, who hold a dependence on
the public bounty to be incompatible with the rights and liberties
of an American citizen, whose deep and cherished consciousness
of independence determines them rather to starve the intellect
of their offspring, than submit to become the objects of public
charity. . . .

Another radical and glaring defect in the existing public
school system is the very limited amount of instruction it affords,
even to the comparatively small number of youth, who enjoy its
benefits. It extends, in no case, further than a tolerable proficiency
in reading, writing, and arithmetic, and sometimes to a slight
acquaintance with geography. Besides these, the girls are taught
a few simple branches of industry. A great proportion of scholars,
however, from the causes already enumerated, acquire but a
very slight and partial knowledge of these branches. . . .

In a republic, the people constitute the government, and by
wielding its powers in accordance with the dictates, either of their
intelligence or their ignorance, of their judgment or their caprices,
are the makers and the rulers of their own good or evil destiny.
They frame the laws and create the institutions, that promote
their happiness or produce their destruction. If they be wise and
intelligent, no laws but what are just and equal will receive their
approbation, or be sustained by their suffrages. If they be
ignorant and capricious, they will be deceived by mistaken or
designing rulers, into the support of laws that are unequal and
unjust.

It appears, therefore, to the committees that there can be no
real liberty without a wide diffusion of real intelligence; that the
members of a republic should all be alike instructed in the nature
and character of their equal rights and duties, as human beings,
and as citizens; and that education, instead of being limited as
in our public poor schools, to a simple acquaintance with words
and cyphers, should tend, as far as possible, to the production of a
just disposition, virtuous habits, and a rational self-governing
character.[5]

Regardless of the pressing social problems and the zealous arguments persistently put forth by reform leaders, resistance to the
common school idea was not to be easily overcome. A predominant
segment of the monied powers believed neither in Jefferson's sociopolitical views nor in the pragmatic expansion of those views by
Jackson. The entrenched social views held by the opponents of the
common school were not to be swayed by any rhetoric on democratic
principles. Their opposition was based to a large extent on a prin-
cipled economic posture that held that no man should have to pay
for the education of another man's child. This was a prevalent argument, but an argument too simple to betray the underlying social
attitude of many who used it. Many of the powerful opponents of

[5] As quoted in Cubberley, op. cit., pp. 559–560.

the common school held an elitist attitude that enabled them to
explain away industrial poverty or any other social inequalities as
inevitable—Social Darwinism yet unnamed. For example, in response
to the pronouncements of the educational reform movement the
Philadelphia *Gazette* published the following editorial on July 10,
1830:

> It is our strong inclination and our obvious interest that literary
> acquirements should be universal; but we should be guilty of
> imposture, if we professed to believe in the possibility of that
> consumation. Literature cannot be acquired without leisure, and
> wealth gives leisure. Universal opulence, or even competency, is
> a chimera, as man and society are constituted. There will ever
> be distinctions of conditions of capacity, of knowledge, and
> ignorance, in spite of all the fond conceits which may be tried, to
> the contrary. The "peasant" must labor during those hours of
> the day, which his wealthy neighbor can give to the abstract
> culture of his mind; otherwise, the earth would not yield enough
> for the subsistence of all: the mechanic cannot abandon the
> operations of his trade, for general studies; if he should, most of
> the convenience of life and objects of exchange would be wanting;
> langour, decay, poverty, discontent would soon be visible among
> all classes. No government, no statesman, no philanthropist, can
> furnish what is incompatible with the very organization and
> being of civil society. Education, the most comprehensive,
> should be, and is, open to the whole community, but it must cost
> to everyone, time and money; and those are means which everyone
> cannot possess simultaneously.[6]

The social philosophy expounded in the Philadelphia *Gazette* editorial was subscribed to by a majority of what historian Arthur
Schlesinger, Jr. calls the "possessing classes" of the day. Not that they
were the only opponents of the common school, but they were the
most influential. The opposition of others, such as rigid sectarians
or rural residents, was based on positions not so totally incompatible
with the reform movement. In any event, the resistance to reform
was eventually to be overcome both by the real social press and the
egalitarian zeal of many of the reform leaders. But, again, the direction would have to come from a state level. Even with the limited
provisions for local school districts allowed by many states before
1830, it was clear that little would or really could be done at a local
level. Legally, the responsibility for education rested with the state.
And the battles for schools that were fought and eventually won were
ultimately fought in the legislative halls of the states.

Pennsylvania is a fair example of the development of state involvement in the establishment of a public school system. The charge

---

[6] As quoted in David B. Tyack (ed.), *Turning Points in American Educational History*
(Waltham, Mass.: Blaisdell Publishing, 1967), p. 146.

made by the Philadelphia Workingmen's Association in 1830 that Pennsylvania was "destitute of any provisions for public instruction," except those made for paupers, was a charge obviously based on fact. According to an 1829 report of the secretary of the Commonwealth, over 60 percent of the state's children "were growing up in ignorance because no schools were within their reach." [7] Of the 400,000 children of school age, fewer than 150,000 were receiving any education at all. Nor was this situation unique to Pennsylvania. Even in New England the situation was somewhat the same. Whatever provisions had been made were simply permissive and for the most part provided free schooling only for paupers, which, as has been pointed out, was most ineffective. In the same report cited above it was estimated that in thirty-one of Pennsylvania's counties a total of only 4,477 poor children had received any instruction at all in 1828.

Pennsylvania's slim effort to provide minimal education for the poor was set forth in an 1809 law that allowed for such children to be educated at the expense of the counties—if the counties so chose. The law was not mandatory. Opposition came from all quarters. It was opposed by the rich, whose taxes would support the program, and by the poor, who rejected the stigmatizing effect of the law. Nor was the law acceptable to the humanitarian societies, who saw it as a block to any real progress toward expanding education. Even though the 1809 law was grossly ineffective, falling far short of even its limited goals, it remained in effect until 1834. But by the 1830s, however, Pennsylvania, as well as the rest of the country, had begun to make definite advances of social adjustment. It was a period when movement in politics as well as in ideas was toward democratic social reform. Expanded suffrage, the establishment of labor organizations, the continued activities of humanitarian organizations all began to have their effect on educational legislation.

Pressed by the inadequacy of its educational commitment to meet the needs of the time, Pennsylvania made a significant, if limited, move toward educational reform in 1834. Led by a governor who was an ardent advocate of free schools, the Pennsylvania legislature set up a program that provided a basis for a state system of public schools. The 1834 law did fall short of statewide effectiveness. Again, it was permissive legislation, but it did lend legal sanction to local districts to tax for the establishment and support of common schools. Of the 987 school districts in the state, 742 had put the law into effect by 1837. [8]

Although it might be argued that the motivation behind the Pennsylvania school law of 1834 was varied, it is clear that the new spirit of Jacksonian democracy was the carrying force. This spirit was evident in a report to the legislature by a legislative education committee in 1834:

[7] As quoted in Donehoo, op. cit., p. 1340.
[8] Ibid., p. 1610.

A radical defect in our laws upon the subject of education, is
that the public aid now given, and imperfectly given, is confined
to the poor. Aware of this, your committee have taken care to
exclude the word poor from the bill which will accompany this
report, meaning to make the system general, that is to say, to
form an educational association between the rich, the comparatively rich, and the destitute. Let them all fare alike in the
primary schools, receive the same elementary instruction, imbibe
the republican spirit, and be animated by a feeling of perfect
equality. In after life, he who is diligent at school will take his
station accordingly, whether born to wealth or not.[9]

The almost unanimous support of the 1834 bill (only one senator
opposed it) seemed to indicate that the common school forces in
Pennsylvania had won a lasting victory. But the enemies of the free
school system immediately began work to have the law repealed the
following year. When the legislature assembled in 1835, the Senate
quickly repealed the 1834 law. It was expected that the House would
also be in favor of repeal since many of the counties in the state had
sent in petitions for repeal. But, rather than repeal the 1834 law, the
House accepted, and finally forced the Senate to accept, a bill that
went even further than the previous law. There was an adamant
minority of free-school supporters in the House. The credit for
victory clearly belongs to Thaddeus Stevens, perhaps the most ardent
of the supporters. Speaking to the House in support of the 1834 bill,
Stevens argued on the democratic principle that:

If an elective republic is to endure for any great length of time,
every elector must have sufficient information, not only to
accumulate wealth and take care of his pecuniary concerns, but
to direct wisely the Legislature, the Ambassadors, and the
Executive of the nation; for some part of all these things, some
agency in approving or disapproving them, falls to every freeman.
If then the permanency of our government depends upon some
knowledge it is the duty of the government to see that the means
of information be diffused to every citizen. This is a sufficient
answer to those who deem education a private and not a public
duty—who argue that they are willing to educate their own
children, but not their neighbor's children.

In a more direct fashion Stevens lashed out at the monied opponents
of the common school:

I know how large a portion of the community can scarcely feel
any sympathy with, or understanding the necessities of the poor;
or appreciate the exquisite feelings which they enjoy, when they
see their children receiving the boon of education and arising

[9] *Ibid.*, pp. 1610–1611.

in intellectual superiority above the clogs which hereditary
poverty had cast upon them. . . . Sir, when I reflect how apt
hereditary wealth, hereditary influence, and perhaps, as a
consequence, hereditary pride, are to close the avenues and to
steel the heart against the wants and rights of the poor, I am
induced to thank my creator for having, from early life, bestowed
on me the blessing of poverty . . . for if there be any human
sensation more ethereal and divine than all others, it is that which
feelingly sympathizes with misfortune.[10]

Although not the first, the Pennsylvania struggle to establish a
public school system may be looked on as a turning point for American
education. Other states followed, and by 1850, the right to tax for
the support of public schools was firmly established in most states.
Assurance for the systems was gained, again at a state level, with the
passage of compulsory attendance laws—first in Massachusetts in
1852 and subsequently in all states by 1918. The structural objectives
of the common school movement were realized. Of necessity they
were achieved at a state level, but in varying degrees the states assigned to the local districts the responsibility of management and
partial financing of the schools. To a great extent the structural
patterns that developed have been maintained. Obviously, there
have been modifications with time and population growth.

state control of schools

State involvement in education, both in terms of control and funding,
has grown immensely from its early cautious and sometimes parsimo-
nious concern. Along with legislative provisions that allowed for
extension of education in all directions came the development of specific educational administrative functions at the state level. Although
the states have been autonomous in structuring their educational
systems, there are patterns of structure that can be applied generally
to all states. This is particularly true in viewing the administrative
structures that have developed within the states. It might be argued
that the tight state bureaucracies that have developed are the inevitable result of the rapid growth of education since 1920. But regardless,
there has been a maintenance of the local character of schools, except
in the larger cities where local bureaucratization has been a more
stifling form of centralization than at the state level. This too, of
course, is a direct responsibility of the state who legally sets up the
size and type of district patterns.

In view of the fact that states have the ultimate legal responsibility
for education, even to the point of designating the degree of local
involvement, it is important to understand something of the general
characteristics of state educational structures.

[10] *Ibid*., pp. 1344–1345

state legislatures

Although state legislatures seldom seem directly involved with running the educational systems of their respective states, in a legal sense they are the ultimate power in educational decision making. The only instances where their decisions might be overruled are in cases where legislation is an abridgment of either the state or federal constitution as decided by either state or federal courts. Because of the legislative function in education, the schools of a state are to some extent within the control of the people, at least potentially, if not always in fact, through the ballot.

The extent of the legislature's control over a state's educational system can best be seen by the nature of its functions. Among its most important functions are the following:

1. Basic legislation providing for schools.
2. Direct or indirect control over the size and composition of local districts and their management; determining the size of local school boards, qualifications for members, terms of office, and methods of selection.
3. Establishing taxing power limits for local districts.
4. Direct or indirect control over the administrative structure of local administration.
5. Determining the length of the school year.
6. Determining the age limits for compulsory attendance.
7. Establishing distribution patterns of state monies to local districts.
8. Determining the type of state administrative structure to run the system.

Although the legislatures have the final authority over education, the actual administration of school programs is delegated to other agencies in the states. While the methods of determining the agencies and the assignment of their duties vary among the states, there is some similarity in their structure. The most general pattern consists of a state board of education, and a chief school officer who administers the state department of education.

state boards of education

The most basic agency for broad planning and operation of a state's school system is the state board of education. From 1834, when the Massachusetts State Board of Education was established with Horace Mann as its secretary, state boards have been set up in all but two states, Illinois and Wisconsin. Among other things, state boards may have the delegated power to regulate teacher certification, adopt rules and regulations for schools, and prescribe minimal standards. Working within the legislative provisions, most state boards are responsible

lor formulating the educational policies for their states. Some
boards, of course, function as nothing more than political yes-men to
either the governor or state political bosses. But where the boards
are given delegated power by the legislature, their formulated rules
and regulations have the force of law.

Size and Method of Selection

Although the sizes of state boards vary from three to twenty-three
members, most states have boards that range in size from five to nine
members. The methods of selecting members for the state boards of
education are varied also. In a majority of the states the members
are appointed by the governor. In other states they are either elected
by popular vote or vote of the legislature, appointed by the chief
school officer, or serve as ex-officio members because of other specified offices held. The type of selection by states is shown in Table 3.
Along with with general state boards of education, many states have
several special-purpose boards whose duties pertain to specific areas
of education.

chief state school officers

The task of implementing and administering the school policies of a
state set out by the state boards of education and the legislature rests
with the chief school officer of the state. The title for the office may
be superintendent of public instruction, superintendent of schools,
superintendent of education, or commissioner of education. The important difference among the chief school officers, however, is not
their title but the kind of leadership they give to the state's educational system. Students of school administration contend that the
method of selection has a great deal to do with the potential of the office. There seems to be general agreement that selection by popular
election is less likely to provide as able an administrator than are
other methods of selection, such as appointment by the state board or
by the governor. Table 4 shows methods of selection by states.

Although the specific duties of the chief state school officers vary
from state to state, they generally involve broad supervisory authority
over the public schools of a state. In some instances the officer has
limited authority over higher education.

The office achieved early importance and dignity when Horace
Mann was appointed secretary of the Massachusetts State Board of
Education in 1834. At that time the extent of state involvement in
education required little more than one man to oversee the schools.
In most states that was the extent of state supervision. Horace Mann
was the sole member of the department in Massachusetts. Even by
the turn of the century the median number of staff members in state
departments of education was two. With the vast expansion of educational programs since 1920 it has been necessary to expand the admin-

TABLE 3 *Methods of Selecting State Board of Education*

States	No state board	Appointed by chief school officers	Ex-officio member-ship	Appointed by gov-ernors	Elected by people or legislature
Alabama				x	
Alaska				x	
Arizona			x		
Arkansas				x	
California				x	
Colorado					x
Connecticut				x	
Delaware				x	
Florida			x		
Georgia				x	
Hawaii					x
Idaho				x	
Illinois	x				
Indiana				x	
Iowa					x
Kansas				x	
Kentucky				x	
Louisiana					x
Maine				x	
Maryland				x	
Massachusetts				x	
Michigan				x	
Minnesota				x	
Mississippi			x		
Missouri				x	
Montana				x	
Nebraska					x
Nevada					x
New Hampshire				x	
New Jersey				x	
New Mexico					x
New York					x
North Carolina				x	
North Dakota			x		
Ohio					x
Oklahoma				x	
Oregon				x	
Pennsylvania				x	
Rhode Island				x	
South Carolina				x	
South Dakota				x	
Tennessee				x	
Texas					x
Utah					x
Vermont				x	
Virginia				x	
Washington					x
West Virginia				x	
Wisconsin	x				
Wyoming		x			
Total	2	1	4	31	12

TABLE 4 *Methods of Selecting the Chief State School Officer*

State	Appointed by board	Elected by people	Appointed by governor
Alabama		x	
Alaska			x
Arizona		x	
Arkansas	x		
California		x	
Colorado	x		
Connecticut	x		
Delaware	x		
Florida		x	
Georgia		x	
Hawaii	x		
Idaho		x	
Illinois		x	
Indiana		x	
Iowa	x		
Kansas		x	
Kentucky		x	
Louisiana		x	
Maine	x		
Maryland	x		
Massachusetts	x		
Michigan	x		
Minnesota	x		
Mississippi		x	
Missouri	x		
Montana		x	
Nebraska	x		
Nevada	x		
New Hampshire	x		
New Jersey			x
New Mexico	x		
New York	x		
North Carolina		x	
North Dakota		x	
Ohio	x		
Oklahoma		x	
Oregon	x		
Pennsylvania			x
Rhode Island	x		
South Carolina		x	
South Dakota		x	
Tennessee			x
Texas	x		
Utah	x		
Vermont	x		
Virginia			x
Washington		x	
West Virginia	x		
Wisconsin		x	
Wyoming		x	
Total	24	21	5

istrative staffs working under the chief school officer. Today state
departments of education or departments of public instruction are
large bureaucratic structures. In some states they have become obstacles to eductional innovation because of the usual bureaucratic
penchant for following established patterns or because of the institutionalized self-defensiveness of bureaucracies.

In the twentieth century state controls of education have expanded
greatly. For the most part, with the legal responsibility for education
that rests with the state and the scope of education today, the expansion is understandable.

local control of education

Even with the expanded state supervision of schools the local communities in most states have been given the responsibility of operating
their own schools. Although the pattern of school districts varies
from state to state, the organization of administration in the districts
is patterned somewhat like that at the state level. The decentralization is provided for by state legislation or constitutional provisions.
In a strict legal sense, the local administrative structure functions as
a state agency. The state delegates the responsibility for operation of
the schools to the local areas, defining specifically the geographic and
political character of the local districts.

school districts as political units

Due to both geographical and historical factors the resultant geo-
political characteristics of the local units of school organization vary
throughout the states. Although the term *district* is usually applied
to any local unit, the actual designation of the local units by the states
falls generally into five broad categories, with many internal modifications not noted here:

1. *The district.* In most of the western states, as well as in Michigan,
   Delaware, Ohio, and New York, the state designated units of local
   school organization are referred to as districts. The districts vary
   from those that operate no more than a one-teacher school, or perhaps no school at all, to highly populated areas, such as some of
   those in New York. In many states there is also some overlay of
   administration at a county or regional level.
2. *The county.* In most of the South, as well as in Nevada and Utah,
   the local unit is assigned at the county level. Obviously, such
   county units range in population from a few hundred to several
   million.
3. *The town and township.* Some type of town or township organizational units are found in the New England states as well as in
   Pennsylvania, New Jersey, and Indiana. There are also some in

Illinois, Iowa, and Michigan, states primarily organized on the *district* system.

4. *The state.* Hawaii is the only state with a single state system that directly governs all of its schools. Alaska has a modified state system that governs only the schools outside of about thirty cities and villages, which have local governance.

5. *City systems as separate units.* In most states, regardless of the pattern of local structure, the larger cities operate somewhat independently as local *district* systems. When one considers the vastness of the educational structures in cities such as New York, Chicago, Boston, and Detroit, the designation of local district seems somewhat absurd. The degree to which any large bureaucratic administration can be responsive to the community is obviously limited, which has been more than adequately displayed in the recent press for community control of schools within the large cities.

administration of local units

Although there is a great diversity in the size and character of local unit organization, the administration of the units mirrors, somewhat, the administrative structure at the state level. There are local equivalents of state boards of education, elected by the local citizenry or, as in some of the larger cities, appointed in one way or another. Although in a legal sense the local school boards are agents of the state, they are responsible to the people of the districts they serve as well as to the state. Working within the framework of state laws and regulations, the local board has the function of carrying out the educational program set out by the state. Although their powers vary, they generally have the broad power to tax for schools, hire personnel, and direct the educational program. In all but the smallest districts the local boards appoint an executive officer or chief school administrator to carry out the school program. His duties include administration of the total instructional program, management of the budget and expenditures, and administration and supervision of personnel. The degree to which the administrative duties are delegated to others in some form of bureaucratic hierarchy is relative to the size of the local unit.

financing education

Since the beginning of public school systems in the United States, one of the growing problems has been the question of finance. In terms of dollars it is a large problem. The cost of elementary and secondary public schools in the United States for the 1969–1970 year was about $38 billion. If one includes the nonpublic schools and colleges, the total outlay amounted to about $65 billion. Obviously, it fell far short of the needed commitment in view of societal problems. But

the question that faces society in educational financing is how to meet
the needed commitment—not whether society is able. There is no
question that two or three times the amount now spent for education
in the United States could be spent if we rearranged our priorities.
This is not to imply that the quality of education is measured only in
dollars, but, all other things held constant, it can be the determining
factor. If some districts find that it is necessary to spend $1,200 per
year for each pupil in order to provide a good educational program,
then it is obvious that a district that spends only one-fourth that
amount would be providing a great deal less of educational opportunity to its children. Basically, it is the question of equality of educational opportunity that is as much at issue today as it was during the
common school movement.

The early common school ideals held that education was a public
responsibility. To some extent the spirit of that idea has been accepted. Most people accept, though occasionally grudgingly, the right
of a community or state to tax for schools. But not so widely accepted is the idea that there should be an equal offering of education
to all. Consequently, the quality of educational offerings varies greatly
within states as well as among them. Wealthier local districts with
greater tax-paying ability can provide more money for education than
can poor districts. For the most part state plans for equalizing educational offerings have done little more than provide for minimal offerings, even though the states have been assuming a progressively
greater share of the support of education. The differential of school
expenditures between wealthier and poorer districts is still extensive
in most states.

The problem of inequality of educational opportunity at the national level is even more acute than at the state level. The differential
of states' abilities to provide for education can be seen in Table 5.
States with high tax resources can afford a great deal more for education than can poorer states. Attempts to give federal aid to provide
for some equalization among the states has continually met with political and ideological opposition.

The basic question involved at both the state and federal level is
whether or not education is to be looked upon as a public rather than
a private responsibility. Obviously, the designation of *private* interest
here is not as narrowly defined as it was in the common school movement. *Privatism* might now be more broadly applied to a community
rather than to an individual. In this sense one might look at the wide
differential of school expenditures between wealthy and poor districts
as an example of this expanded privatism. The wealthy district assumes little responsibility for the education of those outside its own
district. In the national arena, a wealthy state assumes little responsibility for the fiscal problems of other states. In terms of state effort
it is readily apparent from Table 5 that many of the poorer states
make a substantially greater effort to provide for education than do

TABLE 5 *State Income and Educational Expenditures*

State	Per capita income—1967	Educational Expenditures— above, within, or below national average	Expenditures for all education of state and local governments as percentage of personal income—above, within, or below national average
U.S. Average	$2,963	$500–$600	About 6.0%
Connecticut	3,690	Above	4.1
Illinois	3,532	Average	4.2
Delaware	3,529	Average	5.9
Nevada	3,497	Average	6.1
New York	3,497	Above	5.0
California	3,497	Average	6.4
New Jersey	3,445	Average	4.2
Alaska	3,421	Above	7.3
Massachusetts	3,271	Average	4.0
Michigan	3,269	Average	6.4
Washington	3,222	Average	6.5
Maryland	3,204	Average	4.9
Hawaii	3,124	Average	5.5
Indiana	3,076	Average	6.2
Ohio	3,056	Average	4.5
Rhode Island	3,047	Average	4.5
Iowa	2,992	Average	6.5
Wisconsin	2,973	Average	6.4
Pennsylvania	2,968	Average	4.6
Colorado	2,916	Average	8.2
Oregon	2,908	Above	7.2
Nebraska	2,905	Below	5.5
Minnesota	2,904	Average	7.6
Kansas	2,862	Average	6.3
Missouri	2,817	Below	4.6
New Hampshire	2,808	Below	4.6
Wyoming	2,739	Above	8.0
Montana	2,623	Average	7.5
Florida	2,614	Below	5.3
Virginia	2,605	Average	5.3
Vermont	2,595	Average	6.7
Arizona	2,544	Average	8.0
Texas	2,542	Below	6.2
Utah	2,485	Below	9.4
Maine	2,477	Below	4.8
Oklahoma	2,452	Below	6.3
Idaho	2,445	Below	6.1
South Dakota	2,420	Below	7.5
New Mexico	2,385	Average	9.1
North Dakota	2,384	Below	7.6
Georgia	2,379	Below	5.2
North Carolina	2,277	Below	5.7
Louisiana	2,277	Average	5.9
Kentucky	2,227	Below	5.4
Tennessee	2,227	Below	5.6
West Virginia	2,176	Below	5.6
Alabama	2,088	Below	5.6
South Carolina	2,052	Below	5.6
Arkansas	2,010	Below	5.4
Mississippi	1,777	Below	6.6

Source: Adapted from: National Education Association, *What Everyone Should Know About School Financing* (Washington, D.C.: NEA, 1968), p. 50.

some of the wealthier states. Mississippi, for example, expends a greater percentage of its available income for education than does New York, but it is only able to provide about one-third as much as does New York.

Although both state and federal financial resources have been increasingly given to the schools, the continued inequality of educational offerings within and among the states is a matter of growing concern. If the demands that society places on education are to be met and if equality of educational opportunity is to be achieved, some fundamental changes must be made in the patterns of school financing.

patterns of educational support

Perhaps the greatest diversity in American education is found in the patterns of financial support for public schools. They range from an almost totally local funding pattern, as in Nebraska, to a predominantly state funding pattern, as in Alaska. The national average of state support for 1967–1968, as can be seen in Table 6, was about 40 percent, an increase of about 20 percent since 1940.

The state with its broader tax base is better able to meet the increasing costs of education than is the local community, whose major source of revenue has been the property tax. Nonetheless, as has been mentioned, the increase in state support has not yet been able to sufficiently reduce the existing wide differences of educational expenditures among school districts. Conservative legislatures, persuaded by influential lobbying groups, have not been willing to view education in an egalitarian sense in terms of money. With increased state aid wealthier districts are able to spend a great deal more money for their

TABLE 6 *Percent of Revenue for Public Elementary and Secondary Schools from State Governments, 1967–1968*

Hawaii	84.4%	Arkansas	46.2	Maine	33.3
Delaware	74.4	Pennsylvania	44.2	Ohio	31.6
North Carolina	66.6	Florida	43.7	Vermont	31.4
South Carolina	65.9	Indiana	42.0	Kansas	30.6
New Mexico	64.0	Minnesota	41.5	Montana	28.4
Alabama	62.3	Idaho	40.8	New Jersey	28.3
Washington	61.9	Alaska	40.4	Oregon	27.3
Georgia	61.6	**UNITED STATES**	**40.3**	Massachusetts	26.7
Louisiana	60.3	Maryland	39.8	North Dakota	26.4
New York	54.8	Virginia	38.8	Wisconsin	25.3
Utah	52.0	Nevada	38.3	Oklahoma	25.2
Tennessee	51.0	Arizona	37.5	Iowa	24.0
Kentucky	50.7	Wyoming	37.5	Colorado	23.5
Texas	50.3	Connecticut	35.1	Illinois	22.7
Mississippi	50.2	Missouri	34.2	South Dakota	13.7
West Virginia	49.7	California	34.0	New Hampshire	9.4
Michigan	49.6	Rhode Island	33.3	Nebraska	3.9

Source: National Education Association, *What Everyone Should Know About School Financing* (Washington, D.C.: NEA, 1968), p. 47.

schools while some poorer districts cannot maintain even minimal standards. State equalization formulas, which have the implied purpose of bridging the gap between rich and poor districts, for the most part are shams that are often devised as a result of lobbyist pressure of wealthier districts and pressure from established special-interest lobbying groups. The seriousness of the problem was brought out in the 1968 *Report of the National Advisory Commission on Civil Disorders*. The commission is commonly known as the Kerner Commission. It reported that:

> State contributions to city school systems have not had consistent
> equalizing effects. The Civil Rights Commission found that,
> although state aid to city schools has increased at a rate
> proportionately greater than for suburban schools, states
> continue to contribute more per pupil to suburban schools in
> seven of the twelve metropolitan areas studied.[11]

Citing Detroit as an example of the suburban–city differentiation, the commission reported that twenty-five suburban school districts surrounding the city spent up to $500 more per pupil per year for education.[12]

Such elitist practices are bad enough in wealthier states, but in the economically poorer states the problem is greatly magnified. Even if sound equalization programs were in effect, such states as Mississippi, South Carolina, Alabama, and others would still be financially unable to provide for schools at the level of the national average. The educational needs of children in Mississippi are no less than the needs of children in New York. The only practical means by which to narrow the gap of educational differences between rich and poor is through increased federal funding of education.

federal aid to education

The issue of federal aid to education has long been controversial but never so much as in the 1950s and 1960s. The increasing financial demands of widely expanded educational programs since World War II and the inability of many districts, as well as states, to meet these demands has brought about a greater need for utilizing the broad taxing powers of the federal government. Constitutionally, the federal government has the right, and the responsibility, to provide for the general welfare of the people. Today, perhaps more than ever before, there is little question that education, regardless of its shortcomings, is seen to serve the welfare of the people. In many instances the

---

[11] *Report of the National Advisory Commission on Civil Disorders* (New York: Bantam, 1968), p. 435.
[12] *Ibid.*, p. 434.

unwillingness or inability of states to assure even a minimal standard of education for all children can be overcome only by federal aid. In this sense it might be useful to note that while we use the term *aid* we do not consider it as a temporary ameliorative for educational problems, but as a necessary addition to the financing pattern of American education.

Even though federal aid to public education grew between 1960 and 1969 from about 3.5 percent to about 8 percent, the total federal expenditure for public elementary and secondary schools for 1969 was less than $2.5 billion, about one month's expenditures for the Vietnam war and about 3 percent of the yearly military budget. There is no question that in the United States in 1969–1970 the military establishment was given financial priority over the gravest domestic problems. That alone, though an important factor, did not account for (and does not account for) the failure to provide more federal aid to education. Again, it is not because of financial inability. There have been solid oppositional blocks to federal aid for education. Their power has been effectively applied, through lobbyist activities, either to block any significant legislation or, in some instances, to render it to their interests.

Historically, the most persistent and organized opposition to federal aid to education has come from conservative groups such as the National Association of Manufacturers and the United States Chamber of Commerce, both of which have highly organized and well-funded lobbying activities. Added to these are groups such as the Southern States Industrial Council, the Investment Bankers Association, the Daughters of the American Revolution, and the American Legion. In general terms their opposition is based on the argument that federal aid to education will certainly bring federal control and thus discourage local initiative. They also refute the idea that some states do not have the financial ability to afford adequate systems of education. If one analyzes the position of some of these groups on other federal expenditures, it is evident that their concern is more private than public. They are more than ready to accept, indeed lobby for, federal monies for research and other projects that would benefit them directly. Therefore, the case might well be made that the opposition to federal aid from such conservative groups is based on a privatist view of education. They are opposed to state increases in educational expenditures as well as to federal aid. Their fear about state or federal programs is that such programs might provide money for the poorer districts where it is most needed. Unfortunately, in the past too many members of Congress have felt a responsibility to these self-interest groups rather than to the welfare of the people.

To some extent the opposition to federal aid was overcome in 1965 with the passage of the Elementary and Secondary Education Act. However, even this act fell far short of the vital needs of education, especially in urban areas, as pointed out by the Kerner Commission:

Federal assistance, while focused on the innercity schools, has not been at a scale sufficient to remove the disparity. In the 1965–1966 school year, federal aid accounted for less than 8 percent of the total educational expenditure. Our survey of federal programs in Detroit, Newark and New Haven during the school year 1967–1968 found that a median of approximately half the eligible school population is receiving assistance under Title I of the Elementary and Secondary Education Act.[13]

Significant increases in federal aid are likely to meet with continued opposition from conservative forces regardless of the pronounced need.

Although the conservative economic groups have been the most persistent opponents of federal aid to education, they have not been alone. What might be termed as qualified opposition has also come from the South and the Catholic Church. The southern states, although desperately in need of aid, have generally opposed federal aid for fear that it might carry with it a greater enforcement of the Supreme Court's 1954 desegregation decision. Since the passage of the 1964 Civil Rights Act, any aid is dependent upon compliance. The Catholic Church has simply opposed any federal aid programs that did not include expenditures for their schools. Such inclusion in the Elementary and Secondary Education Act and the earlier National Defense Education Act removed their opposition, at least to these two specific acts.

Opposition to federal aid for education did not completely prevent federal programs for such aid. Long before the 1958 National Defense Education Act, programs of federal aid were established. Such programs were primarily aimed at levels other than the elementary and secondary schools. As can be seen in the following list of selected examples, the history of federal aid to education spans many years:

1. *The Ordinance of 1785.* Provided that a specified amount of land be reserved for the maintenance of public schools in each state being admitted to the Union.
2. *The Morrill Act of 1862.* Provided that each state receive, for each of its congressmen, 30,000 acres of land, the sale of which was to provide for the establishment and maintenance of agricultural and mechanical arts colleges. Supplemented by later legislation.
3. *The Hatch Act of 1887.* Provided for the promotion of agricultural science by appropriating $15,000 annually to each state and territory that had an agricultural college.
4. *The Smith-Lever Act of 1914.* Provided funds for the purpose of providing the farmer and the housewife with the results of agricultural and scientific research.

13 *Ibid.,* p. 436.

5. *The Smith-Hughes Act of 1917*. Provided federal monies for vocational education in the secondary schools.
6. *The Vocational Rehabilitation Act of 1920*. Provided funds for rehabilitating handicapped persons. Supplemented by later legislation.
7. *The Servicemen's Readjustment Act of 1944*. Provided direct aid to World War II veterans for furthering their education.
8. *The National Defense Education Act of 1958*. Provided funds to strengthen education in science, mathematics, and languages. (Discussed below).
9. *The Elementary and Secondary Education Act of 1965*. Provided funds for public schools, especially in poorer districts. (Discussed below).

Although important as historical precedents, the programs of federal aid to education before 1958 were relatively small and for narrowly defined purposes. Even the 1958 National Defense Education Act was an emergency measure, narrowly categorized. It did little to meet the real needs, especially of the poorer districts. The most significant legislation that was at least designed to begin to meet some of the needs of education in the poorer communities and states was the Elementary and Secondary Education Act of 1965. The passage of this act increased significantly the federal share of public school costs. It also provided some aid for nonpublic schools as did the National Defense Education Act. This act of 1958 was narrowly conceived to upgrade certain curricular areas. It was the education act of 1965 that was more broadly fashioned to meet the general needs of schools. Since both acts are significant items in a discussion about federal aid, we shall examine fully their major points.

national defense education act

The National Defense Education Act (NDEA) was signed into law in September 1958. Although the program was conceived to some extent before Sputnik, its passage was undoubtedly spurred by Russia's space shot. As the title suggests, the act was put forth to insure trained manpower for national defense. Although the act expresses the purpose of extending educational opportunity to all, it had little provision for upgrading education in poor districts. As it related to the public schools, its main concern, especially in the beginning, was for expanding programs in the sciences, mathematics, and foreign languages. After a great deal of voiced concern about its narrow curricular choices, the act was amended in 1963 to include some provision for the social and literary subjects. For the most part, the act was to provide relatively little for general public education, and even this more for the purpose of developing special abilities than for equalizing opportunity. The act displays no educational altruism, as perhaps can be seen by the various provisions of the act that were categorized into ten titles:

Title I. General provisions.

Title II. Loans to students in higher education.

Title III. Financial assistance for strengthening science, mathematics, and modern language instruction. In 1963 expanded to include history, civics, geography, English, and reading.

Title IV. National defense fellowships. Awarded in fields determined to be important to national defense.

Title V. Guidance, counseling, and testing. To identify and encourage able students at the high school level. Also included expenditures for operating counseling and guidance institutes of training at colleges and universities.

Title VI. Language development. To establish centers for research and studies in order to obtain more teachers of important but rarely taught languages.

Title VII. Research and experimentation in more effective utilization of television, radio, motion pictures, and related media for educational purposes.

Title VIII. Area vocational education programs. To prepare skilled technicians in certain vocations deemed necessary for national defense.

Title IX. Science information service. To provide scientists with centrally located and rapidly available information.

Title X. Improvement of statistical services of state educational agencies.

The NDEA authorized more than $1 billion to be spent over a four-year period. Since then various titles of the act have been refunded in lesser or greater amounts. Titles II and III have received the greatest amounts, with titles V and VI following.

Although the NDEA has increased the federal role in education, it was only partially and indirectly concerned with the general problems of education in impoverished areas. It was conceived and legislated in a conservative sense, following more the social and educational philosophy of an Admiral Hyman Rickover than a John Dewey. Its effect on the problems of urban schools was negligible (nor was it intended to be anything more).

elementary and secondary education act

Concern for urban problems in education by the federal government was not shown until passage, in 1965, of the Elementary and Secondary Education Act (ESEA)—the most significant piece of legislation in the area of federal aid to education. The act, signed into law in April

1965, was not only the largest commitment, $1.3 billion, made by the federal government, but also the first that provided some degree of general rather than strictly categorical aid to schools. It places relatively few limitations on the types of programs that local communities may devise. The proposed programs must meet with approval, but they are not narrowly restricted to predescribed programs. The major purpose of the act was to strengthen school programs for educationally deprived children in low-income areas, and for this purpose it allotted the greatest share of money. The act was categorized into five titles, the first of which really displays the major intent:

Title I. Financial assistance for special educational programs to local areas that have high concentrations of children from low-income families. Some provisions for private as well as public schools. ($1.06 billion)

Title II. Funds for school library resources, textbooks, and other instructional materials. Available to both public and private schools. ($100 million)

Title III. Funds for supplementary educational centers and services to meet needs defined by local areas. Also for local educational agencies to create innovative programs to meet local needs in elementary and secondary schools. ($100 million)

Title IV. Funds for educational research and training. ($22.5 million)

Title V. Funds to strengthen state departments of education. ($25 million)

the future of federal aid

The Elementary and Secondary Education Act represents the most comprehensive federal effort toward alleviating the vicious educational neglect that has attended poverty. To be sure, even that effort has far from adequately met the problem, but it has at least set a direction. Whether or not it is followed by expanded funding depends a great deal upon the nature of Congress and subsequent administrations. It also depends on the nature of the opposition.

To some extent, the opposition from parochial schools has been removed by their inclusion in recent legislation. This could, of course, change in the future. It is likely that at some point the provision made for parochial schools in federal legislation will be questioned as to its constitutional validity. Until 1968 a citizen could not challenge federal statutes simply because they were taxpayers. Then, however, the Supreme Court ruled that such suits could be brought against the federal government if on the Establishment or Free Exercise clauses of the First Amendment. If such a suit arises, it will then be up to the Supreme Court to decide.

The opposition to federal aid from conservative groups is likely to continue, and perhaps increase, in view of the growing needs for such aid. Although the arguments generally include questions about the need for federal aid or the financial ability of the federal government to provide for the needs, the most potent and most widely propagandized argument put forth by these groups is that of *federal control*. This is especially true from the ultraconservative groups, whose usual polemics paint federal control in ominous tones, implying that with federal aid will come a loss of freedom.

This is not to imply that the question of federal control is not worth discussion; obviously, it is. But the issue, as raised by the ultraconservatives, like all other issues they raise, is not discussed for purposes of clarification, but for frightened suasion. A case in point of the alarmist diatribe aimed against federal aid to education is a statement by Max Rafferty, Superintendent of Public Instruction of California (until 1970!):

> But the kind of federal aid most people think of when that
> term is used is the multi-billion-dollar kind which brings
> Uncle Sam into the local school picture with both feet,
> barging into such non-specific and generally fuzzy areas as
> salaries and construction. It's this particular Pandora's Box,
> redolent with threats of national control and an end to
> grassroots government, which the recent Federal Aid to
> Elementary and Secondary Education Bill has now opened.[14]

The interesting aspect of this is that America's Future, Inc. for whom Dr. Rafferty wrote the piece above and other things, is an ultraconservative organization whose primary function is that of attempting to establish some degree of control over American education through self-imposed censorship of textbooks.

The question of federal control is in need of discussion, not in simple terms of whether it is good or bad but in terms of its nature and scope. Some kind of control is necessary with public expenditures at any level. It does not seem unreasonable for the federal government to insist on certain regulatory practices or standards when financial aid is being offered, nor is it without accepted precedent. Federal housing, highway programs, as well as many others, insist on certain standards. Controls are imposed by the Pure Food and Drug Act, and the Securities and Exchange Commission is a regulatory agency. And lack of defined controls has produced many massive problems in the area of air and water pollution, for example. We do not mean that extensive federal control over education is desirable, nor has it been either attempted or achieved by federal aid programs. Carefully written into the opening statement of the National Defense Education Act is the intended limitation of federal control.

[14] Max Rafferty, *Our Schools Today: As They Are; As They Should Be* (New Rochelle, N.Y.: America's Future, Inc.), p. 3.

> Nothing contained in this Act shall be construed to
> authorize any department, agency, officer, or employee of the
> United States to exercise any direction, supervision, or
> control over the curriculum, program of instruction, admin-
> istration, or personnel of any educational institution or school
> system.

With such limitations explicitly set forth it obviously is possible to define the necessary limits of control that must accompany federal aid to education. And to some extent it might be argued that federal aid rather than restricting liberty might better assure a measure of it for those who are now robbed of it because of inadequate educational funding.

federal government in the educational structure

Although the federal government has no direct control over the various states' systems of education, nevertheless, it fits into the structure of education in the United States. In terms of direct control, for example, the national government is responsible for education in Washington, D.C., in the territories, and on federal reservations. And, as has been noted, its involvement with the financing of education has increased significantly. It is in this dimension that the United States Office of Education (USOE) functions most directly. Essentially, the USOE, directed by the commissioner of education, has responsibilities in the following areas:

1. To collect information on education in the states and other countries.
2. To provide services to local, state, national and international agencies of education, such as compiling national statistics and conducting surveys.
3. To provide consultation to local or state systems on problems of financing, administration, reorganization, curriculum, and so forth.
4. To recommend and encourage minimal educational standards and programs for the states.
5. To administer federal grants to local, state, and national programs.

The USOE grew out of department status that it had originally been given with its creation in 1867. Due to opposition from some states the Department of Education became the Bureau of Education in 1870 under the Interior Department. In 1929 it was retitled the Office of Education, and in 1939 it was transferred to the Federal Security Agency. Since 1953 it has been under the Department of Health, Education, and Welfare. The head of the USOE, like the cabinet members, is appointed by the President with Senate consent. The office was dignified by its first commissioner, Henry Barnard, whose annual reports remain as important historical documents on American education.

The functions of the USOE have grown immensely since its beginning, but its greatest increase in power has come about in the 1960s with the increased federal funding of education. In 1965 it was reorganized into five main bureaus: Higher Education, Adult and Vocational Education, Elementary and Secondary Education, Education for the Handicapped, and Research, all of these with a number of lower divisions. With the apparent projected involvement of the federal government in educational funding, the USOE will undoubtedly broaden the scope of both its responsibility and influence. The question, of course, is whether or not it can avoid becoming as much of a politically manipulative agency as have other federal agencies. The means by which it handles its growing programs will indicate the value of its influence on American education.

topics for inquiry

1. Education in Presidential Platforms
2. Proposed Ideas For Family Allotments for Education
3. The Radical Right and the Public Schools
4. Extent and Administration of Federal Programs in Your District
5. School Tax Structure in Your District
6. State Equalization Formulas in Your State
7. Sociopolitical Backgrounds of Your Local or State School Boards
8. Range of Expenditures Among Suburban and Urban Districts in Your Area
9. Minimal Standards of Your State
10. School Law as it Affects the Teacher

subjects for discussion

1. The issue of federal control is sure to be a continuing argument against federal funding of education.
   a. Is it a real threat? How?
   b. Would federal control be more restrictive than state control?
   c. Would a nationally enforced code of standards be good or bad for education in the United States?
   d. Does federal aid imply federal control?

2. Recent federal aid to education programs have included some monies for parochial as well as public schools.
   a. Does this aid or hinder the public schools?
   b. Should federal monies be given to states not complying with the Supreme Court's desegregation order?
   c. Should federal aid be given to parochial schools for religious instruction? If not, how would such aid be controlled?
3. Some observers take the position that the public schools have continually failed to serve the needs of lower-class children. They maintain that current educational problems stem not from the fact that the schools have changed, but precisely because they have not.
   a. What evidence seems to support or refute the charge in today's schools?
   b. If the charge can be supported, is the failure due to accidental or purposeful direction of the schools?
   c. Does the charge suggest the possibility of a continuing elitist attitude in the country?

selected readings

BUTTS, R. FREEMAN, and LAWRENCE A. CREMIN. *A History of Education in American Culture.* New York: Holt, Rinehart and Winston, 1953.
   A detailed and scholarly treatment of the development of American education. The authors bring into play much of the social and political history that has had a significant effect on educational development.

SCHLESINGER, ARTHUR M., JR. *The Age of Jackson.* Boston: Little, Brown, 1945.
   A broad scholarly view of the period that gave impetus to the common school movement.

TYLER, ALICE FELT. *Freedom's Ferment.* New York: Harper & Row, 1962.
   An exciting reading adventure into the various social forces and reform movements from the colonial period to the Civil War.

   Any one of the three books listed below offers a comprehensive set of documents that makes interesting and illuminating reading. The editors, all of them educational historians, offer perceptive commentaries and arrangement of topics that give meaning to their selections.

CALHOUN, DANIEL (ed.). *The Educating of Americans: A Documentary History.* Boston: Houghton Mifflin, 1969.

RIPPA, ALEXANDER S. (ed.). *Educational Ideas in America: A Documentary History.* New York: McKay, 1969.

TYACK, DAVID B. (ed.). *Turning Points in American Educational History.* Waltham, Mass.: Blaisdell, 1967.

5

THE NEW POLITICAL SCIENCE OF AMERICAN EDUCATION

the power structure

Power is the capacity to affect decisions in a way favorable to its possessor's disposition and interests. In brief, power is the capacity to get done what you want done. Absolute power, which does not exist in the real world (although some have caused a lot of trouble trying to acquire it), would be the capacity to get anything you wanted done when and where you wanted it. Power in the American community is *limited power*. These limits are constitutional, legal, political, and social.

Individuals in a free democratic society exert at one level an equal power, that is, the power in the ballot—one man, one vote. In the real community in many important areas of decision making power is nowhere nearly so equally distributed. A relatively few individuals possess a very large capacity to influence decisions. In the main, most others merely respond to their decisions. Certain factors tend to endow their possessors with extra power to affect community decisions, such as:

1. Possession of large properties, especially properties with extensive employment rolls.
2. Control of finance, especially through banking and credit institutions.
3. Family connections, an established position in the decision making community.
4. Access to the media, especially through the ownership or control of a newspaper or radio or television station.
5. Personal prestige, an earned or otherwise attained reputation for unusual capacity to get

things done, or for dedication and energy, or perhaps even for knowledge and sagacity.

A network of acquaintance, of cooperation, and of general agreement usually exists among the majority of those who share in these factors. This network constitutes a formidable organization (though the organization may be quite informal) for getting a good part of what it wants done, done and for preventing decisions that it deems unwise or detrimental to its interests. This network with its capacity to affect decision making far beyond its numerical strength is called the *power structure*. In a small rural community, for example, it might include the village banker, the owner of the grain elevator, a handful of wealthy farmers, the publisher of a weekly paper, and a "distinguished" citizen or two.

The local school board in such a community may or may not have on its roster any of the foregoing members of the community's power structure. It probably will be elected democratically in elections where, except in unusual circumstances, a minority of the qualified electorate participate. In our typical community then the five-man board might be made up of (1) the cashier of the local bank, (2) the assistant manager of the grain elevator, (3) a local merchant who had established his business on a loan from the bank, (4) the wife of the newspaper publisher, and (5) a college graduate, former school-teacher, who married a farmer whose mortgage is held by the local bank.

Is the power structure of the community represented on the school board, or is it not? The question is not necessarily to be taken in a negative sense. The voters, those who cared enough to vote, may have elected five persons whom they believed to have the ability to make policy decisions that would give the community a good school for its children. The power structure of the community may, indeed, agree with that generally stated goal. As long as the board does not hand down decisions that run counter to the tacit position of the local power structure, the school board will have its support, even if the structure is not in complete agreement with the board's decision. In other words, the school board "rules" for minor decisions.

On major decisions, however, how often do you think the school board will fail to consult the power structure? The consultation need not be direct, the school board knows what the power structure wants. In this case it wants a school. It likes something to be proud of—winning teams, a scholarship or two; it wants stability, a sense that things are running smoothly; it wants efficiency and economy; it wants its school to be accredited so that its students can count on entering college without undue hazard. The board is also keenly aware of what the power structure does not want. It does not want drastic change; it does not want to be challenged; it does not want radical new notions of curriculum or method, unless there is a good chance of federal money or favorable publicity; above all, it does not want higher taxes.

If the school board has to seek a tax increase or a bond issue for necessary plant or for meeting the increased costs of education, the consultation with the power structure will be real and personal. In cases where taxes—monies—are concerned the power structure will demand to be directly involved in decision making. And its wisdom will conventionally be asserted in just these terms: not one penny more than you can avoid.

If the power structure were put on the defensive, if its members sat together on the platform of the local school (which does not happen) to justify its decisive role in what the community does or does not do, it would state its case thusly:

"We are your friends and neighbors. We furnish the capital that your businesses run on, that built your houses. We raise the fundamental commodities, the crops, from which the real wealth of our community comes. We handle and market these crops. We pay a large share of the taxes. We want good schools, just as you do. We think we have good schools, and we do not think fads and frills and a lot of crazy notions are going to make them any better."

In a large and complex metropolis the power structure is just as real, but the complexity and dimensions of interests served will be much greater. But the process by which the structure makes its wants known and the justification for its position remain the same.

The process—that is, the method of consultation—through which the power structure gets what it wants done (and not much more gets done) is the *system*. Another term often used in conjunction with the system is the *establishment*. The term is often used loosely and variously. Education is said to have an establishment. Communities are said to have an establishment. Both friendly and hostile critics refer to a national, an American establishment. Just what is the establishment? Within any defined area of complex decision making, the establishment is the power structure and its designated agents and spokesmen who use the system to get what it wants and to prevent what it does not want.

(This is not an attack on system, as such, or an attack on The System, in the worn popular vocabulary. It is a specific analysis of *a* system, a relatively undemocratic and bureaucratic one, which has mushroomed along with the seam splitting growth of the cities and has developed beyond the reach of the historical system of control of popular education.)

the case for community control

A key demand in the cities, and of the black community in particular, is community control of schools. Let us look at the pros and cons of this issue. Community control would mean the development of a new political science for urban education. Perhaps more appropriately stated, it would mean the application of classical American educational political science to the control of the schools.

Local control and local support of education have been time-honored principles in the American educational scene. Although American society has developed in complexity and populations have increased, local control of education as a basic feature has remained considerably intact. Statewide controls aimed at assuring sound minimum standards of instruction, materials, building codes, and teacher certification have been enacted and enforced, as we have already noted. The states also have enacted varied forms of equalization systems. In effect, the states intruded upon the principle of local support by using the tax power to restore some measure of equality of educational opportunity among the richer and poorer districts. The principle of local control was not greatly intruded upon, except for the maintenance of minimum standards. In fact, equalization through a measure of statewide tax support was indeed a means for assuring the success and continuation of local control. Local boards of education could then exercise their classic functions: determining local school policies, planning building programs, hiring and firing administrators and teachers, devising curricula and choosing textbooks (within varying limitations from state to state).

In the rapidly growing cities, local control came to be quite a different matter from the function of the principle in towns and rural areas. Local control as practiced in a rural area when applied to a city bred centralization. In texts on education and in education courses alike, the case for local control had often been bulwarked by negative evidence of the effects of *centralization* on education. The ministries of education of European nations operating highly centralized systems were often cited to illustrate the disadvantages—the remoteness of the wielders of educational power from the popular will; the unresponsiveness of school authorities to parental concerns, important or trivial; the deadly uniformity of curriculum and textbooks without adaptation to regional, ethnic, cultural, or social differences; the growth of bureaucracies of self-serving functionaries; the regimentation of the teaching force; the lack of accountability of education to any one other than to the political rulers. These characteristics of *centralization* were consistently (and quite correctly) pointed out to be debilitating to educational enterprise, and quite fortunately largely lacking in the American system due largely to the prevalence of local control.

In fact, in the American culture a common feature and a distinctive one has been a widespread and general feeling of *closeness to the schools*. This feeling has been a live aspect of the common culture whether 10 or 80 percent of the electorate voted in the school election, the size of the vote depending on the issues. The citizenry, especially the parents, have been nurtured in the conviction that the schools were theirs, not merely in theory but in practice and actuality.

A whole culture of participation in the life of the school has developed, seemingly as a direct product of local control. Parent-Teacher Associations, Citizen's Councils on Education, and parents' committees abound bringing communication and advices upon education of varying worth and practicality to bear, but always making their presence felt. Activities of the school, especially athletics, often make the school a center of community interest, an important element of general civic élan and morale. These elements of the American school culture are so common that they scarcely need remarking. They are, however, remarkable on two scores: they exist nowhere else to any such degree; they have very considerably ceased to exist in the great cities of the nation.

While educators were teaching the phenomena of centralization as debilitating factors remote from these shores, the American cities were growing to metropolitan dimensions. Unnoticed, the characteristics usually ascribed to European ministries of education crept into the operation of urban schools: bureaucratization, senseless uniformities and conformities, remoteness and inaccessibility, reduction of teacher forces to a civil service mentality, unaccountability. It took a dramatic crisis to bring the condition to light. Events have not yet been critical enough to bring effective change.

There is, for example, New York City [1] whose Board of Education at 110 Livingston Street controls the education of a populace larger than that of Ireland, Israel, and Denmark combined. Its budget for elementary education exceeds that of England, or for secondary education, of France; its total expenditure for education exceeds that of Italy or Switzerland or Holland or Belgium. Nor does New York stand alone. Twenty cities in this nation have boards of education (often unelected) which administer school systems with larger budgets, greater enrollments, and larger teaching forces than many nations of the earth. This is *centralization*, and where it exists, the typical characteristics are sure to appear.

Today it is mainly urban education that is in critical trouble, and when the critics give their analysis of the urban problem, it falls into the pattern of the classical analysis of centralized control.

Since centralization is recognized as a main factor of the urban school problem, the logical question is why does the system not change. Change can take place if enough people agree on the desirability of change and on what change is desirable and if they invest enough time, energy, and money to bring it about. In smaller cities, in towns, and in rural areas this can happen—not easily, but not against impossible odds either. The system is accessible to their

---

[1] In 1970 New York City began to decentralize its board of education. It established 33 local school districts whose boards are locally elected. However, all funds are distributed through the central board and there is still one city-wide contract with teachers and it is negotiated by the central board.

wishes if these are held onto and effectively acted upon; the system is within their control. But such is not the case in a city as large as New York or in one as small as Pittsburgh. The system is not accessible; the school board members are not elected.[2] Issues may only be brought to large public attention in ways that are not a part of the system. School officials may give credence to organized protest or ignore it, according to their own appraisal of its strength or merit. They may be wise or unwise in appraising the popular will. That indeed, is just the point: it puts the whole burden on their wisdom, not that of the public. The public, where local control is the viable process, is not listened to by choice. The public is in control. Its measured voice, counted soberly at the ballot box, is the ultimate accountability. The fundamental decisions are made publicly—in simple terms, democratically.

Centralized systems on the defensive often misstate this process as "public dictation of school policy." This is a mislabeling of democratic decision making. Dictating is only done by entrenched minorities in a position to ignore the majority will. There is no point in arguing who can estimate best or more responsibly appraise the majority will. The only thing to do is to count it—that means elections.

Centralized systems on the defensive often make the claim that they have the capacity for change. They have expertise; they have research; they have the good interests of the child and the public at heart. These are the familiar appeals of all governing elites. Even when they are well intentioned, they are naïve with respect to the fundamental and unchanging attributes of centralized power, of bureaucracies. The remoteness gap is not to be closed by "beefing up" the public relations department; school authorities' responsiveness is not measurable in units of personal "contacts"; the organizational thrust for orderliness cannot discipline itself to the necessities of diversity; closed systems of bureaucracies always reward and promote the self-serving; teachers must lose their initiative and creativity in such a system; accountability is a farce when it means substantially accountability only to yourself. Changes of administration within such a system always mean mere "palace revolutions" with new personnel wielding the same power, doing similar things under new labels, substantially ignoring or being in ignorance of the public will.

There should be no apprehension that the desire to exert control over the schools would create an atmosphere hostile to the schools. To the contrary, where the community does control its schools (which is in the overwhelming majority of the nation's school districts), the atmosphere of school-community relations tends to be positive and friendly. A power structure exists everywhere and some of its influences are exerted behind closed doors. But issues do come out in the open, and then a defined system of public debate and public resolution

[2] Local school boards are now elected in New York. In 1970, the central board is not, but will be as soon as a constitutional question as to the proper method can be decided.

is available. Angry confrontations, public name-calling, disrupted meetings, attempts to prove weight of support by volume of noise, a plethora of self-certified spokesmen—these are aspects of process when citizens are disenfranchised in decision making, when public institutions are unaccountable to electorates.

The climate around the typical locally controlled school is not devoid of problems, but it is a climate in which problem-solving can take place. In fact, where community control exists, the words *control* and *power* are not much exercised. Where the people know the reality of *closeness to their schools*, influences and opinions may be brought to numerous more or less responsive ears, a network of formal and informal and generally friendly communication exists. The decision-making process tends to be open, understood, and in consequence is reasonably calm and orderly.

The drive in the cities for community control has been centered in the black community. Harlem and newsworthy Ocean Hill-Brownsville in New York, the Hill district and Homewood-Brushton district in Pittsburgh, the Chicago South Side—all designations of ghetto black neighborhoods—are cases in point. The abundant reasons for the disaffection of such areas with centralized school administration have been made clear.

This drive encounters not only the generalized opposition of the status quo, the intrinsic indisposition of large organizations to change, but specific areas of well-defined opposition.

In Pittsburgh, for example, the Board of Education has been more than a little unresponsive to public appeal. An appointed board, which historically has chosen to send most of its own children to private schools, makes the policy decisions for the city. It is a school system with a woefully inadequate physical plant, a salary schedule inferior to most of its surrounding suburbs, and a comparatively unexamined curriculum. The board in 1967 brought the school system to a halt by refusing to enter into collective negotiations with its teachers—result, a teachers' strike.

The public schools of Pittsburgh have the stubborn loyalty of many who choose to send their children to them, but this loyalty is joined with enthusiasm in very few. In the black community rampant criticism and widespread hostility approach the norm. A few years ago the Pittsburgh Board of Education announced its intention to build a few enormous secondary schools, designated as Great High Schools.

The intentions behind the program were good. The will to start somewhere in reconstructing the antiquated physical plant must be credited. The effort to qualify for what then appeared to be imminently available large federal monies seemed timely. The stated aim of creating high school districts large enough to draw from cross-sectional populations in social class, ethnic, and racial terms was apparently high-minded, though somewhat out of touch with reality.

The announced decision, however, far from unifying public support for a bold new venture, brought into the open many unconsidered factors, many grounds for objection that had apparently not been considered or had been cavalierly dismissed. The Great High School plan (now abandoned) did elicit some support, but it also raised a great deal of skepticism and much open hostility among black constituencies. It divided the public at a time when policies to create harmony were sorely needed.

Pittsburgh is used not as a sorry example but as a meaningful instance of the rigors of the urban educational dilemma and the consequences of a process for educational decision-making that is not rooted in democracy.

The issue, again, is not the matter of the wisdom or unwisdom of the Great High School, but the ineffectiveness of nonparticipatory decision-making, which is inherent in a centralized school system of such magnitude.

The defense of centralization is sometimes made in terms of an abstraction—the efficiency of large organizational aggregates. This is an admissable appeal in the case of a large successful business. By its success it is vindicated, but a bankrupted enterprise can not justify its management in terms of devotion to an abstraction.

Centralization is the consistent characteristic of the American school systems that fail to educate many of their students, and do poorly with most of the rest. As we have noted, it is the large cities that have highly centralized educational systems. And it is in these urban centers that schooling is on the verge of educational bankruptcy.

Decentralization, community control, or local management of schools do not necessitate the establishment of districts so small as to be weak, ineffective, or inefficient. If New York City were divided into 200 community controlled districts (and so many would not be necessary to achieve effective decentralization), it would still provide constituencies of 50,000 per school district. Too few? Most of the best school systems in the nation are operated in districts this size or smaller.

An effective decentralization plan was proposed for our main example—Pittsburgh—in an urban education class at the University of Pittsburgh. It is so good, so workable a program, that with suitable modifications for local situations, it could be profitably adopted as a model across the country. Under the plan Pittsburgh's schools would be divided into several community-controlled areas. Seven to ten of these would create relatively meaningful community constituencies for the schools. No district would have a population of fewer than 60,000, which is a figure larger than that of any of the good to excellent suburban systems surrounding the Steel City.

The Pittsburgh Board of Education, reconstituted and limited in functions, would persist. Each district would, however, possess large areas of autonomy in clearly defined functions. The district boards would be elected within the districts. The central board would include representatives from each district board, members elected at large, and proportional representation of teachers' organizations enrolling 500 or more members. School elections would be on a nonpartisan ballot and conducted at a different time than other elections.

The responsibilities of the central board would be primarily to:

1. To collect funds and to allocate budget. Budget allocation would be based on per pupil basis, plus sophisticated formulas carefully derived to correct long-standing educational inequities and give attention to pressing problems of educational needs. (The precedents for such *equalization* are abundant).
2. Conduct research and collect statistics—the highest priority going to studies of the foregoing matters.
3. Develop building programs, largely contingent upon considerations in points 1 and 2.
4. Establish salary scales, in accordance with points 1 and 2.
5. Recruit and qualify teachers and establish a personnel resource to be utilized by the districts in hiring teachers.
6. Seek special grants and federal funds; to conduct in-service educational programs.
7. Interpret the schools to the community at large, lobby, and publicize educational needs and accomplishments.
8. Operate a city-wide program of audiovisual and educational communications resources.
9. Effect liaison and communication among the districts of the city system.
10. Keep accounts and audit district finances.

The central board would, therefore, perform a number of useful, dignified, professional functions. But it *would not* (1) impose policy regulations upon the administration of district schools, (2) impose curriculum or conduct a curriculum division, (3) conduct city-wide testing programs, (4) supervise instruction, nor (5) hire or assign teachers.

The district boards, therefore, would actually operate their schools. Their functions would be to:

1. Provide for the administration of their schools.
2. Plan and develop curricula.
3. Hire and assign teachers.
4. Provide for instructional supervision.
5. Allocate budgets.
6. Conduct testing programs.
7. Study educational needs and keep these clearly in the foreground of the central board's attention.
8. Develop pupil personnel services and special programs according to school and community needs.

9. Develop continuing programs to enhance school-community *close-ness*.

Such a program, modified to meet varied needs, could be the beginning of a true educational renaissance for the American city.

a new conceptual model for the school

This re-conceptualization is intended to serve as an instrument to restore perspective as to the real purpose of the schools. It should clarify the priorities and value system within the institution.

A restatement of the meaning of the school would assert as central to every consideration of the school its fundamental obligation to be educational—to be consistently and effectively an institution that nurtures learning and fosters youth development. These purposes may be stated variously, but they are never quarreled with or denied. Despite the verbal consensus as to the purposes of the schools, they *do not* state the actual governing principles of the school as it appears to function in contemporary America.

The central purpose of the school has quite generally become obscured or lost in a confusion of educationally irrelevant considerations. Among these irrelevancies are the following:

The idea that the school's purposes may be accomplished on the basis of institutional efficiency is a major offender. In other words, if the school is well kept, is a smoothly functioning organism, then it may be assumed that education is taking place. This is a vacuous and typical institutionalist's assumption. Those who think efficiency makes for education demand that schedules of buses, and lunches, and classes are well made out and punctiliously adhered to; that teachers and students are properly in such places they are scheduled to be—or elsewhere only with proper excuses and credentials in hand; that supervisors are diligently out and about upon their appointed rounds; that guidance officers are busy giving tests and compiling folders and files; and that researchers are keeping the computers humming. All these frequently have little bearing upon learning, and all may be taking place in an institution where little learning is going on. They are not what school is all about, though the general delusion holds it to be so.

Get this, these things are not bad happenings; they just do not define a school. A school's meaning does not lie in the province of institutional functioning.

Another matter irrelevant to the purpose of the school, and related to the foregoing, is *the idea of the school as an instrument for administrative satisfaction.* The school is not an arena for the exercise of power. This sounds obvious. What then has happened to make it worth saying? As schools have developed from small simple institutions to large complex systems, their central purpose has been lost in practices that have no bearing on education. Power, the capacity to make or withhold decision, has been assigned in large bundles to persons trained in running institutions. The administrator, who has useful supportive functions in a school well conceived, becomes a primary perpetrator of irrelevancy when he mistakenly comes to view the school as an instrument for exercising administrative talent. Such an individual sees the school as primarily a place to enjoy power and among his greatest satisfactions is exercising this power with finesse and artistry. The most skilful wielders of power do not always have pictures of Napoleon on their office walls (they may even have John Dewey's portrait there). They like to be seen as "good guys," or firm but fair captains of taut ships, great organizers, and especially as statesmen and men of educational vision. These latter qualities, however, are not necessarily demonstrated by the ability they have: to get along smoothly with school boards; to keep the complex administrative staff happy and functioning as a team; to preserve control over the faculty while maintaining the image of a friendly father-figure; to make a cheery speech to a luncheon club and maintain good public relations for the schools. These are the attributes of men who hold and enjoy power, and know how to perpetuate it.

Leadership and statesmanship and vision are another matter: leaders take risks, get shot at; statesmen know reverses, sometimes gain obloquy rather than compromise a cause; men of vision have known martyrdom.

Many administrative attributes are valuable to a school governed to an educative purpose. However, the meaning of the school is not to be found in the skilful manipulation of power.

Also irrelevant to the purpose of the school is the welfare of the teacher. Do not die of shock as this is being said. We do not say that the teacher's welfare is irrelevant to the teacher, or to the community, or to society. But the schools do not exist to provide employment at public expense for a good share of the annual harvest of college graduates. The schools, and teachers like others tend to forget this, do not exist for the teachers.

The teacher's relevancy to education lies in his professionalism: his continuing study of students and problems of learning, his developed ability to devise and conduct learning experiences.

Relax a little and understand: We are not making a case for starving or exploiting teachers. The teacher's quest for better wages and working conditions is legitimate. It is proper that teachers be well and fairly paid as the crucial professionals in the school. However, a faculty may be well paid and educationally inept. The purpose and meaning of the school is not to be defined in terms of teacher "welfare."

Beyond, though including teacher welfare, lies an overriding irrelevancy: *the idea of the school as a dynamic bureaucracy, a place where adults fulfill themselves in upward-bound careers.* That adults find satisfaction in their jobs in schools is not undesirable, but it is only about one-twentieth relevant to the school's meaning (1:20 being a generous statement of the ratio of adults to children in the school). For many in the school system getting ahead becomes the all-consuming goal. Every action and every thought are planned with "promotion" as the goal. True teaching and the students become secondary considerations.

There is a hierarchical structure of the school through which the aspiring individual must go. It does invite the misconception that schools are professionally to be thought of as places where educated adults aspire to get ahead. Teachers aspire to improved status and better pensions at the very least; the more ambitious strive to become department heads or supervisors. Then they plan and conspire to qualify as assistant principals, assistant principals to be principals, and principals by varied routes through the chairs of administrative staff positions to the office of superintendent.

To want to get ahead is thoroughly approvable, but the purpose of the school is not to be defined as an arena where adults fulfill their career needs.

Thus far, the tone of the discussion might be called negative. However, the authors have been describing the "Common Conventional Model" of the schools in the United States today. The model—and the concepts behind it—has generated most of the practices, none of them bad in themselves, that have led to one very damaging outcome: *the loss of central attention to what the school is all about.* Though some teaching and learning undeniably goes on, most of the adult time and energy and personal involvement is directed to one or more of these four fundamentally irrelevant notions about the school, stated in review:

1. That institutional efficiency defines the purpose of a school.
2. That administrative gratification spells the purpose of a school.
3. That schools exist primarily to serve the teacher's welfare.
4. That schools exist mainly as dynamic bureaucracies in which adults seek personal satisfaction and career development.

This is how the authors state it, and that is very much how it is. It is, in sum, a gross conceptual error. We hope a new generation of educators will see the purpose of the school more clearly and govern themselves to that purpose. The reconceptualized school may be a well-running institution, where administrators are happy and fulfilled in ways satisfying to the mature, where teachers are paid and used as professionals, but where bureaucratic vying, conniving, and striving is minimized to insignificance—and where the purpose of all activity is directed to the goal of the school.

What is that goal? To educate the children. There is really no other reason to keep a school than this. It is a purpose simple to state. To educate, of course, is not so simple. But to study the meaning of *to educate* and to try to accomplish that meaning should be the governing principle upon all that takes place in the school. To take education seriously will indeed make a big difference in the school.

Education brings the *students* to the *center* of the scene. In recognizing this basic premise of true education once again, all activity in the school and the system will be directed to the students (see Figure 4). The center is not where the students are in the typical school today. The student is the low man on the totem pole. The student is perceived variously, but commonly as an object to be worked upon, molded, manipulated, processed. The student is raw material, product, "the kids," future employee, future college student, future this or that. The student is sometimes appreciated, even praised, as he fulfills promptly and with docility the adult expectations that are laid out for him.

But the pervasive attitude of the school toward the student is one of uneasiness, of dread. The student, even well-shorn and neatly dressed, is known to be untrustworthy. He talks; he reports on the school outside. He is at best an incipient troublemaker: Mr. Duffy's favorite is ever Miss Grimby's demon. He shows unconstructive attitudes, forgets to veil his boredom, shows signs of sulkiness, looks like he would wish to make a critical comment. Students can "get out of hand," spread false rumors, give the school a bad name—even lead a student protest and demonstrations.

The lowly student is a large inspiration of institutional paranoia. His presence in such great numbers, far larger than the adult population of the school, is frightening, and for cause. The student is not

FIGURE 4 *A Reconceptualization*

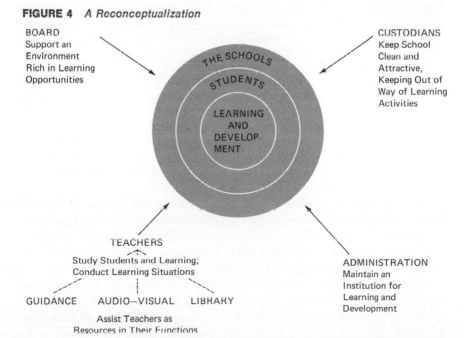

BOARD
Support an
Environment
Rich in Learning
Opportunities

THE SCHOOLS

STUDENTS

LEARNING
AND
DEVELOP-
MENT

CUSTODIANS
Keep School
Clean and
Attractive,
Keeping Out of
Way of Learning
Activities

TEACHERS
Study Students and Learning;
Conduct Learning Situations

GUIDANCE   AUDIO–VISUAL   LIBRARY

Assist Teachers as
Resources in Their Functions

ADMINISTRATION
Maintain an
Institution for
Learning and
Development

partner to a single one of the irrelevant purposes by which most of the adults are governed. He cares little for schedules and even less how administrators "get their kicks." What teachers are paid, or who gets promoted to the downtown office is not his concern. The student knows only one good reason for being in school—*to get an education*. When that reason ceases to engage him, when he discovers that the school takes him none too seriously in this regard, he will find diversions. One thing he cannot do is involve himself in the adult games that dominate the school. Potentially, every student constitutes a hazard to adult ambition in the school because he has no possible stake in it.

Put the student in the center of things and all this begins to change.

new power forces in education

Three new power forces have entered the educational decision-making scene since the 1950s. These are teacher power, student power, and black power. In this section we shall consider them in terms of the development of a new political science for education.

teacher power

Traditionally, the only power the teacher has exerted has been power over children. In the traditional hierarchical school this power could be almost an absolute within the classroom. Its instruments were familiar: the capacity to punish, to grade, to pass or fail. The student had little opportunity to appeal if the power were exercised unjustly. He stood at the bottom of the power structure. In case of an issue between a student and a teacher, two conventions of behavior commonly were exercised. The teachers "stuck together," and the administrator "backed up the teacher." This was simply the way the system worked.

Since the teacher had little or no power in any other direction, strong psychological persuasions tempted her to fulfill her ego needs at the expense of the children. Elsewhere in the school, the teacher was much more accustomed to taking orders, to following regulations, and to complying with other peoples' directives rather than to shaping decisions or participating in making them.

Teachers were very considerably coerced by the communities that employed them. They were held by convention, if not by regulation, to conformity in matters of dress style, coiffure and make-up, and general comportment. Contracts even stipulated regulations as to dating, number of weekends to be spent in the community, and bans on smoking and drinking. Community expectations were often enforced by strong pressures in matters of teaching Sunday school classes and sponsoring community activities and as to public places not to be frequented.

In school the teachers conformed to schedules as rigidly enforced as those for the students. Even in areas of professional competence, the teachers' choices were curtailed. What to teach and when and how to teach it were matters of prescribed syllabuses, and the force of supervision was mainly employed to assure that these things were done "by the book."

The administration made the decisions, with or without the "advice" of teachers' committees. The matter of salary was largely a matter of school board decision. Theoretically, the school administrator represented the faculty in presenting its case for improved remuneration. In this role, the administrator was, to say the least, in a position of conflicting interest. His obligation to the community was to run the schools as efficiently and economically as possible. The school board was his employer; it held the power to hire and fire him. In cases of disagreement between teachers and employers, the administrator was faced with a pressing reality: the board held power over him; the teachers simply did not. This condition did not tend to make the administrator the most militant of bargainers on behalf of teachers.

All in all, teachers prior to the 1960s were a timid profession. The major organization of teachers, the National Education Asssociation, was administrator-dominated and held deep biases against trade-union tactics, such as collective bargaining with the implied coercion of the strike. As a matter of fact, teachers themselves were biased against these devices. Teachers with rural antecedents held organizations like unions suspect; urban teachers seeing teaching as a ladder to middle-class respectability also held a similar bias. The idea of teacher solidarity was not a governing principle, except, as we have seen, when the issue was a matter of students against teachers.

Thus, teachers were essentially powerless. They heard many good words spoken publicly in their behalf, but they remained disgracefully underpaid, generally patronized, and ego-starved. If a teacher ventured in class too far into the arena of controversial issues, if she wore a dress too short, or if he betook himself for coffee to a neighborhood cafe on his "free period," that teacher might once be warned; if he persisted, be dismissed "for cause." If a teacher looked about for support in such a case, the sympathy was likely to be in short supply, expressed if at all most personally and privately. "If you don't like the way we do things here, you can always move on" was the common attitude, even of the teaching force itself.

But the teaching force has changed its stance. Higher educational standards have brought more vigorous minds into the profession. An increase of men determined to make teaching a life work— and to push for rewards which render it possible—has had an effect. The rising cost of living in a society educated to its own affluence and habituated to consumership and a high standard of living lit fires under teachers' economic aspirations. And the success of militancy, first espoused by the small American Federation of Teachers, taught its own lessons of the fruits of vigorous organization.

Teacher power has emerged as a growing reality on the educational scene. Its first effects have been twofold: (1) a public demonstration of the capacity of teachers to make their presence felt and (2) a dramatic upward rescaling of salaries and working conditions of the teaching force. The future course of the exercise of teacher power is uncertain. It is safe to predict, however, that the voice of the teacher in educational decision making will be heard increasingly.

The first goals of teacher power have usually been the classic ones: better wages and working conditions. But basic to the teachers' demands has been a desire to be recognized on a basis of parity with other governing forces in the school, especially with the administration. Teacher organizations are increasingly concerned with active involvement in educational decision-making processes. Their concerns are expressed not merely in terms of more adequate salary schedules, but in terms of curriculum change, support for instructional conditions to make good learning possible, and new methodologies. Teacher power in whatever form of organization gives itself added dimensions of public and professional respect when it zeroes in on one primary objective: better schools. In one critical arena of decision—what shall become of the instructional dollar—teacher power may well be mobilized to prevent further dehumanization of the schools; when the issue becomes clear, teacher power may insist that instructional budgets be mobilized to support better teaching in smaller classes and that expensive gadgetries and depersonalizing hardwares not cannibalize the budget to the advantage of suppliers and the neglect of the child.

student power

The student in both school and college has had even less voice in education than his teachers. He has been in the hierarchy of the school "the low man on the totem pole," which position has been a matter of rather common agreement. After all, the school exists to give him an education; his job, therefore, in school is to get an education. His presence in the school, in fact, the necessity for his being educated, derives from certain facts about him: he is young; he is immature; he is ignorant.

Although these realities are true to a degree, the position of the student in the school is not therewith beyond appeal or beyond complaint. In addition to being young, immature, and relatively unlearned, he is also fully human. He not only goes to school, he lives a good part of his life there. Like his parents, his teachers, and school officials, he walks on the ground and breathes the air. Like them, he is getting older every day. He does vary greatly in the degree of his maturity, but this is not necessarily because of chronology. He does know some things better than others.

Among the things he knows is when a shoe pinches. He knows when he is being treated unfairly. He recognizes it when he is subjected to indignities. Not less than adults he has ego needs. If he is subjected to injustice in school, he has a hard time finding an institutionalized avenue for seeking justice. The best he can do is find a friend at court, a teacher perhaps who will "go out on a limb" for him, or to develop a power play, if power is available in the form of a social contact of parents with an administrator or school board member. In operation this is a defective mechanism. It is largely available to a select minority, which ordinarily is in least need of it.

Schools have universally placed the student in a powerless role. Variations in the school's control of students have been in terms of the benevolence or intelligence of its exercise. To be sure, student government has been a conventional device to give some appearance of "democratic citizenship education" to the school or campus. But such governments have largely been form without substance. When the areas of active decision making "allowed" to students are carefully scrutinized, it is apparent that the exercise of power is limited to those matters that really have no significance. Or worse, the students are "persuaded" to take on themselves the onus of enforcing the rules and regulations of the school that they simply endorse but do not create.

The progressive education thrust did attempt to change somewhat the governing *ethos* of the school. It tried to win respect for the "felt needs" of students. It inaugurated methodologies that brought the students into the learning process. It focused attention on the quality of the school as a place for living. It sometimes pushed student government into areas of real responsibility. Yet its influence was limited and transient.

The student is in a peculiar position with respect to power. His choices are severely limited. Even to opt out is very costly. If he makes this choice through bad behavior or truancy, while still of legal school age, he is only in effect choosing residence at another altogether more disagreeable institution. If he *drops out*, after arriving at legal school-leaving age, he finds himself entering life with severely curtailed options and opportunities. In a very real sense, "to make it" he must use the institution. The price exacted is that he must in transit let the institution use him pretty much as its wisdom dictates.

As to attaining power, he is under the most severe of handicaps. He cannot withhold his presence, except to bring about his own ruin. The law and the economic scene define the condition. He can petition for consultation and dialogue, but arguing from no defined strength gives him little bargaining power. Furthermore, traditional educational philosophy formidably buttresses the stance of those who simply assert that he has no business or no competence in discussing the whats, whens, and hows of his learning.

In the lack of institutionalized modes of asserting the student's presence other than by responding "here" at roll call, the course of the rise of student power has been chaotic. Its exercise and its successes have been largely found on the college and university campus, where the students are less young, less immature, and less ignorant. At college where the student is present by a somewhat freer option, he has some choice over the withholding of his presence. Even at college the student in quest of power to affect educational decisions has been forced not so much to work within the institution as to challenge it.

The principal instrument of challenge has been confrontation. Confrontation is not synonymous with violence. Sometimes it is orderly, but orderly process is not built into confrontation. Confrontation arises out of frustration for lack of built-in processes of open communication and participation in decision making by defined means. The climate fostering confrontation is not uninviting to irrationality and violence. The drive to student power has sometimes exhibited both characteristics. Because of this it is not to be concluded that student power is inherently irrational and violence prone.

The challenge of student power to institutions has been disruptive. That students can bring classes to a halt, bring down administrations, excite sympathy and hostility has been demonstrated. Concerted student demonstration has proved capable of instituting processes of long-postponed change. It has also showed that the larger society can be excited to exert the police power to keep institutions operating and even to be considerably repressive on occasion.

Among changes brought about by student efforts have been:

1. Reorganization of administrative structure, e.g., Columbia University.
2. Gains of real decision-making power in regard to regulation of student life, campus publications, and dormitory management.
3. Limitation or abolition of ROTC courses.
4. Curriculum change—new programs, freer electives, pass-fail grading, among others.
5. Student representation on faculty and administrative committees; in rare instances even student membership on governing boards.

The press for student power has not proceeded in a campus vacuum. It exists in a complex of social and political problems and issues. Student activists have been influenced by many social forces, such as the unpopular war in Vietnam, the awareness of the influence of the military-industrial complex, and the plight of the urban populations. Activists have been affected by these matters, and they have demanded that education bring them centrally into their curriculum. In other words, they have insisted that the curriculum be relevant to the issues of the day.

It must be pointed out that student militancy enlists a wide range of persons. The search for responsible roles in decision making seems only just and mature. Among student activists are also to be found, however, a number of destructive agents whose philosophy, of whatever origin, is characterized by two untenable positions: (1) that the colleges and universities are hopeless and deserve only to be destroyed and (2) that the ways of democracy are rotten and corrupt and the only road to progress is to be shown by enlightened elite minorities. The familiar old rhetoric of the authoritarianism of the left has been restated by neo-Marxist Herbert Marcuse, who has become something of a prophet to some elements of the student power movement.

Student power is on good grounds when it seeks participation in institutional progress and when it presents its case for relevance. If student power will relate itself broadly to the pursuit of a more successful democracy, it will succeed, but it will diminish to a forlorn little coterie of frustrated agitators if it espouses causes that have no relevance to American democracy.

black power

Black power is not merely a school or campus phenomenon. It represents a sociocultural force that has come to school. It has both a community and an academic base, and these are in close communication. The complexities of the black power movement are especially germane to questions of urban education and will be explored more fully in that context in Chapter 14.

Of all sectors of the community, and of all constituencies of the school, none has been so dominated, none has been as powerless as the black citizenry. Black people have exhausted their patience with this condition and have taken direct action to attempt to change it.

Since all other avenues led into blind alleys of disappointment and betrayal, black people have turned to confrontation as their instrument of obtaining their rights. Confrontation has taken place in public gatherings, in churches, in school board meetings, in governmental hearings, on campuses, and in the streets. The climate again has been one that invites irrationality and violence, but this does not equate black power with these. As for violence, it is a simple fact of American history that the black American was traditionally dealt with in violence. His human dignity, his ego, and his person have been consistently violated. Such violence as he has dealt has been no measure of what he has received. The basic assumptions of black power are neither irrational nor violent:

1. That black people are fully human.
2. That they want for themselves and their children what all good people want.
3. That they do not deserve by virtue of race and color a subservient and outcast role in American society.
4. That they must take their own responsibility for actions to improve their condition, since others are glib with promises and tardy with actions.
5. That they acknowledge no special deficiencies or incapacities for taking charge of their own destinies.
6. That they must be taken fully into account wherever decisions are made that effect them, and that they will seek to make for themselves those decisions that mainly or solely effect them.
7. That where long-standing neglect and bias have severely curtailed their opportunities, they deserve special accommodation and concern to alter drastically and suddenly this state of affairs.
8. That if the cause is just, a long American tradition asserts that the pursuit of justice is not to be forever frustrated but to be pursued "by all means necessary."

In the lower schools the thrust of black power has been for community control, more black teachers, and black studies. At the college level it has sought a wide range of changes including more open admission policies; more black students, more black professors, more black administrators; programs of black studies; Afro-American library facilities; and more respect for black athletes as individuals.

The results have been far-reaching. Some elements remain controversial. The nature of and uses of black studies are debated even among black educators. The eventual goals of black power, whether toward integration, separation, or black nationalism remain moot issues. But change is taking place. In 1969 Michigan State University announced the selection of a black educator, Clifton R. Wharton, Jr., as its new president. Black power, along with teacher and student power, is taking its place in the new political science of American education.

the directions of power

Because the previous pages have examined teacher power, student power, and black power, the authors have not intended to idealize "power" per se. The stress, rather, has been to indicate that power in education does exist. Traditionally, it has been focused at the top and has been directed from the top downward. This is not the way of democracy. Democracy acknowledges power but also distrusts it. Democracy attempts to distribute power, to create conditions of shared power. It seeks to prevent any group from exercising its power unduly at the expense of others. It creates conditions for debate, for deliberation, for negotiation, and for compromise. It is by definition "participatory." It asserts that governing should be by "the consent of the governed."

Since in education many of these precepts have been neglected, and the political science of open institutions has eroded through lack of use, ruder instruments for participating in decision making have appeared. The principal instrument of the new scene is *confrontation*. We have noted its use by the black community and by students too. Teachers have also made use of it; the New York teacher strike in 1968, for example. Confrontation appeared on the scene when other instruments were denied or used but grudgingly. Sometimes it is an effective instrument, but it is not altogether trustworthy. It does invite irrationality and violence, and these invite greater conflict and repression.

To create a new political science for education is actually to attempt to bring new power forces into a legitimatized pattern for shared power and responsible decision making. First, we must understand these new power forces. Hence, there follows an analysis of how confrontation can be used to create a dialogue in which justice is served and in which irrationality is minimized and violence is truly self-defeating.

issues

The new education of the 1970s must be concerned with issues. This is partly because the issues have thrust themselves upon the school, and partly because society to some degree has come to expect education to resolve its issues. The school resides in a society troubled with all sorts of issues. The only way the school could avoid issues would be to shelter itself from reality—from life itself. Such a course has been followed too often. But the school can no longer allow itself a splendid detachment from the real affairs of the world, nor will the school be allowed such a choice if it should so prefer.

The assumptions in the above paragraph are arguable, and much argued. They constitute the base for some of the issues unavoidable in education. The school is forced by circumstance, even if reluctantly, to take a stand one way or another upon them.

When issues arise, there will be contesting parties, and vested interests will be involved. Persons will see themselves as standing to gain or lose according to the way the issue is settled. Moreover, the decision at stake will be seen differently by varied parties. Sometimes this will be because some parties have a better knowledge of relevant facts, a better information base than others. To the extent that this is true, the sharing of knowledge may bring the contending parties closer together, though information alone seldom totally resolves issues. Vested interests cannot bear the onus as the sole cause for the disagreement. Issues persist around the facts themselves, not merely because of vested interests, but because the facts themselves look different to different people. Facts are weighed and perceived not just in themselves, but in terms of a person's background, his culture, his experience.

If the school sits in an environment ridden with many issues that it cannot, even if it would, avoid, then when issues come to school, the school must be ready for them. To be ready in this sense means that the school must possess a sophisticated understanding of the social process by which issues may be encountered, inquired into, and to some degree resolved. In other words, the school, being an educational institution, *must learn to educate about and among issues.*

The school is not ordinarily sure of itself on these grounds. It is usually quite strong as a gatherer and purveyor of facts and information, but the simple relaying of facts seldom resolves issues. The school also, and quite appropriately, holds to the method of reason. It holds dear, as it should, the disciplines of science and objectivity. Issues, however, have arisen from circumstances where these disciplines have little if at all been applied. Issues arise where people have perceived the conditions that affect them to have been quite unreasonable, even unbearably so. People do possess intelligence; they are capable of reason. But in decision making people are not only influenced by reason. Many attributes of irrationality affect their views. Deep-rooted cultural and social biases contend with reason as a base for their viewpoints. Emotional factors enter in—feelings, angers, hatreds, preferences, greeds, fears. These are part of being human, too, along with a potential for using intelligence by the dictate of reason.

The school is reasonably successful in gathering and teaching facts, as we have indicated. It has some success in developing some of the discipline of reasonableness. However, it has proven awkward and even inept in dealing with the human responses that spring from the affective, the emotional. It has been afraid of emotion, tongue-tied with respect to basic drives—the powerful hungers of its students— and utterly at a loss when confronted with the vast potential of man for irrationality.

Thus, the school must extend its methodological competence if it is to assume its rightful role in resolving issues. It cannot, as it so often has tried to do, educate by attempting to rule the emotions out of its consideration; nor can it by quarantine forbid the irrational from its premises. Along with intelligence, the emotions come to school with every student, teacher, administrator, or any other person who enters its doors. So what can the school do? It can study the fuller realities of what it means *to educate.* It can apply its favorite dictum more broadly. "To take the learner from where he is" has a great deal of verbal acknowledgment. It is a dictum fairly well applied in the cognitive realm, in developing sequences of studies, of progressions for acquiring information. To be effectively applied, however, the whole person must be acknowledged and "taken from where he is." Such a course involves not only taking into account the state of his knowledge, but also the state of his experience and the shape and depth of his feelings.

In the main, issues are not contests of facts; they are contests among persons. None of the people concerned may have all the facts, and varied parties may possess differing sets of facts. Yet even though many facts are shared by the parties, different circumstances impose many views upon the facts, upon what they mean, and upon what ought to be done about them. This will be true in issues between generations, religious groups, students and teachers, teachers and school boards, blacks and whites, and "hawks" and "doves." It is true for all "contestants" in all issues.

Issues are a result of circumstances long allowed to move in directions that have deeply divided persons from one another. They will be deeply divided not only in their view of their facts, but in their feelings about them. Back of issues, however, are not merely *differing* circumstances. The circumstances have often been a product of some persons being controlled or dominated by others, so that conditions are better for some than for others. When teachers organize to seek power, they perceive that conditions for some, perhaps administrators, have been better than for them. Young people rebelling at home, school, or college may feel the same. Black people perceive this more sharply perhaps than any other. Difference of condition means not merely wide variation in material goods. It means variation in respect accorded, freedom in decision making, and basic equality. Thus, when we speak of feelings being involved, we do not imply simply feelings about conditions.

There are also feelings about persons. Persons make conditions; persons persist in doing things to others for the sake of their own advantage. Persons exploit, hold down, ignore, withhold respect from, abuse, and hurt other people. These things are sometimes done unwittingly, being the product of ancient cultural habits and traditions. Thus, children have been held down, ignored, and sometimes abused; women have been held to expectations that denied their full human potential; black Americans have been done the full range of economic, social, cultural, and psychological injury. These things have been done by some in a sense unknowingly. "Parents are supposed to dominate their children"; "Woman's place is in the home"; "Negroes are all right in their place." The culture has offered easy cliches to afford refuge for those who would not take the trouble to examine facts. Meanwhile, conditions for the ignored become unbearable.

confrontation

Eventually, the ignored, the people whose condition has become unbearable, must make reality visible. The method that they have found to be most effective in modifying the unbearable circumstances is confrontation, as we have already indicated. In confrontation the reality that is made visible is not alone the conditions but also *how people have come to feel about them*. Included in the feelings are feelings directed against others. Hatred for persons who have either directly or passively contributed to injustices done or perceived to have been done is deeply felt and broadly expressed.

Issues result in confrontation as a result of three factors:

1. Inequitable circumstances long ignored.
2. Verbal acknowledgment of disparities without attendant action.
3. Stubborn resistance to change because of vested interest or deep-seated bias.

When confrontation does occur, there are generally two alternative courses of action—an approach to the issue that brings people and the divisive conditions closer together or the course that leads to further division and subsequent destructive actions. A more complex analysis of alternatives of the latter course may be posed as repression and power struggle. Parties that dominate, or think they can dominate, simply refuse to address the issue. In other words, they direct all efforts to *repress* the issue. They use whatever power they have of cajolery, purse, or police to prevent change, to keep things as they are. Sometimes, the attitude behind repression is justified in quite moral terms. "Things are really not so bad"; "People get what they deserve out of life"; or, simply, "The public be damned; ain't I got the power." If social process is perceived simplistically as merely a contention in power, or if it is the only kind of social process by which change can take place, the issue may be resolved in a *power struggle*. The ultimate in power struggle may be naked power, armed force, violence, and revolution. Sometimes when the oppressors are relatively weak, representing historical institutions that have outrun their usefulness, genuine social change may take place, as when oligarchic power is overthrown to create a more democratic base of social control. More often, power struggle results in repression, if entrenched forces prevail, or in simple new tyrannies where access to power is transferred to another group who use another set of the same devices of control and protection of power.

The alternatives of repression or power struggle for settling an issue are indicative of either a lack of democracy or a breakdown of its processes. Democracy intends to institutionalize processes by which change may take place on bases more comprehensive than mere power struggle. It would be naïve and erroneous to contend that aggregates of power do not exist and legitimately contend, but open social process allows power relationships to be altered without parties destroying one another or bringing chaos to the entire society in the wake of their contention. There is a third alternative for resolving issues—

to seek justice. Criteria for this are not lacking. What has been lack
ing is the consistent application of the criteria. This approach presumes that social change that is generally beneficial can take place.
It assumes that the principle of "the greatest good for the greatest
number" is workable. It does not assume that what is best for most
can be denied to any.

Each of the alternatives discussed has a parallel course in the
school. *Repression* takes the form of denying issues access to the
curriculum. *Power struggle* turns the curriculum into propaganda
rather than inquiry. That is, the school teaches the view of circumstance that the dominant power forces holds or approves. The way
of *justice* is to educate. The school holds open and fair forum on the
issues. By so doing it performs its basic contribution to a free society:
the education of persons who will know how to address to issues and
to resolve problems by the methods available or made available. Thus
the school provides an education that provides equality for all and
that assures a decent cohesiveness among varying groups for them
to seek their varied purposes in harmony with and not constant contention against others.

The school must have a sophisticated knowledge of the reality, the
process, and the use of confrontation. The school may say, "Our
method is dialogue, not confrontation." This sounds good, but it is
naïve. The sophisticated school will say, "To arrive at dialogue is our
goal. We understand, however, that when issues have become crucial
and urgent, confrontation is inevitable. Only if we understand the
process of confrontation, can we hope to arrive at the goal of dialogue."

The assumptions we make with respect to the school in relation
to confrontation are: (1) that freedom is a virtue and a necessity;
(2) that freedom is not widely trusted as a virtue in the school and
far from understood as a necessity in the educative process; (3) that
freedom has its disciplines, is not automatic; and (4) that the learning
of these disciplines may be painful.

To repeat, confrontation is the process by which those who have
suffered from conditions which have become unbearable attempt to
make others, including those whom they hold responsible, aware both
of their condition and their suffering from it. In confrontation the
confronter and the confronted stand widely separated by circumstance. And, very significantly, they often perceive themselves to be
even farther apart than they actually are. In confrontation, there is
a period in which the perceived distance actually grows larger. In
confrontation, the first priority in expression often goes toward com-
municating emotion: "I want you to know how I feel—and what I
want you to know how I feel is I hate you." Confrontation does not
tend to make exceptions to its generalizations. Confronters are deeply
experienced in being stereotyped: "Children should be seen and not
heard"; "Women are intuitive and sensitive, but not logical and pre-

cise"; "Colored people are cheerful, full of rhythmn, and lazy." The generalizations thrown back in confrontation may give the confronted their first experience of the bite in being stereotyped: "You can't talk to anybody over thirty"; "All men are spoiled overgrown children"; "Every white man is a racist."

The confrontation is likely to be full of anger: on the confronter's part, because he perceives both his entitlement to it *and* because he deems it important to show just how he really feels; on the side of the confronted, because some people are talking whether he had invited them to or not, because if invited by him they transgress far beyond the boundaries of manner and substance that were his assumed ground rules, because some reality is hard to face, *and* because he perceives himself as being attacked unfairly in terms of motives, responsibility, or stereotyping.

The confronted squirm and suffer in the process because they are hearing things that they never wanted much to hear said in ways incredible to their experience. Then the defenses appear: "You have me all wrong"; or "You can't talk to me like that"; or "How can you lump me in with all those others?" (all those parents, all those male chauvinists, all those white racists).

When the school accepts an obligation to educate among issues, it necessarily must accept confrontation. It needs to be able to see two fundamentals and act upon them:

1. Confrontation has very little base of trust. Its minimum is the bare one—people willing to sit in a room and to communicate hostility in an atmosphere of general hostility.
2. More is present, however. The contenders do have certain things in common—a lot of human intelligence, a good deal of common as well as uncommon experience (not much referred to in this phase), a lot of people who would rather live than die. Above all, the basic reality is that here are members of the same species, who are the same in their basic drives and want very much the same things out of life. (This is a fact not merely obscured, but denied by bias. It is, nevertheless, a reality that can give the school a fair promise that confrontation may arrive at dialogue instead of dissolution of the group.)

from confrontation to dialogue

Dialogue is a desirable goal, but it is not an end in itself. Parties that have control of affairs often propose dialogue, but their conception of dialogue is not the fundamental one. "Let's sit down and talk things over" in this context generally carries the veiled assumption "then you will get your complaints off your chest and will go away and forget about them, and we won't have to do anything about them."

Properly conceived, dialogue is a process, a means of getting things accomplished. Through dialogue (1) people may educate one another to some part of their separated experience. (2) People may educate one another to understanding the scope and depth of their feelings that have been muted or hidden. (3) People may discover common denominators of purpose. And, all important, (4) programs may be developed cooperatively; action may be initiated.

Dialogue differs from confrontation in these respects:

1. Confrontation is preoccupied with announcing and asserting; dialogue lends itself equally to listening and qualifying its assertions.
2. Confrontation uses its emotions as both subject matter and justification of its argument; dialogue comments upon its emotions to help to clarify the conditions in which communication is taking place. ("When you put it like that I feel better about you"; or "I think you ought to know that coming on that way turns me off.")
3. Confrontation asserts basic distrust; dialogue presumes at least limited confidence—if not in persons, at the minimum in communication.
4. Confrontation stereotypes, addresses itself to an aggregate adversary; dialogue individualizes, addresses itself to persons.
5. Confrontation seeks flaws and elements for ridicule in the adversaries' statements; dialogue listens for evidences of sense and rationality to which to make its basic response.

The school must not perceive confrontation, on the one hand, to be evil and dirty and dialogue, on the other, to be clean and virtuous. They are two modes of human communication. Institutionally, dialogue, if preferred, should be sought by creating the circumstances hospitable to it. Institutionally, it would appear that the school would prefer dialogue as a goal and process since dialogue employs the method of reason. It can analyze problems and promote solutions. Through dialogue decisions can be made that result in improvements, not destruction.

If confrontation is the process to which the school must attend, then educators will be well advised to look at the conditions from which it stems. Delay, repression or fast talk will presumably not alter these conditions. If dialogue is the goal, as it should be, it must be arrived at by a sophisticated discipline. The school must recognize that confrontation exists, that there has been a loss of confidence by the confronter, and that confrontation *can* lead to dialogue.

Recognition of confrontation does not imply sanction or consent to destructive or violent behavior. It means recognition that the conditions or causes are real and that an urgency for communication is at hand. To bring the confronted and confronter together is impossible unless the third party—the school—realizes that the confronter has lost confidence in the confronted and that margins of trust and respect, if present at all, are minimal.

For confrontation to move to dialogue, school officials must be alert to the opportunities that will enable the school people to persuade the two camps to enter into a dialogue. To do this, they must be able to:

1. Establish a minimum confidence that response to confrontation is not by preference going to be flight or repression.
2. Suggest opportunities for response, not to cite past virtues.
3. Prove the capacity to listen, even to abuse, with disciplined calm and to try to hear evidences of reason, that is, to try really to hear things that they had never heard before.
4. Try to give evidence that there are men in the institution who are not afraid to make an appearance in the midst of trouble.

The knowledge that confrontation can move to dialogue also suggests that the educator:

1. Not make confrontation a basis for decision and action.
2. Respect the confronter and the injustice done to him.

In his knowledge that dialogue can eventuate, the educator, to repeat, *must not* make confrontation a basis for decision and action. For example, nonnegotiable demands must be neither rejected nor adopted—they must be listened to. Dialogue can be achieved. Then negotiation can take place, and negotiation improves all decisions and actions.

The educator must respect the confronter in the knowledge that injustice is real and personal and that one person used unjustly is case enough to trouble the just man. He must give his moral energy, however, to justice, not expediency. The response to confrontation must not be in tune with the nasty old cliche "The squeaky wheel gets the grease." Confrontation does rise from the conviction of injustice done, but it also comes about from deep seated angers that reason can no longer soften. Therefore, often not justice is sought but preference, not merely redress of wrongs but punitive actions.

Administrative capitulation to confrontation has been as erroneous as repression. Both postures fail to realize that dialogue is the proper and feasible goal to be sought.

A knowledge of the process and its dictates will not assure easy solutions of hard issues in troubled times. However, the worst crises, the ugliest scenes, have appeared where educators and public authorities appeared to have no understanding of basic processes or the deep dictates of reason. These principles constitute guidelines that, in another sense, afford a new political science for education.

topics for inquiry

1. The Power Structure in Your Community
2. Local-State Relationships in the Control of Education in Your Community and State
3. Closeness to the Schools, or the Lack of It, in Your Community
4. The Meaning of Efficiency in Educational Terms
5. Confrontations and Outcomes: A Case Study
6. How Teacher Power Works
7. The Origin and the Concept of Black Power
8. Varied Views on Student Power
9. The Meaning of Dialogue
10. The Group Dynamics Movement

subjects for discussion

1. Stage a sociodrama in which the roles represent two groups in confrontation: students versus parents, blacks versus whites, teachers versus school board. Let the confrontation run a full course. Observe it in light of this chapter. What happens? Does the situation move to dialogue? What changes took place? Ask the role players to talk about how they felt changes in themselves or about the other side as the situation developed. Discuss the implications.
2. There is no obligation for you to agree with the authors in any editorial position that they assume. Where do you take issue with positions taken in this chapter?
3. How might the generation gap be perceived as a necessity for moving from "confrontation to dialogue"? What could a participant in such a confrontation do to facilitate achieving dialogue?
4. Should teachers ever strike? Under what circumstances?
5. What was the most open communication session you ever participated in? How did it develop? Were your reactions positive? How could institutions foster more open communication?
6. Discuss the functioning of the school board in your area. How is it composed? How much public interest is there in school affairs? What issues generate public interest? Is the school board responsive to public concern? In what ways?

selected readings

BENDINER, ROBERT. *The Politics of Schools: A Crisis In Self-Govern-ment.* New York: Harper & Row, 1969.

> An effective analysis of the issues of decentralization and local control. Bendiner comes to well-argued conclusions that are quite opposite to those of the authors of this text.

BLAU, PETER M. *Bureaucracy in Modern Society.* New York: Random House, 1956.

> An evaluation of bureaucracy in general. The exposition extends and illuminates the analyses within our chapter.

FEUER, LEWIS S. *The Conflict of Generations.* New York: Basic Books, 1969.

> Subtitled *The Character and Significance of Student Movements.* These phenomena are studied in historical and international perspective.

LUNDBERG, FERDINAND. *The Rich and the Super-Rich.* New York: Lyle Stuart, Inc., 1968.

> The comprehensive work on the concentration of wealth and economic power in the United States and the facts on the distribution of the American affluence. This work is the up-to-date successor to Gustavus Myer's classic *History of the Great American Fortunes* and Lundberg's own *America's Sixty Families.*

MILLS, C. WRIGHT. *The Power Elite.* New York: Oxford, 1956.

> A penetrating analysis of how the system works.

ROGERS, CARL. *Freedom to Learn.* Columbus, Ohio: Charles Merrill, 1969.

> A "practical" handbook on how to achieve true dialogue in the classroom.

ROGERS, DAVID. *110 Livingston St.* New York: Random House, 1969.

> A full-fledged case study of precisely how a centralized urban education structure operates.

TAWNEY, R. H. *The Acquisitive Society.* New York: Harcourt, Brace, 1920.

> A modern classic. States the underlying motivations of man in institutional life. To read Tawney, as with Veblen, is a necessary step to achieving a truly relevant modern education.

VEBLEN, THORSTEIN. *Theory of the Leisure Class.* New York: Macmillan, 1899.

> Our nomination for one of America's top five great books. He sees institutional reality with uncanny clarity and an anthropological perspective. Though originally printed in 1899, you will not find a more *relevant* book on contemporary America.

> *Note:* Relevant at this point will be the previously cited works by Callahan, Kimball and McClelland, Whyte, and Parkinson.

6

RELIGION AND THE SCHOOLS: THE CON- TINUING DEBATE

One of the most persistent issues involving education in the United States has been the question of separation between church and state as it relates to the schools. From the very beginning of the struggle to establish the common school through the present, the church-state issue has been a central point of controversy. The principle of separation is defined in the First Amendment in these words in what is known as the Establishment and Free-Exercise clauses:

> Congress shall make no law respecting an establishment of religion, or prohibiting the free exercise thereof:

This principle of separation, which many hold to be a firmly established tradition in American society, continues to press for interpretation with respect to its application to education. In essence, the central question involving the schools is whether or not certain practices carried on in a state's educational program are in violation of the Establishment Clause of the First Amendment.

The fact that the Establishment Clause has been interpreted in various ways by differing segments of society is, of course, the pivotal point of the controversy. What, precisely, was the intended meaning behind the Establishment Clause? Under the Constitution the Supreme Court has had the obligation of bringing interpretive rulings to the specific cases and in doing so it has found it necessary to seriously consider the state of religious affairs in this country during the colonial period and at the time of the drafting of the Constitution.

religion in colonial america

In its extremest form the establishment of religion in colonial America meant, in practice, that public funds could be used to support a particular church and that the government could legally enforce a particular church's orthodox doctrine. Under this system the colony used its powers to levy taxes upon all persons, regardless of their religious beliefs, to finance the established church. The colony in many instances also used its powers to give legal and moral support to the established church by prohibiting the practice of any other religion or, for that matter, public statement of any other belief.

The most severe examples of this strong establishment of church and state were those to be found among the Puritans in the New England colonies during the seventeenth century. The tenacity of their views and the argument of justification for them are evident in many of the writings of that period. Nathaniel Ward, for example, in his book, *The Simple Cobbler*, published in 1647, voices the theocrats' views on religious intolerance. In a section entitled "Against Toleration" Ward argued:

> That state is wise, that will improve all pains and patience rather to compose, than tolerate differences in religion. . . .
> He that is willing to tolerate any religion, or discrepant way of religion, besides his own . . . either doubts of his own or is not sincere in it. . . .
> That state that will give liberty of conscience in matters of religion, must give liberty of conscience and conversation in their moral laws. . . .
> Experience will teach Churches and Christians, that it is far better to live in a state united, though a little corrupt, than in a state whereof some part is incorrupt, and all the rest divided.[1]

The argument for theocracy was also put forth in strong terms by John Cotton:

> Democracy, I do not conceyve that ever God did ordeyne as a fit government eyther for church or commonwealth. If the people be governors, who shall be governed?[2]

In regard to the schools of the New England colonies it is clear, both in the stated purposes for the schools and in the practices therein, that the prevailing establishment ideal was the guiding factor. The religious intent of education was evident in all of the early New England colonial school laws, the most renowned of which is the Massachusetts act of 1647, commonly referred to as "The Old Deluder, Satan, Act." The preamble to the act directly points up its religious intent:

[1] Nathaniel Ward, *The Simple Cobbler*, in Norman Foerster (ed.), *American Poetry and Prose, Part I* (Boston: Houghton Mifflin, 1947), pp. 31–32.

[2] As quoted in Thomas Jefferson Wertenbaker, *The First Americans 1607–1690* (New York: Macmillan, 1927), pp. 93–94.

The Massachusetts Law of 1647

It being one cheife proiect of ye ould deluder, Satan, to keepe men from the knowledge of ye Scriptures, as in form^r times by keeping y^m in an unknowne tongue, so in these latt^r times by perswading from ye use of tongues, y^t so at least ye true sence & meaning of ye originall might be clouded by false glosses of saint seeming deceivers, y^t learning may not be buried in ye grave of o^r fath^rs in ye church and commonwealth, the Lord assisting o^r endeavo^rs, —

It is therefore ord^red, y^t ev^ry towneship in this iurisdiction, aft^r ye Lord hath increased y^m number to 50 household^rs, shall then forthw^th appoint one w^thin their towne to teach all such children as shall resort to him to write & reade, whose wages shall be paid eith^r by ye parents or mast^rs of such children, or by ye inhabitants in gen^rall, by way of supply, as ye maior part of those y^t ord^r ye prudentials of ye towne shall appoint; provided, those y^t send their children be not oppressed by paying much more y^n they can have y^m taught for in oth^r townes; & it is furth^r ordered, y^t where any towne shall increase to ye numb^r of 100 families or household^rs, they shall set up a grammer schoole, ye m^r thereof being able to instruct youth so farr as they shall be fited for ye university, provided, y^t if any towne neglect ye performance hereof above one yeare, y^t every such towne shall pay 5 £ to ye next schoole till they shall performe this order.[3]

വ@ഓഓ@ഓ@ഓ@ഓ@ഓ@ഓ*@ഓ@ഓ@ഓ@ഓ@ഓ@ഓ

Spiritual Milk

For AMERICAN BABES,

Drawn out of the Breasts of both *Teftaments,*
for their Souls Nourifhment.

By JOHN COTTON.

Queft. *W*HAT hathGod done for you?
Anf. God hath made me, he keepeth me, and he can fave me.

Q. *What is* GOD ?
A God is a Spirit of himfelf and for himfelf.

Q. *How many Gods be there ?*
A. There be but One GOD in three Perfons, the Father, the Son, and the Holy Ghoft.

Q. *How did God make you ?*
A. In my firft Parents holy and righteous.

Q. *Are you then born Holy and Righteous ?*
A. No, my firft Parents finned, and I in them.

Q. *Are you then born a Sinner !*
A. I was conceived in Sin & born in Iniquity.

Q. *What is your Birth Sin ?*
A. Adam's Sin imputed to me, and a corrupt Nature dwelling in me.

Q. *What is your corrupt Nature ?*

An ALPHABET *of Leffons for* Youth.

A Wife Son makes a glad Father, but a foolifh Son is the heavinefs of his Mother.

B ETTER is a little with the Fear of the Lord, than great Treafure and Trouble therewith.

C OME unto Chrift all ye that labour and are heavy laden, and he will give you Reft.

D O not the abominable Thing which I hate, faith the Lord.

E XCEPT a Man be born again he cannot fee the Kingdom of God.

F OOLISHNESS is bound up in the Heart of a Child, but the Rod of Correction fhall drive it from him.

G RIEVE not the Holy Spirit, left it depart from thee.

H OLINESS becomes God's Houfe forever.

I T is good for me to draw near unto God. 4

---

[3] As reprinted in Ellwood P. Cubberley, *Readings in the History of Education* (New York: Houghton Mifflin, 1948), p. 299.

[4] *Ibid.,* p. 315.

Since teaching children to read also meant teaching them the Puritan religion, it is obvious that the schools would assume a religious direction in practice. And the best means to teach reading and Calvinism was the New England Primer, which first appeared about 1690 and was in use in various editions through the early nineteenth century. The catechetical intent of the Primer is seen in the excerpt from an alphabet lesson.

Whatever their reasons, (e.g., need of security in hostile environment) it is clear that the ruling theocrats took harsh measures to maintain their control. Although there were many examples of the theocrats' intolerances, none stands out as do the Salem Witch Trials of 1692 and 1693. By this time the power of the ruling class, which had been challenged earlier by dissenters such as Ann Hutchinson and Roger Williams, as well as by many lesser-known figures, was slipping. It was apparent that the ecclesiastical social order that the rulers had attempted to maintain was not able to repress the spirit of democracy and individualism. Samuel Tory in his election sermon in 1674 was undoubtedly reflecting the leaders' concerns even at an earlier time when he noted: "Truly, so it is, the very heart of New England is changed and exceedingly corrupted with the sins of the Times . . ." [5,6]

It is against this slipping of power that the Salem Witch Trials are to be seen; a frantic attempt of the Puritan theocracy to revitalize and maintain its power over the citizenry who were becoming progressively disenchanted with the strength of the "establishment." The statistics of the trials are impressive enough evidence to hold that the rulers saw in the whole affair a means by which to strike fear into the hearts of men. Nineteen were executed; at least one died under torture; more than fifty had confessed in order to escape execution; and some two hundred were held in prison awaiting trial.

Although the witchcraft trials were most certainly an attempt at restating power, the decline of theocracy in Massachusetts had already been certified by a new charter brought back from England in 1692 by Increase Mather. The new charter contained the provision that the electorate was no longer to be limited to members of the covenant but broadened to include propertied members of every Christian sect except, of course, Catholics. The limitation of franchise to the elect had been the cornerstone of the theocracy, enabling power to be maintained by a few. Such remnants from an earlier feudal arrangement were to be irrevocably lost in the press of liberal ideals. Although the extreme form of Calvinist theocracy in New England had been virtually unseated by 1700, the church-state relationship was not completely lost. For even until 1833 citizens of Massachusetts were taxed for the support of Protestant religion, the assumption being, obviously, that a multiple establishment was a great deal more

[5] Lindsay Swift, "The Massachusetts Election Sermons," Col. Soc. of Mass., Publs., Vol. I, p. 402, as quoted in Wertenbaker, op. cit., p. 110.
[6] See also Cotton Mather, Magnalia Christi Americana, Ibid., pp. 109–110.

tolerable than a single establishment, even though the multiple establishment included only Protestant denominations.

Establishment practices were by no means limited to the New England colonies. The southern colonies maintained, in general, the pattern of establishment of a single church, the Anglican, until the Revolution, at which time establishments were either replaced by multiple-establishment patterns, such as in Maryland and South Carolina, or erased completely as in Virginia.

disestablishment begins

Virginia's direction was significant. The involvement of Thomas Jefferson and James Madison in the controversy over establishment patterns in that state was to affect the nation's course in the years to come. After the Revolution there was a strong conservative bloc in the Virginia legislature for a multiple-establishment pattern. Jefferson and Madison pleaded persistently for a total separation, and eventually their position was carried. The influence of both Madison's and Jefferson's arguments is evident not only in the drafting of the First Amendment to the Constitution but also in the arguments of the Supreme Court in later decisions involving questions of church-state relationships.

The thrust of Madison's position is eloquently put forth in his "Memorial and Remonstrance Against Religious Assessments" delivered to the Virginia General Assembly in 1784. His arguments are most relevant to today's church-state issues. Opposing a bill that would provide public monies for teachers of the Christian religion, Madison argued:

> . . . we maintain . . . that in matters of religion no man's
> right is abridged by the institution of civil society; and that
> religion is wholly exempt from its cognizance. True it is,
> that no other rule exists, by which any question which may
> divide society can be ultimately determined, but the will of
> the majority; but it is also true that the majority may
> trespass on the rights of the minority.
> . . . Who does not see that the same authority which can
> establish Christianity, in exclusion of all other religions, may
> establish, with the same ease, any particular sect of
> Christians, in exclusion of all other sects? That the same
> authority that can call for each citizen to contribute three
> pence only of his property for the support of only one
> establishment, may force him to conform to any one
> establishment, in all cases whatsoever?
> . . . What influences, in fact, have ecclesiastical establish-
> ments had on civil society? In some instances they have
> been seen to erect a spiritual tyranny on the ruins of civil
> authority; in many instances they have been seen upholding
> the thrones of political tyranny; in no instance have they
> been seen the guardians of the liberties of the people.

> Rulers who wished to subvert the public liberty may have
> found an established clergy convenient auxiliaries. A just
> government, instituted to secure and perpetuate it, needs
> them not. Such government will be best supported by
> protecting every citizen in the enjoyment of his religion with
> the same equal hand that protects his person and property;
> by neither invading the equal rights of any sect, nor suffering
> any sect to invade those of another.[7]

Madison's views have been cited as points of argument in most of the
Supreme Court cases involving church-state questions, as have been
the arguments of Jefferson. The most widely cited separation arguments of Jefferson are those that appeared in his Bill for Establishing
Religious Freedom, which was introduced to the Virginia legislature
in 1779 and passed in 1786. As in Madison's argument, Jefferson's argument also promotes ideas that can be seen as constituting the essence
of both the Establishment and Free-Exercise clauses of the First
Amendment. His bill proposed:

> That to compel a man to furnish contributions of money
> for the propagation of opinions which he disbelieves and
> abhors, is sinful and tyrannical; that even forcing him to
> support this or that teacher of his own religious persuasion,
> is depriving him of the comfortable liberty of giving his
> contributions to the particular pastor whose morals he would
> make his pattern, and whose powers he feels most persuasive
> to righteousness; and . . . that our civil rights have no
> dependance on our religious opinions . . . that the opinions
> of men are not the object of civil government, nor under its
> jurisdiction. . . .
>   We the General Assembly of Virginia do enact that no man
> shall be compelled to frequent or support any religious
> worship, place, or ministry whatsoever, nor shall be enforced,
> restrained, molested, or burthened in his body or goods, on
> account of his religious opinions or belief. . . .[8]

The complete disestablishment that Jefferson and Madison argued
for was attained in nine of the thirteen states through constitutional
provisions by 1800 and in the remaining four by 1833, when Massachusetts made a constitutional provision against multiple establishment. However, even with this and the fact that disestablishment had
been ruled for at a national level by the First Amendment in 1789, the
issue was obviously not settled. For one thing, the First Amendment
was not made applicable to the states until 1868 with the ratification
of the Fourteenth Amendment and even then rarely applied until the
twentieth century. Even this application would not settle the problem, especially in regard to education.

[7] As quoted in Herbert M. Kliebard, *Religion and Education in America: A Documentary
History* (Scranton, Pa.: International Textbook, 1969), pp. 50–51.
[8] *Ibid.*, pp. 56–57.

religious issue in the common school struggle

From the very outset of the struggle to establish the common school in the various states during the first half of the nineteenth century the religious question was at issue. Previous to the establishment of state systems of public education the schools, for the most part, had been in the hands of religious organizations and private entrepreneurs, many of which received public tax monies. It is not surprising, therefore, that a transition from church-controlled schools to a state system of education would carry with it religious issues. To some degree the issues were present in the early development of all state systems of education. Perhaps the substance of the issues at the time can best be seen in light of the fact that the United States during the first half of the nineteenth century was predominantly Protestant. Therefore, the "secularization" of the schools, as seen by the leaders, meant, for the most part, that there would be no proselytizing for any particular sect nor any tax support of separate church schools. It did not mean that the leaders were about to exclude practices such as prayer and Bible reading, generally acceptable then to most Protestant denominations. But even with this maintenance of general Christian features in the schools, schools were charged with "ungodliness." The most notable dispute carrying this charge occurred in Massachusetts during the 1830s and 1840s while Horace Mann was secretary to the state board of education.

Horace Mann's position in regard to teaching religion reflected to a great extent the prevailing nonsectarian proposals for public schools. He did, indeed, favor the use of the King James Bible in school, and in no way did he consider this as a sectarian practice nor, obviously, as an irreligious practice. However, for his advocacy of nonsectarianism he was charged by some dogmatic fundamentalists as being, at worst, an atheist and unfit to direct the schools. The controversy was carried on with fervor by Frederick A. Packard, secretary of the American Sunday School Union in Philadelphia, and Matthew Hole Smith, a Calvinist preacher from Massachusetts. Both Packard and Smith turned the issue into an anti-public school campaign. This might lead one to question whether or not even then the issue was to be seen as a convenient and fiery symbol for opposing the common school rather than a literal controversy. For whatever reason, the controversy became so intense that a legislative attempt was made in 1840 to abolish the state board of education in Massachusetts.

Much of the controversy involved in Mann's fight with the fundamentalists was primarily centered on his nonsectarian position, which was made very clear in his First Annual Report (1837).

> . . . To prevent the school from being converted into an
> engine of religious proselytism; to debar successive teachers

in the same school, from successively inculcating hostile
religious creeds, until the children in their simplemindedness
should be alienated, not only from creeds but from religion
itself; the statute of 1826 specially provided, that no school
books should be used in any of the public schools "calculated
to favor any particular religious sect or tenet." [9]

His concern was apparently not groundless, for in his Twelfth
Annual Report (1848) he refers to the conditions that he found in the
Massachusetts schools in 1837, his first year as secretary and a decade
after the law prohibiting sectarian instruction:

> . . . I found books in the schools, as strictly and exclusively
> *doctrinal* as any on the shelves of a theological library. I
> heard teachers giving oral instruction, as strictly and purely
> *doctrinal*, as any ever heard from the pulpit, or from the
> professor's chair. And more than this: I have now in my
> possession, printed directions, given by committeemen to
> teachers, enjoining upon them the use of a catechism, in
> school, which is wholly devoted to an exposition of the
> doctrines of one of the denominations amongst us. These
> directions bear a date a dozen years subsequent to the
> prohibitory law. . . . [10]

Obviously Mann's efforts to maintain what was to him a nonsectarian school system did not set well with his fundamentalist adversaries. Against their charges of ungodliness in the schools Mann put
forth this argument in his Twelfth Annual Report:

> . . . If the Bible, then, is the exponent of Christianity; if the
> Bible contains the communication, precepts, and doctrines,
> which make up the religious system, called and known as
> Christianity; if the Bible makes known those truths, which
> according to the faith of Christians, are able to make men
> wise unto salvation; and if the Bible is in the schools, how
> can it be said that Christianity is excluded from the schools;
> or how can it be said that the school system, which adopts
> and uses the Bible, is an anti-Christian, or an un-Christian
> system? [11]

It is apparent that the religious issue as it appeared in the controversy in Massachusetts in the 1840s had more to do with the question
of singular versus multiple establishment than it did with total disestablishment as provided for by the First Amendment or as is the
case today. Of course, the country was predominantly Protestant at
the time. The Catholic population, which has been estimated at about

[9] *Ibid.*, p. 67.
[10] *Ibid.*, p. 76.
[11] *Ibid.*, p. 83.

1 percent in 1800, did not increase significantly until around the middle of the nineteenth century, and other non-Protestant church membership was even smaller.

catholic concern

The preceding discussion is not to imply that there were no protestations from the Catholic Church in regard to the religious issue in education. Obviously, the Church would strongly oppose the use of the King James Bible in the public schools. To the Catholic mind the schools were sectarian, and this position was clearly stated in the Pastoral Letter of 1843:

> . . . We have seen with serious alarm, efforts made to poison
> the fountains of public education, by giving it a sectarian hue,
> and accustoming children to the use of a version of the
> Bible made under sectarian bias, and placing in their hands
> books of various kinds replete with offensive and dangerous
> matter. This is plainly opposed to the free genius of our
> civil institutions.[12]

A Pastoral Letter of 1884 recognized that the public schools must maintain a secular character and encouraged its members to support Catholic schools. The statement, however, spoke of the recognition not in Catholic but in Christian terms and in a sense lent support to church-state separation while at the same time condemning the public schools.

> The friends of Christian education do not condemn the State
> for not imparting religious instruction in the public schools
> as they are now organized, because they well know it does
> not lie within the province of the State to teach religion.
> They simply follow their conscience by sending their children
> to denominational schools, where religion can have its
> rightful place and influence.
> Two objects therefore, dear brethren, we have in view, to
> multiply our schools, and to perfect them. We must multiply
> them, till every Catholic child in the land shall have within
> its reach the means of education.[13]

trend toward secularism

To some extent the Pastoral Letter of 1884 reflects a general trend found toward the end of the nineteenth century to accept the public schools as secular institutions. By 1900 Massachusetts was the only state that required by law morning prayers and Bible reading. Of

[12] *Ibid.*, p. 88.
[13] *Ibid.*, p. 93.

course, many other states had school systems with similar practices but without either statutory compulsion or sanction.

What seemed to be a definitely progressive trend toward achieving complete secularization in the public schools came to an abrupt reversal in 1913 with the passage of legislation in Pennsylvania requiring that Bible reading and the Lord's Prayer be a daily practice in the schools. By 1946 thirteen states had laws requiring Bible reading in the public schools. Also, by this time, other practices involving the church-state question had become a part of the American school scene. Along with the issue of religious ceremony in public schools came the issue of public monies for church schools. It is to these specific issues and the Supreme Court's rulings on them that we next turn our attention.

the supreme court and the issues

Since 1923 the United States Supreme Court has had to weigh the constitutional legality of a number of specific practices in the educational systems of the states. These fall into two general categories of questions, both to be weighed essentially against the First Amendment:

1. Does a state have the right to expend public funds for the support, direct or indirect, of religious schools?
2. Does a state have the right to permit or legislate for religious practices or instruction to be carried on in the public schools?

The problem is one of determining whether or not specific practices constitute an abridgment of the Establishment and Free-Exercise clauses of the First Amendment as interpreted by the Supreme Court. The cases selected for discussion here illustrate the major issues and to a great extent display the general trend of interpretation given to the First Amendment by the Supreme Court. The first cases discussed relate to the question of public aid to religious schools. The other cases involve the questions of religious practices or instruction in public schools.

public aid to religious schools

The practice of public aid to religious schools has assumed a variety of forms in the United States. Until recent years such aid for the most part had been limited to indirect state support such as providing transportation or textbooks to parochial school children in certain states. More recently, with the National Defense Education Act of 1958 and the Elementary and Secondary Education Act of 1965, tax monies have been allotted directly to parochial schools, although the funds have been categorized for curricular areas determined to be

Case	State	Year	Issue in Question	Court's Decision	Vote	Amendment Grounds
Mayer v. Nebraska	Neb.	1923	May a state compel exclusion of curriculum from private schools? (No question of state's right to set standards)	NO	7–2	14th
Pierce v. Society of Sisters	Oregon	1925	May a state compel all children to attend public schools?	NO	9–0	14th
Cochran v. Louisiana	La.	1930	May a state supply textbooks to parochial school children?	YES	9–0	14th
Minersville v. Gobitis	Pa.	1940	May a state compel a child to pledge allegiance to the flag? (Reversed in 1943)	YES	8–1	1st
W. Va. Bd. of Ed. v. Barnette	W. Va.	1943	May a state compel a child to pledge allegiance to the flag?	NO	6–3	1st
Everson v. Bd. of Ed.	N.J.	1947	May a state provide transportation for parochial school children?	YES	5–4	1st
McCollum v. Bd. of Ed.	Ill.	1948	Is religious instruction allowed on school property?	NO	8–1	1st
Zorach v. Clauson	N.Y.	1952	May children be released from school time for religious instruction off school property?	YES	6–3	1st
Engel v. Vitale	N.Y.	1962	May a state composed prayer be voluntarily recited in school?	NO	6–1	1st
Abington v. Schempp Murray v. Curlett	Pa. Md.	1963	May the Lord's Prayer and Bible reading be a part of a school's exercises?	NO	8–1	1st
Cent. School District v. Allen	N.Y.	1968	May a state supply books for parochial school children?	YES	6–3	1st

FIGURE 5 *Significant Supreme Court Rulings on Religion-Education Issue*

secular in nature. The federal involvement has not yet been challenged due to a 1923 Supreme Court decision that held that federal
taxpayers could not challenge federal statutes on constitutional
grounds simply on the basis of their standing as taxpayers. However,
this ruling was reversed in part by a 1968 decision which allows for
challenge on the grounds of abridgment of the Establishment or Free-
Exercise clause. This will undoubtedly open the way for the challenge
of federal programs that include parochial schools.

The challenges made at the state level have involved the practices
of providing transportation and books for parochial school children.
In both instances the Supreme Court has ruled that such practices
are not of direct benefit to a religious school but rather of benefit to
the child. In light of the "child benefit" theory the Court has held
that such practices, therefore, are not in violation of the First Amendment. The two cases discussed below, spanning twenty-one years,
point up the Court's consistency on the child-benefit theory.

Everson v. Board of Education (1947)

The charge was brought against Ewing Township, New Jersey. The
Ewing school board, acting pursuant to a New Jersey statute, authorized reimbursement to parents of the cost of bus transportation for
their children. (The reimbursement was limited to those attending
public or parochial schools.)

> Whenever in any district there are children living remote
> from any schoolhouse, the board of education of the district
> may make rules and contracts for the transportation of such
> children to and from school, including the transportation of
> school children to and from school other than a public
> school, except such school as is operated for profit. . . .

The plaintiff in the case held that the reimbursement of children
attending parochial schools was in clear violation of the First Amendment and also of the Fourteenth. In September 1944, the Supreme
Court of New Jersey ruled that the practice was unconstitutional in
that it aided religious schools. In October 1945, the Court of Errors
and Appeals of New Jersey reversed the lower court's decison, holding
that such a practice was in support of and supplementary to the school
attendance laws of New Jersey, and within the state's constitutional
rights.

On appeal from the plaintiff, the United States Supreme Court
heard the case and rendered its decision in February, 1947. The Court
was sharply divided, five members upholding the New Jersey statute
as being constitutionally valid and four members dissenting. While
the majority opinion, delivered by Justice Black, rested its argument
to a great extent on the child benefit theory, it nevertheless handled
cautiously the question of the Establishment Clause. It was this that

led Justice Jackson to open his dissenting opinion with a caustic comment:

> The Court's opinion marshals every argument in favor of
> state aid and puts the case in its most favorable light, but much
> of its reasoning confirms my conclusions that there are no good
> grounds upon which to support the present legislation. In
> fact, the undertones of the opinion, advocating complete and
> uncompromising separation of Church from State, seems
> utterly discordant with its conclusions yielding support to their
> comingling in educational matters. The case which irresistably
> comes to mind as the most fitting precedent is that of Julia,
> who, according to Byron's reports, "whispering 'I will ne'er
> consent'—consented."

The majority opinion was written by Justice Black and concurred in by Chief Justice Vinson and Justices Reed, Douglas, and Murphy. The minority was composed of Justices Frankfurter, Jackson, Rutledge, and Burton. Dissenting opinions were written by Justices Jackson and Rutledge and concurred in by Justices Frankfurter and Burton. Excerpts from the opinions are set forth below in juxtaposition in order to parallel the Court's arguments on various points.

Majority Opinion
(*Justice Black*)

Since there has been no attack on the statute on the ground that part of its language excludes children attending private schools operated for profit from enjoying State payment for their transportation, we need not consider the exclusionary language; it has no relevancy to any constitutional question here presented. Furthermore, if the exclusion clause had been properly challenged, we do not know whether New Jersey's highest court would construe its statutes as precluding payment of the school transportation of any group of pupils, even those of a private school run for profit. Consequently, we put to one side the question as to the validity of the statute against the claim that it does not authorize payment for the transportation generally of school children in New Jersey.

Minority Opinion
(*Dissenting—Justice Jackson*)

The New Jersey Act in question makes the character of the school, not the needs of the children, determine the eligibility of parents to reimbursement. The Act permits payment for transportation to parochial schools or public schools but prohibits it for private schools operated in whole or in part for profit. . . . Refusal to reimburse those who attend such schools is understandable only in the light of a purpose to aid the schools, because the State may well abstain from aiding a profit-making private enterprise. Thus under the Act and resolution brought to us by this case, children are classified according to the school they attend and are to be aided if they attend the public schools or private Catholic schools, and they are not allowed to be aided if they attend private secular schools or private religious schools of other faiths.

(Justice Rutledge)

I have chosen to place my dissent upon the broad ground I think decisive, though strictly speaking the case might be decided on narrower issues. The New Jersey statute might be held invalid on its face for the exclusion of children who attend private, profit-making schools. I cannot assume, as does the majority, that the New Jersey Courts would write off explicit limitations from the statute. Moreover, the resolution by which the statute was applied expressly limits its benefits to students of public and Catholic schools. . . .

(Justice Black)

The due process argument that the state law taxes some people to help others carry their private purposes is framed in two phases: The first phase is that a state cannot tax A to reimburse B for the cost of transporting his children to church schools. This is said to violate the due process clause because the children are sent to their church school to satisfy the personal desire of their parents, rather than the public's interest in the general education of all children. This argument, if valid, would apply equally to prohibit state payment for the transportation of children to any non-public school, whether operated by a church or any other non-governmental individual or group. But, the New Jersey legislature has decided that a public purpose will be served by using tax-raised funds to pay the bus fares of all school children, including those who attend parochial schools. The New Jersey Court of Errors and Appeals has reached the same conclusion. The fact that a state law, passed to satisfy a public need, coincides with the personal desires of the individuals most directly affected is cer-

(Justice Jackson)

It is of no importance in this situation whether the beneficiary of this expenditure of tax-raised funds is primarily the parochial school and incidently the pupil, or whether the aid is directly bestowed on the pupil with indirect benefits to the school. The state cannot maintain a Church and it can no more tax its citizens to furnish free carriage to those who attend a Church. The prohibition against establishment of religion cannot be circumvented by a subsidy, bonus or reimbursement of expenses to individuals for receiving religious instruction and indoctrination.

The court, however, compares this to other subsidies and loans to individuals and says, "Nor does it follow that a law has a private rather than a public purpose because it provides that tax-raised funds will be paid to reimburse individuals on account of money spent by them in a way which furthers a public program. . . ." Of course, the state may pay out tax-raised funds to relieve pauperism, but it may not spend funds to secure religion against skepticism. It may compensate individuals for loss of

tainly an inadequate reason for us to say that a legislature has erroneously appraised the public need.

It is true that this court has, in rare instances, struck down state statutes on the ground that the purpose for which tax-raised funds were to be expended was not a public one. . . . But the court has also pointed out that this far-reaching authority must be exercised with the most extreme caution. . . . Otherwise, a state's power to legislate for the public welfare might be seriously curtailed, a power which is a primary reason for the existence of states. . . .

This "establishment of religion" clause of the First Amendment means at least this: neither a state nor the Federal Government can set up a church. Neither can pass laws which aid one religion or prefer one religion over another. Neither can force nor influence a person to stay away from church against his will or force him to profess a belief or a disbelief in any religion. . . .

No tax in any amount large or small, can be levied to support any religious activities or institutions, whatever they may be called, or whatever form they may adopt to teach or practice religion. In the words of Jefferson, the clause against establishment of religion by law was intended to erect a wall of separation between church and state.

We must consider the New Jersey statute in accordance with the foregoing limitations imposed by the First Amendment. But we must not strike that statute down if it is within the State's constitutional power even though it approaches the verge of that power. . . .

The First Amendment has erected a wall between church and state. That wall must be kept high and impregnable. We could not approve the slightest breach. New Jersey

employment, but it cannot compensate them for adherence to a creed.

(Justice Rutledge)

This case forces us to determine squarely for the first time what was "an establishment of religion" in the First Amendment's conception and by that measure to decide whether New Jersey's action violates its command. . . .

Not simply an established church but any law respecting an establishment of religion is forbidden. The Amendment was broadly but not loosely phrased. . . .

The Amendment's purpose was not to strike merely at the official establishment of a single sect creed or religion, outlawing only a formal relation such as had prevailed in England and some of the colonies. Necessarily it was to uproot all such relationships. But the object was broader than separating church and state in this narrow sense. It was to create a complete and permanent separation of the spheres of religious activity and civil authority by comprehensively forbidding every form of public aid or support of religion. . . .

Two great drives are constantly in motion to abridge, in the name of education, the complete division of religion and civil authority which our forefathers made. One is to introduce religious education and observances into the public schools.

has not breached it here.

The other to obtain public funds for the aid and support of various private religious schools. . . . In my opinion both avenues were closed by the constitution. Neither should be opened by the court. The matter is not one of quantity to be measured by the amount of money expended. Now as in Madison's day it is one of principle, to keep separate spheres as the First Amendment drew them; to prevent the first experiment upon our liberties; and to keep the question from becoming entangled in corrosive precedents. We should not be less strict to keep strong and untarnished the one side of the shield of religious freedom than we have been of the other.

The judgment should be reversed.

Central School District v. Allen (1968)

In 1965 the New York State Legislature passed a law that required local school boards to purchase textbooks and lend them to students of private schools as well as to those of public schools. The law was challenged, on grounds of the First Amendment, by the Board of Education of the Central School District, which brought suit against James E. Allen Jr., who as Commissioner of Education in New York was responsible for implementing the statute. The case came to the United States Supreme Court by way of the New York Court of Appeals, which had held that the statute was constitutionally valid.

The United States Supreme Court upheld the lower courts ruling that the practice was constitutionally valid by a 6 to 3 decision based again on the child-benefit theory. Much of the Court's argument was based on the language of the Everson case, although two of the justices who had upheld the Everson decision dissented in this instance. The majority opinion was delivered by Justice White. Dissenting opinions were delivered by Justices Black and Douglas.

Majority Opinion
(Justice White)

. . . The statute upheld in Everson would be considered a law having "a secular legislative purpose and a primary effect that neither advances nor inhibits religion." We reach the same result with respect to the New York law requiring school books to be loaned free of charge to

Dissenting Opinion
(Justice Black)

. . . I believe the New York law held valid is a flat, flagrant, open violation of the First and Fourteenth Amendments. . . .

I know of no prior opinion of this Court upon which the majority here can rightfully rely to support its holding this New York law con-all students in specified grades. The express purpose of 701 was stated by the New York Legislature to be furtherance of the educational opportunities available to the young. Appellants have shown us nothing about the necessary effects of the statute that is contrary to its stated purpose. The law merely makes available to all children the benefits of a general program to lend school books free of charge. . . . Thus no funds or books are furnished to parochial schools, and the financial benefit is to parents and children, not to schools. . . .

The major reason offered by appellants for distinguishing free textbooks from free bus fares is that books, but not buses, are critical to the teaching process, and in a sectarian school that process is employed to teach religion. However this Court has long recognized that religious schools pursue two goals, religious instruction and secular education. . . . Nothing in this record supports the proposition that all textbooks, whether they deal with mathematics, physics, foreign languages, history, or literature, are used by the parochial schools to teach religion. . . . We are unable to hold, based solely on judicial notice, that this statute results in unconstitutional involvement of the State with religious instruction or that . . . this is a law respecting the establishment of religion within the meaning of the First Amendment.

stitutional. In saying this I am not unmindful of the fact that the New York Court of Appeals purported to follow Everson v. Board of Education, *supra,* in which this Court, in an opinion written by me, upheld a New Jersey law authorizing reimbursement to parents for the transportation of children attending sectarian schools. . . .

As my Brother Douglas so forcefully shows, in an argument with which I fully agree, upholding a State's power to pay bus or streetcar fares for school children cannot provide support for the validity of a state law using tax-raised funds to buy school books for a religious school. The First Amendment's bar to establishment of religion must preclude a State from using funds . . . to purchase books for use by sectarian schools, which, although "secular," realistically will in some way inevitably tend to propagate the religious views of the favored sect. Books are the most essential tool of education since they contain the resources of knowledge which the educational process is designed to exploit. In this sense it is not difficult to distinguish books, which are the heart of any school, from bus fares, which provide a convenient and helpful general public transportation service. . . .

This New York law, it may be said by some, makes but a small inroad and does not amount to complete establishment of religion. But that is no excuse for upholding it. . . .

I still subscribe to the belief that tax-raised funds cannot constitutionally be used to support religious schools, buy their school books, erect their buildings, pay their teachers, or pay any other of their maintenance expenses, even to the extent of one penny. . . . And I still believe that the only way to protect minority religious groups from ma-

jority groups in this country is to
keep the wall of separation between
church and state high and impregnable as the First and Fourteenth
Amendments provide. The Court's
affirmance here bodes nothing but
evil to religious peace in this country.

It is obvious, from the decision in the two cases cited, that to some
degree the doors have been opened for public support of religious
schools if that support can be argued on the child-benefit theory. Such
legislation is most often the result of powerful and persistent lobbyist
activities as well as political maneuvering on educational bills at both
state and federal levels. It is no secret that Catholic opposition has
effectively played its part to defeat federal aid proposals that did not
include provisions for the parochial school. Perhaps this was Justice
Black's thought in his dissent of the *Central v. Allen* decision when he
stated that:

> The same powerful sectarian religious propagandists who
> have succeeded in securing passage of the present law to
> help religious schools . . . can and doubtless will continue
> their propaganda, looking toward complete domination and
> supremacy of their particular brand of religion.

Although the Court has been willing to grant constitutional legality
to certain practices of public funding for religious schools they have
been strong, however, in their opposition to religious instruction or
practices in public schools.

released time for religious instruction in public schools

Religious instruction in variously arranged programs had by the 1940s
become a practice in a significant number of public schools in the
United States. In 1948 and again in '951 the Supreme Court was
obliged to rule on two different types of programs. The decisions in
these cases were significant in that they established a clearly defined
separationist view, which in one instance was based on the Establishment Clause and in the other on the Free-Exercise Clause. The two
cases discussed here are the *McCollum v. Board of Education* (1948)
and the *Zorach v. Clauson* (1952).

McCollum v. Board of Education (1948)
    The point in question in the McCollum case was whether or not a
released-time program for religious instruction on school property
was permissible under the terms of the Establishment Clause of the
First Amendment.

In 1940 the Champaign County (Illinois) Board of Education granted permission for religious instruction in grades four through nine in the public schools. The program was worked out in conjunction with a group made up of Protestant, Catholic, and Jewish citizens. Students were to be excused from regular classes one period or so a week to attend religious instruction. Each faith was to have its own class, and any pupil not participating was to attend a class in regular secular studies.

The plaintiff, Mrs. Vashti McCollum, whose son was in the schools, charged that the joint program violated the First and Fourteenth amendments. The Illinois State Supreme Court upheld the school board.

The United States Supreme Court reversed the ruling, by an 8 to 1 vote, holding that the practice was not permissible under terms of the First Amendment. Justice Black delivered the majority opinion. Justice Reed was the lone dissenter.

Majority Opinion
(Justice Black)
The operation of the State's compulsory education system thus assists and is integrated with the program of religious instruction carried on by separate religious sects. . . . This is beyond all question a utilization of the tax-established and tax-supported public school system to aid religious groups to spread their faith. And it falls squarely under the ban of the First Amendment. . . .

Here not only are the State's tax-supported public school buildings used for the dissemination of religious doctrines. The State also affords sectarian groups an invaluable aid in that it helps to provide pupils for their religious classes through use of the State's compulsory public school machinery. This is not separation of Church and State.

Dissenting Opinion
(Justice Reed)
I find it difficult to extract from the opinion any conclusion as to what it is in the Champaign plan that is unconstitutional. . . . None of the reversing opinions say whether the purpose of the Champaign plan for religious instruction during school hours is unconstitutional or whether it is some ingredient used in or omitted from the formula that makes the plan unconstitutional. . . . From the holding and the language of the opinions, I can only deduce that religious instruction of public school children during school hours is prohibited. The history of American Education is against such an interpretation of the First Amendment.

The phrase "an establishment of religion" may have been intended by Congress to be aimed only at a state church. . . . Passing years, however, have brought about the acceptance of a broader meaning, although never until today, I believe, has this Court widened its interpretation to any such degree as holding that recognition of the interest of our nation in religion, through the granting . . . of opportunity to pre-

sent religion as an optional, extracurricular subject during released
school time in public school buildings, was equivalent to the establishment of a religion. . . .

. . . I cannot agree with the
Court's conclusion that when pupils
compelled by law to go to school
for secular education are released
from school to attend the religious
classes, churches are unconstitution-
ally aided.

In the McCollum case the Court's primary argument was on the
point of use of public school buildings for religious instruction, but
they also argued that the state compulsory school machinery aided
the church. The second point, however, was apparently not to be
held as a pivotal point of the argument, for in the subsequent *Zorach
v. Clauson* case of 1952 it was discounted by the majority.

Zorach v. Clauson (1952)

The question in the Zorach case was whether a released-time program for religious instruction carried on outside of school property
was constitutionally valid. The case related specifically to a New
York City program that excused public school pupils from a part of
their school schedule each week to attend religious instruction in
their churches. Students not participating remained in their classrooms.

The one major difference between the Zorach case and the McCollum case was, of course, that the religious instruction was to take
place off school property. On the basis of this factor the Court ruled
by a 6 to 3 decision that the practice was constitutionally valid. The
majority opinion was presented by Justice Douglas. The dissenting
opinions, one of which was written by Justice Black, argued the point
that the compulsory school machinery was aiding the churches, an
argument proposed by the majority in the McCollum case.

Majority Opinion
(Justice Douglas)

It takes obtuse reasoning to inject
any issue of the "free exercise" of
religion in this case. No one is
forced to go to the religious classroom and no religious instruction is
brought into the classrooms of the
public schools. . . .

There is a suggestion that the
system involves the use of coercion
to get public school students into

Dissenting Opinion
(Justice Black)

. . . Here the sole question is
whether New York can use its compulsory education laws to help religious sects get attendants presumably too unenthusiastic to go unless
moved to do so by the pressure
of this state machinery. . . . The
state thus makes religious sects
beneficiaries of its power to compel
children to attend secular schools.

religious classrooms. There is no evidence in the record before us that supports that conclusion.

Any use of such coercive power by the state to help or hinder some religious sects or to prefer all religious sects over nonbelievers or vice versa is just what I think the First Amendment forbids.

We are a religious people whose institutions presuppose a Supreme Being. We guarantee the freedom to worship as one chooses. We make room for as wide a variety of beliefs and creeds as the spiritual needs of man deem necessary. . . . When the state encourages religious instruction or cooperates with religious authorities by adjusting the schedule of public events to sectarian needs, it follows the best of our traditions. . . . To hold that it may not would be to find in the Constitution a requirement that the government show a callous indifference to religious groups. That would be preferring those who believe in no religion over those who do believe.

The Court's validation . . . rests in part on its statement that Americans are "a religious people whose institutions presuppose a Supreme Being." This was at least as true when the First Amendment was adopted. . . . It was precisely because eighteenth-century Americans were a religious people divided into many fighting sects that we were given the constitutional mandate to keep Church and State separate.

. . . Before today, our judicial opinions have refrained from drawing invidious distinctions between those who believe in no religion and those who do believe. The First Amendment has lost much if the religious follower and the atheist are no longer to be judicially regarded as entitled to equal justice under law.

The significance of the dissenting opinion in the Zorach case is not to be overlooked, for to a great degree the arguments foretold the Court's direction in the 1960s on the prayer and Bible reading issues.

religious ceremony in public schools

The issue of religious ceremony in the public schools has never been so heated as it has been in recent years. With the Supreme Court's rulings in *Engel v. Vitale* (1962) and *Abington v. Schempp* (1963) banning prayer and Bible reading in the schools, the issue became so crucial that it led to two major attempts at constitutional revision.

Engel v. Vitale (1962)

At issue was a practice in the Hyde Park schools of New York State where a prayer, composed by the New York State Board of Regents, was required to be recited by each class at the beginning of each school day. The prayer read as follows:

Almighty God, we acknowledge our dependence upon Thee, and we beg Thy blessings upon us, our parents, our teachers and our Country.

Although provisions were made for nonparticipation by those not wanting to take part, the practice was challenged on the grounds that it was in violation of the Establishment Clause of the First Amendment. The United States Supreme Court reversed the decisions of New York's lower courts and ruled by a 6 to 1 decision that the practice was unconstitutional. The majority opinion was delivered by Justice Black. The lone dissenting position was written by Justice Stewart.

Majority Opinion
(*Justice Black*)

. . . the constitutional prohibition against laws respecting an establishment of religion must at least mean that in this country it is no part of the business of government to compose official prayers for any group of the American people to recite as a part of a religious program carried on by government.

There can be no doubt that New York's state prayer program officially establishes the religious beliefs embodied in the Regent's prayer. The respondent argument to the contrary, which is largely based upon the contention that the Regent's prayer is "non-denominational" and the fact that the program, as modified and approved by the state courts, does not require all pupils to recite the prayer . . . ignores the essential nature of the program's constitutional defects. Neither . . . fact . . . can serve to free it from the limitations of the Establishment Clause, as it might from the Free Exercise Clause, of the First Amendment. . . . Although these two clauses may in certain instances overlap, they forbid two quite different kinds of governmental encroachment upon religious freedom. The Establishment Clause, unlike the Free Exercise Clause, does not depend upon any showing of direct governmental compulsion and is violated by the enactment of laws which establish

Dissenting Opinion
(*Justice Stewart*)

The Court does not hold, nor could it, that New York has interfered with the free exercise of anybody's religion. For the state courts have made clear that those who object to reciting the prayer must be entirely free of any compulsion to do so. . . . But the Court says that in permitting school children to say this simple prayer, the New York authorities have established "an official religion."

With all respect, I think the Court has misapplied a great constitutional principle. I cannot see how an "official religion" is established by letting those who want to say a prayer say it. On the contrary, I think that to deny the wish of these school children to join in reciting this prayer is to deny them the opportunity of sharing in the spiritual heritage of our Nation. . . . What is relevant to the issue here is not the history of an established church in sixteenth-century England or in eighteenth-century America, but the history of religious traditions of our people, reflected in countless practices of the institutions and officials of our government.

an official religion whether those
laws operate directly to coerce non-
observing individuals or not.

The stand of the Court in the Engel case was clear in its opposition
to any degree of encroachment on the Establishment Clause. The fact
that the Regent's prayer was nondenominational might, in a narrow
sense, be an argument that its official use did not stand as example of
the government respecting the establishment of a single church. But,
as pointed out earlier in this chapter, a multiple establishment was
also prohibited by the Establishment Clause. The ruling in the Engel
case met with a great deal of public agitation, but its argument was
clear and sound. It portended the direction that the Court was to
take in the following year with its ruling on Bible reading and the
Lord's Prayer in the schools.

lord's prayer and bible reading in school

Abington v. Schempp (1963)
Murray v. Curlett (1963)

By 1963 a significant number of states either required or allowed
their public schools to have Bible reading and recitation of the Lord's
Prayer as part of their daily exercises. The two state laws on which
the Supreme Court rendered their decision opposing the practice were
those of Pennsylvania and Maryland. The Court ruled on both in one
decision since the cases were on the same issue. In both instances
the question was whether or not a state could require or allow any
kind of religous ceremony to be carried on in its schools even though
provisions allowed for nonparticipation. In both instances such provisions had been made previous to the Court's hearing. The plaintiffs
charged that the practice was unconstitutional on the basis of the
Establishment Clause of the First Amendment. The Court in an 8 to
1 decision held for the plaintiff and ruled that the practice of Bible
reading and prayer in the public schools was unconstitutional. The
majority opinion was presented by Justice Clark. The lone dissenter
was Justice Stewart. The full decision of the Court summarizes very
effectively the recent history of adjudication of questions involving
church-state-school relationships. Only brief excerpts are offered
here.

Majority Opinion
(Justice Clark)
. . . the Establishment Clause has
been directly considered by this
Court eight times in the past score
of years and, with only one Justice
dissenting on the point, it has con-

Dissenting Opinion
(Justice Stewart)
. . . what is involved is not state
action based on impermissible categories, but rather an attempt by the
State to accommodate those differences which the existence in our so-

sistently held that the clause with-
drew all legislative power respecting religious belief or the expression
thereof. The test may be stated as
follows: what are the purpose and
the primary effect of the enactment?
If either is the advancement or in-
hibition of religion then the enactment exceeds the scope of legislative
power as circumscribed by the Constitution. . . .

The conclusion follows that in
both cases the laws require religious exercises and such exercises
are being conducted in direct violation of the right of the appellees and
petitioners. Nor are these required
exercises mitigated by the fact that
individual students may absent
themselves upon parental request,
for that fact furnishes no defense to
a claim of unconstitutionality under
the Establishment Clause. . . . Further, it is no defense to urge that
the religious practice here may be
relatively minor encroachments on
the First Amendment. The breach
of neutrality that is today a trickling
stream may all too soon become a
raging torrent and, in the words of
Madison, "it is proper to take alarm
at the first experiment on our liberties."

. . . In the relationship between
man and religion, the State is firmly
committed to a position of neutrality. Though the application of that
rule requires interpretation of a del-
icate sort, the rule itself is clearly
and concisely stated in the words of
the First Amendment.

ciety of a variety of religious beliefs
makes inevitable. The Constitution
requires that such efforts be struck
down only if they are proven to entail the use of the secular authority
of government to coerce a preference among the beliefs.

. . . religious exercises are not
constitutionally invalid if they simply reflect differences which exist in
the society from which the school
draws its pupils. They become constitutionally invalid only if their administration places the sanction of
secular authority behind one or
more particular religious or irreligious beliefs.

To be specific, it seems to me
clear that certain types of exercises
would present situations in which
no possibility of coercion on the
part of secular officials could be
claimed to exist. . . .

Although the decisions of the Supreme Court on religion in the
schools were argued on solid constitutional grounds they have nevertheless met with a practiced opposition. Obviously there are some
institutional positions that would hold intrinsic opposition to the
Court's decisions. There are also some patterns of regional interests
that can be accounted for. In many instances, though, the issue has
become a convenient emotional perch from which to attack not only
the Court, but the schools as well. Many of the perennial foes of the

public school have found something to either replace or to revitalize
their older, tiring arguments. Others have found an issue that can be
effectively utilized for many nonrelated political purposes.

religious institutional positions

It is to be expected that particular religious institutional positions
regarding the issue of religion and education will be varied in accordance with specific practices in question. It is also to be expected that
on the issue of religious instruction in the schools, which was ruled
out in the McCollum case, one would find some agreement by the
major religious institutions. In a sense, their mutual interests were
met in the Zorach case. But beyond this area of partial agreement
the picture of unity breaks apart. On issues involving public monies
for parochial schools or religious exercises in public schools the single
institutional positions are in accordance with their particular interests.

It is not surprising that the Catholic Church in America has been
the most vocal and persistent in its attempts to get public tax monies
for its schools. To some extent it was given encouragement by the
Supreme Court decision in the Everson case. Since that time the efforts to obtain public monies, either state or federal, have increased
significantly, and with some success as is evidenced by the New York
textbook plan as well as by the National Defense Education Act of
1958 and the Elementary and Secondary Education Act of 1965. The
latter two programs have included allotments to parochial schools for
special areas defined as secular in nature. Federal programs that do
not include Catholic schools thus far are likely to meet an early death
in Congress with Catholic opposition adding the needed strength to
the Southern states-rights block.

In pressing for tax support for schools the Catholic Church most
often bases its argument on the grounds that its schools save the taxpayers a great deal of money and that its members are doubly taxed
for education. The former argument stands without question, but it
is subordinate to the schools' purposes. The second argument, however, does not stand. The only compulsory taxation is governmental.
Monies paid by Catholic parents are voluntary contributions for the
support of a private, sectarian school that they choose along very
personal lines. (Their right to choose a private education was guaranteed by the Supreme Court's decision in the Oregon case in 1925.)

Instances of Protestant denominations and Jews subscribing to
public support for their schools have been rare as compared to the
Catholic position. Protestant and Jewish leaders have largely opposed
programs of public support for religious schools on the grounds that
it abridges the Establishment Clause. However, the Protestant position on the Establishment Clause has not been so consistent in apply-
ing it to the question of prayer and Bible reading in the public schools.

institutional position on prayer and bible reading

Certainly it can be argued that until the Abington-Schempp case the public schools in many parts of the country were Protestant in nature. That is, they allowed religious practices that were exclusive of Jews, Catholics, other religious or nonreligious minorities, as well as atheists. The point of exclusion, however, was not the basis of the Supreme Court's decision in the Abington-Schempp case. The decision was based on a clear interpretation of the Establishment Clause in its multiple sense. The Court could not have logically ruled otherwise. But the religious institutional positions on the issue of prayer and Bible reading in public schools are not as clearly defined as are their positions on tax support for parochial schools. In a sense, one would expect the Catholic position to have supported the Court's ruling, but in many instances its leadership spoke out in opposition. Cardinals McIntyre of Los Angeles and Spellman of New York spoke harshly of the decision. Even Cardinal Cushing of Boston demanded an amendment to the Constitution permitting Bible reading in the schools.[14] Where before the Catholic Church had found the schools to be sectarian, they now charged them with secularism. One would have thought that the trend toward neutralism would have been welcomed by the Church.

The Protestant reaction has, of course, been varied not only in accordance with denominational differences, but also with regional differences. For the most part the northern Protestant leaders have supported the decision on prayer and Bible reading. In some instances this was true even before the Court's ruling. In May, 1963, the General Assembly of the United Presbyterian Church declared its opposition to religious observances in public schools. The National Council of Churches in June, 1963, stated a similar position.[15] Of course, this stood only as the official institutional position in these instances.

There are, to be sure, communities as well as individuals in all parts of the country that oppose the Court's ruling. But in many instances the flaunted opposition is seen by some as a convenient camouflage for more serious concerns. For example, the southern Dixiecrats' continued and, at times, vicious opposition to the Court's decision might be their way of striking at the Court that handed down the 1954 decision against racial segregation. The concerted efforts of southern Dixiecrats and northern conservatives have continually brought forth attempts at amendments to the Constitution that would, in a sense, reverse the Court's decisions. The most prominent of the proposals toward this end have been the Becker Amendment and the Dirksen

---

[14] Paul Blanshard, *Religion and the Schools: The Great Controversy* (Boston: Beacon Press, 1963), p. 117.
[15] *Ibid.*, p. 117.

Amendment, both of which would repudiate the Court's decison. This in itself would be a tragic reversal toward establishment if a constitutional convention were called and one such amendment ratified. More tragic would be the attempts at further constitutional revision in the area of civil rights. There is no doubt that this is uppermost in the minds of a significant number of southern legislators, who would like to turn the clock back on civil rights. All critics of the Court's decision on prayer and Bible reading are not to be aligned with civil rights opponents, but the flames of controversy over the issue are continually being fanned by various groups whose underlying concerns seem not to be prayer, but states' rights.

Critics of the Court's rulings on religion in the schools often charge that the ruling benefits the minority groups. This would, of course, be true if the Court had allowed for a minority religious program to be carried on; if the Bible were replaced by the Koran or the Torah, the Lord's Prayer by the Fatiha or the Shema. However, the Court ruled against any religious exercises in the public schools. Therefore, the public schools are to be neutral in matters religious.

This neutrality has often been the basis of a second and more widely used argument by critics of the Court. They charge that without religion the schools are thus robbed of their ability to develop moral and spiritual values. Implied is the belief that a short daily prayer and a few passages from the Bible somehow constitute the schools' involvement with moral questions. If this were the case, if the schools' delusions were so great, then removing this crutch of morality might in a sense move the schools toward a more realistic and meaningful encounter with moral questions.

Without a doubt the church-state issue in education is one which will remain critical. Some school districts have openly violated the Supreme Court's rulings, thus displaying their lack of understanding of the Establishment Clause or their disagreement with it. The issue of public monies for parochial schools is also an issue that will be in need of continual ruling. Although the Court's language allowed that the school curriculum might include teaching about religion in a comparative or historical manner, it is obvious that any critical approach to the subject would meet with some disagreement from one group or another.

In the light of history the road to religious neutrality in the public schools has been a difficult one, but it has been traveled. The progress thus made speaks clearly of the vitality of our Constitution.

topics for inquiry

1. The Pattern of Decisions Regarding Religion Made by Individual Supreme Court Justices
2. The Relationship Between Public and Parochial Schools in Your District
3. Admissions Policies and Practices of Parochial Schools
4. The Origins of Reaction Against the Supreme Court Ruling on Prayer and Bible Readings
5. Educational Costs in Public and Parochial Schools in Your Area
6. Your District's or State's Curricular Plans for the Study of Religion as a Subject
7. Comparison of Public School and Parochial School Editions of Textbooks
8. Released-time Practices in Your District or State
9. Cooperative Busing Plans Between Public and Parochial Schools in Your Area or State

subjects for discussion

1. On the questions of public monies for busing and textbooks the Supreme Court draws a distinction between aid to religion and child benefit.
   a. Is the distinction tenable?
   b. What are some arguments against it?
   c. Should such issues be argued on legal or pragmatic grounds?
2. If public monies are given to parochial schools, should they also be given to private secular schools? Are these schools different in a legal sense?
3. Some critics of the public schools have suggested a new pattern of public funding for education. One plan proposes to have a stated amount, say $600, for each child, alloted to the parents for education. They would then select a school, religious or secular, for their children.
   a. What would be some of the advantages and disadvantages?
   b. What could be some of the social consequences of such a plan?
   c. If such a plan were put in effect, what might be some of the results in a competitive business sense?

selected readings

BLANSHARD, PAUL. *Religion and the Schools: The Great Controversy.* Boston: Beacon Press, 1963.

> Illuminating details about the immediate institutional responses to the Supreme Court's rulings on prayer and Bible reading in the schools.

DUKER, SAM. *The Public Schools and Religion: The Legal Context.* New York: Harper & Row, 1966.

> The legal aspect of the religion-education issue with limited but pertinent excerpts from the Supreme Court decisions.

KLIEBARD, HERBERT M. *Religion and Education In America: A Documentary History.* Scranton, Pa.: International Textbook, 1969.

> A valuable source book with extended Supreme Court Decisions. Also presents some important historical developments with supportive documentation.

LAWRENCE, JEROME, and ROBERT E. LEE. *Inherit the Wind.* New York: Boston Books, 1960.

> An intriguing dramatization of the Scopes Monkey Trial of the 1920s. It is important for its historical value and its psycho-sociological analysis of fundamentalism.

MILLER, ARTHUR. *The Crucible.* New York: Boston Books, 1959.

> A fascinating and historically accurate drama about the Salem Witch Trials that furnishes an illuminating view of day-to-day early New England life.

SIZER, THEODORE R. (ed.). *Religion and Public Education.* Boston: Houghton Mifflin, 1967.

> A valuable collection of essays on the philosophical and theological aspects of the religion and education issues.

STARKEY, MARION L. *The Devil in Massachusetts.* New York: Knopf, 1949.

> A delightful scholarly account of the Salem Witch Trials. The writing style brings forth the mood of the times.

7
THE
SCHOOLS
AND THE
PUBLIC: THE
PUBLIC
AND THE
SCHOOLS

Each weekday morning about 200 million Americans get up and go. Where do they go? In many directions—back to their kitchens and household chores; out to play, off to the office, the assembly line, the store, the shop, the mill, the filling station, and so on ad infinitum. Many routes, many jobs, to be sure, but three out of ten are going to the same place—to school. No other institution or occupation enlists nearly so large a fraction of the population. Thus the startling generalization that: *America's Number One occupation is going to school* is indisputable.

Of these 60 million school-goers, about 51 million are children heading for kindergarten or high school, or way-points between. Nine million are adults, of whom over 7 million are students at college and university (whom we choose to classify as adults, in the conviction that they should be so regarded) and about 2.7 million are teachers, supervisors, and administrators. Sixty million and more when you include those who attend school as as "avocation." This is a big country, but that is still a lot of people. It is more than the population of either France or Great Britain— and all going to school.

Just to man the elementary classrooms there are about 1.25 million elementary school teachers. That means there is about one teacher to thirty pupils at this level. Which means that on the average this teacher does not exactly have a soft touch as far as teaching load is concerned. If each teacher were paid the most modest baby-sitting rate of 50 cents an hour for the seven hours daily that he was in charge of these children over a 180-day school year, the an nual salary simply for assuming this level of care would be $9,450. This is cheaper than most baby-sitting, but it is considerably greater than the average teaching salary in 1970. Furthermore, it is generally assumed that the teachers' responsibilities and trained capacities will somewhat exceed those of baby-sitters. The children are not, of course, evenly distributed among the teachers. Miss Evers, in the suburbs, may greet the new day with a smile anticipating the pleasure of working with fifteen to twenty-five children in her second-grade classroom in the shiny new school. Miss Nevers too may enjoy the children, but she may head for the bus or subway on the way to the urban school with a more preoccupied look on her countenance as she contemplates on how many of them—perhaps forty, fifty, or even sixty—there are to enjoy, and presumably to teach.

where we find ourselves

In the United States we find ourselves living in a great nation and a situation made up of many contradictions. We live in affluent society, the richest in history in material terms. Yet one-fifth of our families live below the poverty level—and that defined as below $3,500 per year.

We live in a land, as Lincoln put it a century ago, "dedicated to the proposition that all men are created equal." Yet 23 million black Americans know that equality in every practical sense has traditionally been denied them—at the ballot box, in education, in the job market, in housing, in acceptance, and in the recognition of their human dignity.

We live in an advanced era of technology and science. Research has put an end to the dread of polio, diphtheria, small pox, tetanus, scarlet fever, and other ills. Yet we find billions to send men to the dreary face of the moon, but not enough millions to complete the research on cancer or the common cold. Research has spelled out the connection between cigarette smoking and lung cancer, emphysema, and heart disease. Yet busy enterprisers still spend millions in a conscienceless effort to peddle their cigarette death dealers. Technology has given us television, put it in practically every home. Yet this miracle for communication is chiefly employed to convey junk and to sell soap.

We live in a world where it would be job enough to feed and to shelter the human billions. Yet the common game of the nations is to squander their budgets on the unproductive and unnourishing armament industry.

We live in a world that knows from history that wars are madness. We live for the first time in history with the capacity to eradicate human life from the planet. The Soviet Union and the United States both possess the capacity for "overkill"—this strange word means more than enough deadly stuff to kill everybody. Yet nations plan for war and improve armaments "defensively," as though it were sane and sensible to plan for the suicide of mankind.

We live in a nation that prints "In God We Trust" upon its coins and insists on saying "one nation under God" in its pledge of allegiance; in a nation where the religious establishment is so rich that its buildings are among the most magnificent structures in every community. Yet to suggest that in business, or in politics, or in international affairs, or in labor relations the discipline of religious teaching should greatly affect decision-making would be commonly regarded as pure simple-minded nonsense.

In a word, with these and so many other contradictions in mind, it must seem that as a civilization we are just not putting our know-how together very well. These contradictions are at least hurting and dividing us; at worst, unless we learn to put it all together, they can kill us. That is where we live. And the big excitement about taking on a job in education is that you might play a part in putting it together. Nothing could be more worth working and living for.

the burden of cultural pluralism

Cultural pluralism is an American fact of life and one of the nation's primary characteristics. It enriches the nation, lends variety, extends its reaches, multiplies the richness of its arts. It also poses many problems. Cultural pluralism makes life better for Americans; it also makes it harder. It is not customary to speak of cultural pluralism as a burden, but burden it is. One of the hardest things about being an American is having to live, and learning to live, in a community of such diverse cultural backgrounds. The common denominators of American culture are considerable and need to be noted:

1. A common language comprehensible to all. One contribution of the mass media, building on what the school accomplished, has been to pull usage and pronunciation together. This and the mobility of modern America, assures that its spoken medium will strengthen as a common tool, rather than diminish due to the centrifugal forces of isolation and provincialism.
2. A general agreement that the United States is a good place to live — with some exceptions. To live here constituted a choice for most at some historic time—with the exception of Afro-Americans, who mostly were brought to our shores for other peoples' reasons.
3. A general consensus that its framework of constitutional democracy is preferable to other systems of government.
4. A general consensus that its economic system, loosely labeled free enterprise, with private property rights and the protection of these under the law, is generally preferable to other more limited and controlled systems.

5. A general—but a woefully inadequate—understanding of its history and its basic institutions.
6. A common culture of broadly utilized instruments: baseball, football, and other sports; cinemas and drive-ins; drug stores and supermarkets and shopping centers; television; automobiles. The psychologically unifying aspects of these could easily be overrated. All they say, in general, is that Americans like them.

Cultural pluralism cuts in many directions; it does not slice simply in one dimension. Its dimensions are ethnic, religious, educational, social class, economic, and political, among others. In a classroom two students might reflect similar cultural origins:

Parents: Upper-middle class
Religion: Protestant Methodist
Education: Both parents college graduates
Ethnic: Anglo-Saxon

Such students might be predicted to be quite similar in outlook and quite compatible personally. But this is not necessarily true. Other factors—such as political differences, personality traits, occupational variations, differing views of church, different home practices in child-rearing—complicate the patterns and reduce predictability to riskiness.

Two students whose backgrounds were congruent except for one factor, *race*, might be presumed to have very different outlooks and aspirations because of that *one factor*. They might, but if you have observed widely among people, again they might not.

The lack of congruence in any identifiable category might lead to a prediction of utterly dissimilar persons and a probability of considerable incompatability. The odds are no doubt increased that these things will be so. But, again, it ain't necessarily so. The individuals—for example, two fifteen-year old boys who have no similar categories—are human, and human inclusiveness encompasses all categories. Both, despite differing class, religious, racial, economic, and family backgrounds, are human. The common denominator of *humanness*, based on universal hungers, needs, aspirations may dwarf all other considerations.

Getting around in a culturally pluralistic society is difficult sometimes. It means frictions over preferences, misunderstanding of the uses of unfamiliar words and phrases, a different calendar of holidays and meaningful events. But universal education brings together at best all the children of all the people. Its greatest job is to teach them the binders, the common denominators of humanness. It has to develop the understanding that there are many manners of fulfilling them but that the needs of all men are common needs. A large support for this basic function of democratic education exists. However, many fear and dread it—and oppose it bitterly.

the educational establishment

The American educational enterprise is big. Over 7 million are enrolled in its colleges and universities. High school enrollment in 1970 was over the 14.5 million mark. And the elementary schools number approximately 37 million pupils. Over 2,677,000 teachers constitute the instructional force. The figures cited include both private and public education.

Such a vast structure is expensive. The average teacher salary was $8,300 per year in 1970 and quite sure to increase. For the same year annual expenses for higher education totaled about $23 billion (almost as costly as putting two men briefly on the moon). The public sector of elementary and secondary education (90 percent of the total) cost about $38 billion dollars annually. Education is so expensive that its annual total cost is actually *over half* that of the nation's military budget.

Education in the United States is not a huge hierarchical structure. In considerable degree the most effective operational power resides at the local level. The states by constitutional reservation hold educational authority. In this country there is no national ministry of education.

The United States Office of Education in the Department of Health, Education, and Welfare (USOE of HEW) prior to World War II was small, lethargic, and not influential. Its functions were nominal— mainly, to collect statistics and to give advice. Professionally, it generally was held in friendly disregard. Today the USOE has real power, real influence, and generates from time to time the whole gamut of reactions from high regard to contempt. The change in posture is due to money and programs. The federal government in 1969 appropriated $3.7 billion for aid to education (not all administered by USOE). Two acts of Congress, the National Defense Education Act and the Elementary and Secondary Education Act, have translated the office into an operational agency. It awards large contracts, conducts major research programs, distributes funds, conducts workshops and institutes, purchases materials and equipment, influences curriculum in cities and towns throughout the land, and hires personnel by the thousands. Such is the stuff of power.

Having money, program, and power, the USOE has become involved in politics. Contrary to theory, but in fact, the USOE lobbies for appropriations and extended programs and power. It has employed power and also has been caught in the middle of political power plays with respect to school desegregation, award of contracts, urban educational policies, and many other educational matters. It is embroiled in a tangled web of academic politics, especially in the award of research grants and contracts.

Washington, D.C., as the capital of the nation is the abode of much power in education. Not all of it is centered in government, but all "factions" with an "interest" in education are located in D.C. because the seat of government is there. Over one hundred agencies of the federal government are involved in education. The National Institute of Health (NIH) and National Science Foundation are important research agencies. The Pentagon administers billions for training and education. The federal Department of Agriculture and the Department of the Interior have long directed educational programs. The latter is responsible for education of American Indians.

Non-governmental educational agencies in Washington are led by two institutions: the National Education Association (NEA), focus of public school activity and influence, and the American Council on Education, legislative watchdog and lobbyist for the organized force of higher education.

the national education association

The largest and most influential organizational force in the nation, the NEA is a comprehensive federal-type organization with an effective line structure. It is *also* a confederate association of affiliated organizations with varying degrees of autonomy. All activities are centered in the family structure in Washington, D.C.

The most powerful of the affiliated organizations is the American Association of School Administrators (AASA). For many years the AASA dominated the structure and decision-making of the NEA, but its influence has greatly diminished, if not ended. The rise in strength of the Department of Classroom Teachers has been a factor in the undermining of the AASA domination.

The growth of NEA from its humble origins in 1857, and its membership of 2,332 at the turn of the century, to its present massive membership is shown in Figure 6. The Representative Assembly, the body of delegates which serves as the legislative and policy body of the association, now exceeds the total membership in 1910.

The size of the Representative Assembly is a formidable obstacle to legislative achievement. It is a body that meets annually for about one week, which consists of over twelve times the number of members of the Congress of the United States. The brevity of the legislative session plus its unwieldy size shifts great power and influence onto the executive branch, consisting of the Board of Directors, and the smaller Executive Committee. Much effective power resides in the permanent secretariat of over 1,300 staff members directed by the Executive Secretary. Between 1893 and 1970 only six people had held this position, a period in which there have been fourteen different occupants of the office of the President of the United States. The administrative responsibilities, the residual influence in year-round management, and the established continuity of the office combine to make the $50,000

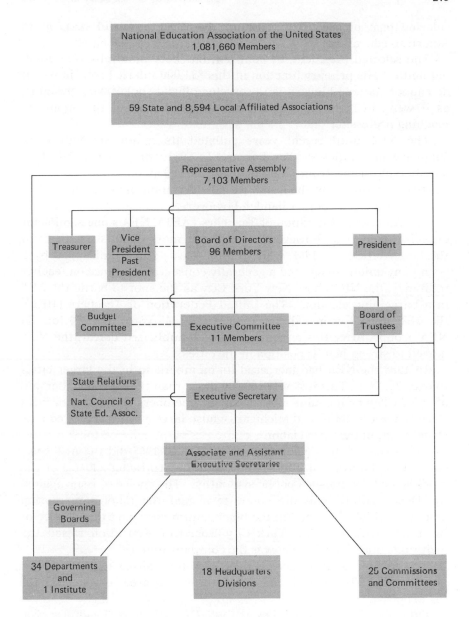

FIGURE 6 *The Organizational Structure of the National Education Association*

Source: National Education Association, *NEA Handbook* (Washington, D.C.: NEA, 1968), p. 19.

salaried post of executive secretary the most powerful position in American education.

The selected president, by contrast, has become a relatively nominal figure. His primary function in this $21,000 salaried role, in which he cannot succeed himself, is to serve as official spokesman, engaging, as it were, in high-level public relations on behalf of the organized teaching profession.

The NEA until recent years enlisted its major strength from smaller communities and rural areas. In 1961, only 22.1 percent of its membership came from cities of over 100,000 population. A city of thirty, sixty, or ninety thousand, we would remind metropolitan readers is not exactly a country hamlet, however.

The American Federation of Teachers (AFT), NEA's one significant organizational rival, however, has enlisted most of its strength from the larger cities. In 1961, while the NEA was still handicapped by a "company-union" image and a generally conservative stance on teacher militancy, the NEA chose New York City as the spot to battle the AFT in a bargaining election. The United Federation of Teachers (UFT), the AFT affiliate, won a decisive victory, 20,045 votes to 9,770 for the NEA group. After this crushing, and well-publicized defeat, the NEA moved to strengthen its position in the cities.

In 1968 the NEA had increased its membership in the larger cities to over 250,000. This is nearly 100,000 more than the total membership of the AFT, which counts almost half its members in the three states of New York, Illinois, and Michigan, whose largest cities are, of course, strongholds of organized labor.

The strike of the UFT in New York City in 1968 did the AFT little good in the interorganizational contest. The protracted closing of the city's schools diminished public sympathy. The choice of issue against the Ocean Hill-Brownsville board tarnished the union's reputation among black teachers and in the black community, and the alliance of the union with the New York City Board of Education raised the legitimate question, "Who now is the company union?"

The AFT periodically makes overtures for uniting with the larger organization. To date, the NEA has shown no great enthusiasm for the proposal.

Other headquarters affiliates at the NEA include national organizations of school subject fields, such as the National Council for the Social Studies (NCSS), the National Council of Teachers of Mathematics (NCTM), the National Science Teachers Association (NSTA), and the Music Educators National Conference (MENC). Exceptional in its absence from this roster is the National Council of Teachers of English (NCTE), which preserves an isolation all its own.

Other institutions in the educational establishment include the influential accrediting agencies. Accreditation is the process by which standards of institutional quality in schools and colleges are maintained with respect to qualified faculty, facilities, and program. The

National Council for the Accreditation of Teacher Education (NCATE) exerts strong influence on the preparation of teachers. The regional accrediting agencies—such as the North Central Association, the Middle States Association, the Southern Association—form a network for the maintenance of professional standards across the nation. The practical advantages of accreditation include at the school level: facilitation of transfer of credits from school to school, a positive asset in the recruitment of professional staff, and recognition of credits for college admission. At the college level, these things operate similarly. Furthermore, the prestige factor is enhanced at this level, and the recognition of credits becomes particularly important for admission to graduate and professional schools. The graduate of the nonaccreditated school or college may achieve all these things, but usually with added difficulties.

These organizations and associations relate to the formal educational enterprise, to the schools. They help to build cohesion and coordination into the "educational establishment."

the state of public information

However, that the American public is not informed and educated exclusively by its schools is an established fact. The other sources of information are the media, the common culture, and the circumstances. The *media*, of course, are the instruments by which varied messages and symbols and images are transmitted from an originating source to the receiver. They include newspapers, magazines, billboards and posters, radio, television, and books. The *common culture* may be defined as what most people think and feel about most things most of the time. *Circumstances*, in our context, stand for reality, or the way things are, or are becoming, or have become. Of course, these three information sources tend to mix and to relate to one another.

The question arises, Is the American public well informed? It is a good question, which we can extend and illuminate—but not answer definitively. But it is a question that teachers and educators should consider.

For purpose of analysis the question can be approached from the fourfold categorization of a complete education proposed earlier: the humanistic-ethical, the vocational-utilitarian, the scientific-quantitative, and the creative-aesthetic. Each of these dimensions may be considered in view of certain evidences, positive and negative, with some of the ambiguities and contradictions pertinent to them. Then the effects, the contributions, the limitations, the distortions of the informing sources may be examined. By this approach it may be possible to achieve a sort of composite view of the educational profile of the public and some view of the adequacy and quality of the sources that inform it.

The *humanistic-ethical* dimension of learning suffers from no lack of good intent. There is scarcely any cultural isolation so extreme or cultural deprivation so severe that anyone is at a loss for the "good" words and "good" concepts that Western civilization has developed as basic codes for human conduct. It seems unlikely that vast numbers of people suffer from lack of instruction that lying, stealing, killing are wrongdoings.

Then, how do we account for the fact that so much general behavior contradicts the readily available instruction? It is nothing new that man in all his complexity is hard to govern. Powerful human drives exist that are counter to the governing restraints that civilization would impose. These drives include biological urges, visceral hungers, demands for recognition, and culturally supported traits of acquisition and ambition. If circumstances do not permit the fulfillment of these drives in legitimate and socially approved channels, there is much in the human person that dictates that he go after what he wants either deviously or directly outside those channels.

Contradictions deep within the nature of the learner are neither minimized nor dismissed, but it is our intent to point up another root to the problem. There are also contradictions in the messages delivered by the media, the common culture, and circumstance. These are by no means as simple, direct, and unequivocal as the Decalogue or the lessons taught in Sunday school.

As a matter of fact, there is often a colossal ambiguity within the institutions that themselves purport to transmit messages of urgent, unalterable truth. The churches, an intrinsic part of our culture, are related to things of the spirit; yet they have built themselves some of the most impressive material edifices upon the scene. They own empires of land and property. They lend money, take rents, and operate businesses. This tends to obscure the meaning of such texts as "You cannot serve God and Mammon." And the public reflects the fact that the point is thoroughly confused in its mind.

One would suppose that of all literal truths the one taught most literally and unequivocally would be "Thou shalt not kill." It is almost beyond doubt that the crime of murder is instructed, by religious teachers and at a mother's knee, with the utmost of repugnance toward the deed. But, the message as received by the public from all sources is by no means clear-cut. Given a nation's sanction, a regimented mass of men wearing similar suits of clothes may kill upon a vast scale and receive public acclaim, even be regarded as heroic for extra devotion and efficiency at the task. The public has no unequivocal instruction on war, although the official view tends to be a favorable one when the circumstances as interpreted by the officials warrant it.

And the public still kills in the name of repressing killing in a diminishing number of states that still practice capital punishment. Regardless of other dimensions of the argument, this must surely tend to confuse the public about the commandment "Thou shalt not kill."

What about the sanction of killing people by other means—tobacco, air and water pollutants, for example? Society not only countenances such murder in the private, unofficial sector, but also allows the public solicitation of victims. It awards good incomes and even great fortunes to those involved.

Our purpose is not at this point to take issue with the by-products of the way people earn a living. It is to show contradictions in the "curriculum" for modern Americans. From the evidence it would appear that a consistent and meaningful directive on killing is hard to define. Could that help to account for the amount of gleeful and witless violence that troubles our society?

The *vocational-utilitarian* dimension is of primary importance within the common culture. Folklore and ancient wisdom alike sanction elementary principles about the importance of work. The notion that income must come from an honorable source has traditional support. The idea that life is to some degree justified by and connected with productive effort resides in the culture. But it is obvious even to the child that the most useful deeds are not the best rewarded. Some of the most frivolous, and indeed, some of the most antisocial, are.

The contradictions of affluence are evident everywhere. Farmers, workmen, manufacturers—all have learned to restrict production to increase their cash returns. It all comes under the heading of economic necessity, but it does tend to induce contradiction in young minds.

The *scientific-quantitative* dimension is constantly being abused by the general public. Reasoned arguments can be brought to bear against the idea that science constitutes the sole method of intelligence. Yet contradictions to sense that have no reasoned basis abound in the common culture. It is incredible that a people who has sent its emissaries to the moon still constitutes a lucrative market for the hocus-pocus of soothsayers, fortune tellers, horoscope casting, and astrologers. To the extent that this is playful, it is as harmless as laughing over a message in a fortune cookie. But it is not playful in the aggregate. It is a big business promoted by cynical men for profit and sometimes a petty racket. To fool around in the realm of magic is worse than a by-pass of the method of intelligence, it is a rejection of it.

How silly it seems to be writing such words in 1971! Yet a true and full report requires it. It is not so much that we begrudge the charlatans their rice bowls or their fortunes. It is that responsible educators must identify and go to work on behaviors that deprive man of his surest chance of perceiving his fate and somewhat mastering it, and that is through the use of—not the rejection of—his intelligence.

The public is much informed in the *creative-aesthetic* dimension, which is not to say well informed. But, at least, in the common culture an individual is amid a plethora of stimuli, which is not always true in school. Music of sorts is everywhere; he can hardly get away

from it. Pop art has improved even the packaging of his most transient consumer goods. Who would venture a definitive view on the
state of American taste or the condition of the arts in the republic?
At any rate, there is abundance. In sum, the American seems to know
what he likes, at any given moment. And he backs his judgment up:
he buys a lot of what he likes. Ordinarily, however, he is inarticulate
when it comes to saying why.

   Still, the educated man has usually had a rationale for all of his
choices. He has been able to talk somewhat sensibly about his preferences, even in the aesthetic realm. So most gingerly in this realm, on
the sole criterion of his inability to express himself on the subject,
though he buys and consumes much art, we hazard the opinion that
the American in general is less than adequately developed in this dimension.

the media as educators

In certain fundamental areas the education of the person is much
more accomplished by the mass media—television, radio, newspapers,
magazines—than the school. These areas in which the principal
weight of instruction is carried by nonschool agencies are:

1. The report and analysis of meaning of events in the world.
2. The development of knowledge of political behavior and the formation of political attitudes.
3. At home, civic issues such as transportation, housing, air pollution.
4. The shaping of tastes and aesthetic judgments in such matters as
   music, art, foods, fashions, home decoration.
5. The introduction to new participants and new ideas in the world of
   literature and culture.
6. The direction of interests in entertainment: what is going on, where
   it is, what it is about.
7. Consumer education: what to buy and where to get it.

   This is a formidable curriculum. When you look it over, it seems
to leave the school a fairly limited function, which might be summed
up as:

1. Teaching skills of the three Rs.
2. Keeping children institutionalized and certified for the next levels
   of formal schooling.

   If these two items are all there is to formal education, then the
multibillion-dollar annual investment in the schools looks like a rather
bad bargain. We must examine the functions of the media and the
schools more closely.

   This first critical point must be the limitations upon the media as educators. In the main, their competence is limited to reporting, gaining a large audience, exciting, entertaining, and selling. The media do all the things set forth, and more too, but they do them with severe limitations of competence and motivations that disqualify them as educators. The function of the media in basic terms is to sell: first, to sell themselves, get viewers, enroll subscribers; and second, to sell products, to advertise. *Selling* is the root of the matter. The media, no matter what is learned from them, exist to sell, *not* educate. And they are masters at selling. An economic system based on mass consumership could scarcely exist without the media, without advertising. And the key to successful advertising is mass audience, through mass appeal.

Herein lies the key to the educational disqualification of the media, which is threefold:

1. They direct themselves to the mass rather than to the individual.
2. They seek to use—even to abuse—the individual by getting him to do something primarily for someone else's advantage, while lulling or conning him into the belief that it is to his own advantage.
3. They are directed to the irrational. They appeal to the primitive and relatively uncontrolled aspects of human behavior.

With regard to the first disqualification when applied to the schools, it is always an error to refer to the American establishment of schools as mass education. The schools reach large aggregates, but in basic purpose and theory they are not masses, merely large numbers of persons. The aim of education is not to condition mass behavior; it is to develop self-aware individuals who know how to make intelligent choices for their own advantage in a developed sense of social responsibility.

The media at every hand exploit the person. Beginning with the little children, they keep the environment emblazoned and raucous with the carnival sight and sounds of the barkers and hawkers of goods. We recommend that each student watch so-called "children's programming" for a week (around 4 to 6 daily, plus Saturday and Sunday mornings).

The predictable outcome for a reasonably intelligent viewer of children's TV programs, for example, is an emotional revulsion ranging from annoyance to nausea and moral indignation. The programing itself is not the principal issue. That nine-tenths of it is repetitious nonsense is not remarkable; that is the approximate ratio of the same commodity on adult programing. The moral horror lies in the selling. The audience is the innocent, the children from two to twelve or thereabouts. Observe, first, the subtlety of identification of the good guy, the program M.C., the big brother, or the mother-father figure with the peddler of goods. Then notice the tone of the sales pitch, the insistence, the hard sell quality, the blandishments, the playing upon childish vulnerabilities. Be vigilant also for phony invocations of educational attributes of the product.

Overall, the consequences of selling and seducing children into the market are long term, and they produce exactly what is intended: a new crop of adult consumers who are witless and defenseless in the marketplace, puppets who respond to every command of the advertiser puppeteer and who are often surprised in the cold gray dawn of bill collection season at the wonders wrought in their hours of semi-hypnosis. The American is being educated to get his consumer satisfaction in the *act of buying*, in the kick of acting out the impulse which the manipulators have both created and triggered in him. His satisfaction in the use of his purchases will probably be meager: they will not last long, nor work very well. That to the well-conditioned consumer is not important. It is not the article purchased which is the sought-satisfaction; it is the next act of buying, which will give him a brief ecstasy and a fleeting moment of escape from his daemon. The aim of the media is not to satisfy a realistic appraisal of wants and needs—but to create an incurable addiction to buying.

The media do play a fundamental role in reporting the events of our time and informing us somewhat on their meaning. Newscasting does sensationalize to gain an audience and often exalts the trivial, especially when nothing particularly important bids for the front page or for broadcast time. It is also true that the media are big business and that great cities have become merely one- or two-newspaper towns. Thus, *their interpretation* of what is important or what should be played up or down is printed. The benefits of competition are often lacking.

But the media cannot be solely blamed for playing down the real issues and playing up the relatively unimportant. Politicians, even candidates for the presidency, avoid the real issues and allow themselves to be packaged and peddled like detergents. Indeed, inquiring reporters and TV commentators stubbornly persist on behalf of the real story and in the public interest in trying to break through the sheltering facades to get at some of the essence of the man and his stance.

Often when the media perform their function most objectively, when they simply report and show the facts, they then incur most fully the wrath of those who would choose to inform the public only through the carefully edited text or the official release. Thus the howls of anguish when at a national convention the television cameras were trained simply on what went on, showing among other things a mayor and a police force in action. And, of course, when the events took place, the media men, who are trained observers and obligated to report and are *free* by constitutional guarantee, said things: things that were responsive to events as they saw them and things upon which it was both their professional and their moral responsibility to comment.

It is undeniable that turning the glare of merciless exposure upon public figures in the execution of their public offices is a fundamental obligation of the press and other media in a free society. Sometimes, through commercial influence and lack of competition, they exercise it none too well. But when cries of anguish go up, even in the highest places, it may be confidently assumed that the media are not exercising their basic function badly, but rather in the view of some, much too well indeed. Thoughtful citizens, and educators particularly, concerned with the general enlightenment must ever be concerned that the media perform fully and freely, that never must there be any general dread that the public will be too well or too fully informed.

Television is overall both our most potent and our most ill-utilized medium. But it has known hours of great use. With consummate dignity it took the nation into the national tragedies in the deaths of John Kennedy, Martin Luther King, Jr., and Robert Kennedy. With powerful documentaries it has illuminated the issues of Viet Nam, of air and water pollution, of population problems, of the racial crisis, of the state of the schools. We need no more tragedy, but much more depth-reporting of profound problems. TV even carried the world along on man's first trip to the moon.

But there is one medium that the educated man must hold in highest esteem—*the book*. This is but a reasoned favoritism. It should not be so regarded on the sole basis that the book includes the greater part of man's recorded heritage and is the memory of civilization, for now the film, the tape, and the recording archives join in this function.

The book commands this esteem because it is the full-dimensioned medium. It explores in deeply reasoned complexity all the facets of life. It is available for instant rerun, over and over. It is at hand at any hour of day or night. It is replete with competitive versions of all things and all matters. It explores in depth, and offers not one, or two, or three alternative documentaries, but a dozen or even a hundred documented alternatives on everything that matters.

The book is the hardest earned product of the human mind. Its production is the most laborious. Its publication undergoes the most critical scrutinies. Its reaches are the most profound. The processes of scrutiny, of review, and of criticism are the most rigorous. No other communication is in a form so permanent or so readily at hand to turn back upon, to argue with, to disprove, to utilize. It cannot be readily cast aside. When the attack comes upon the book, when the censors and the book-burners move in, then history and historical-minded man know that barbarism is on the march, that civilization is again at stake.

Thus, the great task for the teacher is to teach to read and to read well. But further, it is to inculcate the joy in reading. For man to get at the facts, the full facts, he must get at the books. They are many; they are varied. Among them is the truest and fullest report of human intelligence. The American public reads not enough, nor does it select its reading well at all. This spells a central job for the schools.

the public views its schools

The *public* sector of American education enrolls over 37 million elementary school students and nearly 14.5 million in high schools. The expenditure annually on public education exceeds *$33 billion*.

This is a major investment. How does the public view the schools to which it entrusts the education of 88 percent of its children? The results of the first national public opinion poll that sought to find answers to this question were published in 1969.[1] The outcomes are illuminating.

The public at large, as one might expect, reveals itself to be less than well informed about the schools themselves; on the subject of education the public is quite ill informed. Predictably, parents with children presently in public school were better informed than the public at large, but not impressively so.

Even at the simple level of knowing the names of local school officials, the degree of information was shockingly low. A majority, 56 percent, of respondents, did know the name of the local superintendent of schools. Only a large minority (47 percent) could name the principal of the neighborhood elementary school. Two out of five could name the principal of the high school, but only one in four could identify the chairman of the school board.

The public's primary concern about its schools is focused on a presumed lack of discipline, an old standard complaint often echoed in PTA meetings. Discipline at 26 percent had the highest rating among perceived problems. It has probably been reinforced by the widespread phenomena of juvenile delinquency and student unrest (which, we hasten to add, are not the same thing) and the attendant and frequently exaggerated attention given these by the news media.

Other areas identified as problem areas were facilities (22 percent), teachers (17 percent), finances (14 percent), integration-segregation (13 percent). That only 4 percent of the respondents identify curriculum as a major problem and that 4 percent also state "There are no problems" indicates that the public has a dim notion of the reality of the schools' problems.

In the face of much professional and even more published critical opinion that the schools overregiment and rule the students, a mere 2 percent of the public consider the schools too strict. About half (49 percent) feel that the schools are not strict enough. Interestingly, criticism of insufficient discipline is greatest in the big cities, greater

[1] *I/D/E/A/ Reporter* (Melbourne, Florida: Institute for the Development of Educational Activities, 1969).

among blacks than whites, and greater among lower income group parents.

A sidelight on discipline is revealed in attitudes toward regulation of dress. Only a large one-third (36 percent) express a view of satisfaction with the relaxing of dress codes. Over half (53 percent) come out for greater regulation of dress, while only 7 percent advocate less regulation. The better educated were less critical of the way children dress. The general view on dress and general strictness might be worth considering when persons express wonderment at youth's perception of a generation gap.

The views held by the general public with respect to discipline are not surprising. Many schools with no distinction in terms of academic achievement have achieved public esteem on no better grounds than that they make the children "toe the line." The same can be said of prisons. Many a teacher of poor scholarship and atrocious methodology has achieved community status as a fine teacher, simply by attaining a reputation for "being tough on the kids."

Attitudes expressed toward teachers and teaching showed a good deal of esteem for the profession. In fact, when asked, "Would you like a child of yours to take up teaching as a career?" the response was 75 percent affirmative. As to teacher salaries, the largest group (43 percent) believed them to be just about right. Only 2 percent contended that they were too high, whereas a third (33 percent) of respondents said salaries were too low. On the question of automatic pay increases, opinion was about equally split between yes and no.

By a fairly narrow margin, the teacher's right to join a labor union was supported (45 percent to 40 percent). But to the question, "Do you think teachers should have the right to strike?" the negative response was an overwhelming 59 percent, in comparison with a 37 percent affirmative voice. A critical view of the teaching force might be implied when one considers that 52 percent thought their local public school system has a hard time getting good teachers, and 38 percent said "yes," along with 22 percent "no" and 40 percent "no opinion," to the query as to whether some local teachers should be dismissed.

Thus, it appears that the public is generally supportive toward its schools but not well informed enough to exert constructive critical pressure for their improvement. This is a general national descriptive summation. It does not say nor imply that a given community cannot take, or has not taken, the time and trouble to involve itself in a well-informed way for school improvement. As to financial support, 49 percent had expressed themselves as being opposed at the time to more school taxes, while 45 percent would support higher taxes for schools. This opinion has been reflected in many elections on school bond issues in recent years. It might be read as a reaction to the total tax burden, not necessarily as a rejection of the obligation to support public schools.

In the main, citizens express high regard for teachers. They tend to believe that they are underpaid (but not so badly that they would discourage a child from becoming one). Citizens are willing in large numbers to serve on school boards and show quite a lot of interest in school affairs. In conclusion it must be repeated that they have a great deal to learn about their schools specifically and about the whole field of education in general.

to educate amid complexity

Education takes place amid complexity; education is full of complexity. In the midst of all this complexity, there is a great deal of assertiveness, the posing of simple answers for complex problems. In giving attention to the dialogue and debate, the assertions and counterassertions, concerning education, in our view it is well to be aware of two dispositions of the human mind that lead to errors of equal and opposite kind: one is to make the complex simple; the other to make the simple complex.

Assertion of simple solutions to complex problems is rampant on the education scene. We all have heard many absurd oversimplifications spoken confidently as verities. For example:

"The overindulgence of children under progressive education and permissive child-rearing is responsible for most of the crime and juvenile delinquency today; *therefore*, if the schools would just crack down on the kids, make them behave and work hard, and parents wouldn't be afraid to use the old razor strap where it would do the most good, the problem would be solved."

"Grades are unfair and give false goals for motivating students; *therefore*, if you abolished the grading system, students would be motivated purely. Then the problem would be solved."

"There are a lot of troublemakers and agitators on the campus; *therefore*, throw them out of school and student protest will disappear."

"Too many children do not learn to read well or at all; *therefore*, adopt my system (or buy my series of textbooks), and the problem will be solved."

"The application of technology has made industry wonderfully productive, and has even put men on the moon; *therefore*, apply technology to education, and the problem of the schools will be solved."

Such statements and many others are often said as printed here and are widely quoted. They are bad thinking. True thought does not express itself so neatly; good thinking does not attempt to render the complex absurdly simple.

To appreciate the complexities of educational problems, consider the realities of complication in certain issues that are often approached by simple arguments around polarized positions. Where arguments are centered at two extremes, the rational comment is not necessarily, "Well, the truth lies somewhere midway between the two." Truth is not the average of two absurdities. In a polarized argument one position may be much better than another. It may have facts and evidence to support it; the other position may have little but illusion and false hopes. The point is really that you cannot simply argue your way to the solution of problems. To work your way through complexity requires the disciplines of logic and evidence. In the three cases that follow partisanship, for example, obscures or ignores the complexities of the situation.

CASE I. One position holds that athletics are an important part of education and should be encouraged; the other contends that athletics are commercialized, have nothing to do with education and, therefore, should be abolished. Each position has arguments to sustain it. One way to base a decision would be to see which side could come up with the longest list of sustained arguments and select it. Arriving at your decision with this as a basis is not good reasoning, however. It ignores the complexities of interrelationships between the two cases and pushes for a simple either-or solution.

Let us examine some of the underlying complexities. Athletics do enjoy overemphasis. Coaches often make more money than distinguished professors. But athletics were important in the educational scheme of ancient Athens. Coaches and partisan public will do and support almost anything to win, but a winning team now and then can do wonders for the morale of a school and the community of support around it. Winning does thrive in an atmosphere of intense competition, but in team sports to win requires much practice in the lessons of cooperation and subjecting self-aggrandizement to the discipline of team effort. Participation in athletics may distract students from their studies even to the point of academic failure on occasion, but it also holds some students in school who would never remain there otherwise and holds them to at least minimum standards of academic achievement.

One could readily extend the complication of the realities. If a school really wanted to make sense of its athletics program, it should follow a procedure similar to the one outlined below:

1. Define its educational objectives clearly.
2. Establish ways in which an athletic program might contribute to these objectives.
3. By critical comparison, determine whether in any of these instances

some other aspect of the school program might more effectively or
economically serve the educational objectives.
4. Establish an athletic program tailored to the foregoing analysis.
5. Maintain a continuing scrutiny (A) to assure that the program was
accomplishing its goals as planned (which might have little to do
with won-lost compilations) and (B) to guard against the extension
of the program into activities that were either not related to the
school's educational goals or, at worst, were positively contradictory
to them.

Such a procedure applies the problem-solving method to the athletic issue. It would be the rational approach. It would not drive
athletic programs from the schools, but it would drastically alter
them. It would be an excellent and desirable procedure, but it is not
likely to take place on a broad scale for several reasons: (1) the athletic establishment is a powerful and deeply entrenched vested interest
in education; (2) administrators and policy-makers are usually men,
and American men in general are so boyish in their love of games that
their emotions put them conveniently in the coat pockets of the athletic establishment; and (3) the support of the common culture for its
games is profoundly irrational and the general public gauges success
by such crude competitive standards that it would not permit an objective educational approach to the problem. But again, in educational terms, it would be a good thing to do.

CASE II. One position holds that vocational education is essential and
should be extended greatly because students who graduate without a
vocation are at a loss in the world; another holds that vocational education is inferior and educates for second-class citizenship and should
be abolished. Both cases are bolstered by sophisticated arguments,
but none of the arguments seems to solve the problem. Both sides
have unresolved elements of contradictory realities to sustain them.
Many students leave high school, and college too, ill-equipped in
terms of salable skills for entering the job market. However, premature job orientation can narrow the student's range of occupational
choice into those with poorer pay and lower career ceilings. A capacity to do a job for decent pay is a first requirement for getting the
children of the poor out of the poverty trap, but a definition of vocation that shunts these children into the permanent lower echelons
does tend to freeze them into a lower-class status. Vocational education should not be perceived as a catch-all for the low-motivated and
the ill-adjusted as it so often is. Nor should it be used as an educational dumping ground. The case for a good liberal education as a
necessity for all is classic and persuasive in a democracy, but many of
the goals of a liberal education can be achieved in a *good* program of
vocational education.
Again the argument has raged in either-or terms, but the realities

do not shape up that way at all. The method of problem solving would suggest the following approach:

1. The school would have to determine its educational objectives.
2. It would determine to what extent a vocational objective is a part of a good education for all its students.
3. Holding to the disciplines of free choice and equality of opportunity, it would seek to develop an educational program that would maximize these for all students.
4. In developing specific aspects of vocational education in the school, it would study its entire curriculum to assure that the objectives of good education in the vocational dimension might not be more effectively and economically served elsewhere.
5. It would maintain a continuing scrutiny on these special aspects of program to assure that the purposes sought were being achieved and that extensions were not developing which either did not contribute to these goals or were positively detrimental to their achievement.

In practice such procedures have been used somewhat. The obstacles to such a method come largely from (1) the vocational educators, who are a powerfully entrenched and sophisticated vested interest group, and (2) the liberal-arts-oriented professionals, who persist in maintaining a patronizing attitude of academic snobbery. These "fraternities" have not contributed to constructive dialogue. However, rational solutions in this area have strong supports in the common culture. American civilization values the practical; its history has put a premium upon the utilitarian. The comprehensive high school is itself a rough solution to the issue. It is in the comprehensive school that the climate is most favorable to an analytical educational approach to the problem.

CASE III. Argument rages between those who say that grades are necessary and inevitable and those who maintain that the grading system gets in the way of learning and must be abolished. Here, too, the situation is loaded with complexity.

Efforts to change the grading system have encountered strenuous opposition forces that seem to render the effort futile. E–G–F–P report cards became some time ago A–B–C–D. A change to Satisfactory–Unsatisfactory may become another four-point scale when pluses and minuses begin to creep in next to the S. The same thing may happen on Pass–Fail grading, when the adjectives high and low begin to appear to qualify the *pass*. It is true that skilled gamesmen may be good grade-getters but mediocre learners, but it is also true that good learners sometimes get good grades. Some teachers oppose grades because of legitimate opposition to extrinsic and corruptible motivation devices. However, others would be happy to be rid of grading simply to escape the rigors of defining objectives and the appraisals of achievement that go along with fair use of a grading system. Grades are gross appraisals, often corrupted by teacher preferences, punishments and rewards for conduct and hard work, and irrelevancies like neatness and penmanship. An objective evaluative report, on the other hand, may be specific, diagnostic, and useful. Grades are paradoxical: they are both powerful inducements to conformity and expressive indicators of individual differences. Pupils loathe and love them. They shun invidious comparisons that set them apart from or at odds with their fellows; and they love to make good-better-best judgments and to receive praise.

The grading system is constantly under fire. The absurdities and cruelties within it are in part due to four factors: (1) a lack of refinement in its instruments and procedures, (2) the judgmentalism of adults and teachers toward students, (3) the corruption of the academic achievement measure with extraneous disciplinary factors, (4) the overstress of the competitive at the expense of the diagnostic.

The schools may or may not abandon the grading system. They will at the expense of educating philosophically abandon evaluation and appraisal. It is as true as ever that the "unexamined life is not worth living." This applies to the part of it lived in school. The golfer may not enter tournament competition, but he is rare who never counts his score, or compares it with par, or the performance of another player. The job is not to endorse a grading system, or to abandon it, but to make sense of evaluation and appraisal. To do this, a school would have to proceed somewhat as follows:

1. To determine its educational objectives clearly.
2. To analyze in each aspect of its program what contributions are sought toward realizing those objectives.
3. To create instruments that validly and reliably measure achievement among these.
4. To devise appropriate means of reporting gains toward these objectives in meaningful useful terms. Such communication would be addressed to teachers, parents, and students in such terms as would be most useful and appropriate to each.
5. To exercise constant scrutiny that both the instruments of measurement and those of communication were serving the educational objectives of the school, were not going outside of them, and, above all, were not doing things positively detrimental to their achievement.

The time and money spent on testing and research about testing indicate that the question has been attended to. The great body of evidence of abuse, and the large protest against it, is demonstration that many efforts have been ill-conceived and executed.

The application of the problem-solving method would no doubt drastically restructure grading and evaluation systems in the schools and might even dictate their abandonment.

It is our opinion that the best procedure to follow in resolving educational issues is the problem-solving method. It is rational; it is the method of intelligence. Teachers and other educators will dwell among dozens of issues similar to the case studies in this chapter. For them the choice is to be stridently partisan and argumentative or to be analytical, rational—and intelligent.

topics for inquiry

1. "Melting Pot" versus Cultural Pluralism
2. The Case for Joining the NEA
3. The Case for Joining the AFT
4. How the Common Culture Supports Science
5. How the Common Culture Rejects Science
6. Television and the News
7. Television and the Child
8. Public Support of Education in Your City or State
9. The Changing View of the Teacher
10. Dress Codes: Pros and Cons

subjects for discussion

1. Devise a survey seeking opinions as to the quality of the schools in your area and indications of perceived problems. Get a group of citizen responses; see how their views compare with the views in the text. Or administer the same instrument to two groups— education students and noneducation students. Compare outcomes. Discuss implications.
2. Conduct a study of commercial children's TV programing in your area for a week. Analyze the content of programs and commercials. Make a time check on ratio of programing to advertising. Do your observations bear out the authors' contentions in this chapter?
3. Identify an issue about education similar to the three "cases" in this chapter. Divide the class: let one group choose sides to debate the issue; let another group approach the issue by a problem-solving analysis. Compare outcomes. Which approach seems to get farther? Discuss implications.

selected readings

BOULDING, KENNETH E. *The Meaning of the Twentieth Century: The Great Transition.* New York: Harper & Row, 1964.

A profound work on what we call the curriculum of modern man.

"Collision Course in the High Schools." *Life Magazine,* May 16, 1969.

The issue of *Life* of which use was made in one section of this chapter. Worth looking up.

FRANKEL, CHARLES. *The Case for Modern Man.* New York: Harper & Row, 1956.

Presents a hope based on bitter experience.

ROSENBERG, BERNARD and DAVID M. WHITE. *Mass Culture: The Popular Arts in America.* New York: Free Press, 1957.

A very good source book with an objective and critical approach.

RUSSELL, BERTRAND. *Unpopular Essays.* New York: Simon and Schuster, 1950.

Included to show the sense that sometimes must be made in the face of a general addiction to nonsense.

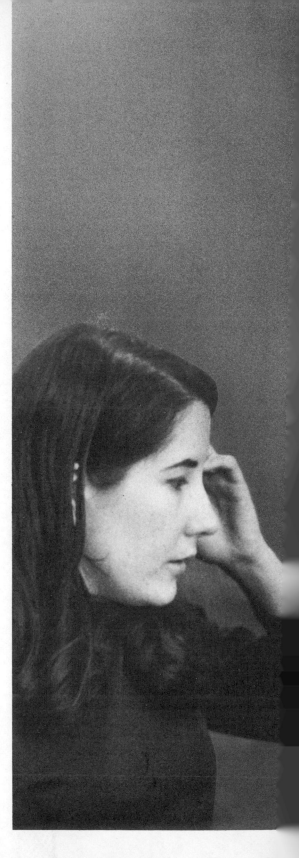

8
THE
PRACTICE
OF
EDUCATION

the act of teaching

Is teaching an art or a science? This question once enjoyed lively debate and dialogue. It is essentially, however, one of those impossible either-or propositions. The teacher is at once an artist, a scientist, a manager, and a technologist, at the very least. The teacher's function is summed up and synthesized as an organizer and guide of learning activities.

Art in teaching is real. Teaching is *creative*. It brings into existence new elements, things that were not there before. It restructures so that newly discovered functions may persist and operate in suitable forms. It creates awareness, which allows the learner to recognize the sense and meaning of his experience and to make use of it.

In the exercise of his art, the teacher is well advised to take note of where his talents lie and to work to develop those that will give more meaning to his teaching. A capacity to dramatize, for example, is an asset to creative teaching. But the priority should be given to dramatization of meaning, of the learning situation, and of the students. The classroom does not exist to fulfill the frustrated thespian urge of the teacher; this misuse leads to much bad lecturing. Whatever capacity the teacher has for drama, it should be used on behalf of the class, not for the indulgence of his own ego.

If there is an art essential to good teaching, it is that of communication. Let the study of this art be concentrated on the neglected aspect, which is *listening*. The schoolteacherish mode of listening, nonetheless, is to be avoided. Bad

listeners often have very sharp ears for picking up trivial errors at
the expense of larger sense. This skill is the beginning of the artful
"put-down," which is so much the stock in trade of bad teaching. The
good listener hears the sense and seizes upon it for a creative act of
teaching. A classroom dialogue observed in a geography class in Ecuador illustrates good listening turned to consummate effect in teaching.

> "What can you tell us of the United States of America, Pablo?"
> the teacher questioned.
> "The United States is a republic in Europe whose people are
> mostly farmers and it is pretty big."

Oh, Pablo, what the schoolteacherish listener could do to you!
"Pablo, what a strange thing you tell us. The United States is in Eur-
ope. Tell us, then, is China in South America? Farmers, indeed; the
United States has its people mostly in cities. It is a great industrial
nation. I think you must read your book again ten times tonight."
But this was a teacher who responded,

> "Well, Pablo, you have told us some good things about the United
> States. It *is* big. Did you know it is about as big as Brazil?
> And yes, there are many farmers there, as in Ecuador. But did
> you know, Pablo, that even more North Americans live in cities
> than on farms. I believe you know the names of some cities in
> the United States?"
> "Miami, New York?"
> "Yes, Pablo."
> "Paris."
> "Well . . . , no, Pablo."
> "Los Angeles?"
> "Yes, of course!"
> The teacher continued, "You know you are very right to say
> the United States is a republic, but did not your tongue slip
> when you said it is in Europe?"
> "North America?"
> "Of course, that is right. But most of its people came from
> Europe at some time, so you were partly right after all."

Thus, constructive teaching holds to what is correct and builds
upon it. The teacher who would build confidence in his students lets
them down gently in their errors. Destructive teaching seizes upon
what a student says that is wrong and criticizes it.

Science, too, is at the center of teaching. The supreme contradiction, it would seem, would be when a science were taught unscientifically. This does happen. It happens when the teacher's science is
merely his subject, when he neglects the science in learning. Science
does not ignore relevant evidence. Thus, when science teachers neglect to gain and use knowledge about their learners, they are perform-

ing unscientifically. Science is a means of discovery. Therefore, when learning is all cut and dried, when even laboratory is a cookbook exercise, science is scarcely operative in the classroom.

The method of science is appropriate to any classroom, except in the graphic and performing arts—and these too have uses for it. Science is a major method of intelligence. Inquiry can scarcely be precise and disciplined without reliance upon it.

Teaching, too, is *managerial*. If it be reduced simply to this, the teacher is led in the direction of general business and officiousness. That is not the point. The classroom is a complex institution. It has many people, furniture, materials, physical conditions, tools and instruments. Many functions in the classroom necessitate a variety of forms. Therefore, to some extent, the teacher is a manager, an administrator.

To organize is the key. The schoolteacherish conception of organization is a limited one that implies keeping things neat, having everything in on time, shades drawn symmetrically. These are small matters, and they may even get in the way of good organization. Good administration rests on more basic principles. It seeks the development of general responsibility. It delegates responsibility, which surely suggests a virtue in cooperative planning. It divides labor, which can get some of the classroom burden off the teacher's back. It establishes priorities, which says both that some things must come before others and that some things deserve more time. The good manager is skilled in assessing resources and mobilizing instruments.

In the seventies, as earlier, the teacher is a technologist. He must be a student of technique, and he must know the uses of the tools that technology offers him. The act of teaching is not the sum total of a large number of techniques any more than surgery is. Technique, though, is vital to a surgeon, and to a teacher also. Questioning is a technical matter as well as an art. (The artist, indeed, is at a loss without technique.) Test construction in the absence of developed technique leads to the cardinal errors of unreliability and invalidity. There are techniques of discipline that may be studied and used, though the study of justice is ever necessary lest the techniques be debased to authoritarian uses.

With respect to technology, the teacher must know not merely the claimed utility of proposed instruments, but he must also know the research that led to their development and the reasons for their use. Tools exist to serve the purpose of the craftsman. They do not exist to be used as often or as broadly as possible simply to prove their utility. (But the teacher can take it for granted that films and tape have vindicated classroom uses.)

The hazard in technique is that it can be too self-conscious or employed as an end in itself. Effective teaching is the goal; appraisal of teaching must be based on totality of impact not on observation of a matrix of techniques. A reference to games will make the point. An athlete will not become a champion unless he has mastered the necessary elements for success in a game. He will not, however, in most sports be judged a winner on critics' ratings of a pattern of separately identified techniques. It may be absurd in the light of all experience to high jump by flipping over the bar backwards, but if he clears the bar at highest mark, he will get the gold medal (just as he did in Mexico City at the 1968 Olympics).

Every game tends to become stylized. The governing assumption is that a given style, a set of frozen techniques as it were, has proved itself to be the most effective way to win the most games. This parallels certain professional efforts to reduce teaching to an analysis of its microaspects. But in football, for example, experimentation and rejection of old governing styles went so far that it dictated a redesignation of the position of the players themselves.

The teacher may profitably analyze his strengths and shortcomings. It may be essential to build competence where lack of it ruins teaching effect. But the season for a teacher, as for a baseball team, is a long one. Playing it day by day in good morale, taking the losses as they come, with a calm view of the main objective is the governing discipline.

But if a teacher or a supervisor is conscious mainly of microaspects of teaching, he is sure to lose track of the name of the game: *effective teaching*. The job is to study the game, build on strength, reject neurotic perfectionism, hold to central purpose (desire), and give a decent and a limited amount of attention to the improvement of details of technique. It would be nice if every quarterback were a perfect all-round practitioner of all the football skills and a paragon of virtue for youth to emulate, but a man can become a superstar if he is superb in only two dimensions—throws the ball consistently straight and true and keeps his head under fire. Teaching is more complex, and a good deal rougher all in all than pro-football, but the point should be obvious to the reader.

practical morale building

Teaching breaks the spirit of more teachers than it drives from the classroom. It does not have to do so, but it can. It is a job that puts formidable demands on the person. It is one of the most taxing jobs in terms of human relations. You must not merely relate to students; you must be responsible for them. "And," as one young teacher put it, "the children are so constant!"

That is it. They are out of sight, but not out of mind—or even sound, even when a "free period" allows a retreat to the teacher's lounge. An elementary school teacher will relate to thirty or forty children all day long; a secondary school teacher from 100 to 200 different students in the course of the day. Suggestions, questions (some that will drive you up the wall), compliments, needlings, pleasantries, effronteries, jokes, jibes, persuasions, cajoleries, problems, secrets, confidences—all will be encountered by a teacher at any level during one school day. After one of the frequent more active days of "relating," a teacher will find himself slumping away from school convinced that there is nothing left of him. His personality, he feels, has been beaten to insignificance by the constant barrage of persons who have leaned, probed, depended, and hit upon it through the day.

A teacher also dwells among his peers—his colleagues. These are, in the main, very nice people, but, like all of us, they do have their idiosyncrasies. They are generally much more supportive than burdensome.

The teacher has to (or rather, should) endure at his job. The big element in developing staying power in the face of all the factors that can demoralize one is pursuit of a model of instructional practice that allows the individual to function in the ways most supportive of personal growth and satisfaction. A good model allows both the teacher and the students to live a good life during the school day. There is no more basic and more enduring support to good morale than this. The teacher must never forget that the good instructional model is one that is supportive of personal growth and satisfaction, not for the teacher, but for the *student*. Thus the student must be central in the development of a model—not in the sense that he is the object to be developed or shaped, but in the sense that he is involved in the direction of the process.

instructional models: past and present

Most proposed instructional models, past and present, have been built on the premise that the student is an object to be treated with step-by-step predeveloped procedures. To be sure, Parker, Dewey, and others proposed student-centered models, but for the most part rigid formalization has had a secure stay in the schools, even with the entrance of new ideas or models that held promise for expanding the educational process and making it more meaningful. In a sense there has been a continuing dualism in instructional models. There have been those that have proposed an expanding concept of education and those that have pressed for a continually narrowing concept. In some instances the latter approach has turned progressive innovations into rigid systematization in the name of efficiency.

In setting down historical models of instruction one could obviously include an array of specific types. Our purpose, however, is to present a sample of the more illustrative models that significantly influenced either educational thought or instructional practices in American schools. To some extent they stand as examples not only of attempts to standardize teaching practices but of educational purpose as well. In another sense they illustrate what seems to be a continuing attempt to rigidly systematize and mechanize the educational process.

moral didacticism: the mcguffey readers

In 1836, just in the formative years of the common school movement, the first McGuffey Reader was published. The subsequent volumes were to enjoy nearly a century of popular use. Fifty million copies were sold before McGuffey's death in 1873; by 1920 the sales had reached 122 million. Nor has their popularity yet died. There are still a number of conservative organizations that call for the use of McGuffey's Readers today. They see in them a possible rebirth of what they felt was one of the great stabilizers of nineteenth-century America. The moral lessons of the McGuffey Readers were intended not only to inculcate a moral common denominator but also to shape a national character. The individual, not the social order, was on trial in life. Sobriety, thrift, industriousness, perseverence, honesty, and so on, were taught to be the guaranteed paths to success.

Two excerpts from McGuffey Readers (see pp. 240–245) illustrate the moral didacticism that characterized most of the lessons. Although they are not instructional models in the strict sense, nevertheless, they display the general approach of teaching throughout much of the nineteenth century and part of the twentieth century.

Much has been written about the McGuffey Readers by those who read them as students in the latter part of the nineteenth century, mostly laudatory testimonials to the moral value of the lessons. One caustic commentary, however, was provided by Clarence Darrow, who would have used the McGuffey Readers during the 1860s. In his book, *Farmington,* he refers directly to the second illustration:

> If we scholars did not grow up to be exemplary men and women, it surely was not the fault of our teachers or our parents—or of the schoolbook publishers.
>
> When I look back to those lessons that we learned, I marvel that I ever wandered from the straight path in the smallest possible degree. Whether we were learning to read or write, studying grammar or composition, in whatever book we chanced to take, there was the moral precept plain on every page. Our many transgressions could have come only from the fact that we really did not know what these lessons meant; and doubtless our teachers also never thought they had any sort of relation to our lives.

How these books were crammed with noble thoughts! In them every virtue was extolled and every vice condemned. I wonder now how the book publishers ever could have printed such tales, or how they reconciled themselves to the hypocrisy they must have felt when they sold the books.

This moral instruction concerned certain general themes. First of all, temperance was the great lesson taught. I well remember that we children believed that the first taste of liquor was the fatal one; and we believed that not one drop could be taken without leading us to everlasting ruin and despair. There were the almshouse, the jail, and the penitentiary square, in front of every child who even considered taking the first drink; while all the rewards of this world and the next were freely promised to the noble lad who should resist.

As I look back today, it seems as if every moral lesson in the universe must have grown into my being from those books. How could I have ever wandered from the narrow path? I look back to those little freckled, trifling boys and girls, and I hear them read their lessons in their books so long ago. The stories were all the same, from the beginning to the end. We began in the primer, and our instruction in reading and good conduct did not end until the covers of the last book were closed. . . .

One other story that has seemed particularly to impress itself upon my mind was about two boys, one named James and the other named John. I believe that these were their names, though possibly one was William and the other Henry. Anyhow, their uncle gave them each a parcel of books. James took out his pocket-knife and cut the fine whipcord that bound his package, but John slowly and patiently untied his string and then rolled it into a nice little ball (the way a nice little boy would do) and carefully put it in his pocket. Some years after, there was a great shooting tournament, and James and John were both there with their bows and arrows; it was late in the game, and so far it was a tie. James seized his last arrow and bent his bow; the string broke and the prize was lost. The book does not tell us that in this emergency John offered his extra piece of whipcord to his brother; instead, the model prudent brother took up his last arrow, bent his bow, when, lo and behold! his string broke too; whereupon John reached into his pocket and pulled out the identical cord that he had untied so long ago, put it on the bow, and of course won the prize!

That miserable story must have cost me several years of valuable time, for ever since I first read it I have always tried to untie every knot that I could find; and although I have ever carefully tucked away all sorts of odd strings into my pockets, I never attended a shooting-match or won a prize in all my life.[1]

[1] Clarence Darrow, *Farmington* (New York: Scribner, 1932), pp. 59–62.

THIRD READER.   **111**

LESSON XLII.

BEWARE OF THE FIRST DRINK.

1. "Uncle Philip, as the day is fine, will you take a walk with us this morning?"

2. "Yes, boys. Let me get my hat and cane, and we will take a ramble. I will tell you a story as we go. Do you know poor old Tom Smith?"

3. "Know him! Why, Uncle Philip, every body knows him. He is such a shocking drunkard, and swears so horribly."

4. "Well, I have known him ever since we were boys together. There was not a more decent, well-behaved boy among us. After he left school, his father died, and he was put into a store in the city. There, he fell into bad company.

5. "Instead of spending his evenings in reading, he would go to the theater and to balls. He soon learned to play cards, and of course to play for money. He lost more than he could pay.

6. "He wrote to his poor mother, and told her his losses. She sent him money to pay his debts, and told him to come home.

7. "He did come home. After all, he might still have been useful and happy, for his friends were willing to forgive the past. For a time, things went on well. He married a lovely woman, gave up his bad habits, and was doing well.

8. "But one thing, boys, ruined him forever. In the city, he had learned to take strong drink, and he said to me once, that when a man begins to drink, he never knows where it will end. 'Therefore,' said Tom, 'beware of the first drink!'

9. "It was not long before he began to follow his old habit. He knew the danger, but it seemed as if he could not resist his desire to drink. His poor mother soon died of grief and shame. His lovely wife followed her to the grave.

10. "He lost the respect of all, went on from bad to worse, and has long been a perfect sot. Last night, I had a letter from the city, stating that Tom Smith has been found guilty of stealing, and sent to the state-prison for ten years.

11. "There I suppose he will die, for he is now old. It is dreadful to think to what an end he has come. I could not but think,

THIRD READER.   **113**

as I read the letter, of what he said to me
years ago, 'Beware of the first drink!'

12. "Ah, my dear boys, when old Uncle
Philip is gone, remember that he told you

the story of Tom Smith, and said to you,
'Beware of the first drink!' The man who
does this will never be a drunkard."

DEFINITIONS.—3. Hŏr′ri bly, *in a dreadful manner, terribly.* 4. Dē′çent, *modest, respectable.* 9. Re şĭst′, *withstand,
overcome.* 10. Sŏt, *an habitual drunkard.* Guĭlt′y, *justly
chargeable with a crime.*[2]

[2] McGuffey Reader, Third Reader, Eclectic Series, pp. 111–113. As reprinted in Harvey C.
Minnich (ed.), *Old Favorites from the McGuffey Readers* (New York: American Book,
1936), pp. 67–69.

LESSON XVI.

2. Ex-am′ine; *v.* to look at carefully.

5. Sig′ni-fies; *v.* to be important.

22. Prize; *n.* a reward for excellence.

30. Ev-er-last′ing; *adj.* lasting
always.

WASTE NOT, WANT NOT.

Utter distinctly each consonant in such words as the following: *parcels, exactly, string, yours, three, excellent, afterward,
arrows, marksman, settled, pronounced, rules, trial, prudently.* See
Ex. IV, page 15.

1. *Mr. Jones.* Boys, if you have nothing to do, will
you unpack these †parcels for me′?

2. The two parcels were †exactly alike, both of
them well tied up with good whip-cord. Ben took his
parcel to the table, and began to examine the knot,
and then to †untie it.

3. John took the other parcel, and tried first at one
corner, and then at the other, to *pull* off the string.
But the cord had been too well secured, and he only
drew the knots †*tighter.*

4. *John.* I wish these people would not tie up their
parcels so tight, as if they were never to be †undone.
Why, Ben, how did you get *yours* undone? What is
in your parcel? I wonder what is in mine! I wish I
could get the string off. I will *cut* it.

5. *Ben.* O no, do not *cut* it, John′! Look, what a
nice cord this is, and yours is the same. It is a *pity*
to *cut* it.

6. *John.* Pooh! what signifies a bit of †pack-
thread?

7. *Ben.* It is †whip-cord.

8. *John.* Well, *whip-cord* then! what signifies a bit of whip-cord? You can get a piece of whip-cord twice as long as that for three cents; and who cares for three cents? Not I, for one. So, here it goes.

9. So he took out his knife, and cut it in several places.

10. *Mr. Jones.* Well, my boys, have you undone the parcels for me?

11. *John.* Yes, sir; here is the parcel.

12. *Ben.* And here is my parcel, father, and here is also the string.

13. *Mr. Jones.* You may *keep* the string, Ben.

14. *Ben.* Thank you, sir. What ⁺excellent whip-cord it is!

15. *Mr. Jones.* And you, John, may keep your string, too, if it will be of any use to you.

16. *John.* It will be of *no* use to me, thank you, sir.

17. *Mr. Jones.* No, I am afraid not, if *this* is it.

18. A few weeks after this, Mr. Jones gave each of his sons a new top.

19. *John.* How is this, Ben? These tops have no strings. What shall we do for strings?

20. *Ben.* I have a string that will do very well for *mine.* And he pulled it out of his pocket.

21. *John.* Why, if that is not the whip-cord! I wish I had saved *mine.*

22. A few days afterward, there was a ⁺shooting-match, with bows and ⁺arrows, among the lads. The prize was a fine bow and arrows, to be given to the best ⁺marksman. "Come, come," said Master Sharp, "I am within one inch of the mark. I should like to see who will go nearer."

23. John drew his bow, and shot. The arrow struck within a quarter of an inch of Master Sharp's. "Shoot away," said Sharp; "but you must understand

THE ECLECTIC SERIES.   65

the rules. We settled them before you came. You are to have three shots with your own arrows. Nobody is to ⁺borrow or lend. So shoot away."

24. John ⁺seized his second arrow; "If I have any luck," said he; —but just as he ⁺pronounced the word "*luck*," the string broke, and the arrow fell from his hands.

25. *Master Sharp.* There! It is all over with you.

26. *Ben.* Here is my bow for him, and welcome.

27. *Master Sharp.* No, no, sir; that is not fair. Did you not hear the rules? There is to be no lending.

28. It was now Ben's turn to make his ⁺trial. His first arrow missed the mark; the *second* was exactly as near as John's *first*. Before ⁺venturing the last arrow, Ben very prudently examined the string of his bow; and, as he pulled it to try its strength, it *snapped*.

29. Master Sharp clapped his hands and danced for joy. But his dancing suddenly ceased, when careful Ben drew out of his pocket an excellent piece of cord, and began to tie it to the bow.

30. "The everlasting whip-cord, I declare!" cried John. "Yes," said Ben; "I put it in my pocket to-day, because I thought I might want it."

31. Ben's last arrow won the prize; and when the bow and arrows were handed to him, John said, "How ⁺valuable that whip-cord has been to you, Ben. I'll take care how I waste any thing, hereafter."

Exercises.—What is this lesson designed to teach? Which of the boys preserved his whip-cord? What good did it do him? What did the other boy do with his? What was the consequence? What did he learn from it?

In the thirtieth paragraph, what two *nouns* are there? In what number are they both? What is number? See Pinneo's Primary Grammar, page 45, Art. 77.[3]

sheldon's object lessons: pestalozzi formalized

In Chapter 3 mention was made of Sheldon's Oswego Normal school and the formalization there of Pestalozzi's ideas about education. The Oswego Movement had an important if short-lived influence on teaching during the 1870s and 1880s. Although Sheldon assumed a Pestalozzian basis for his "object lessons," the rigid formalization promoted a mechanistic approach for teachers. In his *Manual of Elementary Instruction* (1868) he set down the introductory rules for the lessons:

All lessons should be given in accordance with the following principles, which were laid down by Pestalozzi:
1. Activity is a law of childhood. Accustom the child to do—educate the hand.
2. Cultivate the faculties in their natural order—first form the mind, then furnish it.
3. Begin with the senses, and never tell a child what he can discover for himself.
4. Reduce every subject to its elements—one difficulty at a time is enough for a child.
5. Proceed step by step. Be thorough. The measure of information is not what the teacher can give, but what the child can receive.
6. Let every lesson have a point; either immediate or remote.
7. Develop the idea—then give the term—cultivate language.
8. Proceed from the known to the unknown—from the particular to the general—from the concrete to the abstract—from the simple to the more difficult.
9. First synthesis, then analysis—not the order of the subject, but the order of nature.[4]

On the following four pages are two of the model lessons taken from Sheldon's manual.

It is apparent that Sheldon's model lessons were not in strict accordance with what he set down as Pestalozzian principles. Nevertheless, they were at least a departure from the strict recitation method characteristic of most American educational practices. Sheldon's work also established an early formal approach of defining the teaching-learning process. To some extent, if only chronologically, the Oswego work heralded a period significant in the development of ideas about curriculum and pedagogy. By the 1890s the public schools in America were well established, and most states had compulsory attendance laws. But it was obvious at the time that the schools in general were still functioning under the old restrictive ideas of education. Rote learning and recitation, harshly imposed, was the prevail-

---

[4] Edward Sheldon, *A Manual of Elementary Instruction*, 6th ed. (New York, Scribner & Co., 1868), pp. 14–15.

3. *Sketch of a Lesson on Shells and their Inmates.*

MATTER.	METHOD.
I. *Use.*—Shells are found in the sea; also in rivers, and some on land. They serve both for the homes and armor of certain animals. These have no bones, and cold, white, or colorless blood, and, being soft, are called mollusks.	I.—Bring before the children some shells. Let them say what they are. Where found? Supply information as to shells found inland, and by reference to them as marine objects, lead children to conclude that wherever they are found the sea must once have been. Show an oyster shell containing its inmate. Children state the use of the shell. The last use brought out by reference to its defenceless condition without it. Let a child press the oyster; then press his own chin or forehead. The difference, and its cause. What they can say of the oyster. (S. R.): "The oyster has no bones." Another difference discovered by touch. Its cause. (S. R.): "The blood of the oyster is cold." Refer to the color of our blood. Cut the oyster, to show the watery liquid. (S. R.): "The blood of the oyster is colorless." Children told that all animals living in shells resemble the oyster in all these points, and on account of their soft, boneless structure, are called mollusks. Children dictate the matter of this head. (W. B.)
II. *Of what composed.*—Shells are formed from the animals which inhabit them. They are composed of three substances: 1, lime, a sort of chalk, which the creature obtains from the water; 2, a glue given out by it from its own body—this varies in color, and gives color to the shells; 3, part of the	II.—Refer to storms at sea, the waves dashing the shells against rocks, &c., and lead children to see that shells require to be made very strong. Show a specimen of the lime as one constituent part. Where the animals can find such a substance. Refer to the limestone rocks of coasts, and coating inside teakettle. Whether this substance alone would make a good shell (too brittle). What more required—some substance not brittle, the reverse of brittle, to mix with it. Show glue. Let children recognize it as an animal substance, and show the quality on which its use as a constituent part of the shell depends.

skin of the animal, which lines these. The shells, when broken, may be made new again. The new pieces are brighter in color than the old.

Tell children that the glue used to make the shell comes from the animal itself. Note the beauty and color of the various shells. Let the children name the colors, and try to account for their appearance. Give information. Let them give examples of similar variations in other classes of Nature's works (birds, stones, &c.). How the animal obtains the shell—it is part of itself; grows with it. Refer to broken shell. These objects, which are very liable to be broken, can be repaired. Appearance of the new piece on the shell. Refer to a new piece of material put upon an old garment, &c.

III. *Different kinds of Shells.*—Shells are very numerous. There are many thousand different kinds. These are divided into three classes, viz. :—
1, those of one piece;
2, those of two pieces;
3, those of three pieces.

III.—Bring the children specimens of each kind. Let them discover how they differ in structure, and classify accordingly. Matter of the lesson dictated by the children, and placed on the board.

[5] *Ibid.*, pp. 133–134.

5. *Sketch on Flavors.*

MATTER.	METHOD.
I. *Flavors.*	I.—1. Developed by experiment with sugar. Children give the term. No definition given.
1. Some things are sweet to the taste.	
2. Some things are luscious to the taste.	2. Developed by experiment with molasses. Children describe the flavor. Term and general definition given: "Anything which is extremely sweet, is said to be *luscious.*"
3. Some things are bitter to the taste.	3. Developed by experiment with quinine. Children give term. No definition given.
4. Some things are acid to the taste.	4. Developed by experiment with cream of tartar. Children give the term. No general definition given.
5. Some things are acrid or alkaline to the taste.	5. Developed by experiment with soda. Term and general definition given: "Anything that has a burning, bitter taste, is said to be *acrid.*" Children told that soda is one of the substances called alkalies, whence we sometimes speak of its taste as *alkaline.*
6. Some things are saline to the taste.	6. Developed by experiment with the blue and white papers called Seidlitz powders, after the flavor of each powder has been separately ascertained. Term and general definition given: "Anything having the taste of salt is said to be *saline.*" A saline substance can be obtained by combining an acid and an alkaline substance.
7. Some things are brackish to the taste.	7. Developed by putting a little salt in water. Children describe the taste. Term and general definition given: "Anything that has a slightly salty taste, is said to be *brackish.*" Refer to springs in the desert.
8. Some things are astringent to the taste.	8. Developed by experiment with alum. Children describe the effect on the mouth. Term and general definition given: "Anything which draws up or contracts the mouth is said to be *astringent.*"

9. Some things are pungent to the taste.

9. Developed by experiment with mustard. Children referred to scents of the same character. Give the term. General definition given: "Anything which has a hot, biting taste, is said to be *pungent*."

10. Some things are aromatic to the taste.

10. Developed by experiment with cinnamon. Children being referred to scents of the same character, give the term. General definition given: "Anything which has a hot, strong, pleasant taste, is said to be *aromatic*."

11. Some things are savory to the taste.

11. Developed by reference to gravy, &c. Children describe the flavor. Term and general definition given: "Anything with a rich, saltish, pleasant taste, is said to be *savory*."

II.—The sense by which we discover each of these qualities, we call *taste ;* the quality itself we call *flavor*.

II.—Developed by writing two sentences on the board, in each of which the word *taste* is used in a different sense. Children say how used. Are told that there is another word which expresses the quality, and what advantage there would be in using it. Teacher writes the general term *flavor* above the list of specific flavors, which have been written on the board as given.

III.—Things having a flavor are said to be *sapid*. Things having little or no flavor are said to be *insipid*. Things having a highly agreeable flavor, are said to be *delicious*. Things having a disagreeable flavor are said to be *nauseous*.

III.—Terms and definitions given. Examples found by children.

Summary.—1. Children read the list of flavors, and in turn give examples.

2. Teacher gives the definitions in any order, children giving the term which expresses each definition.

3. Teacher erases the list of flavors, children supplying it.[3]

----

⁶ *Ibid.*, pp. 136–137.

ing "method" of teaching.[7]   Parker's work, or for that matter, Sheldon's, had little direct influence on teaching practices if we heed the historical accounts of teaching at the time.   If Sheldon's work was at all influential, it had obviously developed into an even more rigidly devised system than he had intended.   No doubt the conservative forces of the post-Civil War period had a great deal more influence on the direction of education than did the progressive innovators. Though not announced as an underlying philosophical premise as it had been in Calvinism, the belief in the innate depravity of man still seemed to be somewhat in force in the general approach to education. However, there were continuing movements to define the act of teaching in accordance with newly developed philosophical and psychological ideas.   Perhaps the most important and lasting in its influence was the Herbartian movement.

herbartianism: a science of teaching

Toward the close of the century American educational thought, and to some extent practice, were to be influenced by another European pedagogical movement based on the work of Johann Friedrich Herbart (1776–1841).   Herbart's ideas, carried on and further developed by his European followers, especially Tuiskon Ziller and William Rein at the University of Jena, were introduced into American education mainly through the work of Charles DeGarmo and Charles and Frank McMurray.   Herbartianism proposed a system of instruction to be applied by teachers in any area of study.   Essential to the system as it was to develop were the five stages or formal steps through which pupils were to be taken: (1) preparation, (2) presentation, (3) comparison and abstraction or association, (4) generalization, and (5) application.   An important element was Herbart's idea of *apperception*, which in its basic sense meant relating new ideas or knowledge to that which the pupil already possesses.

The following excerpt from *Introduction to the Herbartian Principles of Teaching* by Catherine I. Dodd point up some of the ideas for instruction that developed out of Herbartianism:

> *The Method of Imparting Knowledge*
>   Before we can attempt to teach anything to children, we must know how ideas grow in their minds. Herbart and his followers studied the mental processes by which children take in ideas, and, with these laws to guide them, they worked out the theory of the Five Formal Steps. . . .
>   We often talk of our particular *methods* of teaching, as though the mind could acquire knowledge in a dozen different ways and the teacher had the privilege of choosing in which way

---

[7] An apt description of the strict and punitive method of teaching has been cited on p. 77 in an excerpt from the writings of Joseph Rice.

the pupil should get his ideas. There is only one true method, and that corresponds to the laws according to which the child's mind works. . . . The only way in which children can acquire ideas is by following the universal law by which all discoverers have arrived at their conclusions. To proceed from particulars to the general, and back again to the particular. . . . The theory of the Five Formal Steps is an expansion of this principle. . . .

Teachers are apt to magnify the influence of instruction and to consider it the chief factor in education. The child and the natural contents of his mind are overlooked, and instead of finding out what thoughts and ideas already exist in his mind, and correcting, arranging and adding to them, the teacher often endeavors to force upon the child a mass of uninteresting facts which have no connexion with the child's mental life, and hence are unintelligible and uninteresting to him.

Herbart points out that in every child there exists a circle of thought [apperceptive mass] which he has acquired from Experience and Intercourse. This circle of thought is to be extended by instruction.[8]

A model lesson illustrates how the ideas were to be put into practice by the teacher:

Mathematical Geography

A series of lessons on the measurements of the earth, its motions, its position with regard to the Sun, Latitude, Longitude, use of Ships' Compass, use of Sextant Chronometer, Maps, Charts, form suitable lessons in connexion with Columbus. The simple charts and instruments he used are compared with the instruments in use in the present day, and his slight astronomical, mathematical, and geographical knowledge compared with the fuller knowledge of our own times.

Aim.—How can a sea captain or a sailor find the position of his ship at sea?

I. *Preparation.*—Shape of the Earth. A sphere.

It rotates from West to East.

It completes a rotation in twenty-four hours.

The earth is divided into 360° longitude.

The children gave these facts readily from their knowledge gained in previous lessons.

II. *Presentation.*—(*a*) Light a candle and hold an orange on a knitting-needle before it so that the light falls on it.

Half of it is in the full glare and half in the shade.

The candle represents the sun, the orange the earth. The part in the glare represents daylight, the part in the shade night.

Which part is having noon? The part exactly opposite the light.

Cause the orange to rotate, and the pupils will observe that

[8] Catherine I. Dodd, *Introduction to the Herbartian Principles of Teaching* (New York: Macmillan, 1906), pp. 8–9, 29–30.

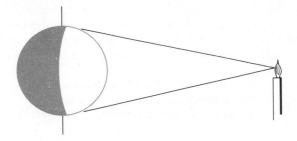

various parts of the earth have noon at different times.

Recapitulate.—Various parts of the earth have noon at different times.

(*b*) Mark the meridian of Greenwich, and cause the orange to revolve as the earth revolves on its axis, and require the pupils to notice whether the eastern or western portion has its noon first.

Recapitulate.—Places West of Greenwich have their noon later than places East of Greenwich.

(*c*) *Exact difference in time.*—If it takes the earth 24 hours to rotate through the 360 degrees, how long will it take the earth to rotate through 1 degree?

$$\frac{24 \text{ hrs.}}{360} - \frac{1440 \text{ min.}}{360} - 4 \text{ minutes.}$$

Recapitulation.—One degree of longitude is equal to four minutes in time.

(*d*) What will be the time at Bordeaux when it is 12 o'clock at Greenwich?

Position of Bordeaux, West of Greenwich (refer to the map). Being West it will have its noon later than Greenwich.

Bordeaux is 1° West of Greenwich, therefore it will be 11.56 at Bordeaux when it is 12 o'clock at Greenwich.

Problems.—What time is it at Genoa when it is 12 o'clock at London?

What time is it at New York when it is 12 o'clock at Greenwich?

What time is it at Greenwich when it is 4 o'clock at Bombay?

(*e*) Examine places near the same meridian.

Examples found on the map by pupils:—

> London and Timbucktu.
> Pekin and Perth in Australia.
> Berlin and Capetown.

Recapitulation.—Places on the same meridian have noon at the same time.

General recapitulation of the matter in presentation.

III. *Association.*—Associate with knowledge of previous lessons on Latitude, method of finding the time by observing the altitude of the sun, use of Chronometer and Sextant.

How can we discover the time of a certain place? By knowing the longitude.

How can a sailor find the longitude? By knowing the Greenwich time and comparing with the ship's time.

How can a sailor know the Greenwich time? By consulting a chronometer.

How can he find the ship's time? By observing the altitude of the sun.

Why is a knowledge of longitude not enough to fix the position of the ship? Longitude only shows how far the ship is East or West of a given point. Pekin and Perth in Australia are in the same longitude.

What fixes its position North or South of Equator? Latitude.

How does the sailor find his latitude? By discovering the sun's altitude, and by consulting a Nautical Almanack.

Having found his longitude and latitude what must he do further? Consult his chart or map.

IV. *Generalization.*—The exact position of a ship may be discovered by obtaining a correct observation of the longitude and latitude, and finding the exact point on a map or chart.

Application.—A number of problems bearing upon a knowledge of latitude, longitude, and arithmetic were given to be solved.[9]

There is no doubt that the Herbartian movement had a significant influence on American education. To some extent the idea of a core curriculum and unit studies show a Herbartian influence. But, as was the case with the development of Pestalozzianism, much of the subsequent development of the original ideas brought about a great deal of rigid formalization in instructional practices. Preactive lesson plans that plotted out in exact steps the learning experiences for children were not far removed from the earlier structured approach. Neither of them took into account the importance of student involvement. They seemed to have been based on the assumption that the student is merely a passive recipient of ideas, something to be molded or developed.

programmed instruction

The ultimate of this instructional approach has appeared more recently in the form of programmed instruction developed by the behaviorists. Excerpts from a programmed textbook display the behaviorists' views of the instructional process. The illustration of a

[9] *Ibid.,* pp. 156–159.

programmed unit, taken from the same book illustrates how those views are transposed into practice.

Programmed Learning

Learning should be fun. However, in the early stages of learning a subject, students make many mistakes. As a result, they often conclude that they do not like the subject. They would be more correct to conclude that they do not like to make errors.

For a long time, educators, psychologists, and people in general thought that it was impossible to learn without errors. Many teachers felt that making errors was, in some mysterious way, "good for you." This idea is now outdated. Recent developments in psychology and education have demonstrated that students can proceed to mastery of a subject with a negligible number of errors along the route. For this to happen, however, the material from which the student learns must be carefully prepared, or "programed," in a special way. The basic idea is that the most efficient, pleasant, and permanent learning occurs when the student proceeds through a course by a large number of small, easy-to-take steps. This is precisely what your self-tutoring course has been designed to do.

This course has been constructed on the basis of learning principles of recognized soundness. It benefits both the student and the instructor. It provides the student with the advantages of a private tutor; at the same time, it frees the instructor from routine lecturing, testing, scoring, and grading duties. This permits a much more efficient use of classroom time than has been possible previously. Students can come to class with a firm grasp of the fundamental concepts and operations in a topic. This permits the instructor to devote more time to laboratory work, enlightened class discussion, and implications and relationships with other areas. New developments in the field or topics of special interest may also be explored.

An examination of the learning situation within this course reveals fundamental differences from conventional study procedures.

First, the student goes through a carefully graded sequence of material which has been demonstrated to produce learning. With conventional textbook and lecture procedures, it is impossible for the writer or teacher to assess accurately at what point the student makes errors or "loses the point." Programed presentations, however, have been evaluated experimentally. This course has been through a series of thorough revisions on the basis of responses actually made by students. In this way, ambiguous statements and instructions have been removed and additional examples have been added to difficult portions. Such a step-by-step analysis and revision of the learning sequence is not possible in the case of textboooks and lectures.

Second, the use of the self-tutoring course insures active participation in the learning process by the student. Since each step in a course requires one or more specific written responses, the instructor can be confident at the end of a course that the student has been responding actively to the material. No comparable assurance is possible when a student has merely attended a lecture or read a textbook.

Third, the self-tutoring course provides the student with immediate confirmation of the correctness of his answers. In this way, the confidence of the student grows, since he can see that he is correct on almost every response. Such rapid confirmation is not possible in the non-programed situation, unless the student has a private tutor. Homework problems and test results simply cannot be scored by the teacher and returned in time to be really effective in helping the student master a topic.

Fourth, the student is provided with a method of proceeding at a rate of his own choosing. The quicker student need no longer be held back. On the other hand, the more methodical student can take as much time as he needs without being embarrassed by the fact that others are proceeding at a more rapid rate. When occasional mistakes are made, the student can correct them in private.

In summary, this course provides the student with a carefully prepared, experimentally tested sequence to proceed through as he gains competence in the topic he is studying. During the learning, he will be responding actively and receiving immediate confirmation of the correctness of his responses. He can proceed as slowly or as rapidly as he wishes. The instructor can be relieved of the more routine aspects of teaching, and be freed to review and elaborate upon the basic understanding of the topic which the self-tutoring course will provide. . . .

Technical Considerations

To the sophisticated "reader" of a course such as this it may seem that there is undue repetition of information and that progress is slow. It should be remembered, however, that the course is not to be "read," but is meant to be "taken" by a student to whom the subject matter is quite novel. It is important to realize that a programed course is not a textbook. If a particular fact is repeated in differing contexts, such repetition was built into the course on the basis of empirical evidence.

Each unit of this course is so structured that it is not possible to skip sequences within a unit without detriment to the learning process. Certain frames may seem too difficult to answer when taken out of context, but these very frames are important building blocks within the structure of the course. These frames will prove to be no more difficult than others when taken within the sequence of the course.

When presenting a concept to a student, it is often necessary to state this concept in a very general form until the student has grasped one of its aspects. Gradually the concept is further defined and limited as the student becomes able to handle it. It is important to realize that no subject matter criticism is valid if based on individual frames taken out of context.[10]

The twenty frames on pages 258–262 were taken from a fifty-five frame unit on spelling in a recent textbook. (The student writes his answer in the empty box, then uncovers the box on the left to check his answer.) [11]

The kind of programmed instruction shown on pages 258–262 is characteristic of the linear type program, the type used most frequently in programmed materials. The other type of programming, branching or intrinsic, involves the use of multiple choice alternatives for response. Norman Crowder, the major developer of intrinsic programming, explains his basic approach this way:

The criterion for whether a particular topic is programmable (in the branching technique) is whether there is anything that can be usefully said to a student who has made an error. If we can say to the student who has erred: (a) your answer is wrong; (b) this is *what* is wrong with your answer; (c) this is *why* this feature of your answer is wrong; (d) this is how you go about figuring out what the right answer is; and (e) now go back and try again, then we are dealing with programmable material.[12]

The examples on pp. 262–264 illustrate his ideas in practice.

As has been pointed out, the models used for illustration here are but a few of the many that could have been selected. They were selected to point up the degree of formalization and predesign that has characterized so much of education.

To be sure, there have been many alternative approaches or models developed that would remove such formalization and bring the student to the center of the educational process, but they are not reducible to neatly packaged illustrations. Their purpose and scope is much more broadly conceived. Their essential ingredient is student involvement. Such a student-centered model is given in the next section (beginning on p. 265).

---

[10] Robert Glaser et al., *General Science Biology and Chemistry* (New York: Groller, 1967), Vol. I.

[11] Lyn Sandow, *Modern English: Spelling* (New York: Grolier, 1968), pp. 1–1—1–4.

[12] Norman Crowder and Grace C. Martin, *Arithmetic of Computers* (New York: U.S. Industries, 1960), pp. 1, 4, 8.

1. Say

p

It begins with the letter (p / b / t) .

2. Say

b

It begins with the letter (t / b / c) .

3. When you write a word, you use letters to stand

for the sounds in the word.

sound

When you write **b** , you are writing a letter that

stands for a (word/sound).

4.

sound

The letter **t** stands for a _____ .

5.

sound

The letter **p** stands for a _____ .

6.

sounds	When you say a word, you are putting (letters/sounds) together.

7.

letters	When you write a word, you are putting down _____ that stand for sounds.

8. Words are made from sets of letters.

Spell

cat	

9. cat

sounds	These letters stand for _____.

10. The letters must be put together in the right way.

no	Does **tca** spell [image] ? (yes/no)

11.   Circle the word that spells

sun   uns   sun

12.   Circle the word that spells

hat   ath   hat   aht

13.   Circle the word that spells

ball   allb   blla   ball

14.   The letters that are used to spell a word:

                                         A. may be written in any order.

B   B. must be written in the right order.

15.   Say

c   This word begins with the letter (c /k) .

16.   Cane does not begin with k.

| same | Sometimes different letters stand for the _____ sound. |

17.

| no | Can you spell [cat] like this: kat? (yes/no) |

18.

| cat | A grown-up kitten is called a _____ . |

19.   Say oat.
       Say kit.

| yes | Do these words start with the same sound? (yes/no) |

20.

| yes | Can the letters c and k stand for the same sound? (yes/no) |

1

LESSON 1

The Powers of Numbers

A modern electronic computer performs complicated mathematical calculations in a matter of seconds. Inside the computer, electrical impulses are translated into a number system which differs considerably from the one commonly used in pencil-and-paper mathematics.

To understand how a computer uses its unique system of numbers to perform such amazing feats, we will have to spend some time dissecting and examining more closely the number system we already know.

Our familiar number system uses ten different numerals: 0, 1, 2, 3, 4, 5, 6, 7, 8 and 9. Each single numeral is called a digit. Because the system uses ten different numerals or digits it is called the *decimal* system (Latin *decem* = ten). The arithmetic we learned in school is decimal arithmetic.

We are so familiar with the decimal system and decimal arithmetic that the decimal system may seem to us the "natural" system. Actually it is only one of many systems of writing numbers.

Now here is a question on the material you have just read. Select what you believe to be the correct answer and turn to the page number indicated to the right of the answer you choose.

Would you say that the two numbers 492 and .29 are both written in the decimal system?

ANSWER

Both 492 and .29 are written in the decimal system. **page 4**

Only .29 is written in the decimal system. **page 8**

4
[from page 1]

YOUR ANSWER: Both 492 and .29 are written in the decimal system.

You are correct.   The word "decimal" refers simply to the fact
that our common number system uses only ten different numerals,
or digits.   With these ten single digits (0, 1, 2 . . . 9), we can count
up to 9.   Beyond 9 we must use combinations of these numerals,
such as 1 and 0 for ten (10), and 1 and 1 for eleven (11), etc.
Do you know, or have you ever heard of, a number system for
representing quantities other than our familiar 10-digit decimal
system?

ANSWER

Yes.   **page 14**

No.   **page XIV**

I'm not sure.   **page** ~~THL~~ ~~THL~~ 1111

8
[from page 1]

YOUR ANSWER: Only .29 is written in the decimal system.

Well, let's see.
You once learned that

$$.29 \ = 29/100,$$

and $$.4 \ \ = 4/10,$$

and $$.333 = 333/1000$$

Fractional quantities such as .29, .4, and .333, written with the aid of the "decimal" point, are called "decimal" fractions. You probably were thinking about this use of the word "decimal" when you decided that the decimal fraction .29 is written in the decimal system and the whole number 492 is not.

The fact that no decimal point is shown does not exclude the number 492 from the decimal system. The word "decimal" means "ten." The decimal system is a number system which uses ten different digits. Both whole and fractional numbers may be written with decimal system digits.

The number 492 and the number .29 are both written in the decimal system because they both use the decimal system digits—which are 0, 1, 2, 3, 4, 5, 6, 7, 8 and 9.

Please return to Page 1 and choose another answer.

Answer to Self-Test Question 1, Lesson 1: Yes.

[13] Norman Crowder and Grace C. Martin, *Arithmetic of Computers* (U.S. Industries, 1960), pp. 1, 4, 8.

a new model for instruction

Since method is implicit in content, a laissez-faire attitude toward the concept of the learning situation must be rejected. Certainly the full dimensions of any school program will not be realized if method or the lack of it: (1) discourages inquiry and creativity, (2) ritualizes procedures, (3) fails to accept individual differences (or perceives or relates to them in superficial terms), (4) ignores scientific or scholarly techniques or attack, (5) maximizes memory and minimizes discovery, (6) neglects the potential for achievement through either the individual or the group, (7) employs teacher resources in a single rather than in a multidimensional role.

A certain schema for instruction best fits this curriculum theory. Its essential characteristics are freedom of movement, flexibility and adaptability, and full employment of all available resources.

Students of methodology will not find the new model so new after all. Its genealogical roots are deep in Quintilian, St. Augustine, Vittorino de Feltre, in Rabelais, Bacon, Locke, Rousseau, Comenius, Pestalozzi, and Dewey. But it acknowledges no debt to Calvin, Marx, Gentile, or Skinner, and little enough to observation of good practice in the schools.

However, Morrison's unit method is significantly used and altered. We do not intend to minimize or patronize his approach by claiming a distinctiveness beyond it. The unit method had both beneficial and revolutionary impact on instructional practice. Most of the instructional situations in the country would be improved significantly if the teacher conceptualized and used the Morrison model of practice. The method did not fail, but it was not widely used because it demanded too much professionalization of teaching.

Our model here is new in scope and purposes. It is a reconceptualization of the basic instructional function of the school and is related to the uses and conception of intelligence. We will use the phrase "built through" to describe the learning situation in this model. The phrase is deliberate and significant; it implies construction, cumulative experience, purposiveness, design, direction, continuity, and eventual completeness.

The five phases include:
1. Exploration and planning
2. Inquiry, activity, and research
3. Presentation, organization, and conceptualization
4. Appraisal and evaluation
5. Utilization, reflection, reconceptualization

EXPLORATION AND PLANNING. The opening phase involves the search for the possibilities of learning experiences within a unit. While the teacher's scholarship is naturally included, it does not preclude the necessity to involve all learners in exploration

and planning. (It is assumed that the teacher too will be an
active, participating learner.) This phase includes assessment
of such study resources as textual accounts, library research,
guests, field study, and projects. It involves review and discussion of what the class, or individuals within the class, already
know or have experienced relating to the unit being planned.
The overview is established; the scope of study is limited and
defined. The hypotheses are set forth as generalizations that
will be examined to discover whether the results of inquiry
(facts or evidence) support them, to what extent, and with what
qualifications. Planning will include preparation of study-guide
materials and the division of labor.

Planning should axiomatically be cooperative. Though most
teachers seem unaware of the skill of cooperation and most
schools devoid of it, it would be anachronistic and patronizing
to set forth a theoretical justification of cooperative planning
and cooperative classroom procedures. Such devices are related
positively to self-realization, initiative, creativity, democratic
attitudes, and motivation. The point here is simply that
exploration and planning are a phase of learning; therefore, to
exclude intended learners from this enterprise is to exclude
them from a part of the intended learning.

INQUIRY, ACTIVITY, AND RESEARCH. Phase 2 implies the study
of evidence and subject matter and the systematic collection of
data: readings, references, projects, field studies. It also
includes the discussion and interchange of knowledge and ideas.

It may be noted that a strand of scientific method runs
through this model, for example, the formulation of hypotheses
in Phase 1 and the systematic collection of data in Phase 2.
However, it is not the sole support of the method, as this model
conceptualizes a complex learning situation, involves groups of
young learners in a context of many social and psychological
factors, and includes content goals that encompass more than
pure discovery.

Nor are the phases sharply cut off from one another. In brief,
they are not "formal steps." For example, somewhere in the
middle of Phase 2 it may be necessary to admit blunders in
direction that require stopping to reassess, turn back, reexplore,
or replan. The central characteristics of each phase are clearly
discernible, but the learning enterprise should be one that
exhibits flow and continuity rather than jerkiness, and spon-
taneity rather than scheduling.

The signal element relevant to the instructional model that
awaits subsequent development is the delineation of content
resources on which the learning situation will be based. A
conceptualization of the substances of experience has been
developed for its intrinsic consonance with this model of
instruction. . . .

In Phase 2 the competence of the teacher as an organizer of
learning is at a premium. The teacher's scholarship is now put

to work by making appropriate resources known and occasionally steering inquiry away from blind alleys and disappointing by-paths. The teacher may give brief, well-planned presentations of material while helping students to develop skills, techniques, and effective use of their time and efforts.

The teacher's most important role is attending to individual differences with constant press toward maximum growth and development. The teacher must be certain that each student finds tasks most appropriate to his abilities, interests, and motivations. This must be defined intersubjectively among individual students, the group, and the teacher, in open communication that reflects phenomenological views of self, situation, and one another.

PRESENTATION, ORGANIZATION, AND CONCEPTUALIZATION. Phase 3 is concerned with bringing together the findings of study, experience, and research in meaningful patterns. It is here that initial hypotheses and assumptions are checked out in light of what has been discovered.

The goals of "generalization" responsibly are confined to the evidence and carefully qualified as to limits and exceptions. If the inquiry has been basically scientific, the generalization may be made quite firm if its limits are strictly defined. In a social scientific setting certain generalizations may be phrased in terms of probabilities or limits of confidence, or something akin to these. But generalizations on moot issues, on humanistic matters, on questions of taste and judgment, or on values must be phrased carefully. When they are not, they may become instruments of semantic or psychological coercion. Dissent as well as consensus is a valid source of generalization.

Conceptualization takes shape here as the articulation and personalization of meaning in a form that is susceptible to use, to growth, and to continuing reappraisal. The students may come to speak of this process in just such terms, but the process is more important than the words. In the actual classroom the process of conceptualization may take place as the learning addresses itself to questions like these:

What conclusions shall we draw from our findings?
What early questions have we satisfactorily answered?
How would we restate our initial questions and hypotheses
    if we had known at the beginning what we know now?
On what matters have we found less evidence than we were
    seeking and what should we do about it?
What implications, if any, do our findings have for action?
What avenues or interests have we opened for further study?

APPRAISAL AND EVALUATION. Phase 4 directs attention to two questions: (1) How have we done? (2) What have I learned? The first question implies a procedural review, a critique on the learning method. Such a critique is a basic element in developing skills, scientific attitudes, and critical thinking. It is also a means by which classes grow in learning competence (a rarity in the educational process). The second question implies not merely the vulgar necessity for tests and grades (which ought to be outside the patterns of motivation); it implies that the learner is intrinsically concerned with evaluation of self. It assumes that a participant in a learning situation developed with this model wants to learn certain realities about self and achievement from the process of evaluation and its outcomes.

The ordinary tests employed either in old academic or recent technological models of instruction primarily measure activities in Phase 2, and these usually in a vacuum. Tests are legitimate but severely limited instruments within a learning situation. Testing presupposes a connection between the ability to give back subject matter on cue in an arbitrarily sought pattern and real-life consequence, which should be the outcome of learning.

Typical testing serves to diminish the person. It is a poor basis for self-judgment and often gives him conscious feelings of inadequacy. To know what we do not know is profound learning. For example, to conclude that we cannot learn to ride a bicycle because we cannot name the identifying characteristics of seven manufacturers' types is the kind of false self-conviction toward which the typical academic approach is directed. The test forever doubles back on itself; it says to go back and memorize the items missed. Evaluation reaches forward; it invites the learner to dare, to assess his strength, to try, and to discover what can be done. A child would never learn to walk if he had to pass a test of competence beforehand.

Evaluation in our model eliminates mystic assumptions. This model inquires directly into consequence. It seeks to assist the student in finding out what he has learned by directing his attention toward self-inquiry: Can I do anything now I could not do before? Have I new or improved skills? How can I find out or demonstrate these consequences? Real evaluation is expansive; it moves out, it demands more.

UTILIZATION, REFLECTION, AND RECONCEPTUALIZATION. If the first four phases mainly represent a restructure and extension of earlier reform models of instructional practice, Phase 5 constitutes a radical theoretical departure and innovation. Elements commonly ignored, or at best merely acknowledged in good words and pious hopes, are herein incorporated with the basic intent of instruction.

This is the phase beyond formal learning in the school, but its importance and reality should not be overlooked. Full learning does not take place without this phase. This is so apparent that anyone may acknowledge and dismiss it. But this model for instruction demands that the school not hold optimistic, careless, or laissez-faire attitudes about desirable outcomes. Instruction must deliberately and intelligently improve the likelihood that culminating learning will eventuate.

At this point the model demands consummate teaching (the

utilization of professional know-how at its highest levels) to effect consummated learning (the wedding of behavior and experience). Such teaching perceives that learning is not a capsule to be swallowed, not a set of hurdles to be run, not a bundle of neat generalizations to be wrapped and stored away, not a series of academic exploits to be catalogued, scored, recorded, and forgotten.

The teacher can directly invite realization of Phase 5, as the class progresses from one unit to another, by such leads as these:

1. The next time such a situation occurs, think of what we found out with respect to hypothesis X.
2. Here are some good books on the subject that we have not used, and which you might like to read on your own.
3. Remember the generalization. Since we disagreed, keep looking for evidence and thinking about it.
4. I think we have some clear ideas about this subject now, but remember, things change. Keep your minds open. Some new evidence may develop, which means that we'll have to reconsider and reshape these concepts some day.

Phase 5 must be thought of in harder terms than invitation. The key words, utility and necessity, do not mean the same. Even the most traditional academician warns: "Learn this, it will come in handy" or "You will need to know it in college."

Utility must be a demonstrable as well as a claimed characteristic of learning. Nothing argues harder for articulation of curricula than this. The school must know at every level what it has enabled its students to learn so that it may deliberately give occasion for its use. Does the school too frequently destroy what it has created by denying opportunity for its use? Does it do the following too often?

1. Teach children songs and deny them the chance to sing.
2. Teach them skills of critical thinking and penalize them when they criticize.
3. Nurture them in choice-making and veto their choices.
4. Attend to their physical health and then restrict them to the most sedentary of routines; reward vigor with captivity, as it were.
5. Keep them in school in their biological prime and refuse to deal respectfully or candidly with their expression of sex.
6. Teach them to love to read and give them no time for it. Teach them to paint and take away their brushes and palettes. Teach them to talk and penalize them for speaking their minds.
7. Sometimes teach the real, but usually test the absurd.
8. Speak of individuality and reward conformity.

How shall the child determine what is useful when the use of what he undertook to learn in good faith is so often denied by the very institution that undertook to get him to learn it?

Beyond utility lies necessity; the necessity in learning is its exercise. In our time, three dozen people watched as a woman was murdered, and nobody acted on her behalf. We can assume that many had studied civics in school and had passed the course. Some had probably written good tests, but they failed the ultimate examination. The school had not stressed fifth-phase learning, necessity. In sum, it is that aspect of the new model of instruction which insists that learning in the school must have a life consequence. The fifth phase is no less than the assumption of human responsibility.

The returns for the student who participates in the new model of instructional practice are great. Three specific advantages may be noted:

The skills of learning are made intrinsic. No choice exists between the development of skill and its use. The traditional classroom may make "the skills" its subject matter; that is, it may assign their study and use. The new model exemplifies the skills in action. The automated classroom simply extends the conventional teaching approach; it renders the skills extrinsic and delegates their exercise to the machine.

Students in the new model become searchers and researchers. They locate, record, and appraise resources for learning. They learn to budget time and energy. They acquaint themselves with the devices of cataloguing, indexing, locating information and ideas. They live in the mode of the modern organization, in which they must survive as individuals while operating in a constantly changing panorama of functional subgroupings. The skills of cooperation that the students employ are not utopian; they have social and ethical value, but they are skills in the context of the complex institutional structures in which most people live.

The student finds his learning situation consistent with his evolving discovery of the modern mind. He learns that man is in a predicament, not wholly of his own making, where intelligence and enterprise are his chief resources. He finds similarities in his situation as well. In the conventional classroom his signs of growth are often held against him. In the new model growth is both sought after and counted on.

Obviously, no learning situation can succeed without the student. But many instructional models leave this at the axiomatic level. Student involvement in the new model is real; in fact, student involvement in responsible rather than perfunctory roles is necessary to its success.

The new model brings the student into the pattern of inquiry that is most typical of sophisticated study. Older models are naive and sterile: assign, recite, test, or lecture, discuss, test, or program, study, reinforce, test. These are patterns of learning familiar only within the school. They are not common to man in his natural habitat, life.

The phases of the new model parallel and incorporate the very structure of modern research. Phase 1—exploration and

planning—parallels the design of the project and the statement
of hypotheses. Phase 2—inquiry, activity, and research—is the
accumulation-of-data stage; its classroom instruments may be
those of any research discipline (documentary, survey, statistical,
or field). Phase 3—presentation, organization, and conceptualization—is like the data-processing and reporting stages of a
research project. Phase 4—appraisal and evaluation—
represents the critical intelligence applied to findings of inquiry,
an application both by the researcher and by his peers, on behalf
of both. Phase 5—utilization, reflection, and reconceptualization
—reflects the outcome of research, which includes every step
from rejection to replication to utilization.

What is important is not that the new model teaches the ways
of science, but that it involves the student in the method of
scientific inquiry. Scientific method is intrinsic rather than
extrinsic to the new model. Learning will be experienced as
problem-solving, whether the problem be the determination of
the amount of energy brought to bear by a machine, the creation
of a poem, or understanding the roots of prejudice in a
community. The results of the method will be new knowledge,
deeper perceptions, and experience itself.

Perhaps the most significant feature of the new model is in
its regard to individual differences. Token acknowledgments
have included some allowance for adjustments to individual
differences, but such tokens are often patronizing or exploitative,
or both. Johnnies-come-lately to the educational scene have
waxed excited over a one-dimensional view of individual difference: the fact that some students learn faster than others. But
a footrace does not constitute a full-dimensioned physical
education program; for that matter, though speed is involved
in both, a runner does not train for the Marathon as he does for
the 100-yard dash.

The new model does not do anything to individual differences.
It accepts them, respects them, and liberates them. It puts all
of the complexities of individual differences to good use,
including: biological differences, variations in cultural background, assorted depths of experience, emotional differences,
wide variations in maturity and motivation, varied skills, broad
ranges of developed and potential strengths, disparate capacities
for communication and response, diverse moral and spiritual
sensitivities, and the fact that some work faster than others.
Variety is not a problem; it is the foundation of the method and
includes the complex, diverse patterns of mankind and expression
of the full human potential. When it is reduced to oversimple
dimensions, it results in confinement to tight little boxes,
circumscribing and distorting the human potential, and the
curtailment of learning. Real education recognizes, appreciates,
and uses differences.[14]

[14] Ryland W. Crary, *Humanizing the School* (New York: Knopf, 1969), pp. 117–127.

topics for inquiry

1. The Montessori Method
2. Research on "Effective Teaching"
3. Computer-Aided Instruction
4. The Winnetka Plan
5. The Dalton Plan
6. Teaching Methods in Business and Industry
7. Socratic Method
8. Methods Courses for Teachers
9. Survey of Modern Methods Books and Journals in Your Field
10. Biologically and Chemically Controlled Learning

subjects for discussion

1. The programmed instruction model is built on the premise that learning occurs with certainty when the possibility for error is eliminated.
   a. Do you agree?
   b. Is it a realistic premise for learning?
   c. Does the student play an "active" part in the process?
2. In his book, *Freedom to Learn*, Carl Rogers states his views on teaching:

   > I have a negative reaction to teaching. Why? I think
   > it is because it raises all the wrong questions. As soon
   > as we focus on teaching the question arises, what shall
   > we teach, what, from our superior vantage point, does
   > the other person need to know? I wonder if, in this
   > modern world, we are justified in the presumption that
   > we are wise about the future and the young foolish.
   > Are we *really* sure as to what they should know? [15]

   a. What implications for teaching does Rogers' statement hold?
   b. Does his idea dismiss the need for a method or model?
   c. Could Rogers' view be adhered to even within the subject area requirements?
3. A. S. Neill, in *Summerhill* states:

   > We have no new methods of teaching, because we do not
   > consider that teaching in itself matters very much.
   > Whether a school has or has not a special method for

[15] Carl Rogers, *Freedom to Learn* (Columbus, Ohio: Charles Merrill, 1969), p. 103.

teaching long division is of no importance except to
those who *want* to learn it. And the child who *wants*
to learn long division *will* learn it no matter how it is
taught.[16]

a. Contrary to Neill's assumption is there an implied method or
   model in his statement?
b. Do you agree with Neill that desire obviates method?
c. Suppose a child wanted to learn nothing that the school offered? Which of the two, the school or the child, would be
   taking a narrow approach?

selected readings

BOWER, ELI M., and WILLIAM G. HOLLISTER (eds.). *Behavioral Science
Frontiers in Education.* New York: Wiley, 1967.
> A deep insight into ego processes as involved in education. It
> discusses significant new ideas in educational theory as they ap-
> ply to teaching.

GOLDHAMMER, ROBERT. *Clinical Supervision.* New York: Holt, Rinehart and Winston, 1969.
> Although written for the supervision of teaching, insightful
> views of the teaching process as it often happens. Goldhammer's
> style of writing makes the book read like a novel.

ROGERS, CARL R. *Freedom to Learn.* Columbus, Ohio: Charles Merrill,
1969.
> Strongly developed arguments for freedom in learning. In
> addition, Rogers provides three examples of classroom ap-
> proaches that illustrate his ideas.

SEARLES, JOHN E. *A System for Instruction.* Scranton, Pa.: International Textbook, 1967.
> An incisive analysis of various aspects of both teaching and
> learning.

SHIPELY, C. MORTON, *et al.* *A Synthesis of Teaching Methods.* To-
ronto: McGraw-Hill, 1968.
> A fairly comprehensive, though conventional discussion of
> teaching methods. Many of the specific tasks involved in teach-
> ing are examined.

YAMAMOTO, KAORU (ed.). *Teaching: Essays and Readings.* Boston:
Houghton Mifflin, 1969.
> A fairly comprehensive collection of ideas about the teaching
> process.

[16] A. S. Neill, *Summerhill: A Radical Approach to Child Rearing* (New York: Hart, 1960),
p. 5.

274

9
ASSERTION AND EVIDENCE IN EDUCATIONAL CHOICE

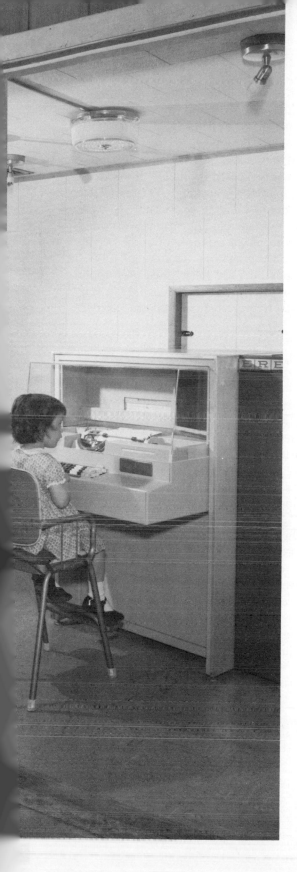

If education were a static enterprise, existing and functioning under an assuring blanket of absolutism, the work of the teacher would be relatively simple. To successfully pursue his profession, he would simply need to attain the absolutes as set down. The teacher, wherever he might be, would then know precisely what to teach and to whom, when to teach it, and, most importantly, how to teach it. However, education, like life, is not static. There are no precisely drawn, and therefore comforting, plans for the teacher to follow. Never has this been truer than in today's rapidly changing world. The most that can be hoped for is some kind of evidence that suggests in pragmatic comparative terms what appears to be the better approach to meet certain needs and aims of education. Ultimately the teacher is faced with the responsibility of choosing how best to perform his work. He might, of course, effortlessly follow the nearest sets of directions without concern as to their appropriateness or validity. Or he might accept the responsibility of making personal decisions about the nature of education and the appropriate functioning of the teacher. Hopefully his decisions will be influenced by the existing evidence in educational research as well as a continuing quest for the philosophical assumptions that underlie education.

It would be utter folly to suggest that the individual teacher has a deciding voice in establishing, in a broad sense, the school program. Except in rare instances, the questions of what subjects shall be taught, to whom, and when are decided by higher levels. The ele-

mentary teacher is given a schedule of subjects to be taught with determined time allotments.   For the secondary teacher the subject
area is self-defined and the time allotments set by the school schedule.
But beyond this institutionally imposed structuring the teacher does
have a great deal of freedom in deciding how best to function in the
classroom as an advocate of the student.   This might mean, at times,
making studied appraisals of insensitive institutionally imposed or
implied practices that tend to work against the student.   It is expected
that such appraisals, and the subsequent choices of alternatives, will
to some extent be based on available evidence in educational research.
What follows in this chapter is offered as an example of some of the
research evidence that speaks to some questions about educational
practices.   In some instances the questions are basic ones that apply
to general educational approaches; in others the questions apply to specific educational practices.   Their relative importance can be decided
by the reader.

education—static or dynamic: authoritarian
or democratic?

In April, 1930, a group of two hundred American educators—teachers,
principals, and professors—met in Washington, D. C., to consider the
problems of the secondary schools in the United States.   As members of
the Progressive Education Association, they were also determined to
improve the high schools.   The elementary schools, stimulated by
early progressive ideas and practices, had already begun to move away
from the rigid and stifling recitation method that had characterized
them at the turn of the century.   The secondary schools, on the other
hand, were functioning as they always had, with rigidly prescribed
curricula where the student too often became a passive recipient.   To
many this would also characterize the high school today.   Then, as
now, however, secondary schools were restricted to a great extent by
college requirements.   In order to explore the problem, the Progressive Education Association established a Commission on the Relation
of School and College.   The result of the commission's work was the
Eight Year Study,[1] which was to begin in 1933.

   In 1931, after a year's investigation the commission cited what it
found to be serious shortcomings of the secondary schools.   These
were some of their findings: [2]

1. Schools failed to give students a sincere appreciation of their American heritage or an insight into the great political, social, and economic problems of the nation.
2. The schools did not adequately prepare students for the responsi-

---

[1] Wilford M. Aiken, *The Story of the Eight Year Study* (New York: Harper and Brothers,
1942).
[2] *Ibid.*, pp. 4–10.

bilities of community life. They were generally autocratic rather than democratic in their organization and functioning.

3. The schools seldom challenged the students to explore on their own. They simply expected them to pass their courses.
4. The schools neither knew their students well nor guided them wisely. They generally showed little concern about students who dropped out or those who graduated.
5. The schools persisted with ineffective and discredited methods, such as assigning meaningless tasks and recitation in spite of what was known about learning theory.
6. The curriculum was far removed from the real concerns of youth, limited to formal subjects that had lost much of their vitality and significance.

The commission's criticisms of the secondary schools were not put forth as a sweeping condemnation. It realized that many of the problems had grown along with the phenomenal growth of high school enrollment in the preceding thirty years. The commission members were also aware that any major curricular reconstruction of secondary education was prohibited by the fact of college entrance requirements. To some extent the restrictive press of college requirements was given official sanction in 1893 by the Committee of Ten on Secondary School Studies who established the unit system in their attempt to standardize high school programs. Although the high school terminated formal education for most students in the 1930s, it was looked upon primarily as preparation for college. Thus any significant attempt at experimenting with changes in secondary education could only come about with the removal of the college requirement press. With this in mind, the commission put forth an experimental plan.

The commission proposed that a number of selected high schools redesign their programs, both in terms of curricular offerings and methods and that they free themselves of the concern for meeting college requirements. This would be accomplished by contractual agreement with a number of colleges that would set aside their regular admission requirements of subjects for graduates of the experimental schools.

Over 300 colleges agreed to take part in the experiment. Thirty high schools from all over the country were selected for the project. They ranged from small private schools to large city high schools. Although the commission provided assistance to the participating high schools, it avoided any chance to dictate policy. Each school was free to develop its own program with a view to achieving what the commission set down as its goals:

The educational emphasis in this plan is based upon a conviction that the secondary schools must become more effective in helping young people to develop the insight, the

powers, and the self-direction necessary for resourceful and
constructive living. We wish to work toward a type of secondary
education which will be flexible, responsive to changing needs,
and clearly based upon an understanding of young people as
well as an understanding of the qualities needed in adult life.

We are trying to develop students who regard education as
an enduring quest for meanings rather than credit accumulation;
who desire to investigate, to follow the leadings of a subject, to
explore new fields of thought; knowing how to budget time, to
read well, to use the sources of knowledge effectively and who
are experienced in fulfilling obligations which come with
membership in the school or college community.[3]

The resultant responses to the commission's aims, which were
to be developed over eight years, were varied. Some schools made
cautious readjustments. Others departed significantly from the formal curriculum organization. However, the general trend in all the
schools was toward a more democratic procedure both in developing
programs and in carrying them out. Principals, teachers, and students together were involved in developing a variety of approaches.
No longer were the syllabuses for courses prepared in the superintendent's or principal's office to be handed out to the teachers. Even
in the less adventurous schools where the traditional course arrangements had been retained, the students were involved in planning their
programs. Some schools utilized the communities as demonstration
laboratories for studying economics, civics, science, architecture, industrial organization, and vocational interests.

It would be impossible here to discuss the variety of approaches
that were taken by the schools, but in general they all emphasized the
following:

1. Some degree of subject integration.
2. Attempts to relate subjects to social problems and adolescent needs.
3. Teacher-pupil planning.
4. Use of a variety of learning experiences adapted to individual interests and needs.
5. Development of social concerns.
6. Development of critical thinking and creativity; individual guidance
   and evaluation.

The specific school programs as well as the development and findings of the Eight Year Study were published in a five-volume report
in 1942.[4]

Although there could have been many means by which to evaluate
the effectiveness of the experimental schools, the original purpose and
intent of the study held for one specific evaluative approach. The

[3] *Ibid.*, p. 144.
[4] *Adventure in American Education* (New York: Harper and Brothers, 1942), Vols. I–V.

success of the experiment was to rest simply on how well the graduates of the schools would perform in college. The essential purpose of the study was to hold up to question the restrictive assumption that success in college depended upon the study of specific subjects for a specified time. If this assumption were baseless, then high schools would have been needlessly restricted to inflexible and often meaningless programs of studies rather than be free to make the schools relevant and exciting for students.

In order to evaluate the study, the 1,475 graduates of the experimental schools were paired with graduates of traditional schools attending the same colleges. Each pair was matched as closely as possible on variables such as sex, race, age, scholastic aptitude scores, vocational interests, socioeconomic background, and other pertinent factors. Under the direction of Ralph W. Tyler, of the University of Chicago, a group of impartial members of college faculties conducted the evaluation. A set of criteria was drawn up against which to measure the matched pairs. The results of the evaluation were impressive, as seen by the following report:

In a comparison of 1,475 matched pairs the Follow-up Staff found that the graduates of the Thirty Schools:

1. earned a slightly higher total grade average;
2. earned higher grade averages in all subject fields except foreign languages;
3. specialized in the same academic fields as did the comparison students;
4. did not differ from the comparison group in the number of times they were placed on probation;
5. received slightly more academic honors in each year;
6. were more often judged to possess a high degree of intellectual curiosity and drive;
7. were more often judged to be precise, systematic and objective in their thinking;
8. were more often judged to have developed clear and well-formulated ideas concerning the meaning of education— especially in the first two years of college;
9. more often demonstrated a high degree of resourcefulness in meeting new situations;
10. did not differ from the comparison group in ability to plan their time effectively;
11. had about the same problems of adjustment as the comparison group, but approached their solution with greater effectiveness;
12. participated somewhat more frequently, and more often enjoyed appreciative experiences in the arts;
13. participated more in all organized student groups except religious and service activities;
14. earned in each college year a higher percentage of non-academic honors;

15. did not differ from the comparison group in the quality of
    adjustment to their contemporaries;
16. differed only slightly from the comparison group in the kinds
    of judgment about their schooling;
17. had a somewhat better orientation toward the choice of a
    vocation;
18. demonstrated a more active concern for what was going on
    in the world.[5]

Although the differences existed consistently for each pair studied, it was found upon further analysis that "the graduates of the most experimental schools were strikingly more successful than their matches. Differences in their favor were much greater than the differences between the total Thirty Schools and their comparison group."[6]

In view of the findings of the Eight Year Study, it would seem reasonable to ask why it has had so little effect on the secondary schools or, for that matter, on college entrance requirements. Colleges still maintain the formal subject requirements, and high schools still structure their curriculum in like order. Even the Thirty Schools had, by 1950, retained little if any of their experimental programs. Of course, the fact that the study was concluded during World War II might well have accounted for its lack of impact on the schools in general. Nevertheless, the results still stand as substantial evidence that education need not be thought of in terms of highly organized and rigidly prescribed subject matter. And the findings of the Eight Year Study have been corroborated by the results of numerous other studies at all levels of education. The evidence strongly asserts the validity of the premises of progressivism discussed throughout this book.

Applied to the schools today, progressivism—or, more appropriately, experimentalism—would have the schools striving continually to determine and meet the needs of students in the contemporary society. It would mean that students themselves would be active participants in the educational process, not mere passive recipients of an imposed step-by-step program.

Even within the present structure of the schools, with the separately defined subject areas, the experimentalist approach has meaning. In its least sense it means that the classroom would become more democratically organized, an arrangement that John Dewey held to be consistent with a preference for a democratic society. In discussing "why we prefer democratic and humane arrangements to those which are autocratic and harsh," Dewey asked this question:

Can we find any reason that does not ultimately come down to
the belief that democratic social arrangements promote a better

[5] Dean Chamberlin *et al., Did They Succeed in College?* (New York: Harper and Brothers, 1942), pp. 207–208.
[6] *Ibid.*, p. 209.

quality of human experience, one which is more widely accessible and enjoyed, than do non-democratic forms of social life? [7]

Aside from the preference for democratic social arrangements, there is also further evidence that supports democratic educational practices. Research in learning theory upholds the validity of the progressive premises about education. According to Goodwin Watson, there is among the various schools of psychology agreement on many aspects of learning theory. Watson put forth some of the well-established principles in a booklet entitled *What Psychology Can We Trust*. Among the principles that he cites as being firmly established by evidence are:

1. The type of reward (reinforcement) which has the greatest transfer value to other life situations is the kind one gives oneself—the sense of satisfaction in achieving purpose.
2. Children are more apt to throw themselves wholeheartedly into any project if they themselves have participated in the selection and planning of the enterprise.
3. Overstrict discipline is associated with more conformity, anxiety, shyness, and acquiescence in children; greater permissiveness is associated with more initiative and creativity in children.
4. Many pupils experience so much criticism, failure, and discouragement in school that their self-confidence, level of aspiration, and sense of worth are damaged.
5. Pupils think when they encounter an obstacle, difficulty, puzzle, or challenge in a course of action which interests them. The process of thinking involves designing and testing plausible solutions for the problem as understood by the thinker.
6. No school subjects are markedly superior to others for "strengthening mental powers." General improvement as a result of study of any subject depends on instruction designed to build up generalizations about principles, concept formation, and improvements of techniques of study, thinking, and communication.[8]

The evidence of the Eight Year Study and subsequent findings that support the progressive premises about education can have meaning for the teacher if they are viewed as a basis from which to proceed. Obviously, there is no precise methodology for teaching to be taken from the evidence. Rather, the study suggests the opposite—teacher-pupil creativity in planning and carrying out educational projects.

iq: prediction or expectation

In his book, *The Tyranny of Testing*, Banesh Hoffman cites a report issued in 1962 by a committee of the American Association of School

[7] John Dewey, *Experience and Education* (New York: Macmillan, 1963), p. 39.

[8] Goodwin Watson, *What Psychology Can We Trust* (New York: Teachers College, Columbia University, 1961), pp. 3–14.

Administrators, the Council of Chief State School Officers, and the National Association of Secondary-School Principals. In their report, *Testing, Testing, Testing,* the committee had this to say about the IQ:

> Often the first question asked about a pupil by a teacher is,
> "What's his IQ?" And the answer, regardless of its accuracy,
> often determines the posture of some, if not all, of his teachers
> toward him. This practice continues despite the innumerable
> examples of frightfully inaccurate IQ scores.[9]

Unfortunately, the committee's charge still holds true regardless of even further evidence that questions the validity of "intelligence tests." Teachers still ask the same question and, what is even more absurd, accept the answer as being an accurate measurement of the student's "intelligence" or "mental ability." The IQ is often accepted with the same degree of certainty as would be a measurement of a person's height or weight. So conditioned have we become to the concept of IQ that it is not unusual to find individuals concerned about what their own IQ is, as though they would therefore be immediately certain as to their level of intelligence. Parents, who have had the opportunity to observe their child functioning "intelligently" from birth, are often concerned about what their child's IQ is. They are reassured if they are told it is above average, disheartened if told it is below, accepting the results of a thirty-minute test as being a magically accurate measurement of "intelligence."

The important fact for education, of course, is that a student's IQ becomes a vitally important entry in his dossier. It is not unusual to hear a school principal characterize his school in terms of the IQ range and median of its students. And the scores are there for the teacher to see, assumedly for the purpose of better enabling him to teach the student, but also possibly enabling him to set limits of expectation for the student. The latter possibility is discussed later in this chapter.

There are some important points that must be considered in any discussion about IQ tests: (1) the intended purposes of the tests, (2) the predictive validity of the tests, and (3) the effects IQ scores might have on a teacher's attitudes about a pupil.

the intended purpose of iq tests

Schools use IQ tests in order to identify presumed levels of ability among students, the assumption being that with such identification a more efficient educational program can be provided. It is assumed that a child's capacity for learning can be measured with the same accuracy that can be expected when one measures the capacity of a container. It is further assumed that with the knowledge of a child's learning capacity the teacher might therefore "teach" with the appropriate levels of expectation.

The stated purposes for IQ tests can be found in the manuals accompanying the tests. In general, they speak in terms of measuring mental ability, thinking power, degree of mental maturity, or abstract intelligence. The results of the tests, some manuals state, may be used to predict the school success of the testees. Thus, teachers will know what achievement to expect of students, administrators may more appropriately group students, and counselors may more wisely advise students.

It is conceivable that for some educational purposes a knowledge of learning capacity might be useful. However, it is questionable, except in extreme instances, that such a complex thing as intelligence, even if defined in functional terms, can be accurately measured by any means, let alone a thirty-minute or one-hour group-administered paper-and-pencil test. Yet, this is exactly what the tests are purported to do—measure mental ability. Of course, the claims are often couched by qualifying language that admits that mental ability cannot be measured directly but only by the effect it has in enabling a pupil to acquire certain knowledge and mental skill. In other words, it is claimed that mental ability can be measured accurately by the use of IQ tests. A certain score on the tests is taken as a measured level of mental ability or mental age. The IQ is then derived by a simple arithmetic equation, mental age divided by chronological age: $\frac{MA}{CA} = IQ$. The only part of the equation that is based on ascertainable fact is the chronological age. The derived mental age is based on statistical analysis of scores achieved by sample populations at various age levels. The scores of particular age groups in the sample population are ordered, and the median score becomes the established norm. Such a procedure assumes not only that differences in learning abilities can be plotted as to range and pattern, but also that any individual child can be accurately positioned in the pattern. The only thing that can be claimed with certainty is that the test scores of a large population assume some kind of normal distribution pattern. An unfortunate and damaging assumption is that the scores can be held as measurements of mental ability, either inherent or developed. It is possible, of course, to simply view the scores as indicators of nothing more than some kind of achievement scores, but this is not the intended purpose of the tests. They are viewed not as achievement tests or diagnostic tests but intelligence tests with predictive validity.

It might be argued that the statistical evidence is proof enough of the tests' validity. But if one looks at the construction of the test items in some tests, the statistical argument can be put aside. Take, for example, the following items, which are not unfair imitations of some test items. They are not meant to stand as examples of all test

items, or indeed all tests, but they are like some items found in a few
of the widely used tests.

1. Which of the things below does not belong?
          cat   deer   fish   horse   camel
  [Obviously, the "right" answer is fish. But what of the child
who would select on some basis other than biological classification? Perhaps geographic classification, or on frequency of
domesticity? Does the mere fact that most people select the
"right" answer make all the other answers "wrong"?]

2. If a child accidentally breaks another child's toy he should deny
it—keep quiet—apologize—hide it.
  [The "right" answer is obviously "apologize." But depending
on his experiences, a child might well "intelligently" select one
of the "wrong" answers.]

3. Rearrange the following words into a good sentence.
        straw   from   birds   fields   the   gather
With what letter does the last word in the sentence begin?
          b   f   t   g   s
  [A "good" sentence here would read—Birds gather straw from
the fields. The "right" answer would be *f*. What happens if
the child selects *s* as the answer? Is not an alternately good
sentence—"From the fields birds gather straw"? It might be
argued that a child with a better grasp of the language than the
test-maker might well make that choice.]

4. What is the usual feeling of a father for his children?
        joy   pity   reverence   contempt   affection
  [A child might well choose any or all of these depending on his
experiences.]

Such internal weaknesses aside, the most important aspect of IQ
tests is their claimed validity as predictors of school success. Many
teachers will vouch for the tests' predictive validity. If a student with
a "low" IQ is doing poorly in school, the teacher is likely to accept this
as his limit. If such a student is doing exceptionally well in school, he
might be looked upon, at times even termed, as an overachiever, as
though a person can somehow achieve more than he is capable of.
Banesh Hoffman [10] cites an appropriate, though extreme, example of
the overachiever phenomenon. He cites the case of a girl who had
been doing nicely in slow regular classes for three years and was rated
at the top of her class in fifth grade. When it was discovered that she
had an IQ of 70, she was put into a class for mentally retarded children despite the arguments of her teacher and test experts.

[10] *Ibid.*, pp. 11–12.

The serious question involved is whether or not the predictive validity of the IQ is somehow assured by the possibility that teachers may use it to set their expectancy levels for pupils and teach accordingly. In other words, is the pupil likely to live up to the expectancy level set for him by the teacher? Is the teacher likely to communicate what his expectancy level for a student is?

These questions were the basis of a revealing experiment by Robert Rosenthal and Lenore F. Jacobson [11] in 1964–1965 in an elementary school in California. The school drew some students from middle-class families but more from lower-class families. The central concept behind the Rosenthal and Jacobson experiment was what they called the self-fulfilling prophecy. The question that they were essentially investigating was whether or not the teacher's expectancy of a pupil's achievement had a significant effect on the realized achievement of the pupil. In the beginning of the 1964 school year the teachers were told very casually that certain pupils could be expected to show significant intellectual gains during the year. The names of the "spurters," however, had been chosen randomly so that the difference between these pupils and the "ordinary" pupils was entirely in the mind of the teacher.

The results of the Rosenthal-Jacobson experiment provide evidence to support their hypothesis that teacher expectancy has a significant effect on pupil achievement. Among the results that they found were the following [summarized]:

On IQ retest at the end of the first year the first- and second-grade pupils—those who were randomly identified as "spurters"—had increased their scores significantly more than did pupils of the control group—those who were "ordinary." About 21 percent of the experimental group had increased their IQ scores by thirty points; only 5 percent in the control group had that large a gain. Almost 50 percent of the experimental group showed gains of at least twenty points; only 19 percent of the control group showed such gain. Nearly 80 percent of the experimental group showed a gain of at least ten points; only 50 percent of the control group showed a like gain.[12]

The researchers also found that at the end of the year teachers described the "spurters" as being happier, more curious, more interesting, better adjusted, and in less need of social approval than the other pupils. In other words, the randomly designated "spurters" were seen to be the better students, and, most probably, as the study

[11] Robert Rosenthal and Lenore F. Jacobson, *Pygmalion in the Classroom* (New York: Holt, Rinehart and Winston, 1968).
[12] *Ibid.*, p. 70.

implies, were approached in like attitude by the teacher. The results
of the study should at least raise the question of the importance of
teacher attitudes about pupils' abilities. Other research has shown
that significant gains in IQ scores can be achieved by enriching the
environment of pupils. But in the Rosenthal–Jacobson study no
changes were made in the programs of the school.

The evidence thus suggests that educators should look very carefully at the concept of IQ as a valid measurement of a student's ability to learn.

ability grouping: learning expedience or social stratification

Closely related to the question of individual ability as measured by
IQ is the question of grouping students by "ability" levels, a practice
that has grown since 1950.

The proponents of homogeneous ability grouping argue their case
on what seem to be common-sense grounds:

1. It allows pupils to work with others of comparable ability and
   therefore advance at appropriate rates.
2. It challenges pupils to do their best in their assigned group, without their becoming discouraged by the work of those of higher
   ability or complacent because others are below them in achievement. Thus their greater achievement potential means greater ego-
   support.
3. It provides greater manageability for the teacher, both in terms of
   methods and materials. Thus it is more efficient.

On the surface, the arguments in favor of ability grouping may seem
plausible. But the evidence which has been provided by research on
the question lessens significantly the plausibility of the arguments.
The claimed effectiveness of homogeneous ability grouping is just not
supported by the facts.

The results of numerous studies that have compared achievement
in homogenous groups with achievement in heterogeneous groups hold
one organization superior to the other in about the same number of
instances; in other instances the studies show no significant differences between the two types of grouping. What the research findings
do suggest is that some factors other than ability grouping may account for the differences in achievement between the two types of
grouping. According to some researchers, the other "factor" is the
teacher, either in terms of personality or procedure. In other words,
the findings suggest that achievement depends on something other
than how children are grouped.

Even if there were empirical data to support ability grouping, one
could still argue against it on other grounds, such as democratic principle. Sidney Hook, for example, writes:

> If we ask then, why we should treat individuals of unequal talents and endowments as persons who are equally entitled to relevant consideration and care—the central idea underlying democratic institutions—we can point to consequences of the following type: it makes for greater tranquility, justice, freedom, security, creative diversity, reasonableness, and less cruelty, insensitiveness and intellectual intolerance than any other social system that has so far been devised or proposed.[13]

With the absence of any supportive empirical evidence for ability grouping the opposing arguments present an incontestible logic. In view of the research, the argument that opposes ability grouping on the grounds that it promotes elitism stands without qualification. Some critics argue, for example, that segregation by ability grouping can be looked upon as a means by which to preserve the principle of social stratification that the movement to end racial discrimination hopes to nullify.

Thus, it must be held that where ability grouping exists, it must either be based knowingly on an elitist position or unknowingly on baseless educational assumptions. In actual practice what seems to occur is that where some students (the gifted) are selected for special attention, the others are segregated for special neglect.

team teaching

After World War II the schools had witnessed various experiments in organizational and instructional reform. The nongraded elementary school, in several forms, had established the possibilities of a viable alternative to the conventional vertical-graded structure. Ability grouping, though not new to the schools, gained in favor after 1957 and, though found wanting, increased even more in the 1960s. Educational television, as well as a surge of interest in audiovisual aids in general, had promised a potentially wider scope for education.

One of the most recent and significant developments in the area of instructional organization has been the innovation of team teaching. Although one might find some historical antecedents to it, team teaching as a significant and popular movement in American education dates back only to the late 1950s. Although teachers in the past have collaborated informally, the new approach was to be a designed cooperation. A significant early experiment with team teaching was begun in 1957 as a joint enterprise between Harvard University and the Lexington, Massachusetts, schools. One elementary school in the district was completely converted to team teaching. Similar programs developed in other parts of the country, and by 1960 some school systems had begun to move beyond the experimental stage, expanding their programs to include more teachers and students. In some in-

[13] Sidney Hook, *Education for Modern Man* (New York: Knopf, 1963), p. 63.

stances new school construction was designed to facilitate team-teaching programs.

team teaching defined

Team teaching as an arrangement of school organization can be considered an alternative to either the self-contained or departmentalized arrangement found in secondary schools and to a growing extent in elementary schools. As an alternative to the self-contained arrangement, team teaching is proposed as a modification that would retain certain advantages of the self-contained elementary classroom while avoiding some of its disadvantages. Robert Anderson's comparison of the different approaches (in his book *Teaching in a World of Change*) is summarized below. Advantages of the self-contained classroom are:

1. The classroom becomes a secure base for both learning and individual development.
2. The child can gain a security of relationships with one adult—the teacher, who sees him in the wide range of circumstance.
3. The child gains a sense of proprietorship—of belonging.
4. The teacher is able to flexibly adjust both time and material to meet the needs of individuals.

Disadvantages of the self-contained arrangement are:

1. The demands on a single teacher to maintain competency in all content areas, which requires both extensive versatility and time for planning.
2. The possibility of personality conflicts between student and teacher that would remain unrelieved for the whole year.
3. The possibility of overdependence upon one teacher.
4. The possible monotony and effects of continuous confinement to a restricted physical environment for the whole school day and year.

It is also contended that the opposite arrangement of departmentalization holds certain advantages:

1. It provides teachers who are more competently prepared in one content area.
2. Specially designed classrooms, such as science laboratories, can be maintained.
3. It allows for more flexible sub-grouping since groups can be drawn from a larger population.

On the other hand, departmentalization seems to have disadvantages, which the proponents of team teaching propose to avoid:

1. It does not allow for integration of the overall school program since teachers function in isolation from one another.
2. It is psychologically unsound since it exposes the child to separate teachers, thus limiting the degree of social entity and security for a child.
3. Its one device for giving a student a base for social entity and security, the homeroom, is generally discredited.

Although the patterns of team teaching vary, the general purposes of the arrangement may be stated as an effort to loosen inflexible arrangements of class size and scheduling to utilize effectively the special competencies of individual teachers, and to encourage cooperation among the teaching staff both in planning and evaluation of programs. The various types of team-teaching patterns that have been used are too numerous to detail. They range from highly structured programs that involve complex planning for large conglomerate groups, small groups, and individuals, including structured teams with designated leaders and aides, to programs that involve perhaps nothing more than informal cooperation and collaboration between two or more teachers.

To some educators a more sensible arrangement than straight team teaching in the elementary school is one that combines a form of team teaching with a self-contained classroom arrangement. Such an arrangement might simply have two teachers of the same grade level switch classes at half-day. One teacher might be responsible for the content areas of social studies and language arts, the other for mathematics and science. The learning groups thus remain intact, while the demands upon the teacher in terms of versatility and preparation time are reduced to sensible levels. Perhaps another advantage of such an arrangement is that it can be worked out by teachers in their own school without a highly supervised and doctrinaire program developed at the administrative level.

Because of the variety of arrangements that have developed under the name of *team teaching*, it is difficult to estimate its effectiveness accurately. For the most part, the research in this area has relied on questionnaires and testimonials from teachers, pupils, and parents and in results of standardized achievement tests, which do not measure achievement in such things as the social studies, science, and the arts. Nevertheless, the evidence from the existing research does imply advantages for some form of team teaching, not as measured by standardized achievement tests, but as measured by teacher and pupil responses.

Most studies report a favorable attitude toward team teaching from a majority of the teachers who have worked in teams of one sort or another. Such attitudes are not unexpected since most of the teachers were volunteers. But many of the programs studied involved some kind of hierarchical structure of team leaders and team teachers. To some, such a hierarchical structure might be expected to produce teacher resistance, but evidently that can be avoided.

Pupil achievement, as measured by standardized tests, shows no significant difference between cooperative teaching arrangements and self-contained classrooms. Therefore, its value has to be weighed not only against its acceptance by teachers, but also against its effect on students in areas other than achievement.

In the area of personal and social adjustment on the part of pupils, the studies have shown that little difference exists between the two arrangements. In general, as in the research on ability grouping, the research on team teaching implies that elements other than organization per se account for pupil adjustment and achievement. To some extent these elements tend to be present more often in the more flexible arrangement of team teaching. To determine just what these are requires closer examination. Such things as teacher personality, pedagogical methods, environmental conditions, and other factors have to be identified and weighed as to their potential influence on the pupil's well being. Perhaps the most decisive "unknown" is the teacher. The teacher, regardless of the system or arrangement, that respects the worth and humanity of *all* children can be successful. An unsound and incompetent teacher will not be redeemed by any type of organization.

the schools and creativity

One of the greatest "success" claims for the American schools has been in the area of creativity. The schools have shown a marked ability *to squelch* it in all but a few of their students. To be sure, it takes them a few years, say three or four, according to the evidence, but their record of success from that time on is impressive. And the "success" here is not to be taken lightly when one considers that they are working against sizable odds. Their task must be directed to every child that walks through the school door. Creativity is as much a part of man's endowment as is intelligence; or, better yet, as research evidence tells us, creativity can be seen as a dimension of intelligence.

For the few "failures," that is, those who seem to hang tenaciously to their creativity, the school assumes the role of a thrice-wronged master, unforgiving and relentless with retributive reaction. Not that it rewards indiscriminately all those whose creativity is successfully stifled. It rewards only those who at the same time "achieve" certain standards of learning and behavior. No doubt the home in many instances aids in the process.

The reader might here ask for something more than what appears to be editorial polemics on the part of the authors. Obviously, some important points beg for verification by supportive evidence, which we intend to furnish. We propose to do this in the discussion of three aspects of creativity and the school: (1) a functional definition of creativity—its dimensions; (2) the school as a force against creativity; and (3) the school's potential to foster creativity.

creativity: its dimensions

It is not unusual to hear someone referred to as a "creative person." There are, obviously, some discernible characteristics of creativity that make possible such a reference. The attributes of creativity are complex and difficult to pinpoint precisely. However, we have available a growing body of literature that provides at least a functional understanding of its nature—not an understanding of what a creative individual is, but an understanding of creativity as a potential in all men.

Pioneering research in the area of creativity has been done by J. P. Guilford.[14] He has developed a model of intellectual abilities based on seventy-five to eighty different factors of intelligence. One of the most important "families" of the factors is divergent production, or divergent thinking—that is, the kind of thinking that allows an individual to freely experiment with taking unconventional meaning from established material or to arrive at unconventional solutions to problems. It is divergent thinking that forms the background of the creative thinker. Not necessarily the opposite of divergent thinking, and also within Guilford's model of intelligence, is convergent thinking. It is thinking that makes the individual seek *the* fundamental meaning or *the* true answer. Obviously, the two are not exclusive of one another, but the balance is of importance here.

Descriptions of the personality traits of the creative individual have been the focus of many studies. A summary of these traits has been provided by Gaston Lebois [15] in his analysis of the research on creativity. Under the headings of cognitive and noncognitive (affective) traits he lists, among others, the following:

> *Cognitive Traits*—sensitivity to problems, fluency and flexibility of thinking, ability to form rich synthesis of ideas, ability to sense one's own ignorance or gaps in knowledge, "childlike perceptiveness combined with a sophisticated mind" and the "capacity to be puzzled, to wonder, and to be surprised," openness to experience.
>
> *Noncognitive Traits*—freedom from persistence, unconventionality, tolerance for ambiguity, interest in the meanings and implications of facts rather than the small details sometimes related to facts, acute self-awareness, a distinct sense of independence, being at home in complexity, "a willingness

---

[14] J. P. Guilford, "The Structure of the Intellect," *Psychological Bulletin*, 53 (1956), 267–293.

[15] Gaston Lebois, "An Analysis and Synthesis of the Concept of Creativity" (Ph.D dissertation, University of Pittsburgh, 1963).

to take a larger calculated risk than the average person," a
lack of fear of the unknown, the mysterious, and the
puzzling.[16]

These traits are not only traits that are basic to creativity but also
are part of what makes up human intelligence.   In terms of the standard instruments that measure intelligence, intelligence is measured as
it relates to convergent thinking.   The relationship between such
conventionally measured intelligence and creativity was the focus of
a study by Jacob W. Getzel and Philip W. Jackson.[17]   From a population of 449 students they selected twenty-six students who were from
the top 20 percent on measures of creativity but not IQ, and twenty-
eight students who were from the top 20 percent in IQ but not in
creativity.   In comparing the two groups with each other and with
the total group they found:

> *Achievement of Subject Matter.*   Both groups did equally
> well as measured by standard tests and better than the total
> group.
> *Teachers' Preference.*   Teachers preferred the high IQ
> students to both the high creatives and the rest of the total
> group.
> *Manner of Response to Projective Pictures.*   High creative
> students offered more responses that were unconventional,
> imaginative, and humorous.
> *Relationship of Teacher-preferred Traits to Student-
> preferred Traits.*   The high IQ student believed his preferred
> traits were also favored by teachers (as they were) and that
> they were predictive of adult success.   The high creative
> student believed his preferred traits were not favored by
> the teacher (as they were not) and were not predictive of
> adult success.

These findings support the contention that schools in general function
in such a way as to discourage or stifle creativity.   The evidence should
not suggest that high IQ students lack creative potential, but only that
the potential has been somewhat stifled.

the school as a force against creativity

Longitudinal studies indicate clearly that in most children creativity
begins to decline at about the age of nine or ten.   The decline begins
just about the time children enter fourth grade, when the school generally takes on a different character.   The fourth grade in most elementary schools marks a shift from the more relaxed structure of

[16] *Ibid.,* pp. 136–137.
[17] Jacob W. Getzel and Philip W. Jackson, *Creativity and Intelligence* (New York: Wiley, 1962).

the primary grades to the more rigidly formalized instruction of the intermediate grades. Of course, with the increasing press on the primary school for content achievement comes the possibility of declining creativity at an earlier age.

If Guilford's concepts of convergent and divergent thinking are used as a basis for creativity, it becomes clear how the school, in most cases, stifles creativity. The usual school encourages and rewards convergent thinking; it discourages and penalizes divergent thinking. The school attempts to condition students to strive for the *right* answer. It may make patient attempts to give adequate explanation as to the *why* of the answer. While this is a great deal better than forced conditioning, nonetheless, it encourages only convergent thinking. A good example is the evaluating of achievement done by most schools. Standardized tests by the millions chart the annual achievement levels of pupils throughout the country. No doubt such tests can be useful for defined purposes, but their use most often reflects the kind of *right-answer* learning that is encouraged in the schools. Such an emphasis almost automatically discourages the *process* of learning by creative involvement, not in all schools, but in a majority of them. Most schools function as if creativity is unrelated to the central purposes of education and thus cannot be their deliberate concern. Or they feel that creativity is restricted to the "creative" arts, thus missing the essential relationship between creativity and problem solving in education.

the school's potential to foster creativity

Research has found that it is possible to develop creativity (divergent thinking) in the school and that there will be a positive effect on learning measured by any standards. But the developing or nurturing of creativity would require certain basic changes in the approach that most schools take. At the very minimum it would mean that the child would be freed from the stultifying press for achievement, defined in narrow terms as getting the *right answers*. Divergent thinking would not only be tolerated but encouraged. In this area the teacher can function with significant effect if he realizes the degree of influence, positive or negative, that his actions have on a student's approach to learning. Ned A. Flanders sums this up well in his study, *Teacher Influence, Pupil Attitudes, and Achievement:*

> Some critics of the public school have advocated that teachers "get tough," tell students what to do, and demand high standards. Our data show that higher standards can be achieved not by telling students what to do in some sort of misguided "get tough" policy, but by asking questions and then using student ideas, perceptions, and reactions to build toward greater student self-direction, responsibility, and understanding. If "getting tough" means helping students face the consequences of

their own ideas and opinions, as contrasted against living with
the consequences of the teacher's ideas and opinions, then
indirect teachers are much tougher.[18]

What Flanders means by "indirect" teaching is the kind of teachers who encourage discovery and reflection by the student—in other
words, the kind of teaching that encourages rather than discourages
divergent thinking. How this might translate into the work of the
classroom is something for the teacher to decide "creatively." One
thing does seem to be implied: the development of creativity must by
its very nature be related to the degree of intellectual and emotional
freedom that is allowed by the school.

programmed instruction

The authors have deliberately chosen to discuss programmed instruction following the discussion of creativity, for in an extreme sense
programmed instruction by its nature stands as an anathema to
creativity. Except in a few contradictory instances, programmed instruction does not propose to foster creativity. We say "contradictory"
since the programmed approach still talks of "shaping" behavior,
which is consistent within the behaviorist theories of learning.
And it is the behaviorist who is the staunchest advocate of programmed
instruction. Words like "freedom" and "creativity" are necessarily
absent from the educational indices of staunch behaviorists.

If we again adopt Guilford's model of intelligence, programmed instruction can be seen as taking the convergent-thinking variable as
the total make-up of intelligence. Although there have been attempts
to develop programs that claim a stake in divergent thinking, again
the essential nature of behaviorism belies such a possibility. The
learner is still taken to a predetermined goal. Like convergent teaching in any form, programmed instruction prods for *the* right answer.
Of course, if teaching for convergent thinking is the pattern in most
schools, then programmed instruction can be viewed as simply attempting to expedite the process. In such a case it might be argued
that programmed instruction, therefore, need be only evaluated on
its relative effectiveness.

Since its development within the last decade, programmed instruction has been given a fair trial. A great deal of research has gone into
its development, and it has had a wide usage. So far, however, there
is no overwhelming evidence that it is any more efficient than conventional teaching. Perhaps that is to be expected if we consider
the fact that it is essentially a mechanized version of "conventional"
teaching. That is, the premise on which both are based is that learning is unidimensional, originating outside the learner, in the lesson or

[18] Ned A. Flanders, *Teacher Influence, Pupil Attitudes, and Achievement,* Cooperative Research Monograph, No. 12 (Washington, D.C.: U.S. Office of Education, 1965), pp. 116–
117.

program. The learner is simply expected to make the "correct" responses.

In the conventional teaching model if the student does not make the correct response, he may be subjected to varying forms of patient prodding or more often coercive pressure, neither of which are foolproof, obviously. In the program-teaching model the student is "conditioned" by the program to give the correct response. One important difference, however, is that the behaviorists stress positive reinforcement. They stand firmly against the abuses of corporal punishment or derision in the classroom. But let us have the program theory speak for itself through one of its early proponents:

> By programed instruction I mean the kind of learning experience
> in which a "program" takes the place of a tutor for the student,
> and leads him through a set of specified behaviors designed and
> sequenced to make it more probable that he will behave in a
> given desired way in the future—in other words, that he will
> learn what the program is designed to teach him. Sometimes
> the program is housed in a "teaching machine" or in a
> "programed text book." If so, the machine or the book is little
> more than a case to hold the program. The *program* is the
> important thing about programed instruction. It is usually a
> series of items, questions, or statements to each of which, in
> order, the student is asked to make a response. His response
> may be to fill in a word left blank, to answer a question, to
> select one of a series of multiple choice answers, to indicate
> agreement or disagreement, or to solve a problem and record the
> answer. As soon as he has responded to the item, he is permitted
> to see the correct response so that he can tell immediately
> whether his has been the right one. But the items are so skill-
> fully written and the steps are so small between them that the
> student practices mostly correct responses, rather than errors,
> and the sequence of items is skillfully arranged to take the
> student from responses he already knows, through new responses
> he is able to make because of the other responses he knows, to
> the final responses, the new knowledge it is intended that he
> should command.[19]

What is described is, according to Wilbur Schramm, a Skinnerian-type program—or, as it is often referred to, a linear program. B. F. Skinner's learning theory, which is based primarily on operant conditioning, places the "learner" in a subposition. That is, the learner is viewed as someone who needs to be "conditioned" to behave in certain ways. Skinner's argument seems to be that any desired behavior, within the organism's range of abilities, can be brought about by operant conditioning, that is by systematic and immediate reinforcement stimulus of the desired behavior or responses. In this

[19] Wilbur Schramm, (ed.), *Four Cases of Programmed Instruction* (New York: Fund for the Advancement of Education, 1964), p. 98.

sense the stimulus reinforcement follows the desired behavior rather than preceding it, as in the classical respondent conditioning of Pavlovian origin. Behaviorist theory takes on complexities, such as determining the nature of reinforcement, that we cannot examine in this brief space. The quote above from Schramm translates the behaviorist theory into programmed instruction. Questions have been raised about the integrity of the relationship between behaviorist theory and programmed instruction. Donald Arnstine [20] makes a penetrating argument on this point.

Although the Skinnerian, or linear program, construction has been the most widely used for programmed instruction, there have been programs developed that modify somewhat the direct sequential pattern. So-called "branching" programs rather than simply "conditioning" for a correct response attempt to explain why an erroneous response is wrong by directing the student to other specified branch frames appropriate to the error. Examples of both are shown in Chapter 8 of this book.

Programmed instruction lays claim to no other source of direction but behaviorist learning theory. By their tautological premises the behaviorists can admit no other learning theory. This perhaps provides intellectual comfort for them, but what does it provide for education? It might be argued that the behaviorist in attempting to define precisely the model by which to achieve desired behavior thereby presents closure to the process of education. In other words, the behaviorist defines the goals of education only in terms of discretely measurable behavior and then limits the process of education to the precise means for achieving that behavior. Thus, he maintains a closed system. Second, if behaviorist theory is seen as the only possible definition of learning, we run the risk of having even the desired behaviors reduced to only those that can be derived from operant conditioning. Thus, the preciseness of the instructional model might be seen as being relative to the preciseness of the desired behavior. In order, then, to achieve what is held by the behaviorist to be ultimately achievable—the precise instructional model—both the elements of the model and the "desired behaviors" might be reduced to whatever degree necessary to achieve preciseness. Some hint of this is apparent in the literature:

> A very evident characteristic of learning which leads to subject
> matter mastery is the increasing precision of the student's
> responses. In learning complex behavior, the student's initial
> of performance is variable and quite crude and rarely meets the
> criteria of subject matter competence. Effective instructional
> procedure tolerates the student's initially crude responses and
> gradually takes him toward mastery. In order to accomplish
> this, the instructional process must involve the establishment of

[20] Donald Arnstine, *Philosophy of Education* (New York: Harper & Row, 1967), pp. 80–81.

successively more rigorous standards or criteria for the learner's
performance. Increasing competence in new learning is
accomplished by gradually contracting the permissible margin
of error, that is, contracting performance tolerance.[21]
In the future, the design of instructional procedures will be
modified as behavioral science and educational practice begin to
be related in a mutually helpful way—a way not atypical of
science and practice in other fields. As this occurs, it is
hypothesized that four main areas of the educational process
will be influenced: (a) the setting of instructional goals will
be recast in terms of observable and measurable student behavior
including achievements, attitudes, motivations, and interests; (b)
the diagnosis of the learner's strengths and weaknesses prior to
instruction will become a more definitive process so that it can
aid in guiding the student along a curriculum specially suited for
him; (c) the techniques and materials employed by the teacher
will undergo significant change; and (d) the ways in which the
outcomes of the education are assessed, both for the student
evaluation and curriculum improvement, will receive increasingly
more attention.[22]

It might well be that the development of programmed instruction
on the basis of operant conditioning holds some promise. Since its
basic premises rest on research in the development of simple motor
skills in subhuman animals, there might be some meaningful transfer
to the human species in the area of skills. For example, effective performance of specific tasks as defined by industry or the military might
be more expediently achieved by programmed instruction. There is
no problem of establishing objectives here; they are established by
the job to be done. Perhaps in this area educational technology has
enjoyed some success.

It has not been successful in the area of complex verbal learning
in the schools. Nonetheless, some critics are willing to admit the possibility of its limited use in certain instances. For example, Maxine
Greene, who is in the truest sense a humanist, admits to this possibility:

It seems to me, therefore, that when we think about curriculum
making in a time of advancing technology, we need to look on
occasion through what is called by some a "person-centered"
perspective. The machine model will be used with increasing
frequency to define behavior; and I recognize that the two
perspectives are incommensurable. Nevertheless, we ought to
be able to preceive a complementarity of the two. . . . If we
think of learning, then, from the point of view of the ego, the

[21] Robert Glaser, "Toward a Behavioral Science Base for Instructional Design," in *Teaching Machines and Programmed Learning, II* (Washington, D.C.: National Education Association, 1965), p. 785.
[22] *Ibid.*, p. 804.

self, or what I prefer to call the person, we will be able to
think of the curriculum in terms of open encounters between
persons and the subject matters they may consciously appropriate
in the course of their initiation into the existing public world.
We will be able to take intentions into account and purposes; we
will be able to confront the significance of selective perception,
of the sense in which each person forms his own world.

Now it is clear that, when we take this perspective—and the
stance it requires of us—we cannot objectify our subject matter;
nor can we quantify or validate or even effectively test. Our
ability to predict will be limited; there will be all sorts of
disturbances and distractions standing in the way of a properly
scientific approach. But the principle of complementarity
permits an alternation of approach; and there is no reason why,
when the perspective of the behavioral sciences is required, we
cannot change the lenses we are using. We ought to do this,
however, to attain very specific ends, ends we consciously define
ourselves.[23]

The essential point in Maxine Greene's statement is that of a conscious self-definition of specific ends. It would mean that the student
might well choose certain kinds of instruments of programmed instruction in the pursuit of specific ends. The choice, though, would
be with the individual. Her position is best reflected by a quote of
Bruno Bettelheim in her paper:

Therefore, it is often felt that control for desirable ends (the
rule of the philosopher kings) is good, or at least not so bad.
But this is a dangerous belief. It neglects the complex and
often serious effects of any external control of man; also the
fact that when the area for free decisions grows too restricted,
it reduces the scope of man's personal responsibility and thus
his autonomy. It assumes that all else counts for little, as long
as "right" decisions are arrived at, and it makes no difference
how you reach them.[24]

The element of control that Bettelheim speaks of is not an unreasonable concern. The behaviorists would see the total school
enterprise as the domain of their instructional theory. One needs
only read Skinner to get an idea of the extent of the behaviorist's
faith in operant conditioning as the only means of instruction. Nor
does he limit it to subject areas. Any prescribed behaviors, social or
what have you, can be brought about by operant conditioning. The
possibility, of course, is that while behaviorist techniques might not be
effective in the cognitive areas of school work, they might be effective in
conditioning for other behaviors. At least this is what Skinner proposes

[23] Maxine Greene, "Technology and the Human Person," in Paul W. F. Witt (ed.), Technology and the Curriculum (New York: Teachers College, Columbia University, 1968), pp.
142–143.
[24] Ibid., p. 140.

in his novel, *Walden Two.* This aspect of social control may or may not be a conscious purpose of Skinner or his followers, but it is an intrinsic implication of their principles and a possible outcome of their methods in any area of learning. Even if the operant-conditioning approach of the behaviorists were a soundly proven method for school instruction, which it is not, would it be thus unquestionably desirable? If it were proven to be effective in all content areas, which its supporters imply, would it therefore have proven itself to be useful? Or are there other considerations? What concomitant "learnings" might take place? Obviously, there is one that is most important to education. That is, the learning about *learning* itself. The programmed lesson on content tells not only what is to be learned but conditions the learner as to *how* it must be learned. In other words, the *process* of learning itself becomes restrictively defined by the instrument itself. And this is no less the intent of the behaviorist than is his purpose of teaching content. Since he sees no other possibility for defining learning except in measurable mechanistic terms, he must logically hold that this is as important a learning as is the "content" of a program.

Donald Arnstine takes the question of the concomitant effects of programmed instruction into a social dimension.

> Whether schooling involves drill work, or the traditional recitation, or the systematic development of those methods that appear in the instructional program, it is attempting to condition students. The kind of "problem" that the student continually meets under these conditions is that of having to supply information on demand. His problem is to complete the unfinished declarative sentence, to select the right alternative, to offer the right faces when asked. . . . Not the least of the unfortunate results of such a habit might be that students, once out of school, would be unconscious of the genuine problems presented by social institutions and group ways of life and thought, just because those problems do not appear as simple demands for information. Such lack of awareness of problems amounts to what is recognized as personal and social insensitivity.
>
> But a narrowing of the sorts of situations one is prepared to deal with as problems is not the only unfortunate habit that might result from effective conditioning. As much cause for concern is the *way* one deals with problems. As noted earlier, the person whose verbal behavior has undergone long conditioning is indoctrinated. He sees the answers to questions as absolute and originating in an unquestioned external source of authority; there are no alternatives. Every question has an answer and there is always a right answer. It would be otiose to observe that scientists and artists cannot work on the basis of such habits of dealing with problems, and that a school that produces people with such habits will not produce scientists and artists. It is equally clear that the everyday problems of living

and working can be but inadequately met on the basis of the
habits of narrowness and dependence on authority that result
from conditioning. . . . When told what to do he responds
promptly; given freedom, he searches for the authority to which
his conditioning has accustomed him.[25]

It should be clear that the question of programmed instruction is
a great deal more involved than simply whether or not it is functional.
Our concerns are not about some simple training grounds for occupations; our concerns are about the school at a time when the increasing
press of technology threatens to enter the schools unquestioned. We
hold no mystical fears of either machines or technology; they are
just *things* produced by man. They have no power in themselves to
control man. A century and a half ago British textile workers had
such fear. They created their mythical King Lud under whose banner
they carried out their destruction of the machines in the factories.
What we need is a reasoned appraisal of the potential of technology
for education. It has a great deal to offer, but not in forms that
simply solidify what is already bad in education.

Another important aspect of the whole question of educational
technology is the part played by American business. There is no doubt
that the corporate thirst for profit sees the field of the knowledge
industry as a satisfying draught. Their presence is well known.
General Electric, AT & T, Westinghouse, Xerox, and IBM, to mention
only a few, have more than just a passing interest in the schools. They
see a potentially good market. This does not mean that their resources cannot be usefully tapped by the schools. But it does mean
that very careful appraisal should be made of what they have to offer.
As it stands now, the knowledge "industry" would have us accept not
only their hardware but their programs as well. Some of their hardware might be useful if designed to specific needs as defined by the
schools. There is no question that industry offers a great deal of
technological know-how, but there is little evidence that it displays
concern for the social welfare without help. The state of our physical
environment is a good enough case in point.

topics for inquiry

     1. Experimental Schools—Past and Present
     2. The "Measurement of Intelligence" Before IQ Tests
     3. The Radical Right's War on Progressive Education
     4. Ability Grouping and Self-Concept Theory

[25] Arnstine, *op. cit.*, pp. 85–86.

5. School Experiences of Famous Artists, Scientists, *et al.*
6. Use of IQ Tests in Other Countries
7. Differing Views of Education in the Utopian Novel
8. Teaching as Indoctrination
9. Industry's "Philosophy of Education": Statements and Deeds
10. Techniques of Animal Training

subjects for discussion

1. John Holt, in his book, *How Children Fail*, asks:

> How can we say, in any case, that one piece of knowl-
> edge is more important than another, or indeed, what
> we really say, that some knowledge is essential and
> the rest, as far as the school is concerned, worthless?
> A child who wants to learn something that the school
> can't and doesn't want to teach him will be told not to
> waste his time. But how can we say that what he wants
> to know is less important than what we want him to
> know? [26]

   a. Does this make sense to you? Should not the school decide what is important?
   b. Is it possible that what a child wants to know could be more important than what the school wants him to know? More important to whom?
   c. Could the school function with this view? Could you? As a student? As a teacher?
   d. Have you ever learned something in school that was not part of the program of studies? Was it meaningful?

2. In his book, *The Technology of Teaching*, B. F. Skinner has this to say about the teaching machine:

> The Machine, like the ——————— ———————, rein-
> forces the student for every correct response, using
> this immediate feedback not only to shape his behavior
> most efficiently but to maintain it in strength. . . .[27]

   a. Two words were purposely omitted. What are some of the possible choices that would meaningfully complete the sentence? Skinner's words here are *good tutor*. Could any others fit as well?
   b. In your own learning experiences do you require immediate reinforcement for every correct response?
   c. Does learning to you mean having your behavior shaped?

[26] John Holt, *How Children Fail* (New York: Pitman, 1964), p. 177.
[27] B. F. Skinner, *The Technology of Teaching* (New York: Appleton–Century–Crofts, 1968), p. 39.

3. Using the traits of creativity discussed in this chapter as a measure, how would you rate yourself as to creativity?
   a. Can you think of any specific or general experiences that might have influenced your "score"?
   b. If a friend were to rate you, how would the scores compare?
   c. Have you ever known any creative thinkers who were school failures? How might they have been successful in school?
4. Let us assume here that the self-fulfilling prophecy idea of Rosenthal and Jacobson discussed in this chapter is valid. In other words, let us assume that teachers and administrators often set expectancy levels for a pupil relative to his IQ.
   a. Could a person, therefore, charge that he is forced to reveal information about himself that may significantly influence the range of opportunities open to him?
   b. Could predictive testing give rise to a meritocracy, a gradual sorting out on the basis of specifically defined and measured intelligence?
   c. If intelligence tests were not used in schools, how would teachers know which pupils were working to the extent of their capabilities?

selected readings

AIKEN, WILFORD M. *The Story of the Eight Year Study*. New York: Harper and Brothers, 1942.
   A summary of the Eight Year Study. It draws from four other volumes in the series of five that set forth the essentials of one of the most significant educational experiments. It provides us with a clear view of the scope of the study and its message of the potential of the schools.

ARNSTINE, DONALD. *Philosophy of Education*. New York: Harper & Row, 1967.
   A penetrating analysis of various theories of learning and teaching. Arnstine discusses in depth the theories under consideration. He takes the options into an analysis of their philosophic assumptions and their social consequences.

GREENE, MAXINE. *Existential Encounters for Teachers*. New York: Random House, 1967.
   A quest for meaningful questions about education as it relates to life. Greene in seeking answers draws on pertinent excerpts from existentialist literature.

HERSEY, JOHN. *The Child Buyer*. New York: Knopf, 1960.
   A penetrating novel that presents some real questions about the direction that education might take in its press for earlier acquisition of specific knowledges and skills via technology.

HOFFMAN, BANESH. *The Tyranny of Testing.* New York: Collier Books, 1962.

A caustic commentary on the testing delirium that has gripped not only the schools but society in general.

HOLT, JOHN. *How Children Fail.* New York: Pitman, 1964.

A journaled recording of a perceptive teacher's experiences with the learning process. The author establishes some important concepts about learning theory through classroom anecdotes.

MICHAEL, WILLIAM B. (ed.). *Teaching for Creative Endeavor.* Bloomington: Indiana University Press, 1968.

An understanding of creativity in the functional-educational sense. Drawing from both researchers and practitioners, it offers an array of highly useful examples which display possibilities of teaching for creativity in all subject areas.

WITT, PAUL F. (ed.). *Technology and the Curriculum.* New York: Teachers College, Columbia University, 1968.

Nine addresses presented at the 1967 Curriculum Conference at Teachers College. The editor has selected comprehensive and thoughtful statements on educational technology and its implications for the schools and teachers.

YOUNG, MICHAEL. *The Rise of the Meritocracy.* Baltimore. Penguin, 1961.

A penetrating satirical essay on the potential hazards in a merit-structured society.

10
THE
TEACHER
IN THE
SYSTEM

The education of the teacher begins long before the college level. It begins when the "future teacher," as a student, enters school at the age of five or six. Through twelve years of elementary and secondary schools the "teacher-student" is exposed to the "process" of teaching at all levels and in most content areas. He observes at first hand as many as twenty-five different teachers. When we look at the time involved, this aspect of teacher education is formidable. For the twelve years it amounts to at least 2,100 days, or 12,000 hours. If the four years of college is added, the time increases by about 2,000 hours. Added to this firsthand experience are the other "lessons" about teaching that are learned from peers and kin as well as from schoolteacher characterizations presented in the popular media of TV, movies, and comic strips. These supplementary sources are, as James Herndon indicates in *The Way It Spozed to Be*, undoubtedly where so many teachers (as students) learn what they think teaching is "spozed to be." And that idea can be the start of a cycle of "spozed to be's" that is often difficult to break.

Thus the student of education might be somewhat conditioned by long exposure to view the teaching process in a particular way. Therefore, his conditioning must be taken into account by the student in his professional education. Preconceived notions about teaching might limit the degree to which the student is able to objectively view new ideas or search for them in his own work. Essentially, the purpose of teacher education is to develop an ongoing concern for the process of education and to develop the ability and drive for inquiry. This does not mean that past observations of teaching are to be discounted. They should be recalled and to whatever degree possible analyzed as to their relationship with new ideas. It is hoped that teacher education can function in such a way as to open up the path for new ideas to develop in relation to today's world. To be sure, it does not always function that way, but like education in general it is in constant need of prodding for relevancy.

professional education: historical development

The development of a specific program of teacher education in America coincides with the development of the public school. With the assumption of responsibility for education by the state came specific requirements for teacher certification.

Before the inception of the public school movement the requirements for teaching were usually specified by the school or district employing the teacher. Some attempts at licensing were made but not effectively enforced. Thus, education for teachers was for the most part simply general education.

In the colonial period the men who were hired to teach in the Latin grammar schools and later the academies were college graduates, schooled in Latin and Greek. Those who taught at the lower levels, such as the primary schools, needed little formal education beyond the level that they were to teach. The lowest level, the dame schools, where only the rudiments of reading were taught, were carried on by women who often had only the ability to read. Of course, there were usually other requirements, such as specific religious affiliation, certain codes of conduct and dress, but essentially there were no standard educational requirements. During the latter part of the eighteenth century some accommodations for teacher education were made in the academies, and for the first half of the nineteenth century they were the major producers of teachers for the lower schools. Even here the preparation was general education. Nor was such education yet required for teachers. There were still no standards for certification; local districts hired in accordance with their own standards or lack of same. With the developing interest in education by the 1820s, however, and with the subsequent press for free public schools came an interest in establishing institutions for teacher education.

The interest in teacher education was influenced by the established work of Pestalozzi and his followers in Europe. But perhaps even more important than a search for a science of teaching was the concern for the state of teacher preparation in any degree. Most elementary schools in the 1820s and 1830s were staffed by poorly educated teachers whose only qualification in many instances was the proper

political-party membership. Since education at that time was literally
under local control, it was the community leaders who established
the hiring practices for teachers.

One of those most concerned about the state of teacher education
during the 1820s and 1830s was James Carter of Massachusetts, who
first as educator and then as legislator was at the vanguard of the
early reform movement that paved the way for Horace Mann and
others. Under his aegis the first state normal school in Massachusetts
was founded in 1839. The term "normal" simply meant model or
rule. Schools so designated were thus thought of as institutions that
could establish rules for teaching. By 1850 Massachusetts had three
normal schools. The nature of these early normal schools can perhaps
best be illustrated by an official statement from Henry Barnard's 1851
volume on normal schools:

organization and operation of the lexington state normal school

The State Normal Schools, of which there are three in
Massachusetts, are designed for those only who purpose to
teach, and especially for those who purpose to teach in
the common schools. The school at West Newton is
for females.

It was opened at Lexington, July 3rd, 1839, with the
examination of three pupils, who were all that presented
themselves as candidates. At the close of the first term it
numbered twelve pupils.

The school continued at Lexington five years. In May, 1844,
having by far outgrown its accommodations, it was removed to
West Newton, where the liberality of the Hon. Josiah Quincy,
Jr., of Boston, had provided for it by the purchase of a
building, formerly used as a private academy, which he
generously gave to the Institution.

The whole number of graduates is 423, nearly all of whom
have engaged in teaching, the most of them in the public schools
of this state.

CONDITIONS OF ENTRANCE.—1. The applicant must be at least
sixteen years old.

2. She must make an explicit declaration of her intention
to become a Teacher.

3. She must produce a certificate of good PHYSICAL, IN-
TELLECTUAL, and MORAL CHARACTER, from some responsible person. It is exceedingly desirable that this condition be
strictly complied with on the part of those who present
candidates.

4. She must pass a satisfactory examination in the
common branches, viz:—Reading, spelling and defining,
arithmetic, grammar, writing and geography.

5. She must give a pledge to remain in the school at least
four consecutive terms, and to observe faithfully all the

regulations of the Institution, as long as she is a member
of it.

6. All candidates for admission must be at the schoolroom on the morning of the day which precedes that on which
the term commences, at half-past eight o'clock. None
will be admitted after the day of examination.

7. Each pupil, at entrance, must be supplied with slate and
pencil, blank book, Bible, Worcester's Comprehensive
Dictionary, and Morse's Geography. Many of the other books
used will be furnished from the library of the school.

STUDIES.—The course of study in each of the State Normal
Schools begins with a review of the studies pursued in the
Common Schools, viz:—Reading, writing, orthography, English
grammar, mental and written arithmetic, geography and
physiology.

The attention of pupils is directed, 1st, to a thorough review of elementary studies; 2d, to those branches of
knowledge which may be considered as an expansion of
the above-named elementary studies, or collateral to
them; to the art of teaching and its modes.

The advanced studies are equally proportioned, according to the following distribution, into three departments, viz:—1. The mathematical, including algebra
through quadratic equations; geometry, to an amount equal
to three books in Euclid; bookkeeping and surveying. 2.
The philosophical, including natural philosophy, astronomy,
moral and intellectual philosophy, natural history,
particularly that of our own country, and so much
of chemistry as relates to the atmosphere, the waters,
and the growth of plants and animals. 3. The literary, including
the critical study of the English language, both in its structure
and history, with an outline of the history of English literature;
the history of the United States, with such a survey of general
history as may be a suitable preparative for it; and historical
geography, ancient and mediaeval, so far as is necessary to
understand general history, from the earliest time to the period
of the French Revolution.

"The art of teaching and its modes," includes instruction
as to philosophy of teaching and discipline, as drawn from
the nature and condition of the juvenile mind; the history
of the progress of the art, and the application of it to our
system of education; and as much exercise in teaching
under constant supervision, toward the close of the
course, as the circumstances and interests of the Model
schools may allow.

Members of the higher classes give teaching exercises
before the whole school, several each week. Members
of the senior class spend three weeks, each, in the public
grammar school of District No. 7, which is connected
with the institution as its Model department.

Pupils who have had considerable experience in teaching,

and are otherwise qualified for it, will be allowed to
enter existing classes.

Pupils who may desire to study the Latin and French
languages, and to prepare themselves to instruct in those
branches usually taught in High Schools, can have an
opportunity to do so, by giving a pledge to remain in the
school for a term of three years, provided the number is
sufficient to warrant the forming of a class.[1]

For the most part the subsequent development of normal schools
fit the pattern of the early Massachusetts schools. By 1900 normal
schools had been established in all forty-five states. By that time
Massachusetts had upgraded its entrance requirements to high school
graduation. Most other states required only two years of high school
for entrance to their normal schools. Most had one- or two-year
teacher education programs. Although there were about 175 such
schools by 1900, they were far from meeting the demands at the time.
In Massachusetts only 40 percent of its teachers had attended normal
schools, and the percentage was even smaller in other states. Some of
the posts were filled by teachers with some college or academy education, but most were filled by teachers who had little academic education since enforced certification requirements had not yet been established at the state level.

After the turn of the century the normal schools grew rapidly in
number, but, more significantly, they were to evolve into teachers'
colleges. Several factors were influential in bringing about this
evolution. Some of the universities and liberal arts colleges had set
up education courses or programs, and thus teacher education gained
respectability. Many normal schools had extended their programs
to four years and had included liberal arts subjects. The extended
high school programs had made it possible for high school graduation to be a prerequisite for normal school admittance.

In 1899 the Michigan State Normal School at Ypsilanti was given
official legislative recognition as a teachers college, the first. By 1905
it had granted B. A. degrees. By 1920 there were forty-six teachers
colleges in the country. From then on their number grew rapidly.
However, the normal school did not entirely vanish. One western
state maintained such programs within the high schools until at least
1957. Some still exist as four-year institutions. Universities, whose
regular programs had been the basis of preparation for high school
teachers, had also begun to develop departments or schools of education. At the turn of the century there were 250 chairs in one or
another branch of pedagogy established in universities. One-fourth
of the liberal arts colleges were offering courses in education. From
1900 on it was simply to be a matter of relating the organization and

[1] As quoted in Marjorie B. Smiley and John S. Diekhoff, *Prologue to Teaching* (New York:
Oxford University Press, 1959), pp. 115–116.

expansion of teacher education programs to the evolving certification requirements of the various states.

Certification requirements for teachers in America today are rigidly adhered to. In all instances the states set specific requirements that must be met before licenses for teaching are issued. Not until the turn of the century, however, were the states able to assume this responsibility. As has been pointed out, it was not until that time that the state began to assume any real degree of centralized control. For many states compulsory education laws had not been in effect very long. Public education, though firmly established in most states, was still in the process of development in others.

Some of the early certification requirements might seem feeble in comparison to today's, but they were important steps then. For example, between 1900 and 1910 a number of states began requiring of elementary teachers a high school diploma. By 1920 not only had most states passed certification laws but these laws also specified certain education courses as part of the requirements. By the 1930s a bachelor's degree was a requirement in an increasing number of states. Today all states require at least a bachelor's degree including a specified number of credits in academic and professional subjects. But this universal minimum has only been achieved in the last decade. For example, in 1957 fourteen states required less than a bachelor's degree for elementary teachers, though all required it for secondary schools. The 1957 elementary teacher requirements of the fourteen states are listed below in college credit hours required:

	Credits	
Alaska	90	
Arkansas	60	
Colorado	60	90 for out-of-state applicants
Iowa	60	
Kansas	60	
Maine	96	
Missouri	64	
Montana	64	from approved two-year institutions
Nebraska	12	for graduates of normal training high schools to teach in rural schools; 60 credits to teach in town schools
North Dakota	32	for rural schools; 64 for graded
South Dakota	30	for rural schools; 60 for town
West Virginia	64	
Wisconsin	64	
Wyoming	60	

All of these states in the 1960s increased their minimal requirements to include the bachelor's degree. At the same time some of the other states increased requirements for permanent certification both at the elementary and secondary level. For example, by 1967 Connecticut, Kentucky, and Washington required a fifth year of education for permanent certification, and Pennsylvania required twenty-four postbachelor credits. The trend is definitely toward increased minimal requirements in all states.

Included in the requirements in all states are specified numbers of credit hours in the professional area. Although again there is variation among the states, the general requirements include studies in educational psychology, historical-philosophical foundations, related methods courses, and student teaching.

teacher education for the 1970s

Teacher education, fortunately, has never been without its critics. Hopefully, criticism will be looked at as an intrinsic aspect of any educational program. Generally, there are two types of criticism, one which is naïvely destructive, the other potentially constructive.

That teacher education is a professional specialization has been the object of criticism from many quarters. Some educators have a condescending attitude toward it. In a sense, their argument often rests on the assumption that teachers need little if any specialized education.

The other type of criticism—the potentially constructive—is aimed not at the idea of teacher education, but at its state. This criticism comes from a concern about the lag of education programs in adjusting to the changing conditions of society. For example, here we are in the 1970s first reacting to social conditions that the schools, as a potent social institution, helped to perpetuate and enlarge by their failure to react to them in earlier decades. Just a partial listing of examples is impressively convincing: racial relations, discrimination, poverty, pollution, depersonalization.

When we talk about schools, we are not talking only about public schools and schools of education, we are talking about colleges and universities as well. To dwell on our failures or to search for a fitting placement for culpability serves no purpose. What we need to do is to look at where we are and where we would like to be, or should be, in education and work to that end. It is in this sense that teacher education must be viewed. We do not propose to go into great detail about the subject but simply to point up some of the general needs.

Of great importance to the teacher's education are the disciplines in the liberal arts. The study of philosophy, general and educational, obviously holds value for a teacher. To know of Plato, Aristotle, Augustine, Kant, Buber, Sartre, and the dozens of other luminaries in philosophy is to become aware of the perennial search for meaning that characterizes man, the philosopher. This knowledge doesn't mean a thing, however, if it fails to bring about some development of the student's own potential to philosophize, or to use a less austere term, to *think*. What else should the study of philosophy be for? But then, what else should the study of anything be for?

Literature has the same purpose as does philosophy. Both have the essential purpose of providing some insight into what the human phenomenon is. Sociology, anthropology, psychology, history, the physical sciences, the fine arts, all, have the essential purpose of providing us with a bit more understanding of the human condition. Full understanding? Complete knowledge? Final answers? Never! But at least a continuation and extension of the development of thinking about the human condition might be attained. In view of the human problems that we face, we need desperately to act out of thought rather than out of blind conditioning. On this point Teilhard de Chardin speaks profoundly:

> In the passage of time a state of collective consciousness has been progressively evolved which is inherited by each succeeding generation of conscious individuals, and to which each generation adds something. . . . It seems that where man is concerned the specific function of education is . . . to extend and ensure in collective mankind a consciousness which may already have reached its limit in the individual.[2]

To give de Chardin an oversimplified, but sufficient, meaning, we take consciousness here to mean *thinking* or *awareness*. So, the general purpose of education, then, is to extend and ensure thinking about life in its totality. Obviously, the approaches taken in schools at any level do not often meet this purpose. As a matter of fact, much of what the schools do seems to be at odds with this purpose.

We have been speaking in general terms about education, not in specific terms about teacher education. What further consideration must be attached to education for teachers? What does the teacher of the 1970s need to know? Or, is it more appropriate to ask, About what does he have to think?

Obviously, the teacher needs to know those experiences in the general educational areas or disciplines that make him aware of man's (his) potential to think. But he also needs experiences that are more specifically aimed at developing thinking about education as a process —a process in which he is to be engaged in the here and now, a process that occurs in a social institution called the *school*. The school exists in a milieu called the *society*, which is made up of numerous other institutions, all of which have given parameters and all of which are inexorably interdependent. In short, the teacher needs to think a great deal about what is going on in the world. He needs to be aware of the fact that the school is not isolated, nor are the students, nor is the teacher.

In essence, this is the purpose of the social-cultural foundations of education courses.   Regardless of specific titles or approaches, be they anthropological, sociological, historical, or philosophical, their purpose is to draw some meaningful relationship between the school and society.   The hope is that such courses will help the teacher better understand (1) the social dynamics within the school, (2) the social, political, and economic forces that affect the schools, (3) the depth of the social problems that affect the schools and vice versa, (4) the value judgments involved in educational problems, and (5) something about himself and his students as part of the milieu.   The hope is that such courses will expand the teacher's cultural awareness.   Perhaps more than ever before that is the name of the game—*awareness*.   Not in the tabloid sense of "being with it," but in a more profound sense of knowing what is going on in man's world, especially as it affects the student and the school.

There are some other, more specific needs for the teacher.   Psychology, developmental and/or educational, should provide some understanding about the educational process.   At their best, courses in these disciplines will provide essential knowledge about the conditions that promote growth in the student, knowledge about the cognitive and emotional developmental stages of children, and knowledge about the various cultural and environmental influences on development.   From them the student should develop some understanding of the alternative approaches to learning theory and their implicit views of man.   All that the student will take away from these courses will hopefully be related to the immediate scene.

Methods courses for teachers, either elementary or secondary, are perhaps the courses most specifically directed toward teacher education.   They have never been without their critics, but perhaps they have never been in as great a need for study than they are today.   Like all other areas of teacher education, the methods courses cannot be approached out of thought patterned in the past.   They too must be based on the new psychological, social, and cultural presses.   At their best, they will offer an array of alternative approaches that might be taken in the teaching of any subject matter.   At their worst, they will attempt to set forth a fixed method of teaching that axiomatically discounts student involvement.

the teacher in the society: pressure groups and academic freedom

The schools in America are politically vulnerable institutions.   They stand as publicly established and financed agencies in the midst of a society diverse in social, political, economic, religious, and educational ideologies.   We need not list the specific dimensions of the diversity here; its character if not its measure is apparent.   In the midst of the diversity the school consequently becomes fair game for pressure from a number of directions.   There is no doubt that the schools are

TABLE 7 *Percentage of Superintendents and Board Members Exposed to Specific Pressures*

Point of Pressure	Superintendents	Board Members
Demands for emphasis on three Rs	59	53
Demands for more courses and subjects	64	47
Protests about views expressed by teachers	49	41
Demands that teachers express certain views	13	12
Protests against tax increases or bond proposals	73	70
Demands for more money for schools	66	52
Protests against expanded or new services	39	35
Demands for new services	63	49
Demands for new teaching methods	29	35
Protests against new teaching methods	43	28
Demands for emphasis on athletic program	58	52
Demands for de-emphasis of athletic program	40	38
Protests about particular textbooks	19	19
Demands that school contracts be given to certain firms	46	24
Demands that teachers be appointed or dismissed for reasons other than competence	46	24

Source: Adapted from Neal Gross, *Who Runs Our Schools?* (New York: Wiley, 1958), p. 49.

influenced in many ways by the varied pressures, especially those from conservative elements. There is also no doubt that this aspect of public control, continual and pervasive, is more important sociologically than is control through the established means of school board elections. Most often the teacher is affected by indirect rather than direct pressure.

School board members, most generally conservative themselves, are especially sensitive and responsive to pressure from organized groups of a conservative bent. They themselves often exert pressure on the schools too. Administrators, next in the pecking order, often respond to pressure applied directly by either social groups or the school boards. An example of the diversity of groups pressuring schools at the local level was provided by Neal Gross in his book *Who Runs Our Schools?* [3] His study involved 105 superintendents and 508 school board members chosen at random in the state of Massachusetts. They were interviewed in order to determine both the sources of pressure on the schools and the most frequent points of concern. Although Gross's study was limited to the state of Massachusetts its results are typical of those found throughout the country. Table 7 shows the sources of pressure that Gross found.

Such pressure on the schools is understandable, and in many instances its purpose might well be for constructive change. Unfortunately, very often the pressure is of a destructive nature. Its purpose is to restrict and narrow the schools' programs. The most frequent points on which Gross found direct pressure are shown in Table 8.

[3] Neal Gross, *Who Runs Our Schools?* (New York: Wiley, 1958).

TABLE 8 *Percentage of Superintendents and Board Members Pressured by Specified Sources*

Source	Superintendents	Board Members
Parents or PTA	92	74
Individual school board members	75	51
Teachers	65	44
Taxpayers' association	49	31
Town finance committee or city council	48	38
Politicians	46	29
Business or commercial organizations	45	19
Individuals influential for economic reasons	44	25
Personal friends	37	37
The press	36	19
Old-line families	30	26
Church or religious groups	28	18
Veterans' organizations	27	10
Labor unions	27	5
Chamber of Commerce	23	5
Service clubs	20	11
Fraternal organizations	13	9
Welfare organizations	3	1
Farm organizations	12	4

Source: Adapted from Neal Gross, *Who Runs Our Schools?* (New York: Wiley, 1958), p. 50.

Obviously, Gross's list of specific points indicates that some pressure might be applied to the schools to bring about constructive change. It is also obvious that much of the pressure is applied in order to curtail or diminish educational programs. In general, these pressures affect the teacher, even if indirectly. Our concern is limited to those specific pressures that relate directly to the teacher's freedom to teach, or more important, the student's freedom to learn—the kind of pressures that have the effect of limiting or constraining free inquiry. Included would be those pressures that attempt to proscribe what might or might not be taught, what material might or might not be used.

The question becomes one of academic freedom on the part of the teacher and the student. Should the teacher be free to encourage inquiry into issues that might be controversial in a particular community or at a particular time? Another question might be whether or not the teacher is willing to grant academic freedom to the student.

It is perhaps something of a paradox to speak with concern about academic freedom in a society that is fundamentally committed to the free play of ideas. Several reasons force this concern. The implication here is not that the schools have ever been systematically or officially stripped of their freedom to delve into controversial issues. On the contrary, they have more often not taken full advantage of the freedom. The conservative social press often has had, and has, a restricting influence on the schools, either from within or without.

In a very real sense the public schools face a dilemma in the question of academic freedom. On the one hand, there is the political reality that the people essentially· control the schools. On the other hand, the educational process thrives only when the student is free to deal with ideas regardless of how controversial they might be. Society in general does not subscribe to censorship of ideas. But in response to the diversity of pressure the schools often avoid many issues that should be central in education. Very often the avoidance arises out of a fear of offending certain self-interest groups, particularly right-wing groups that have historically displayed their invidious tactics of smear or political threat. In regard to these elements, the schools, particularly the administrators, too often have acted out of weakness or fear rather than out of a sensitive reading of public attitude. The records are full of examples where administrators have withdrawn particular books from school use simply because some self-styled censors in the community have complained. *Catcher in the Rye, Brave New World, Grapes of Wrath, A Bell for Adano, Death of a Salesman, 1984, Crime and Punishment, Of Mice and Men, Only Yesterday* are examples of books that have been pulled from classes, reading lists, or even library shelves because of the complaints of an individual or small group.

Teachers have also, on occasion, fallen victim to censorship activities for encouraging free inquiry into ideas. Many of them have been subjected to exhaustive ordeals of needless defense against sensationalist charges made by small but vociferous extremist groups, some of which have an ideological opposition to the idea of public education. The most pervasive educational damage from the censorship activities, however, is the effect on schools in general. There is, no doubt, a great deal of voluntary censorship on the part of teachers and administrators simply to avoid controversy. The statement by a 1951 NEA Committee on Tenure and Academic Freedom is still relevant:

> Presence in the school curriculum of items to which a particular group is sensitive is causing a greater degree of voluntary censorship today than ever before.
> The committee has evidence to indicate that voluntary censorship by administrators and teachers to avoid conflicts with groups is a far more insidious force than the overt acts of boards or legislatures.[4]

The activities of right-wing extremist groups have not abated in the last two decades. In many respects they have become more widely organized, especially in regard to textbooks, which will be discussed later in this section.

In regard to academic freedom for the teacher, what has been specifically lacking is the kind of strong professional stance that would guarantee some degree of security from extremist groups. The NEA has long taken an official stance which holds for academic freedom,

---

[4] "The Erosion of Freedom," *NEA Journal*, 40 (May 1951), p. 321.

but too often in the past the local organizations have been silent on the issue. The principles of academic freedom, as established by the American Association of University Professors (AAUP), for example, have never had real application below the college level. But there is an indication that with the growth of teacher power, the potential for increased assurance of academic freedom will also grow. A 1969 *NEA Research Bulletin* reported that some negotiation agreements have included provisions for academic freedom. For example:

[*From Wyoming, Michigan*]
   In the study of controversial issues in our schools the pupil has four rights to be recognized:

1. The right to study any controversial issue which has political, economic, or social significance and concerning which, at the student's level of maturity, he should begin to have an opinion.
2. The right to have free access to all relevant information, particularly those materials that circulate freely in the community.
3. The right to provide competent instruction in an atmosphere free from bias, prejudice, and external pressures.
4. The right to form and express his own opinions on controversial issues without thereby jeopardizing his relations with his teachers or the schools.

[*From Springfield, Massachusetts*]
   The school committee recognizes that children must be free to learn and teachers free to teach broad areas of knowledge in their search for truth.
[*From Byesville, Ohio*]
   Academic freedom shall be guaranteed to teachers, subject to accepted standards of professional, ethical and statutory educational responsibility.
[*From Bristol Borough, Pennsylvania*]
   The Board of Education hereby respects the professional rights of its employees, including protection from unjustifiable personal attack or violation of the rights of inquiry and academic freedom to teach.[5]

   The same *Bulletin* indicated that of 2,225 agreements only fifty-five had such clauses—a small number, to be sure, but a definite trend that should continue.

freedom to teach or freedom to learn?

An important element in the question of academic freedom that is often overlooked is that of the student's rights. That is the essential

5 *NEA Research Bulletin*, 47 (March 1969), pp. 7–10.

issue—the freedom to learn, which in a sense carries with it the freedom to teach. Even the NEA, in speaking on academic freedom, places it in this context.

> . . . the schools must guarantee the right of the learner to
> have access to all relevant information in studying society's
> unsolved problems.
>   These problems deal with management and labor; local,
> state, national, and foreign governments; communism,
> fascism, isolationism, socialism; public housing; owner-
> ship of public utilities; socialized medicine; universal
> military training; federal aid to education; sex education;
> consumer education; race and religion.[6]

When viewed from the position of the student's rights, the idea of academic freedom takes on a different meaning. In this position it is not so much a teacher's right but rather a responsibility to encourage free inquiry. Here, however, is where many teachers fall down. Academic freedom for students is probably restricted a great deal more by teachers than by the society. In some instances it might well be out of concerned self-censorship, but in far too many cases it is out of a narrow and misunderstood view of the purpose of education. Far too many teachers, at all levels, are unwilling to allow for free inquiry on the part of students. In an important sense this is a far more insidious aspect of censorship than that which comes from outside the school. It not only restricts but also conditions the mind of the student.

Thus, there are two fronts on which the question of academic freedom must be discussed. There is no doubt that the outside pressures for censorship must be met openly; these are real and continual threats. However the basic problem is the restriction on the student's freedom to learn as imposed by the school or teacher. Here is where the teacher must begin with any discussion of academic freedom. He must decide whether or not he is willing to let students wrestle intellectually with such topics as poverty, hunger, racial discrimination, war, nuclear weaponry, population, drugs, sex, and more. If not willing, then he must test his understanding of the principles of democratic life. This has been the central idea in most of the notable statements about academic freedom. Alexander Meiklejohn, for example, held it as so essential to democracy that he argued for the right of communists to teach in the college. Robert H. Baldwin, in an incisive analysis of Meiklejohn's writings states:

> For Meiklejohn, at the heart of the American program of self
> government is the faith that whenever, in the field of ideas, the

advocates of freedom and the advocates of suppression meet
in fair and unabridged discussion, freedom will win.[7]

Nor is it simply in the area of controversial issues that academic
freedom applies. Any time a student's learning in any area is restricted by the teacher or the school his "academic freedom" is diminished. When the school's or teacher's approach is so limited that
it does not encourage the student to search for his own answers,
thoughts, and understandings, then, too, is academic freedom limited.
The educational approach that views the pupil as an object to be
shaped obviously holds little concern for academic freedom for the
student. But most important, of course, is the fact that schools
rarely allow for free and open inquiry into controversial issues. To
repeat, much of the avoidance grows out of either a narrow view of
the purpose of education or an imposed self-censorship as suggested
by the NEA report. In this area the schools or teachers are not alone
in their avoidance of issues. To a great extent their position has
either been supported or directed by the textbooks that they use,
especially those in social studies. There is no question that in most
schools the textbook rather than the teacher determines the content
and direction of a particular course. Thus, any discussion of academic
freedom must take into account the kinds of pressures for censorship
that are applied to textbook authors and publishers.

textbooks and censorship by pressure groups

The most prolonged and organized criticism of history textbooks has
come from the ultraconservative groups. These groups continually
analyze textbooks in search of so-called collectivist, socialist, or com-
munist teachings. In addition, the varied groups make concerted
efforts to pressure the publishers into following ultraconservative
political and economic philosophies.

The problem of group pressures on the writing of history textbooks is not without a long history in the United States. Even before
the Civil War there were instances of publishers complying to meet
the criticisms of particular pressure groups by either issuing two sets
of books, one for the North and one for the South, or by omitting
from all textbooks passages that might have offended the South. For
some years after the Civil War this was a standard practice.

While most of the early attacks on textbooks seemed to stem
mainly from regional interests or biases, those that came after the
turn of the century began more and more to reflect tones of super-
patriotism and militant antisocialism. The success of early pressure
groups in bringing about significant changes in subsequent editions of
particular textbooks is well documented. Howard K. Beale, in his

[7] Robert H. Baldwin, "A Quest for Certainty: An Analysis of the Educational Theory of
Alexander Meiklejohn" (unpublished Ph.D. dissertation, University of Pittsburgh, 1967),
p. 227.

book, *Are Teachers Free* gives several examples of such changes made in textbooks that were attacked by superpatriotic groups in the first two decades of the twentieth century.[8] Such eminent textbook writers as David Muzzey, Andrew McLaughlin, C. H. Van Tyne, A. B. Hart, and E. B. West in subsequent editions of their textbooks had made changes that suggested more than academic revisions. Beale realized the necessity for an author of textbooks to revise in accordance with new developments or findings or to correct misinterpretive passages, but, he states, "a surprising number of the passages found to be changed or eliminated were those most frequently attacked by the patrioteers."

Bessie Louise Pierce, in *Public Opinion and the Teaching of History,* cites examples of textbook changes made in accordance with attacks by the Sons of the Revolution and other superpatriotic groups.[9] She also discusses the part that the Hearst newspapers played in bringing about pressures on authors and publishers. One account of their success appeared in a Chicago newspaper in 1924:

> Among authors to "re-Americanize" their histories were
> David S. Muzzey, who already had made "three mincing
> revisions," Andrew C. McLaughlin, and C. H. Van Tyne,
> who have "at last submitted to the irresistible force
> of nation-wide protest against treason texts and have
> strikingly reversed their views." [10]

The attempts to censor textbooks in the 1920s and 1930s did not emanate solely from superpatriotic groups. There were also significant instances of pressure on publishers from business interests who were concerned with what they saw as "socialism" in the textbooks. One of the most notorious of these instances was that of the public utilities' program carried on in several states.

The censorship activities of the utilities industry were begun by Samuel Insull, a utilities tycoon, who created the Public Welfare and Public Utilities Educational Service, an organization that examined civics and economics texts in use in the public schools of several states. The organization claimed success in blocking the use of certain books. So serious was the problem that the Federal Trade Commission conducted a three-year study and learned that the National Light Association, The American Gas Association, The American Railway Association (which had holdings in utilities), and member corporations had attempted and had often succeeded in placing the utilities' own interpretation of history in school books.

Perhaps the most devastating effects of pressure groups against textbooks were those aimed at texts written by Harold Rugg, former

[8] Howard K. Beale, *Are Teachers Free* (New York: Scribner, 1936).
[9] Bessie Louise Pierce, *Public Opinion and the Teaching of History* (New York: Knopf, 1932), p. 221.
[10] *Ibid.*, p. 222.

professor of education at Teachers College, Columbia University. Rugg's social science textbooks were widely used throughout the country in the 1930s, during which time they met with few adverse reactions. According to Beale, these textbooks dealt with "just the kind of problems people wanted treated, since the depression had aroused men to the existence of these problems." [11] However, by 1940 the Rugg textbooks, so widely accepted for a decade, were being pulled from virtually every school where they had been in use. The instigators of the attacks were the Advertising Federation of America, the National Association of Manufacturers, *Forbes Magazine*, and the American Legion. Even as late as 1958 the American Legion was still referring to the Rugg textbooks as "subversive," almost twenty years after their use by the schools.

The American Legion itself has had a long history of activities in the area of textbook criticism and attempted censorship through pressure tactics. William Gellerman relates that in 1922 the Legion passed a resolution "which condemned the use of textbooks which did not 'give true and adequate accounts of the memorable events which have so long inspired our people to a consecrated devotion to our country' and recommended 'the selection of some appropriate official body for investigation composed of men who are both scholars and patriots and whose decision will be both just and final.' " [12] It seems as though the Legion's proposal has been accepted and is explicitly followed by America's Future, Inc.

After World War II there was an upsurge of ultraconservative groups who attacked textbooks among other things. Even before the Red hunt of the Joseph McCarthy era (1950–1954) there were significant instances of their activities. One such instance of attempted textbook censorship took place in Scarsdale, New York, where a small but vociferous minority brought charges of communism against the local library and textbooks in use at the schools. Fortunately, in this case, the community held a cool head, met the attackers, and refuted the charges. But whether or not there were any effects on subsequent editions of the textbooks that were attacked has not been determined.

In some cases the effects of pressure groups have led to statewide actions of attempted censorship. In Alabama a legislative act required a statement in each textbook that the authors or any authors cited in the books were not known Communists or socialist advocates. In a rare concerted effort the publishers had the law repealed.

Another case of statewide action against textbooks took place in 1961 with the action of the Texas Textbook Committee, which had made charges against fifty textbooks. Several history texts on the list compiled by the committee were charged with various subversive leanings. Subsequently twenty-seven of the fifty books were adopted

[11] Beale, *op. cit.,* p. 271.
[12] William Gellerman, *The American Legion as Educator* (New York: Teachers College, Columbia University, 1938), p. 217.

by the committee. However, the success of the committee's pressure
on the publishers was also disclosed:

> One state official said afterward that all the history books
> were accepted on the condition that certain changes be made in
> accordance with "Texans for America" suggestions. All
> publishers concerned, he said, had agreed to make the changes.
> And he added that the protests should serve to keep the
> publishers on their toes.[13]

The effects of the Texas Textbook Committee on publishers is
further cited by Jack Nelson and Gene Roberts in *The Censors and the
Schools.*[14] They disclose that to some extent such publishers as Lyons
and Carnahan, Ginn and Company, Laidlaw Brothers, and Silver
Burdette made changes in textbooks to suit the committee. They also
cite the claims of a 1961 Florida committee that the publishers were
making changes to suit that committee. As further evidence of publishers' compliance with the demands of pressure groups, the authors
cite a *San Francisco News Bulletin* report that one publisher had
deleted an entire chapter on the United Nations and in its place put a
section from the American Legion *Manual* on flag displays. The
extent of such statewide actions involving textbook controversies
might better be understood when one takes note that between 1958
and 1962 textbooks were under fire in nearly one-third of the state
legislatures.

Many other reports are available about pressure groups bringing
charges of subversion against textbooks. The significant aspect of
most of the cases is the fact that the accusations seem to stem not
from local concern, but from major ultraconservative organizations.
Paul Blanshard suggests that between 1940 and 1950 a pattern of
extremism had begun to emerge that could be identified "on sight"
and that "most agitators who made 'trouble' for local school boards
were not independent citizens expressing their own convictions but
mouthpieces of a reactionary movement against public education."[15]

The notion of interdependence among some of the larger ultraconservative organizations is suggested by the similarities of their
position on certain issues. Such organizations as the American Legion, the Daughters of the American Revolution, the Conference of
American Small Business Organizations, Friends of the Public Schools,
and the National Economic Council assume the same position on
such topics as the United Nations, the Constitution, and "Americanism." And all of them have been active in attacks on textbooks, often
together.

[13] "Textbook Controversy in Texas—A Postscript," *Publishers' Weekly,* 180 (Oct. 23,
1961), p. 21.
[14] Jack Nelson and Gene Roberts, *The Censors and the Schools* (Boston: Little, Brown,
1963).
[15] Paul Blanshard, *The Right to Read* (Boston: Beacon Press, 1955), p. 106.

But the field of ultraconservative organizations is not limited to simply the nationally known groups. Mary Ann Raywid, in her book *The Ax Grinders*, states that there are approximately 1,000 groups highly critical of education in this country, many of which charge that textbooks are subversive.[16] Also suggested is the probability of top-level direction from the national groups whose literature on textbook subversion and textbook analyses have nationwide circulation. The reality of top-level direction is given further credence by the existence of the American Coalition of Patriotic Societies, which is comprised of 125 ultraconservative groups with a claimed membership of over 4 million. Further suggestion of the probability of large organizational direction in censorship pressures is the similarity of issues about specific books in various parts of the country.

One of the first nationally significant groups whose purpose was primarily to examine textbooks for subversive materials was sponsored by the Conference of American Small Business Organizations (CASBO) in 1949. This group, headed by Lucille Cardin Crain, established the *Educational Reviewer*, a quarterly newsletter that cited specific, though not always accurate, passages from textbooks and therefore made the task of local protestors relatively simple. The fact that CASBO, an active lobbying organization, sponsored the group brought action from the Congressional Committee on Lobbying Activities in 1951. In its report the committee stated:

> The long-run aim of this program is obvious, and this is
> nothing less than the establishment of CASBO's philosophy as
> the standard of educational orthodoxy in the schools of the
> nation.

The report also spoke in general terms about the censorship of textbooks:

> We all agree, of course, that our textbooks should be
> American, that they should not be the vehicle for the
> propaganda of obnoxious doctrines. Yet the review of text-
> books by self-appointed experts, especially when undertaken
> under the aegis of an organization having a distinctive legis-
> lative ax to grind, smacks too much of the book-burning orgies
> of Nuremburg to be accepted by thoughtful Americans without
> foreboding and alarm.[17]

The *Educational Reviewer* ceased publication in 1954, but not before it had brought several textbooks under fire in many parts of the country.

In 1958 the large-scale attacks on textbooks came again from two separate but by no means unrelated quarters. The first of these was

[16] Mary Ann Raywid, *The Ax Grinders* (New York: Macmillan, 1962), p. 6.
[17] As quoted in Robert B. Downs, *The First Freedom* (Chicago: American Library Association, 1960), p. 343.

in a book by E. Merrill Root entitled *Brainwashing in the High Schools*, an analysis of eleven American history textbooks, ten of which were charged by Root to be subversive.[18] Root has had a long affiliation with ultraconservative groups and has been a frequent contributor to as well as poetry editor of *American Opinion*, official organ of the John Birch Society. Root's book drew fire from many educators and organizations throughout the country. Nevertheless, by 1962 it had sold over 20,000 copies, and it is still given prominent display in "right-wing" bookstores. Root's work with textbook analysis was extended in 1958 when he joined the reviewing staff of America's Future, Inc., which at that time began their Operation Textbook program.

According to a statement contained in the circulated reviews of America's Future, Inc., its Textbook Evaluation Committee came into being "because of much evidence of socialist and other propaganda in textbooks currently used in our secondary schools." The work of the committee is recommended by the John Birch Society as a source of information about "suspect" textbooks. A relationship between America's Future, Inc., and the John Birch Society is indicated by the fact that several of the reviewers, past and present, have had important connections with the society's journal, *American Opinion*. An even more important link is the fact that two members of the Board of Trustees of America's Future, Inc., are members of the Council of the John Birch Society. There is little doubt that America's Future, Inc. can be labeled as part of the "radical right," that segment of political thought that equates all liberal (and often even conservative) political, social, and economic trends with communism. That America's Future, Inc., follows this line is borne out in the majority of their textbook reviews.

Since 1958 America's Future, Inc., has been the most prolific of any group in its attacks on textbooks, having distributed reviews of more than 400 high school textbooks to an "active" list of educators, board members, parent-teacher groups, and publications of other organizations that can be termed as "superpatriotic." Perhaps their activity can be better understood by realizing that many of the textbook controversies in the 1960s were linked with America's Future, Inc. material. And of course one might assume that there were other controversies which were not made public.

In any event, as early as 1962, Rudolf Scott, president of America's Future, Inc., felt that there was already reason for the organization to be optimistic about its work. By 1966 he held that economic pressure from the organization had brought about compliance by some publishers.

The textbook evaluations that America's Future, Inc., distributes

---

[18] E. Merrill Root, *Brainwashing in the High Schools* (New York: Devin-Adair, 1958).

are from 1,500 to 2,000 words in length and cite specific passages to which they object. While most of the evaluations have been made on high school textbooks, there have also been many made on elementary school and college texts. Their catalogue of available evaluation reports contains over 400 listings. However, not all of the evaluations are negative. Over 100 textbooks are given favorable reviews, and these are given additional listing in a separate catalogue of "recommended textbooks." The organization claims that their recommended list is used by some state adoption committees as well as many local committees. Undoubtedly this organization has established itself as the major force attempting to bring about censorship in textbooks. Their continuing and expanding work seems to indicate that they are a great deal more than simply an ineffective voice of a radical minority.

In order to determine the claimed "success" of America's Future's Inc., operation your authors have investigated nine history textbooks that had received unfavorable reviews by that group. After checking the textbooks for specific criticisms in the reviews, we then investigated subsequent editions of those textbooks to determine whether or not any changes were made that seemed to comply with the specific criticisms in the reviews. In five of the nine subsequent editions changes were made that did seem to comply in varying degrees with the reviews. By no means were the changes shocking reversals, but what is important is that they were specifically related to the exact criticisms. Following is a brief accounting of our findings in the five books:

Textbook A: 1958 and 1964 Editions

Textbook A had the most extensive revision for its subsequent edition. It also had the greatest number of changes significantly reflecting the specific criticisms in the America's Future, Inc., reviews. Of the sixteen specific criticisms in the review of the 1958 edition, twelve were reflected in changes made for the 1964 edition. In eight of the twelve changes the tone of the material was affected by the change. In four instances the tone of the material was not significantly affected even though the changes seemingly took into account the review. The significance of the changes made for the 1964 edition of the textbook was made greater by the fact that the 1964 edition was given a more favorable review by America's Future than was the 1958 edition.

Textbook B: 1960 and 1964 Editions

The America's Future, Inc., review of the 1960 edition of this book cites fourteen specific criticisms about the book. In the 1964 edition there were eight changes made that reflected the criticisms made by the review. In four instances the significance is strengthened by the fact that the immediately related material remained exactly the same in both editions.

Textbook C: 1964 and 1967 Editions

In the America's Future, Inc., review of the 1964 edition of this book the reviewer cites sixteen specific criticisms about the book. In the 1967 edition of the textbook there were six changes made which reflect the specific criticisms. In five instances the significance is strengthened by the fact that the immediately related materials were exactly the same in both editions.

Textbook D: 1960 and 1965 Editions

The reviewer for the America's Future, Inc., detailed eighteen specific criticisms about the 1960 edition of Textbook D. In the 1965 edition of the text six changes can be attributed directly to the review. In three instances the significance is strengthened by the fact that the immediately related materials were exactly the same in both editions.

Textbook E: 1961 and 1967 Editions

The America's Future, Inc., review of the 1961 edition of Textbook E found nineteen specific criticisms of the book. In the 1967 edition of the textbook there were three changes that reflected the specific criticisms. The significance of the three changes is strengthened by the fact that there were no other changes made for the 1967 edition, except for additional material at the end of the book.

It must be pointed out that the changes were not really of any great substance. In many instances they were simple substitutions that reflected the kind of "nit-picking" criticisms of America's Future, Inc., reviews. Following are some selected examples of what we found.

In one review this criticism was made of a 1960 edition of one textbook:

> In the chapter on Andrew Jackson, the unfortunate phrase
> "the common man" (a contemporary cliche making "common"
> synonymous with virtue) is introduced and too much is made
> of it.

In the chapter to which America's Future, Inc., criticism is pointed the phrase "the common man" and "the common people" was used nineteen times. In the subsequent edition, 1964, which followed the review, neither phrase is used at all. But the related textual material remained the same. Here are some examples from the two editions:

1960 Edition	1964 Edition
What was the reason for all this excitement? Andrew Jackson was the hero of the common people. His election was their triumph and they wished to celebrate it with him.	What was the reason for all this excitement? Andrew Jackson was a popular hero. His election was a triumph for his supporters, and they wished to celebrate it with him.

Jackson appealed to the common people not only because of what he had done, but because of the kind of man he was. . . . And Jackson, as the common people knew, believed wholeheartedly in democracy.

Throughout his period in office, Jackson worked hard to give the common man a greater share in the government.

It is important in a democracy that the common man shall have the right to vote and hold public office. But to many Americans, during and after Jackson's administration, it was not enough that the common man take part in his government. They believed that the daily life of the common man should also be improved.

Can you name several ways in which the life of the common man has been improved since Jackson's time?

Jackson appealed to many people not only because of what he had done but also because of the kind of man he was. . . . And Jackson, as all Americans knew, believed sincerely in democracy.

Throughout his period in office, Jackson worked hard to give the people a greater share in the government.

It is important in a democracy like ours that the people shall have the right to vote and hold public office. But many Americans, during and after Jackson's administration, believed that this was not enough. They thought that people should also have the chance to live useful, happy lives.

Name several ways in which the life of the average American has improved since Jackson's time.

In the same review the following criticism was made of the 1960 edition:

> The word "imperialism" does not occur in the index.
> As one looks at pages and topics, however, one finds the
> charge of "imperialism" slipped in. The authors . . .
> say: "For better or for worse, she (America) was now an
> empire with overseas possessions to govern and to defend."
> The charge of "imperialism" is a bit of professional
> propaganda, used by the conquerer of satellites, Communist
> Russia, to discredit and to attack America. . . .

1960 Edition
. . . the United States paid Spain $20,000,000. Finally, Spain agreed to give up its control of Cuba. So by the end of 1898, the United States had colonies extending almost to the shores of Asia. For better or for worse, she was now an empire with overseas possessions to govern and defend.

1964 Edition
. . . the United States paid Spain $20,000,000. In addition, Spain agreed to give up its control of Cuba. [Remainder of paragraph in 1960 edition deleted in 1964 edition.]

The deletion in the 1964 edition of the exact sentence to which the review objects indicates a significant change in compliance with the review. The significance is perhaps further indicated by the fact that there were no other changes made in the particular section dealing with the Spanish-American War.

In another review of a textbook America's Future, Inc., had this specific criticism about the 1964 edition:

> Symptomatic of the "liberal" bias is the treatment of Calvin Coolidge. . . . We are told: "The new President's philosophy of government was simple: economy and *laissez faire*. He acted on the principle that whatever business, especially big business, wanted was good for the country." Certainly Coolidge believed in "economy"—but was that "bad" as compared with the New Deal, Fair Deal, and New Frontier budgets that lead to national bankruptcy? . . .

1964 Edition

The new President's philosophy of government was simple: economy and *laissez faire*. He acted on the principle that whatever business, especially big business, wanted was good for the country. Although the 1920's was a period of rapid concentration of wealth, the antitrust laws were not effectively enforced. Regulatory bodies, such as the Interstate Commerce Commission and Federal Trade Commission, were filled with men who shared the President's own distrust of regulation.

1967 Edition

His philosophy of government was simple: economy and *laissez faire*. To take as little action as possible was with Coolidge almost a principle of life; he once said, "Four-fifths of all our troubles in this life would disappear if we would only sit down and keep still." He is said to have been the only President who slept ten hours every night and took a nap in the afternoon.

Since the paragraphs preceding and following the above excerpts are exactly the same in both editions, the change, especially the sentence deletion, seems to reflect the specific criticism.

In another America's Future, Inc., review, the reviewer commented on a 1960 edition of a text that:

> When Republicans win elections they "control the government" and it is "the Republican reaction. . . ." If Democrats win, they do not "control" the government and it is progress. A peculiarly nauseating passage remains unchanged from the former edition . . . : "In those days the big-business interests of the country were free of government interference, labor was kept in its place, and prosperity was measured by the abundance of crumbs dropped from the rich men's tables." This is not history but partisanship.

1960 Edition

Moreover, Harding's triumphant election in November indicated a

1965 Edition

Moreover, Harding's triumphant election in November indicated a return to the "good old days" of McKinley and Hanna. In those days the big-business interests of the country were free of government interference, labor was kept in its place, and prosperity was measured by the abundance of crumbs dropped from the rich men's tables. The prospect of again being free of government controls won the overwhelming support of the business community. . . .

return to the "good old days" of McKinley and Hanna. The prospect of again being free of government controls won the overwhelming support of the business community. . . .

The deletion of the exact sentence to which the reviewer objects in this instance seems to indicate a clear acknowledgment of the review.

The examples cited are not to be accepted as final evidence of publishers' compliance to America's Future, Inc., reviews. But the changes do appear to be more than simply coincidental.

It is to be understood that authors of textbooks are expected to revise their works in view of new findings, personal interpretations, assumed educational needs, or even to reflect the major societal ideals in any one period. Implied though is the belief that such revision would come about through the author's or publisher's initiative —and not forced by coercive pressure by a particular group, no matter how seemingly insignificant the demands of the group might be. It is apparent that in the America's Future, Inc. reviews, in most cases the specific criticisms originate from a particular political bias that does not coincide with the views of the authors of the textbooks. If the revisions of these textbooks are the responsibility of the authors, as most publishers have indicated, then it is to be assumed that the authors who made the changes were themselves responsive to the criticisms. It is not unlikely that authors, who in response to criticism make changes for subsequent editions of their textbooks, might take such criticism into account when writing new textbooks. And even if the author should choose to completely ignore such criticism, it is highly possible that his publisher would not.

It is most likely that the threat of economic pressure posed by a group such as America's Future, Inc., is taken into consideration by publishers of textbooks. But on the other hand publishers have been vigorously fighting such attempted censorship. A 1962 survey by the American Textbook Publishers' Institute found that publishers of elementary and high school textbooks felt that censorship attacks were a major problem. In terms of economic pressure the problem is especially compounded when one considers the statewide textbook adoption policies of a number of states in the country. More than twenty states, mostly in the South and Southwest, have some type of statewide adoption policies for textbooks. In most instances the committees adopt anywhere from two to five texts in each subject area for selection by individual districts or schools, and in some instances basal adoptions are made. The problem for publishers in such a program of adoption is that a significant portion of the potential market for any particular textbook can be lost for as long as four or five years since books remain on the acceptable list for at least that length of time. The problem is obviously compounded if a particular textbook is specifically blocked in a number of states.

And the thread of censorship in regard to textbooks seems to extend throughout the states where statewide adoption policies are in practice. Alabama, California, Florida, Georgia, Louisiana, Mississippi, North Carolina, South Carolina, Tennessee, and Texas all have state adoption policies. Perhaps for many of these states there would be a degree of natural similarity in regard to ideals that would guide textbook adoption committees. However, when the thread is pulled tighter by a particular group whose function is to pressure publishers for changes in textbooks, as has been the avowed intent of America's Future, Inc., the problem is not simply one of regional bias or attitude, but one of a small minority assuming a relatively powerful economic leverage by which to manipulate publishers. In simple terms, if a publisher sees the possibility of losing a potential market in perhaps ten states, he is apt to make some attempt to regain that potential market. And if, by chance, the means for regaining that potential market are spelled out with a degree of preciseness, as in the reviews of America's Future, Inc., the publishers might find it relatively easy to succumb to the pressure. This is more than just a convenient assumption.

Perhaps the problem of statewide textbook adoption policies would not be so intense if there were not a continuing push by ultraconservative elements in these states for having more lay people appointed to the textbook selection committees. An example of their success in this direction is to be seen in a 1960 legislative act in Mississippi, whereby the governor was given the right to appoint four lay people to each of the seven-member committees. The opening address by the state superintendent to these committees perhaps best indicates the direction of their task:

> In your study of the books offered for adoption please look
> carefully for any alien ideologies that might creep into a
> textbook. In this day when true Americans are fighting for
> survival and for perpetuation of our way of life, we, as
> educators, do not want to aid and abet the enemy by being
> careless in the evaluation of those books that will have a pro-
> found influence upon the mind of our young Mississippians.[19]

If the reviews of America's Future, Inc., had been used by some of the committee members in this instance, the "alien ideologies" would have

[19] James Edward Baxter, "Selection and Censorship of Public School Textbooks" (unpublished Ph.D. dissertation, University of Southern Mississippi, 1964) p. 96.

been readily pointed out for them. Some major textbook publishers
have indicated that America's Future, Inc., reviews have definitely
been used by various state adoption committees.

Whatever the economic advantages for statewide adoption policies
might be, there are obviously profound disadvantages in terms of educational ideals, even without the problem of censorship activities.
They allow for no selection by individual districts, let alone by individual schools or teachers. But with the threat of such activities state
adoption policies become potentially powerful sources of leverage for
censor-minded groups. It is unlikely that in the near future the states
with state adoption policies will change to a less centralized plan of
adoption unless, perhaps, prompted to do so by some overriding consideration such as economic advantages to be gained by such a change.
One, and perhaps the only, means by which to offer such an incentive
would be through a type of federal legislation that would specify certain federal funds available for textbooks with the stipulation that
adoption functions be at some level less centralized than the state
level. Such legislation could hardly be looked upon as an example of
centralized federal control in a restrictive sense since its purpose and
consequences would tend to decentralize control in the area of textbook adoption policies, and furthermore, it would be in the best tradition of competitive free enterprise.

The historical character of federal aid to education in this country
has been one of categorical rather than general aid. In most instances
monies given to the states by the federal government are given for specific purposes and on the condition that the states meet certain requirements. It does not seem unreasonable for the federal govern
ment to insist on certain standards when financial aid is being offered,
nor is it without precedent. In regard to educational aid, the problem
of federal guidelines or rules has been particularly acute because of
the constitutionally implied and historically developed pattern of state
control of education in this country. However, the nature of recent
federal legislation indicates a growing degree of acceptance of the idea
that such legislation, even though categorical and conditional, does
not necessarily imply restrictive federal control. This is spelled out
clearly in the opening statement of the National Defense Education
Act of 1958:

> Nothing contained in this Act shall be construed to
> authorize any department, agency, officer, or employee of
> the United States to exercise any direction, supervision,
> or control over the curriculum, program of instruction,
> administration, or personnel of any educational institution
> or school system.

The National Defense Educational Act of 1958 and the 1964 amendments to the act, however, do earmark monies for certain areas and do
require that certain conditions be met.

In regard to this it is interesting to note that textbooks were specifically excluded from the items covered by the National Defense Educational Act. However, in a more recent public law, Amendments to the Elementary and Secondary Education Act of 1965, textbooks are included in the scope of funded areas. And in Section 123 of the law there are some possibly relevant implications in regard to textbook adoption policies. In the section noted, any state requesting grants is required to submit to the Commissioner of Education a state plan which, among other things:

> . . . sets forth a program under which funds paid to the
> State from its allotment under Section 202 will be ex-
> pended solely for (A) acquisition of library resources . . .
> textbooks, and other printed and published instructional
> materials for the use of children and teachers in public
> and private elementary and secondary schools in
> the State, and (B) administration of the State plan,
> including (i) the development and revision of stand-
> ards relating to library resources, textbooks, and other
> printed and published instructional materials . . . and (ii) the
> distribution and control by a local educational agency of such
> library resources, textbooks, and other instructional materials
> in carrying out such State plan. . . .

Whether or not phrases such as "development and revision of standards" relating to textbooks and "distribution and control by a local educational agency" might be interpreted as having possible relevancy to textbook adoption policies is obviously a question for official legal adjudication and outside the scope of this text. However, there is a possible implication for more explicit conditions to be set in further legislation. As stated earlier, such conditions regarding textbook adoption policies would be liberating rather than restricting. Aside from being a possible deterrent to a growing power of would-be censors, such legislation might also lead to a greater degree of direct teacher involvement in textbook selection in states where existing policies place the responsibility on individuals who in many cases are not only unqualified for the task, but perhaps are also guided by a restricting political bias. It might be argued that in some cases textbook adoption committees at local levels might also be guided by a restricting political bias, even if the committees were to be made up completely of teachers. To some degree this might be true, but the effects in such cases would be limited to the particular districts, and not extended statewide. Under such adoption programs authors and publishers might be less inclined to submit to pressure that lacks the suasive backing of statewide adoption policies.

The significance of the discussion need not be limited to the area of textbooks alone, if one considers that America's Future, Inc., as well as other related groups, represents a particularly narrow view in regard to education in general. For the most part, such groups are generally opposed to any kind of extension in educational spending or any innovative ideas in education. They consistently attempt to equate any part of the educational enterprise to which they object with un-Americanism. For example, they have long viewed progressivism in education as an evil threat to the traditions of America, and have charged it as being the cause of anything from rising crime rates to the alleged weakening of the American character.

Although their charges against the schools and education in general are sensationalistic, they often becloud serious issues such as sorely needed increases in educational spending or curricular innovations. More important, however, such criticism, not viewed and answered objectively, with an understanding of its source, may act as a dangerously restricting force against education at a time when man's needs for freedom in education are greatest. To be sure, textbooks are but one part of the whole enterprise, but in a sense a most important part. When textbooks are restricted by the imposed censorship activities of any group, the scope of education in general is restricted, and more important, the expression of ideas and knowledge, the most necessary and cherished aspects of a free society of men, is threatened.

the teacher and the professional organizations

If this were being written before the 1960s, any discussion of teachers' organizations might well be limited to a brief survey of their historical development, membership, stated purposes, and perhaps some indication of their contribution to American education. But we are in the 1970s and have lived through a decade that has brought about profound and rapid changes in many social institutions.

The events of the 1960s have obviously brought us to a period of intensified conflict in our institutions. The politics of confrontation, of activism, comfortable or not, are always the necessary dynamics of a democratic system. (Please note that confrontation and activism do not necessarily imply violence.) In today's society this has meant that many of the long unattended grievances have been announced more loudly and dramatically, even by groups which heretofore had been relatively nonpolitical in character. Perhaps the most significant evidence of this reality is to be seen in the development of "teacher power" over the last decade.

Before the 1960s the teachers of America, as a group, could have been, and often were, characterized as being politically docile and complaisant, willing to accept their lot without any significant dissent. And this was essentially the role of the teacher as defined by society, and to a large extent by the "profession." The NEA, largest of the teachers' organizations, had, since its beginning in 1857, been mostly dominated by the American Association of School Administrators, one of its affiliates which had always taken a dim view of any show of activism on the part of teachers. The NEA under the administrators' domination was a "safe" organization. This is made clear by the fact that administrators not only encouraged but often required teachers to join. Not that it was simply the case of the superordinate compelling the subordinate to organize, but to organize under a "proper" head. In many instances the encouragement by administrators was simply out of a deep antipathy to unionism, but in another sense it was out of a traditional pattern of paternalism.

Before 1960 teacher strikes were rare occurrences, and seldom if ever did they have official NEA support. Official sanctions by the NEA or affiliate organizations, even against districts, were rarer yet. But during the 1960s the picture began to change. Not only were teacher strikes to occur in increasing numbers, but the NEA, through its state and local affiliates, began to impose official sanctions against districts and even states. An example of the degree of change can be seen in the figures for the 1967–1968 school year. There was a total of 114 strikes involving 1,400,000 man-days. This accounted for 80 percent of the total for the preceding twenty-seven years. Strikes ranging from one day to three weeks occurred in twenty-one states. Statewide strikes took place in Florida, Oklahoma, and Pennsylvania. Of the 114 strikes that year 70 were under the banner of local or state affiliates of the NEA, though not officially supported by NEA. In most instances the strikes were carried out against state antistrike laws, an indication that the laws themselves were under attack.

What had happened, of course, was that the NEA had been moved from complacency to activism by two factors—(1) the press of changing conditions in society and (2) the growing competition of the American Federation of Teachers. Since its beginning in 1916, the AFT had, except in its first few years, always been overshadowed by the NEA. Most of its membership had come from the larger cities, and even there the AFT could not claim the majority of the teachers as its members. But as an affiliate of the American Federation of Labor, it viewed its role as bargaining agent rather than professional negotiator. The results are history. With the AFT winning teacher approval as sole bargaining agent in New York and other large cities, the NEA was induced to shift to a more active role.

On the other hand, the AFT, in order to erase some of the stigma of unionism has moved somewhat toward more statesmanlike negotiation than is characteristic of the AFL in general. For whatever reason, the AFT is no longer looked upon with antipathy by so many teachers. In many districts the AFT and NEA coexist with a growing cooperativeness even though the competition for the role of representation goes on, not only in the cities but in the larger suburban districts as well. The reality of this is made apparent to the new teachers in a district when confronted with the choice of organizational membership. The choice more than ever before has to be made on pragmatic grounds with respect to the particular circumstances. The old ideological dichotomy of NEA or AFT, "professionalism" or "union-ism," is no longer a clear basis for choice. This fact has probably accounted for the recent growth of membership in the AFT.

Undoubtedly, an important sociological factor that has influenced the status of the two teachers' organizations in the past has been teachers' attitudes toward the labor movement. Until the last few decades American teachers had come from middle-class white-collar or farm family backgrounds, neither of which has been particularly friendly to trade unionism. Since World War II, however, a growing number of men and women from blue-collar families have entered teaching. To many people in the labor movement this has accounted for the growth of the AFT in recent years. But their assumption that teachers coming from labor union families will automatically support unionism is perhaps not as valid as it might appear to be. In fact, there is some indication that because of societal role-definition the opposite might well be the case.

This possibility is suggested by the results of one study conducted at a New York state teachers college in 1960.[20] In this instance students from blue-collar families displayed a greater hostility toward trade unionism than did students from farm or white-collar families. The interesting aspect of the study was the fact that the students involved were all social studies majors who had had more than just a superficial knowledge of labor history. Some selected results of the forced-answer questionnaire used in the study are shown in Table 9.

To some extent the results of the study, though limited, indicate the degree to which a press for middle-class attributes are part of the teacher's life style, or part of his education. Doherty sees both at work:

> The old style of life, of course, is the antithesis of the new. . . . It is a world of greasy overalls, of ungrammatical English, and of calendar art. And among all these in-gredients of the working-class syndrome is the union . . . not bad in and of itself, but . . . part of the social accouterment, and it, too, must be sloughed off if there is going to be an easy accommodation to the middle-class style. . . .
>
> The findings . . . suggest that the social and intellectual climate of the teachers colleges is highly conducive to creat-ing in the students identification with the anticipated social class. . . . In college he is learning to make a psychological adjustment to a new style of life, and he has already begun to take on the coloration of the world he aspires to. And in this sleek new world, he believes, people do not take kindly to labor unions.[21]

[20] Robert E. Doherty, "Attitudes Towards Labor," *The School Review*, 71 (Spring 1963), pp. 87–95.
[21] *Ibid.*, pp. 94–95.

TABLE 9   *Responses (in percents) of Two Groups of Students to Items on a Labor-Management Scale*

	Disagreed Completely		Disagreed Slightly		Agreed Completely		Agreed Slightly	
	WC*	BC†	WC	BC	WC	BC	WC	BC
1. Labor Unions are usually run democratically.	26	48	41	26	10	6	23	20
2. There is no more corruption in labor unions than in business and industry.	29	38	33	32	21	18	17	12
3. Affiliating with a teacher's union would be one of the most effective ways for a teacher to improve his professional and economic status.	26	78	71	22	0	0	3	0
4. The dues paid by a union member are almost always used in a way that is beneficial to his own welfare.	23	24	45	34	3	16	29	26
5. Organized labor has retained its idealism, and continues to instill a feeling of elan among its members.	42	58	26	38	7	0	25	4

* White-collar background students
† Blue-collar background students
Source: Robert E. Doherty, "Attitudes Towards Labor," *The School Review*, 71 (Spring, 1963), 92–93.

It is important to note again that Doherty was talking about 1960. The NEA was at that time complacent as compared to today. But what has seemingly happened is that much of its membership though still with a conditioned antipathy to trade unionism was willing to use union strategies while attempting to maintain their "professional" image.

Regardless of the reasons for the change, it is clear that both the NEA and AFT have become powerful organizations for change. The increases in teachers' salary schedules during the 1960s have come about largely because of their activities. But salary is not their only concern. Improved working conditions—which means improved school practices—are also within their realm of concerns. For example, 17,000 Los Angeles teachers in September, 1969 boycotted classes for one day to protest what they felt was a rapid deterioration of that school system. Some of their specific charges were:

1. Classes range upwards of 38, 39, 40, and even 45 students.
2. Teachers' salaries are steadily less competitive, contributing to an educationally disastrous 50 percent turnover each year in inner-city schools.
3. Dropout rates in inner-city high schools average between 30 and 45 percent.
4. Reading scores are well below state and national averages, and are falling a little more each year.

5. There are major shortages of equipment, supplies, and
   textbooks and other instructional material, and much of
   what exists is ancient and in poor repair.
6. Many of the district's ramshackle school buildings have
   safety hazards and unhealthy and unsanitary conditions;
   maintenance is cut back a little further each year.[22]

The Los Angeles teachers pointed out that while these needs went
unmet the school board and administration constructed their own new
building, "air-conditioned, plush-carpeted, and costing nearly $4 mil-
lion." The teachers also served notice to the state government that a
statewide teacher action could be expected unless two actions were
taken before the year's end: a collective bargaining law and a boost of
state support of public education now down to 35 percent from 50 percent a decade ago. That is what is known as the new teacher-power.

The Los Angeles situation is not in any sense unique. In the spring
of 1968 the NEA research division carried out a nationwide teacher's
opinion survey to determine specific problems. The results of that
survey are given in part in Table 10.

In view of the activities of both the NEA and the AFT as the decade
of the 1970s opened, it is very likely that the stated problems will be
future targets for both groups. Also important in the newly voiced
power of teachers' organizations is the expected increase in lobbying
power. Although in force in the past mostly at the state level, lobbying activities will now carry with them a great deal more political clout
than before. Teachers in their lobbying have not restricted themselves
only to legislation for improving the schools. In the future it can be
anticipated that they will extend the limits of their interests at both
the state and national levels. This, too, is a part of the new teacher
power.

TABLE 10 *Major Problems*

	Urban	Suburban	Rural
Large class size	40.4%	33.4%	30.6%
Classroom management and discipline	23.3	10.8	12.1
Inadequate assistance from specialized teachers	22.5	21.0	30.3
Inadequate salary	34.9	24.5	30.3
Inadequate fringe benefits	27.7	22.3	31.3
Ineffective grouping of students into classes	24.3	18.2	24.2
Lack of public support for schools	27.8	17.4	23.7
Ineffective testing and guidance program	21.1	14.2	20.8

Source: NEA Research Bulletin, 46:4 (December 1968), p. 117.

[22] *NEA Reporter* (October 24, 1969), p. 1.

topics for inquiry

1. Censorship Attempts in Your District's Schools and Libraries
2. Textbook Selection Practices in Your District and State
3. Origins and Patterns of Group Pressure in Your District
4. Statements or Provisions for Academic Freedom in Your District
5. Extremist Groups' Literature on the Schools
6. Developing Programs of Urban-Teacher Education
7. Supreme Court Rulings on Academic Freedom and Related Issues
8. Materials Provided for the School by Business and Industry
9. Pressure on Textbooks from the Left
10. Aspects of School Law that Relate to Academic Freedom

subjects for discussion

1. Suppose that as an English or history teacher you have selected a particular book to be used in your course. You are informed by the principal that the book must be withdrawn because of some complaints from the community.
   a. What are your alternatives?
   b. Should you inform your students of the events?
   c. Would the issue itself offer anything valuable for class study?
2. It is felt by some that in dealing with controversial issues teachers should maintain a position of neutrality.
   a. Is this possible?
   b. Is it desirable?
   c. Is it the same as being objective?
   d. Is it possible to be authentic and objective?
3. There has been much discussion in recent years about the issue of teachers' strikes. Some say it is unprofessional; others say it sets a bad example for students.
   a. What is your idea of professionalism?
   b. Could strikes be useful to better the schools?
   c. What lessons might students get from strikes?

selected readings

BEALE, HOWARD K. *Are American Teachers Free.* New York: Scribner, 1936.

————. *A History of Freedom of Teaching in American Schools.* New York: Scribner, 1941.

An incisive view in both volumes of academic freedom in the schools and teaching before the 1940s. The two books offer important insights into social history as well as informative reports on textbook censorship.

BELL, DANIEL. *The Radical Right.* Garden City, N.Y.: Anchor Books, 1964.

An impressive collection of writings by eminent scholars providing a penetrating historical and sociological view of the radical right—a must for today's teacher.

BRAMELD, THEODORE. *Education for the Emerging Age.* New York: Harper & Row, 1965.

A provocative book by one of education's own "gadflies." It presents sound views on teacher education as well as a convincing case for viewing a philosophy of education as a philosophy of politics.

DOWNS, ROBERT B. *The First Freedom.* Chicago: American Library Association, 1960.

An impressive collection of writings on censorship that deals not only with cases but also profoundly with the sociophilosophical questions involved in censorship. Good reading.

NELSON, JACK and GENE ROBERTS *The Censors and the Schools.* Boston: Little, Brown, 1963.

An important journalistic account of some of the most significant censorship activities affecting textbooks since 1930 with particular attention paid to the 1950s and early 1960s.

RAYWID, MARY ANNE. *The Ax Grinders.* New York: Macmillan, 1962.

A well-written and well documented account of the radical right's activities in American education as well as in other areas of society. Provides some informative material on the range of organizations as well as their special activities.

11

THE
STUDENT'S
LIFE

It would be presumptuous to instruct the readers of this text in the details of the student culture. Most of you are a part of it; you have access to the data. The job, therefore, is to assess the data with a view toward making new use of it, to give it an educational function.

the student in society

The student is, first of all, a person. It has been charged that the school calls no person by name, that is, that it fails to recognize and to study the identity of its students. Thus, it is essential to point out: *you do not learn about students by studying students in the aggregate; you learn about students by getting to know a good number of them, one at a time—personally.* On the other hand, you must realize that whatever you come to know about students in general will teach you nothing about any given individual student. Therefore, the limitation on the content of this chapter is clear. It consists of generalizations about students. Thus, by our own contention, the chapter will not help you to know any student. What then can it do? It can help you to comprehend the student's culture. By so doing, one can become somewhat familiar with where the student lives, and to a degree allows the reader to move around in this culture more freely and more surely.

That peer-group approval is a consistent force in the student culture is scarcely arguable. This is a characteristic of the American culture in which the youth culture shares. The authors marvel that the phenomenon of peer-group influence among students is so often remarked upon as a peculiar feature. The whole American society is marked by group organization and association. Businessmen get together in service clubs, housewives in women's clubs, card players in bridge and poker clubs, the list extends *ad infinitum*. Most of the lonely pursuits have vanished, even hunting. The once lonely hunter now goes afield as a member of a sportsman club; he shoulders his weapon as a member of the National Rifleman's Association.

"Peer-group associationism" is broadly characteristic of American culture. Public social behavior is largely observable in group terms. The push downward of these tendencies is illustrated in the Boy Scouts. The Scouts a long generation ago rigorously enforced the twelve-year-old membership rule. Today, two categories of scouting exist below this age. Did you know that the Scouts used to have a category of membership known as Lone Scouts for members in rural or isolated areas? Lone Scouts have gone the way of lonely hunters on the American scene.

In the United States the individual is cloaked in peer-group costume and goes its ways. But there is another side to this coin. Associationism leads to an intense privatism. The American is publicly conformist, privately fugitive from and often bitterly resentful of the group pressures that he does not resist. The smiling, but inner-resentful conformist is in private driven to a profound revulsion against the group. Thus, the other side of the coin of coerced conformity is an intensified individualism verging on anarchism.

This is not the way an open society *should* function. It constitutes an aberration. The good society encourages continuity between public and private identities. The individual in the group is a part of its decision-making process. He does not have to accept its dogmas intact to qualify for membership. Nor does the group attempt to pursue the individual too far; it is not jealous of his time, does not hold him suspect if it observes him in other company, other costume, or other pursuits. The noncoercive fabric of association tends to support the person in the integration of his personality. In his public life he joins the group with his identity uncamouflaged and intact; in his private life he may think of his associations without guilt and resentment. This relationship between society and the individual is a solid base for responsible human behavior.

American culture is a complex one ranging between the two basically conflicting models.

The group does furnish support to a person and lends him a certain degree of company. He may still know an inner loneliness, but he is not too often alone. Probably what the peer group most often does is to support free choice, up to a point, and also put limitations on it.

Very loosely, the student resides in a youth culture. This has a great deal to do with his consumership. It strongly influences the records he buys, the clothes he selects, the length of hair or skirt, the places he goes, the movies he attends.

The film has not profoundly influenced the youth culture. What is true is that the youth culture has profoundly influenced the film. *The Graduate* made the generation gap its subject matter. It did something to communicate about it; it no doubt occasioned a good deal of dialogue upon it.

The Graduate was essentially so documentary that the camera revealed a good deal more than its intent. It was "wild" in that it swung the camera quite candidly on a lot of very real reality. It also revealed a good deal of its own middle-aged, or conventional, perspective. This was nowhere more clearly evident than in the hotel lobby sequence where Benjamin is suddenly depicted in the role of the stumbling, blundering, shy country boy suitor. It was played for high comedy, and it got a lot of laughs; but the comic aspect was the misperception of the scene. For this intrusive and erroneously conceived sequence Gomer Pyle would have been better cast than Dustin Hoffman. The "graduate" was no such blundering, unsophisticated youth. He is the young man who has been established as an honors graduate of an eastern university; he is a member of the sports car set; he is sophisticated enough and independent enough to reject his parents' values and cool enough to carry it off without inducing hysteria. Ultimately, we see him in full determination pounding at the foundations of the most basic institutions of church, family, and marriage itself—and carrying it off—"cool, man, cool."

This "cool cat" is made to look like a blushing, flustered yokel when he is registering for himself and Mrs. Robinson in a downtown hotel. Here, the camera reveals its assessment of the mass culture—not a perceptive view of the way it is. Here the camera adhered to its conventional, conforming role, the scene became the standard Hollywood convention: Sex is funny; sex is amateurish, flirtatious; it never really happens; play it for smirks not for feelings.

Even Mrs. Robinson is sent down two incompatible paths of character development. The phony direction renders her an awkward seductress, yet with a suggestion of the "earth mother" about her (which might come under the heading of "letting Anne Bancroft do her thing"). There was even a suggestion of the old mythology that she might have a good deal to teach the bashful schoolboy. The more real insights are asserted tentatively and lost in the conventional phoniness. The pathos with which age in America clings to and pursues the ways of youth is flirted with and abandoned. It is turned into a middle-age put-down.

There has been a sexual revolution. It began with a revulsion against Puritanism and Victorianism and a preoccupation with Freud. Contraception did not begin with the pill. The automobile was a portable bedroom in today's generation's grandparent's youth. The jazz age was coincident with the roaring twenties. World War II with its vast dislocations of persons and institutions belonged to the parental experience. The sexual revolution is, in modern terms, at least three generations deep. It is well-rooted. Sexual emancipation has not known a single setback since 1920.

That is where the distortion in *The Graduate* lies. Sure, there are still bashful schoolboys, but they are not archetypical of this generation, of a generation of youth reared as this one has been. Sex is matter of fact. The dirty joke belongs to middle age; the smirking, comic film sequence to the 1930s along with the shuffling, shambling "colored" handymen and mammy-type maids.

Another conventional, middle-aged perception in the film is depicted in the final sequence. It is at bottom a time-hallowed formula. The ever-loving true-hearted suitor rescues the bride from the unworthy one at the very steps of the church. In times past, he came astride a western saddle or perhaps in feudal armor, brandishing sword. Benjamin, the graduate, used public transportation. And the switch on the old situation: he rescued her on the wrong side of the altar, after the ceremony. And they set it up for shock! Look at those wild radical kids, making mock of sacred religious symbols, treating the marriage vows as if they had never been spoken. Just where did the media people expect to find the capacity for shock, unless they were deliberately appealing to "the silent majority."

Not that *The Graduate* did not study its subject and report it truly in many dimensions. The empty materialism, the profound rejection of it by youth, the eroded controls of convention, and institutions, and even decency, the pathos of the estranged and alienated. This is the stuff of modern times that the camera could scarcely avoid. And more: the compulsiveness of behavior undisciplined to functional values; the inarticulateness of the rebel in society; and the ambiguity of it all.

The ambiguity of the modern scene is rooted in a conflicting reality. There is much resentment against the establishment, but most want to participate in its material advantages. The life style of youth is not so much unconventional, as emancipated and unrooted (which seem to balance a plus and a minus). There have been folk heroes for youth, and in many arenas youth has found heroic things to do.

A love story for modern well-heeled youth, however, has a hard time being either heroic or tragic. Maybe that is better. Yet it is hard to be sure of any verities except that they be tested.

The plethora of young and campus marriages has no doubt been a social delight and a surcease of frustration, which must be held to be good. The talk of the young about their marriages seldom tells a tale worthy of Sir Walter Scott, let alone of Shakespeare. The authors seem to be the airlines and Macy's, Gimbels, and Marshall Field. Marriage is just the best Christmas ever! A big trip in good company, and all that stuff: the stereo, the color TV, the slick kitchen, and, of course, the checks. It is very nice.

When the "graduate" and the bride (not his, the other fellow's) take off into the west, by municipal bus, there is an ambiguity of circumstance, But there is no question of heroism or tragedy. There is not going to be a fateful duel; the lady's honor is in no peril. They are not destined to languish in a garret or perish of consumption. Those well-heeled, neurotic, materialistic, but vulgarly competent parents are still there. They know how it is; they won't let the children starve; the honeymoon tickets are transferable; annulments can be arranged. The "graduate" has some pride, we know. He will not follow his father's footsteps. It seems a bit too much to ask that Mr. Robinson take him into his business. But all is not lost. We may assume that the "graduate" and his not-so-very-secondhand bride will shortly be enrolled in graduate school.

the generation gap

People nurtured quite differently, in different cultures as it were, often experience a phenomenon known as culture shock. This is frequently experienced by persons taking up residence in foreign countries, especially those not tied to one's native land in a closely related historical tradition. Even movement from rural town to city or vice versa or from region to region may provoke a mild onset of this malaise. Moving across cultural frontiers is upsetting in many ways. The language barrier is only the beginning. Dietary considerations are hazards too, but the variety of the American supermarket and the cosmopolitan range of urban restaurants tend to minimize this factor for the American traveler. The palate adjusts more rapidly than the personality.

It is the weight of all sorts of different expectations that cause the trouble. The stranger in an alien land may well have prided himself on being an adjustable and tolerant individual in his home territory, but now it is a different ball game. He is the minority, perhaps a minority of one. It is his peculiarities that stand out, his ways are socially judged, criticized, condemned—or perhaps tolerated. The new general expectations go far beyond language and diet.

It is the ways of a lifetime historically buttressed that are threatened. They are challenged on so many fronts. The stranger encounters different matters of manners—styles of greeting and departure, expectations about times of arrival and punctuality, the giving of gifts, forms of address. The gentleman in one culture may perform like a boor in another and be made to feel it. The role of religion, the importance of family and position, the relations between men and women, adults and children—complexities in these areas of life are greater still, for example, when a North American from the United States ventures other than as a tourist to Latin America or an Asian country. Unless the stranger takes the trouble to study the new ways and conform to them, his harvest of anxious moments, of angry shouts, and of bent fenders and unnecessary emotional stress is likely to be abundant. (Seldom is it given a stranger to give a whole culture lessons.) He will be subject to complaints of varying types, particularly psychic ones—feelings of vague unease; anxiety; irritability; ups and downs of a manic-depressive quality; a sense of isolation; hostility and strangely triggered tempers. This is homesickness plus.

We accept the generation gap today as a reality which education must reckon with. It too encompasses a "culture shock" similar to that just discussed, a phenomenon today much more pronounced in contemporary America than ever before. Whether it has always existed in some form or another is beside the point. Today it exists to such degrees as to threaten not merely communication between parents and children, but even the working of institutions that have been historically counted upon to provide continuity of culture: the home, the church, and the school. The clichés of extreme disaffection abound: "You just can't talk to anyone over thirty"; "I just can't get through to my children, or my students, anymore." It is our belief that the presence of student unrest and student protest is deep-rooted and general enough to warrant direct and serious attention. It is not our belief that it is simply a passing phase or something that pious wishing will cause to go away. It is a matter of differing cultures at home in the same nation, the same community, even under the same roof.

Culture shock does not just pass away. Sometimes persons persist to the end of their limits; then they either crack up or go home. Sometimes communities of aliens in a strange land will band together in ghettoes of their own choosing—the American colony, the British community—and protect themselves by living their own ways as persistently as possible. Their forays into the surrounding culture will be as tourists, shoppers, businessmen, missionaries—never as permanent residents.

The process of living in a "strange" community is harder, yet more rewarding than living on an island with like individuals. It requires a disciplined living in. It means study of the roots of another culture, an attempt to find out the reasons why other ways of looking at things and doing things make sense to the dwellers in that culture. The greatest discipline is a willingness to learn, to suspend judgment, to cease assertion, and to wait for explanations. The statement tends to be replaced by the question. Listening is a primary tool, listening and participation. For a while participation is forced, uncertain, and awkward. It starts as role-playing, but ends up in being.

The dances of another culture are often derived from unfamiliar rhythms, strange tunes. The postures and movements are not easily acquired. But the learner persists, he listens, he moves, he forgets self and attends to the music and the step. Then, later for some than others, he finds himself at ease and alive in a new style, and he wants to shout "Look, ma, I'm dancing!"

As with dance, so with other matters. And in all matters intercultural, the stranger has one fundamental thing going for him: we are all of one species, one humanity. This bond is not immediate; history and cultures have made many barriers. They do not just fall away. Food is a universal need, but some dishes are strange indeed. Dance is universal, but the steps and rhythms are exotic. The need for recognition is in every person, but cultures vary in the patterns of expression and the awards to this need.

Draw out then from the utter complexity of American civilization one factor for examination, the not-so-simple factor of the contrast between youth and middle age. To try to get some leverage upon the generation gap, look at it with us as a confrontation of two cultures. The two cultures reside so close to one another that they cannot escape one another. Consequently, the only alternatives are conflict or accommodation.

Two cultures, two ways of doing things, two ways of looking at things, is not this too sharp a distinction for persons raised in the same land, even in the same household? The question is a reasonable one, but look also at the sensible evidence.

It is possible to make a rough classification—the chosen aggregates are rough and ready: the *under-thirties* and the *around-fifties*. Plenty of exceptions and many other factors affect the division, but a clustering of experiences and cultural factors and ways of expressing them are, nonetheless, possible for these groups and may be useful in getting at the nature of the problem. It must be remembered that many circumstances of existence have been shared by the members of both groups, that deep bonds do exist, that the cultures coexist, and that some communication with one another does take place regularly. But distinctions do exist, and much communication is bewildered, strained, and even hostile.

First, many things that the "under-thirties" take for granted the "around-fifties" still find surprising, are still adjusting to. Television, for instance, is a universal, but for many of the younger it has been an expectation, a standard part of life, from the very cradle. It is still something new for the "around-fifties"; it was not a part of their nurture. This means something very fundamental. The older generation was accustomed to patience, enforced delays, in getting a full report on things. Even if radio brought the news bulletin, you waited for newspaper or news magazine to give the pictures of it, a week or so for the newsreel to bring a sparing pictorialization. Now be it a flood, a battle, or a ball game, the report is multisensory, immediate, generous, and many-dimensioned. It is the same for all viewers, but it is also different. For the young, this is reality, you get the impact, you encompass it, you react immediately. It has always been that way for them. The elders and all before in history were accustomed to time and distance gaps except for what went on right around them. They are surprised by the immediacy, shocked at being in on so much at the very moment of its happening. They cannot accept the immediacy. They have cultural defenses against it. They still feel apart; they create distances in their minds that no longer exist. If a student revolt

in Paris triggers immediate response in youth in New York or Berkeley, it is an amazement to them. Paris is as far away in their culture
as it was for Lindbergh.

For the elders, in a deeply psychic sense, those broadcasts from the
battlefields of Vietnam are news pictures of something that happened.
(Note the past tense.) They are apart from the immediacy of events
because that is how they had learned it was: you waited for the whole
story; you reacted in patterns of accumulation and delay. To the
young, those broadcasts are going on. They have learned that you are
part of it; that is you fighting, hurting, dying. The reaction and involvement is *now*. The elders speak in bafflement and exasperation
of the "now-generation." It is as though the young had perversely
elected to follow a different calendar. But it was no matter of choice.
The young were born into television, into the *now*. They had no more
choice about it than they had of their race, or social class, or town, or
family. It is a part of their culture. It was not a part of the culture
of their elders or of any generation before in history.

It is not too hard to see relationship between this element of culture and extended views on other matters. *Relevant* is a recent, and
perhaps overworked, word in the common culture. Nonetheless, it
is not a concept likely to diminish in force. Relevant is not simply *in*.
Relevant is a part of the dictates of the culture of the *now*. What is
related in this? What is the good of this? What is the point of this?
Now, not later. If men are dying, if children are starving, if injustice
is visible—if these things are fully reported and can be clearly seen,
you have what you need to know. You are part of it. The response
must be, and is, immediate. The elders have sprung from another
culture that forced them to wait, to ask: "What really happened?"
"What was the whole story?" "Did it really happen?" And the habits
of the other culture affect response to changed circumstance.

The "under-thirties" and the "around-fifties" stem from very different factors of economic expectations. To be sure, both dwell in a pattern of very materialistic expectations. Few of either shun things—
despite those who opt out of the struggle for goods and money. The
young are in the market with more money than children have ever
possessed, expending it on everything from yo-yo's to sports cars.
Both groups are substantially American in outlook. However, they
come from a differing American experience.

The Great Depression is old history to youth; it is an ever-condition-
ing reality to the elders. It hit many of the "around-fifties" in high
school and early college or employment years. It may not have taught
them the meaning of actual hunger, but it did leave enduring lessons
in fear and insecurity. Many families knew the reality of unemployment, still more the dread of it.

For the three-fourths of Americans who share in the national affluence, the years since World War II have been unthreatened economi-

cally. The difference is that the younger take it for granted; the elders can never really believe it will last. Not that they would wish a depression on youth. The elders simply wish the impossible: that the culture of youth contain an element that it does not have—belief in the possibility of being less affluent.

The "around-fifties" appear to youth to have a great docility with respect to the institutions for which they toil. The culture helps to explain this. The options for depression youth were not often expressed in terms of wide vocational choice. It was simply job or no job. The good job was the job you could get. After a while the strictures eased up, but for many of the depression generation the choices were made, the options limited permanently. It was so too of college. The question of the good college was not of its quality or your admission. The good college was the one you could afford to go to, if you could. Most could not. Many decisions had to be postponed; many satisfactions deferred. High school and college students fell in love and wanted to marry, but economic necessity even more than institutional regulations occasioned long delays. The acceptance of deferred satisfaction became a cultural characteristic, which is often confused with virtue.

In general, the ratio of indulgent parents is not known to have changed, although the "over-fifties" generation does not remember much being given to it. It was because their parents at that time did not have so much to give. Cars were family cars borrowed, under terms of varying stringency; seldom were they owned. The recital is unnecessary. Most readers will have heard it from their elders. The point being stressed is: the elder generation does not have much experience in receiving gifts easily rendered.

The "under-thirties" have a general capacity to accept gifts in a matter-of-fact way. It really is a cultural characteristic of the group. This is not to say that it is characteristic to be devoid of courtesy or appreciation in accepting gifts. *But* it is not characteristic to think of a gift as evidencing either love or family sacrifice, for in the experience and the observation of the recipient it may mean neither. If the gift is a car, it may mean really only the expenditure of a spare portion of a family budget, a generous enough gesture.

The trouble comes when the adult giver, reacting from his culture, feels that the young recipient ought to react as he would have reacted in another time and place—another culture—to the gift of a watch, or a bicycle, or an automobile. Cultures being as they are, such things can seldom be.

Youth has not been forced by necessity to defer many satisfactions; therefore, to defer them carries no virtue in their culture.

How will the generation gap be bridged? Not by mere passing of time in all probability. If initiative is to be taken, it would seem that the cultural disposition might be greatest in the youth, among the *now-*

oriented.   However, since the primary instrument for bridging must be *communications,* it seems that the responsibility must be accepted by both cultures.

Understanding might well begin with accepting the concept of two cultures.   This makes the gap a reality, not somebody's guilt.   It has happened; it exists; but no one declared it.   Wars have taken place because of gaps between cultures.   But gaps between cultures are not wars; they are facts of life.   There are other, and better ways of handling facts of life than declaring war over them, especially between those who may be, among other designations, fathers and sons.   The fact of a generation gap does not mean *ipso facto* that adults have declared war on youth, or vice versa.   However, misunderstanding derived from ignorance and culture shock can lead to actual conflict.

To be hopeful at this point is allowable, but not to be unduly optimistic.   The dialogue between the generations is beclouded with bitterness.   The issue is also complicated by psychological factors. Youth does resent imposed controls, restraints, advices.   It hankers for the rights, prerogatives, and possessions of the elders.   It impatiently waits its turn at the high tables.   More is involved than the factors we have indicated.

students and parents view the school

In the May 16, 1969 issue, *Life* magazine reported the result of a Louis Harris poll surveying people's views on the high schoools.[1]   This poll consisted of 2,500 depth interviews among students, teachers, parents, and principals in 100 assorted communities around the nation.   Its data allow interesting comparisons and contrasts among the views of the students with the views of the other respondents.   The disparity between student and parental views is sharp and consistent; in most instances teachers' views stood somewhere between.   The comparison of views with those in the Gallup poll cited in Chapter 7 is also illuminating.

The Harris poll, like the Gallup poll, found discipline a big issue in the minds of parents.   Of the parents 62 percent (but only 27 percent of the teachers) responded "Yes" to the proposition that "maintaining discipline is more important than student self-inquiry."   Support for the statement "homework requiring memorization is good and useful" was strong among both parents (70 percent favorable) and teachers (46 percent).   Only 32 percent of the parents, but 54 percent of the teachers concurred in the opinion that "students are justified in feeling there is too much drudgery."

Parents and students stood far apart on the generation gap with respect to the handling of unruly students.   Almost two-thirds (63 percent) of the parents agreed with the simplistic solution of "crack

[1] *Life,* 66:19 (May 16, 1969), 22–32.

down on them," but only 37 percent of the students endorsed it. The
more humane suggestion, "try to understand them," appealed to 56
percent of the students but to only 35 percent of the parents. Interestingly enough, in percentage terms, teachers stood midway between
students and parents on both matters. The views of school administrators were in practical agreement with those of students in percentage terms.

Of the students 58 percent want more participation in policy-mak-
ing; only 20 percent of the parents want them to have more. That
students should "have more say" in *making rules* was judged affirma-
tively by nearly two-thirds of the students (66 percent) and by less than
one-fourth of the parents (24 percent); *in deciding curriculum* by 63
percent of the students and 35 percent of the parents; *in determining
discipline of students* by 48 percent of the students and 28 percent of
the parents.

Discussion in class of certain aspects of student culture was viewed
by parents with scant enthusiasm. Only 6 percent thought folk rock
music should be so acknowledged, and 17 percent gave the nod to discussion of underground papers and films. Students endorsed these
topics in percentages of 35 percent and 40 percent, respectively. Over
half (52 percent) of the students wanted discussion of black students'
rights in contrast to about one quarter (27 percent) of the parents.
Both groups stood rather close in agreement on sex hygiene (students,
52 percent; parents, 41 percent) and use of drugs (70 percent and 66
percent, respectively) as desirable discussion topics.

The students surveyed were in the main favorable in their judgment upon the schools. Teachers were rated "good to excellent" by
81 percent; 68 percent did not feel that teachers make passing college
tests their main purpose, and a like 68 percent did not feel that teachers were more concerned with tests than with what students learn.
The grade system was judged fair by 65 percent. School meant good
things in general to these majorities. It is not necessarily pessimistic
to point out that significant minor fractions of students failed to
agree in these judgments. It is interesting to speculate as to what
school meant for them.

The students held what *Life* called an "almost universal definition
of what makes a good teacher":

> He's young [which should be encouraging to most readers of
> this text] . . . has a sense of humor . . . listens and understands
> . . . doesn't just go by the book . . . encourages discussion and
> participation . . . treats us like grownups . . . gives us respon-
> sibilities . . . always listens and is free and open with us . . . is
> interested in us, and thinks like a kid.[2]

The students are eager for some methodological changes, though
discussion and dialogue have their basic confidence. In seeking more

[2] *Ibid.*, p. 30.

diverse methods they endorse fieldwork and work in the community. But, says *Life*: "One innovation, however, got an overwhelming thumbs-down from the students: teaching by films and closed-circuit television. The reason, they said, was that it cast them in a passive role and froze out class discussion." [3]

Students' views on curriculum reveal deep ambiguities and contradictions. There is nothing like a majority view, let alone a consensus on the worth of given subjects. A few examples speak for themselves.

English (grammar, composition) was endorsed by the largest group (33 percent) as "most useful," but 14 percent judged it "least useful." It was classified "most difficult" by 21 percent and "most important" by 52 percent, but 25 percent found it "most boring" and 14 percent "most irrelevant."

History (including black) was named by the largest number (18 percent) as the "most irrelevant" subject and by a mere 12 percent as "most important." More dubbed it "least useful"—18 percent—than "most useful"—15 percent—and 19 percent found it "most boring."

Science was found "most difficult" by 22 percent, "most irrelevant" by 13 percent and "most important" by an equal 13 percent. It was deemed "most useful" by 20 percent and "least useful" by another 16 percent.

What sense can one make of the foregoing? Is it not that the central accomplishment of the curriculum is the confusion it creates? The school has a lot of credit in confidence and goodwill among a majority of its students. However, even among these it is failing to get its purposes across. To the extent that it does, its achievements are not congruent with its intent. How can one account for students in significant numbers judging science and history to be irrelevant in this day and age? They are not. Therefore, if they be so judged, have not curriculum and teaching made it so? When views scatter as meaninglessly as these, only one conclusion can be drawn—the school is simply not getting its message across coherently at all.

Bayard Hooper, in the same issue of *Life*, points up the dilemma of education in an article aptly titled, "The Task Is to Learn What Learning Is For." We quote him in full endorsement of his views:

> The dilemma is central to the approaching high school crisis
> today, . . . because most teachers and principals are far too
> cautious ever to allow . . . a controversy to come to a head.
> Indeed, most of them would agree that schools are not the place
> to foster controversy or to challenge prevailing standards. The
> students have begun to realize this. They are beginning to want
> to challenge and change the schools, as their older brothers and
> sisters are challenging and changing the colleges.
>   The *Life* Poll makes clear, however, that most parents feel

exactly the opposite. They think the schools should keep the
children passive and disciplined, and provide them with the
tools that lead to college and a job.

Universal education is something new in the world's experience, new and quite frightening to many people, especially when
coupled with the fact that information doubles every ten years.[4]

the american drug scene and the student

The drug scene today holds a fascination for the youth culture. Speculation on the drug scene and its relation to the youth culture perhaps
is even more fascinating to the "over-thirties."

Drugs are real, prevalent, and dangerous. The facts, the contradictions, and the implications of this need to be faced by teachers
and educators. The problem is complex but not so confused that
rational analysis cannot cut through some of that complexity.

Sense can be made with respect to the drug scene. Whatever sense
can be made should become the property of all teachers This
is obvious because students need mature adults who can make sense
with them on many subjects, and there is no question but that drugs
have become a subject of crucial importance.

The common culture, including both youth and adult segments,
is full of notions about drugs and their consequences. Some notions
are absurd; some are close to the mark. But few of them hang together in any broad pattern of sense. Notions, good or bad, however,
are not safe guides to behavior. What is needed are generalizations
that are central to the evidence and in patterns that have a reasonable
coherence and consistency. Among the notions that are not particularly useful are:

1. "All drugs are equally dangerous, the use of the least dangerous leads surely to the use of the most dangerous."
2. "Some drugs are bad, very dangerous; they have no bearing on
   other drugs, which are not harmful at all."
3. "My use is simply my thing and has no bearing on anyone else. It
   is nobody's business but mine."
4. "My drug is no worse than yours, which says you should lay off
   bugging me about it."

These, and other notional comments, are not unfamiliar. To fill
in specific items in specific situations is probably not difficult. They
are common whenever there is a dialogue on drugs. Not one is a
generalization central to the facts. None are helpful in making sense
of the drug scene.

The most common items in the American drug culture—by which

[4] Bayard Hooper, "The Task Is to Learn What Learning Is For," *Life*, 66:19 (May 16, 1969),
p. 39.

we mean those used, whether legally or illegally, without direct medical advice or prescription—are nicotine, alcohol, marijuana, barbiturates, amphetamines, "psychedelics," and heroin. Not one of these is harmless. Some do have specific uses, however, that may be beneficial in competent medical practice. The hazards in the use of one is neither identical with or equal to that of any other.

In the aggregate, nicotine, used mainly through the smoking of cigarettes, kills more Americans than any other drug. This does not make it the most dangerous to a given individual. Its use is simply the most general. Addiction to it is the most pervasive; therefore, its toll is largest. The evidence on its lethal effects is conclusive, deriving from exhaustive research by the United States Public Health Service, confirmed by much related medical research. The danger is considerably proportional to the degree of use. Thus, the smoker who consumes a pack of cigarettes in two days is less likely to die of lung cancer or heart disease than the one- or two-pack-a-day smoker. But the *addictive* quality of nicotine means that the smoker finds control of the habit at lower levels of hazard difficult to maintain.

Alcohol, in turn, is responsible, whatever its contribution to social graces, for a larger aggregate of human misery than any other commonly used drug in America. It is almost universally available, sold by the most powerful and well-financed persuasions, endorsed by profound cultural traditions. Used moderately, it is hard to convict it of either personal or social damage. Alcohol, however, can be addictive. The hundreds of thousands who have become addicted lack freedom of choice and are made miserable by its enslavement. It figures in assignment to mental hospitals, bankruptcy, family deprivation, and broken homes. The statistical probability for an alcoholic to come to such a state looms large. Alcohol is a factor in half of the fatal highway accidents. It is a most profound illustration of the stubbornness of devotion of the common culture to a favored drug indulgence. Even though enough support was gained in the early twentieth century to accomplish the difficult task of amending the federal Constitution, the power of this drug was past the capacity of legislation to control. Thirst for it caused a tremendous general conspiracy among decent citizens and organized crime that culminated in a pervasive, popular, and extremely profitable lawlessness. Today, alcohol is *the* drug for the "around-fifties" of America—and so it is in many cultures the world over.

For the "under-thirties" the "in" drug is marijuana. It has become the folk drug of the youth culture. As with alcohol, its varieties, its qualities, its uses serve as a central conversational subject among adults, so "pot" or "grass" is a fascination to youthful discourse. It has, like liquor, its lore, its traditions, its in-group vocabulary, its connoisseurs and connoisseuses, its mythology. It is supported by strong loyalties; its sub rosa advertising links it as shrewdly to basic human needs and drives as does Madison Avenue for the liquor industry. Its *addictive* quality is in dispute. That it creates dependency, and that its use may become habitual is not a matter of informed dispute. It is not a convicted killer like nicotine. It is expensive, but it costs no more to "turn on with pot" than to get drunk on beer. Its benefits, however, are grossly exaggerated, and its hazards are much understated.

The barbiturates and amphetamines are too various for present analysis. They include varied forms of "pep pills," "speed," and so forth. Whether for tranquilizing effects or for temporary stimulation, they are only safely to be used under medical prescription. Used in ignorance, they may cause temporary or permanent organic or psychic damage. In overdosage, an ever present hazard in unsupervised use, the consequence may be serious illness or death.

The "psychedelics," LSD in particular, have won a popular spot in the youth culture. Fortunately, they have a much larger place in conversation than in use, though this is not to minimize either the extent of their use nor the hazards in them. The "trip" has entered the folklore and has influenced the popular culture both in cinematic sequences in many films and in decoration. Their *addictive* quality is disputed. The hazards do increase with repeated use. Genetic damage is not established as a sure consequence of use, but the probability is enhanced by repeated use. Psychological damage is not a sure consequence for any given user. It is a probable consequence for some among a number of users. LSD has had limited experimental success in treating mental illness and alcoholism. Its only relatively safe use is under competent medical supervision. In the case of this drug the psychological condition of the user is especially relevant. The largest claims to its "value" lie in terms of enhanced awareness. Its *demonstrated* worth in this dimension is altogether lacking. A common drunk is a good deal more articulate in describing the joys and other particulars of his most recent bender than the person who has made reentry from an LSD trip. Injury to self and others, enhanced paranoia, inadvertent death, and apparent suicide are frequent outcomes of "bad trips," and their frequency is notable especially because this is not a widely used drug.

Hard stuff is mainly *heroin*, "horse" in the dirty vocabulary of the traffic. It is at this point that no debate exists. Heroin has many addicts, many salesmen; it has no defenders. It is *addictive*, so much so that one use (one fix) may set up an addiction. Addiction to heroin is more compelling by far than to nicotine or alcohol. More is the built-in necessity of any addiction. With heroin the pace of stepped-up frequency of use and size of dosage is a fevered one. Many side-effect hazards exist that alone would repel the sane. But none is worth mentioning other than the central fact: To get "hooked" on heroin is a short direct and sure route to complete physical ruin, to loss of any capacity for self-direction, and not uncommonly to death. It is not a matter of probability, or of perhaps one or two of these conse-

quences. It is a complete "wrap-up"; all are a sure and predictable
consequence of addiction, and one usage can lead to addiction!

Some distinctions and common elements among the primary elements in the American drug scene are necessary. First, it is necessary
to clarify the nature of addiction, of dependency, and of habit.

Among the drugs, the addictive include nicotine, alcohol, and
heroin. *Addiction* to one drug is not the same in total consequence
as to another. The addictive quality of a drug is its capacity to create
a physical need in the user for more of the same. The drug itself, in
a sense, cries for more. The addictive capacity of drugs lies in the
nature of the drug not in the vulnerability of the user. The addict
need contribute nothing more than his initial experiment and continued use to the process.

Dependency is another matter. It can be enslaving. But dependency is rooted in the need of the person, not for a specific crutch, but
for something to lean upon. Thus, psychological need may render a
person dependent upon the support of another, or on a set of abstract
dogmas, or on a particular set of circumstances. If marijuana, addictive or not, be turned to as a prop for some psychological need, the
dependency can be real and powerful. It diminishes self; it restricts
freedom of choice at the very least. If the person in psychological
need turns to an *addictive* drug for support, his dependency plus the
potential of the drug make him twice-over a likely prospect to become
an *addict*. Alcoholic addiction is often the product of this two-way
reinforcement. Heroin needs no help from the person.

Habit is a matter that needs to be clarified. Habit is simply the
increased likelihood that actions often repeated will be done again.
It is a fact of life. It makes movement and behavior possible. Habit
formation is a necessary part of human development. When habits
have outlived their usefulness, or become socially unacceptable, standard procedures for reduction or breaking of the habit are available.
The process is difficult, but it is not damaging to the person, nor unduly painful.

All addictions have much in common. The addict will sacrifice
many things to his craving. The cigarette addict will hazard health;
the alcoholic will trade money, job, love, reputation for his need; the
"junkie" lays all these and life too before his addiction. The power
of the drug's necessity is a savage whip-cracker. The cigarette addict
may wake a husband in the night to go on a nocturnal errand to an
all-night service station to quiet a "nicotine fit"; the alcoholic may
abruptly depart a business conference or a family table, because he
"simply must have a drink"; the junkie desperate in need of a "fix"
will steal, sell herself, weep and entreat with a stranger to get the
price of it.

All addicts lose hold on other realities. They are *driven* to self-
delusion. They are always going to quit. They are never really
hooked. Whatever the painful consequence, it is always due to some

other cause than the addiction. They always understate the amount of their usage.

Curing an addiction, difficult always, is not the same as breaking a habit. The pain of separation is real; the addictive drug creates a physical need for its repeated use. "Withdrawal symptoms" are real and devastating. They are part of the process by which the drug puts its strongest coercions on the organism to return to it.

The addict in the battle with his addiction has the same pains as a man in a torture chamber, and a great deal less going for him. The tortured man knows himself, hates his enemy, has conscious purpose to sustain his will. The addict has a diminished self, loves the enemy and longs to embrace it again, and has often lost track of alternative purposes. Alone, he is a poor prospect for recovery. The one thing he has going for him in extremity is whatever will to live he has retained.

These are common elements, but they are not to be treated without distinctions. Rational discourse on the drug scene is utterly obscured by unwillingness to state the sensible distinctions. Addiction to cigarettes has only, in an affluent society, its long-term statistical hazard to life involved. Smoking does not vitally damage the self; though the inability to quit or to stay quit, is somewhat damaging to self esteem. It does not fundamentally alter the personality; beyond irritability at deprivation, it does not trigger profound or violent emotions. Smoking, though addictive, is to a considerable degree simply habitual, and "kicking the habit" is somewhat amenable then to the rules of habit. Junkies and alcoholics are in quite another predicament.

To warn against oversimplification is essential at this point. We are talking within the limits of what is known and are trying to put it together better than the common discourse does it. A lot of things are not known that need to be known. These cannot be talked of as "knowns," nor can they be put into a sensible pattern. The unknowns include (1) why some people use alcohol a great deal and do not become alcoholics, (2) how some addicts "kick the habit" more effectively than others, (3) the full term consequences of such drugs as "pot" and LSD, (4) why persons turn to dangerous drugs in the first place. So back to the sense of what is better known.

Alcoholism is classified by many as a disease. Apparently such a categorization is clinically sound. It is also a cultural gain since it allows for objective consideration without judgmentalism or moralism. Alcoholism is also an addiction. Either or both may be true of a given alcoholic: he may be both dependent on the drug as a support to the psychological problems from which he has sought escape, and he may be "hooked" on the drug. One fact is known of the disease of alcoholism—alcohol has to be absolutely denied in its treatment. The problems (of finance, family, business worry, self-esteem, denial of love, lack of trust in self, or others) that, in the vernacular, may have "driven the person to drink" are only magnified by the "treatment." Stopping the alcohol may not get at the root of the illness, it merely assures that the "cure" will not kill.

Another factor distinguishing among the drugs in the American scene is legality. The evidence that drug loyalty can win out even over constitutional illegality attests to the stubborn persistence of these elements in the culture. Tremendous ambiguity exists on the legal scene with respect to drugs. Two powerful addictive ones are generally legalized, and popularly advertised and sold. Of course, all know the two—alcohol and nicotine. The job of pointing out the hazards in their use is left largely to "education." This is not true of such unlike commodities as marijuana, LSD, and heroin. Possession of "pot" is generally a felony, punishable by prison sentences of up to twenty years.

The undiscriminating quality of such laws is notable. The adult citizen may possess a case each of scotch, bourbon, and gin and rest comfortable in the knowledge of legality and general social approval. His son at college, possessing a little sack of "grass" may, if arrested ("busted"), become a convicted felon, preventing him from the full rights of citizenship and forbidding many avenues of gainful employment among other disqualifications. The purveyor of "horse" at the same time, practicing the most despicable trade in the culture, stands in hazard of *no worse* penalty. Among the other unknowns in the drug scene, this points up another, namely: What sense can be made of this?

The great disparity between the crime and the punishment tends to deprive the law of whatever restraining force sensible legislation might have. Regulations on the sale and use of intoxicants does, for example, have a certain restraining force. But the courts, except in peculiarly vindictive or racially biased instances, often refuse to find grounds to convict for possession of "pot." Even so, the risk of great magnitude, if not high probability, remains. It does not noticeably restrict the use. Nor does it, anymore than did the prohibition amendment in its time, educate in an enhanced respect for law.

What of the things in common within the drug culture? First, the drug culture consists of many subcultures. Each has rites of initiation. Each holds the commodity in highest regard. All, except for junkies who hide for a fix in lonely shame, seek social rituals for usage. The in-group vocabulary is an age-old device of secret societies for conjuring up images of having hold of and of being something special. Songs, folk heroes, and legends abound in each subculture.

Second, each of these drugs tends to give immediate pleasurable reactions, which is its initial appeal and reward, and each has an exaggerated propaganda with respect to the positive consequences. Satisfaction, euphoria, enhanced awareness, sociability, escape—all these are immediate impressions. And each is a general delusion.

Drugs provide none of these, except briefly, and then most treacherously.

Third, traffic in each drug is immensely profitable—not to the user, but to the purveyors. This is true no less of the legal than of the illegal sellers. Drugs are big business on the legitimate Wall Street Board and in the underworld.

Then to the large question—What does this knowledge contain that is useful? How does education affect the student in persuading him not to enter the drug scene as a participant?

Education must be aware of its handicap which is that it must try to counter sensationalism and bias with matter-of-fact evidence. It must understand that it must try to couch its persuasions in reality. It cannot stand simply as the agent for the adult culture because that puts too heavy a load of hypocrisy and contradiction on its back. It must communicate sense, not just another set of biases. We shall concentrate on marijuana ("pot") because it seems to be the focus of adult apprehension and it is where the action is in terms of the student drug culture.

The inquiring student may assert: "Aren't the laws about pot ridiculous?" The response of the informed might be, "They seem to be." But does not the very fact of that possible extreme penalty argue against taking such a long chance?

The student may say, "Isn't it hypocritical for dad to worry about the possibility of my smoking pot when he has two martinis before dinner every night?" And the response might be, "Of course, it is. But in the language you so often use, that's his problem. You have another decision to make."

"But," he continues, "isn't it true that booze and cigarettes are at least as harmful as pot?"

To which, the rational response might be, "There is sure some evidence for such an argument. But what does that say? After all, just because strychnine is a known poison, it doesn't mean that cyanide is therefore a healthy item of diet."

"Yeah," he says, "but they say pot is great. I mean it really turns you on; it makes you more aware of everything."

And there you are at the core of it—the awareness, the mind-expansion "thing." This is where the mystique, the in-group social *fol-de-rol*, the petty argumentation ends. The real case for pot is that it does something to make you more alive—that it expands the mind, enhances awareness.

Here is where education *should* prevail. These are terms that education can understand; they are its very special province, so to speak. What expands the mind? It is attention to the method of intelligence, the admission of all questions, the denial of no evidence, the excitement of all curiosities, the rejection of all irrelevancies. It is the educator who can lead one to all these. What enhances awareness? The focused attention upon reality, the overriding of tensions and fears and biases, the eager trusting of testimony of the ears and eyes and all the senses, the bringing to bear in harmony all of the instruments of perception including experience upon an object or a subject. To be more aware is to neglect nothing, to shun inattentiveness, to scrutinize minutely and patiently; it is to refuse to overlook or to shut out any part of the observed or any part of the observer's reaction. Again, it is the educator who is the most logical person to help the individual broaden his horizon.

However, school more often turns students off than turns them on. It turns tail and runs at signs of real awareness. It denies intelligence, asks its own questions and refuses the students', peddles its own motivations and accepts no wonderment which is the students' own. It touches on everything; yet, it tunes in on nothing. Does the school not do these things much too much?

Now having their awareness blunted by the school, hammered to insensibility by the constant yammer of the media, is there any surprise in the fact that some students are astonished at the sense of liberation from external restraints and pressures they feel when given an artificial assist by a drug? The betrayal is that real awareness is an all-time, not a sometime thing. A real hazard in pot is that the let-down of return leaves the user even more incapable of being aware on his own. But the best argument against pot in the schools will not be in words, no matter how rational. It will be in showing alternatives, in achieving a constant awareness that no drug can even approximate. When the student says of schools, as he does say of an experience in school now and then, "that really turns me on," then it has really given him an awareness that says of pot—or any drug— "Who needs it?"

Another aspect of the drug culture must also be taken into consideration—its roots in protest. What of that? It is associated with protest but, nevertheless, is irrelevant to it. Protest is pretty flimsy if it is either drug-induced or if its expression is in the use of drugs. Student protest makes sense when it makes sense. Its greatest strength is in its exposure of absurdities. However, an absurdity set against an absurdity does not equal sense. It simply doubles the absurdity.

For example, the alleged connection of marijuana with heroin, where the real dread of the adult lies, has been proposed on flimsy evidence to persuade youth through fear. Youth in the main refuses to admit the sense of the allegation in the absence of conclusive evidence. There is a real connection, however, that is neglected in the dialogue and can be persuasive. Youth does dread *horse* and hates the traffic in "hard stuff." The connection lies not in the unproved contention that using pot leads to using "hard stuff," but in the fact of the pusher. The pusher is a slimy little soul who sells drugs for profit. He handles both pot and "hard stuff." He sees a connection; pot gains him access to customers. Furthermore, his profits go to finance the drug syndicates, the Mafia and others who are the entrepreneurs of every variety of organized crime. The profits on pot, like those on heroin, go to support the worst elements in America. The students have not always thought of this, but they can follow the argument. Sure, some pot is home-grown, camouflaged among the tomato-plants, but in no larger part than home-brew in the liquor traffic. Profit creates the drug culture. Profit links the legal and the illicit. The purveyors of drugs, whether legal or illegal, have one characteristic in common—a callous disregard for the health and life of the users.

the school as a life force

The school must, it has been rather well established, give the student recognition. And contrary to the uninformed judgment of the public and the parents, it will do well to foster self-inquiry.

In addition to recognition, it must also give the student understanding. Besides who he is, he must find out where he is and the why and wherefore of it. These are the questions that history and science and literature can illuminate for him.

It is not subject matter competence that we are speaking of, nor mastery of a discipline in the vocational sense. The subjects must be enlivened by the realization that the questions of easy and hard, likable and dislikable, useful or useless, if answerable about a curriculum are signs of a senseless curriculum. The question that governs the live curriculum is *necessity*.

If the matter sounds abstract, even vague, for the moment, rest easy. The nitty-gritty, as they say, is at hand.

In the fall of 1969, on a national TV network, a terrifying interview took place. A well-known newscaster was talking with a young man, a father of two, a discharged veteran of the Vietnam venture. He told of his part in the alleged massacre of Vietnamese villagers by American soldiers. He spoke of rounding up men, women, and children; "Babies?" he was asked. "Babies," he agreed. Then he told how his officer said, "You know what to do with them," and walked away. He said he thought the officer meant to keep them under guard. That got cleared up. The officer returned and gave the order to shoot them—and he did.

> ". . . So you fired something like 60, 70 shots."
> "Right."
> "And you killed how many at that time?"
> ". . . I might have killed about 10 or 15 of them."
> "Men, women and children?"
> "Men, women and children."
> "And babies?"
> "And babies."
> "Why did you do it?"
> ". . . Because I felt like I was ordered to do it. And it
> seemed like—well, at the time, I felt I was doing the right thing.

I really did. Because, like I said, I lost buddies. I—I lost—I
lost a good, damn good buddy. Bobby Wilson. And it was on
my conscious. It was on—so—so after I done it I felt good, but
later on that day it—getting to me."

*   *   *

". . . how do you shoot babies?"
"I don't know. It was just one of them things."

*   *   *

"What will happen to you now?"
"Well, I don't think there can be anything done to me. Cause
I'm out. I'm out."
"And what is your feeling now in retrospect, as you look back
on all of that?"
"Well, it's been on my conscious, and it's going to stay on my
conscious for the rest of my life. But like I said, God punished
me. . . ."
"By?"
"By me stepping on a land mine. So I feel like I've been
punished." [The soldier lost part of a leg in the mine explosion.]

*   *   *   *   *

This man has a god who hands out light sentences. It is not ours
to assert the way of God, but what of human responsibility? A man
may speak of any crime and still show himself touched by his civilization if he speaks of his prompting fears and passions, his awareness
of evil, of contrition and repentence. But in 1969 to hear an American
who has gone to school with us speak with the cool moral illiteracy
of the barbarian chills the marrow.

Is this civilization? Is this the nature of modern man? The long-
delayed revelation of monstrous events now upon the front pages
illustrates how badly the school must have neglected its most necessary curriculum. What grounds have we to claim that he might have
been better taught?

Whatever the school has taught, there are certain deeds that this
man or another might well have taken for his curriculum. He might
well know that World War II was often fought against civilians. Both
sides, taking their cue from the Nazis, rained explosive and fire upon
a hundred cities of man. The target was humanity, men, women,
children, and babies; the military objective, to break its spirit. This
never worked. The only way to break the human spirit is to obliterate
it. And he might well know that the military mind has studied and
perfected that project. Obliteration was the achieved end at Hiro-
shima, an accomplishment of the genius of the nation that gave him
a uniform and a gun and an officer who gave him an order. He might
well have known, perhaps not of the disapproval of many at home,
but of the official sanction and use of napalm on jungle villages. The
torrent of liquid fire which is napalm is not a precisely discriminating
weapon. Despite the hopes of its distributors, it does not cool or
swerve when it encounters an ununiformed person in its path be it

man, woman, child—or baby. This man or another could be far from morally obtuse and still fail to see much distinction between his act and others which have high official sanction.

The military is not, after all, a progressive educator: does not the end, indeed justify the means?

The curriculum he had failed to be instructed by, perhaps because it had never been brought to him, does, nevertheless, exist. "I was given an order" is a phrase that modern man educated to the experience of his time can immediately hold suspect. The Nuremberg trials of Nazi war criminals established a code that indeed there are some deeds, done even within the general hunting license of war, that cannot be justified, that the person must be accountable for. Eichmann used this phrase in his defense; it only gave evidence of his moral degeneracy. The existential view that every man is responsible for his every act in every circumstance is not a generally accepted discipline. But modern man is not naked or alone, or without conceptual support when he chooses to act responsibly.

We are not condemning a man, or thinking of him without compassion. We are trying to raise the questions on which a curriculum of necessity might be based, a curriculum that could make school a life force for its students. They are pressing questions.

In the latter days of World War II, Nazi soldiers massacred a number of Americans, they were soldiers in uniform, at Malmedy. When news of it became known a sense of outrage inflamed the nation. Was it an outrage of moral indignation? Or was it an outrage of national preference—this ought not happen to us? History gives us the chance to answer the question.

What would have happened had a soldier disobeyed his officer at Malmedy or in a little Vietnamese village? Would it have shocked the officer into awareness of his barbarism? Would he have taken the gun into his own hands and done his own killings? Would he have placed the soldier under arrest? Would he have shot him on the spot? Would this be worse than becoming a killer of innocents?

An act of personal responsibility at least opens alternatives. Capitulation before authority demanding unreasonable or evil deeds allows no alternatives a chance to develop. But there is, as long as human responsibility persists, always a choice.

The most terrible phrase in this interview was the laconic, " 'It was just one of those things.' " As if that were the end of it. Oh, God, what a terrible empty irony it would be if that should truly be the end of it. If in the logic of national defense among frightened men all over the world, the strategic culmination of military planning had been achieved, the obliteration of the human spirit—and all men were dead, and in the radioactive rubble a tape recorder played out one time more the song which went—" 'it was just one of those things.' " And there was no one there to appreciate the irony, and none to nod knowingly.

topics for inquiry

1. The Role of the Peer Group in Determining Students' Attitudes Toward (1) Sex, (2) the War in Vietnam, (3) Civil Liberties
2. The Cause of the Generation Gap: Parents' Views Versus Students' Views
3. The Role of the Teenager in the United States Compared with the Role of the Teenager in an African or Asian Nation
4. The Lyrics of the Rock and Roll Music of the 1950s compared with the Lyrics of Acid Rock and Folk Music of 1968–1970
   (In what ways do the lyrics reflect the student culture?)
5. How Madison Avenue on TV Seduces the Teenager to Buy Products
6. Hospital Admissions of Persons under Twenty-one Because of Drugs or Related Problems
   (Visit a local hospital or mental institution and inquire about the number of such persons admitted for problems related to the use of drugs. Compare these statistics with those of 1960, 1965, and 1968. How do they compare with statistics of persons over twenty-one years of age admitted to the same hospital?)
7. Sex and Drug Education in the Elementary School or Junior High
   (Visit at least two elementary schools or two junior high schools to find out what those schools are doing to provide sex education and information about drugs to their students.)
8. The Relevance of the English Curriculum for a High School Student
   (Examine the city or county curriculum for high school English classes.)
9. Concerns Voiced by a Local PTA
   (Attend at least three consecutive PTA meetings at one school in your community.)
10. Concerns of Teenage Members of Religious Youth Groups
    (Visit a youth group meeting at your local church or temple.)

subjects for discussion

1. In 1946 W. H. Auden wrote in *The Age of Anxiety:*
   . . . . To be young means to be all on edge, to be held
   waiting in a packed lounge for a Personal Call from Long
   Distance, for the low voice that defines one's future. The
   fears we know are of not knowing. Will nightfall
   bring us some awful order—Keep a hardware store in

> a small town. . . . Teach science for life to Progressive
> girls—? It is getting late. Shall we ever be asked for?
> Are we simply not wanted at all? [5]

Discuss how you think today's high school and college student would react to this. Does it reflect your feelings? What factors in our culture cause many students to feel this way?

2. Edgar Friedenberg in *The Vanishing Adolescent* states:

> Regardless of the uses to which any society may put
> its schools, education has an obligation that transcends
> its own social function and society's purposes. That
> obligation is to clarify for its students the meaning of
> their experience of life in their society. . . . [6]

Assuming that Friedenberg is correct, discuss the ways in which the school can perform this function.

3. As a beginning teacher you will often be urged by your older colleagues to study the academic and personal records of your students before you meet your class for the first time.
Discuss the ways in which such advice might either be helpful or harmful to you in your attempt to understand your student.

4. Make the assumption that there is no such thing as a "student culture." In behavioral terms discuss the ways in which acceptance of this assumption would affect your teaching.

5. You are a new teacher who has grown up in a small town. Now you are teaching in a public school in New York City, Los Angeles, or Chicago. How do you plan to familiarize yourself with the diverse backgrounds of your students? Discuss a possible step-by-step program that would help you in accomplishing this goal.

selected readings

In addition to the works listed below, books cited at the end of Chapter 14 by Kozol, Holt, Kohl, Schrag, and Herndon are relevant to this chapter.

COLEMAN, JAMES S. *The Adolescent Society: The Social Life of the Teenager and Its Impact on Education.* New York: Free Press, 1961.

A comprehensive and illuminating study of the basics of this important topic.

DENNISON, GEORGE. *The Lives of Children.* New York: Random House, 1969.

A graphic picture of the capacity of students to attend to their own problems when freed to do so. Among the points that an-

[5] W. H. Auden, *The Age of Anxiety* (New York: Random House, 1946), p. 42.
[6] Edgar Friedenberg, *The Vanishing Adolescent* (New York: Dell, 1962), p. 75.

ticipate our own view in Chapter 14: "We do know enough to run good schools, if we only would."

HECHINGER, GRACE and FRED M. *Teen-Age Tyranny*. New York: Morrow, 1963.
   The problem from a point of view that might be termed adult-biased.

KENISTON, KENNETH. *The Uncommitted: Alienated Youth in American Society*. New York: Harcourt, Brace, Jovanovich, 1965.
   Explores the psychological and cultural roots of the generation gap.

NORDSTROM, CARL, EDGAR Z. FRIEDENBERG, and HILARY A. GOLD. *Society's Children: A Study of Ressentiment in the Secondary School*. New York: Random House, 1967.
   Probably the most pertinent work in this set of readings. It graphically portrays the student and his relationship to the contemporary school and focusses with clarity on "what is eating" the students.

REMMERS, H. H., and D. H. RADLER. *The American Teenager*. New York: Bobbs-Merrill, 1957.
   Dated but still illuminating.

SALINGER, J. D. *Catcher in the Rye*. New York: Bantam, 1951.
   Almost a contemporary classic. This work of fiction shows the pain and struggle of an adolescent trying to make sense of himself and the world around him.

SCHREIBER, DANIEL (ed.). *Profile of the School Drop Out*. New York: Vintage Books, 1968.
   Contains, among others, articles by Bruno Bettelheim, Edgar Z. Friedenberg, and Paul Goodman. This anthology comprehensively wraps up the subject.

Three other works of fiction with a lot to say about young people and their relation with school or society that not only are of interest but also good reading are:

CARY, JOYCE. *Charly Is My Darling*. New York: Harper & Row.

GLYN, CAROLYN. *Don't Knock the Corners Off*. London: Pan Books, 1966.

HUNTER, EVAN. *The Blackboard Jungle*. New York: Simon and Schuster, 1954.

12
SOCIETAL
NECESSITIES
AND EDUCA-
TIONAL
RESPONSE

As the old saying goes, if the United States did not have an educational system, it would have to invent one. And it would have to do that practically instantaneously. This brings up an interesting historical point.

When the colonial Americans started schools it was a matter of choice. They wanted access to Scripture; this required literacy, so they chose to build schools. The Founding Fathers established an elective system in government; an elective system works better if voters are informed, therefore, they chose to build schools. But in those days, society functioned to a very large degree independent of its schools. Boys learned trade and vocation largely in the home, on the farm, or in apprenticeship; girls learned their primary vocation—housekeeping—at home. Most of what most people knew of the big wide world—which for most in those provincial days was little enough—its happenings, its wonders, its ideas, its inventions, they learned from conversation, from travelers and visitors, from newspapers, and from the pulpit. And they got along; they managed.

the demands of the great technology

Today society is very largely dependent for its very survival on the Great Technology. Americans are very often disposed to assess their material affluence in terms of what they possess. It is an impressive inventory: 104,702,000 motor vehicle registrations; 1,110,187,000 acres of farm land; 209,292 miles of railroads; 113,910,636,000 passenger miles flown in 1968; 65 million black-and-white television sets and over 20 million color sets; and an impressive score of bathtubs, refrigerators, washers and dryers, and the whole gamut of things in whose possession Americans share a vast abundance quite broadly.

But to perceive the American affluence in terms of its collection of goods, impressive though the inventory may be, is a profoundly erroneous perception. It is a static perception of a dynamic situation.

Perhaps the pop art of our time may symbolize the distinction being made. The music, much of it, of an earlier day was suggestive of things in order, quiet afternoons of attending to or dozing over a string quartet, concerts for people who knew how to enjoy the best music—and who knew their place: from the folk of rank and wealth in the orchestra and the "diamond horseshoe" to the students and the culture-hungry poor in the upper galleries. The situation was in many ways fixed, predictable, in order. The music, though its tremendous range we do not propose to diminish, was itself based upon such solid theoretical principles that its very weight of traditional practice tended to keep expression within bounds, to render innovation beyond those bounds shocking. But, of course, there was innovation: Beethoven, Brahms, Tchaikovsky in their time innovated and suffered temporary misunderstanding and rejection because of the *shocking* things they did. Debussy, Stravinsky, and Prokofiev at the turn of the century moved farther and Hindemith and Schoenberg farther yet. Each exceeded the bounds, but wound up extending the bounds both by practice and even by revision of underlying theory.

The modern world has become noisy. The music of the quiet world of yesterday explored all the capacity of orchestrated sound to provide sensory experience beyond the quiet of the times. Modern music reaches the ears of men who dwell among noise: the din of traffic, the hammers of construction, the whoosh and boom of the jets, the hum of air conditioners, the yak and yammer of unattended television sets, the noises of the neighbors who so often live today on either side and above and below as well. This noise is the common property of most of us.

All this noise is there because there are a lot of people around, and they are doing the things they must do to be there, to get there, and to have what they want. The noise is the sound of utility and production. It is the noise of affluence. Affluence is not so much the concrete "things" that we possess as it is the use of these things (which includes wearing them out), the capacity to keep them useful (to power, to fix, and to repair them), and to replace and extend them.

The music of a show like *Hair*, for example, lives meaningfully with noise. It slams sounds at you, and it comes at you with unpredictable shocking noise which assures that its message will penetrate beyond the noise level of the customary. To get his message across it may be that modern man must either shout and bang it out, or call a few to come up close to whisper together. Modern music does both; *Hair* does the former. It uses the sounds of its time. Eerie electronic whines and vibrations, percussion as raucous as the power-hammers in the streets, beats as throbbing and profound as the drumming of the dynamos, rhythms as frenetic as those of the traffic on the parkways all around.

The noise in which modern man abides is functional. It is a part of the life he has chosen to lead; it is the sound of himself, using what he has made in doing what he wants or has to do and in making more of the same.

If he really wanted quiet, he could turn everything off: his cars, his televisions, his refrigerators, his air conditioners—the lot of it. It would be quiet, blessed relief, for a moment. But he presently would start to sweat. Travellers would fume and presently rage, and perhaps panic. His food would be spoiling. His job would be meaningless. He would cease to survive. He would not last long.

Without the school, however, and this is the real point we are making, there would soon be no noise. For in the affluent America, whose wealth is actually its capacity to use and produce goods, the Great Technology would, indeed, soon come to a halt without those who know how to create it and keep it running.

The productive capacity of the nation is a complex linkage of organizational structures, engineering abilities, industrial plants, and human efforts. Transportation, manufacture, distribution, merchandising all are mutually contributive to production and use of goods. The Great Technology is linked in other ways. The power system is literally tied together in a pattern of local, regional, and ultimately a national grid. Communication likewise serves to tie most households of the nation in a system of practically instantaneous service. Back of the convenient telephone, the flow of air traffic, the movement of trucks, the assembly lines are banks of electronic sorters, knowledge banks, directors—the near miraculous mindlike machines, the computers. The processes of the technological, interdependent modern society have become much too complex to manipulate without these electronic brains. There are simply not enough human hands and minds available to look up and sort out the necessary knowledge to keep the machine going—to count, to locate, to route, to classify the traffic, the traffic in goods, messages, persons, planes, railroad cars, and ideas.

And back of it all, historically and presently, lies human intelligence. Human intelligence created the Great Technology; human intelligence uses its product, not always wisely or even sensibly by any means; and human intelligence must keep it running. The Great Technology was built by effort which was bent to finding out *how*; this effort succeeding became *know-how*, the phrase that in the jargon has come to symbolize the technological capacity of modern man. But The Great Technology is not a perpetual motion machine. New decisions as to its use must be programmed anew. It breaks down, it wears out, it requires inspection, operation, repair, extension, rebuilding. The know-how of human intelligence must be at hand and ready for these tasks.

When a regional power grid gave way in 1967, the great blackout on the Eastern seaboard took place. It occasioned much consternation and inconvenience as well as much improvisation and jest. Most of all, it showed the vulnerability of technology and the dual relationship of machine and man. It pointed up not only the dependence of modern man upon the reliable functioning of his technology, but also, the consistent dependence of its functioning upon the availability of human intelligence with developed know-how. In this case, it required the know-how to define the difficulty, to isolate the problem, and to restore the functioning.

In the total interdependence of modern society there are many interdependent relationships. Those that come first to mind are city and farm, labor and capital, shipper and receiver, buyer and seller, consumer and producer, man and machine. The economy is interknit and interdependent; the society likewise.

In the simpler days of colonial America education was very much an institution *outside* the central necessities of the economy and quite *peripheral* to most of the concerns of society. It was important to some people for reasons meaningful to them, but it was not an absolute necessity for *anyone's* or *everybody's* survival. In today's world education has a different role. Education in the age of the Great Technology has become an *absolute necessity* for anyone's and everybody's survival.

Education in the societal sense is not an outside institution or a matter of choice. It is an integral part of the system, essential to its operation. It is part of the grid; without it the system breaks down, just as surely as if a power source fails and even more drastically and generally. It is relevant to each set of interdependencies. The farm must be a place of sophisticated know-how if each farm worker is to be able to feed a hundred urbanites, for example.

At this point, let us remind you of a previous position. It is true, very true, that in the total societal sense, in the sense of keeping the machine running, education is a basic necessity. Indeed, education is a part of that machine. But that is not all education is. There are two other basic truths about education, modern truths at that, that have already been established. First, education is a process of self-discovery, of individual development, of humanization. Second, education devoted to free inquiry, to the access to all evidence, and to the weighing of all facts is a necessity for the preservation of a free and open society. So we are dealing now with *another* necessity, not the only one. This other is the necessity for survival.

Furthermore, to a large degree, the point with respect to the necessity of education in the *system* is a fact that may be taken as politically and socially neutral. The basic machinery of the modern world, the processes by which its goods are assembled, produced, moved about, repaired, and replaced, may be operated under various systems of political and social philosophy. Hitler, for instance, hitched an extremely sophisticated industrial technology to an utterly debased and decadent ideology. Electric turbines operate on the same principles—physical not political ones—in Niagara Falls, Egypt, Russia, or China. An adventure in space may be directed one day from Houston, another from a laboratory in Siberia; success or failure will in either case depend on the know-how of the engineers, not their politics.

Thus there is a societal necessity and a personal need for education, and the place these meet is simply called JOBS. Not so long ago most jobs were unskilled or semiskilled, requiring no long period of training. But the advance and the spread of technology have meant a drastic decrease in the ratio of unskilled and semiskilled jobs to the total of available jobs. The demand is now not merely expressed in terms of skill, signifying mainly a high level of manual competence; it is a demand for technical competence, which involves both skill and educated know-how.

It is not true, of course, that society is completely automated, or just about to be. There are still millions of work opportunities for the able-bodied and willing that can be adequately mastered within a day or a month without a great deal of schooling. These include the loading and unloading of vans, boxcars, and ships; many assembly-line tasks; waiting on tables, cleaning, and dishwashing; seasonal farm labor; collecting garbage; retail clerking; driving a cab. These too are jobs that society has created, and they are in no true sense demeaning. They are honorable, useful occupations, and they afford a living. In fact, these occupations may in many instances afford an annual income that compares quite favorably with such occupations as teaching, nursing, and social work. The disadvantages are marked, however: (1) the hazard of technological displacement in some, especially on the assembly line, is considerable; (2) the occupations have a short distance between starting point and highest level of achievement; (3) in the main, they are the least rewarding in financial terms; and (4) perhaps most important, they furnish the least challenge to the whole person, the least potential for personal fulfillment and continuing human growth.

Agriculture is an area which clearly illustrates some of the points we are making. The technological revolution in agriculture is not new, any more than it is in manufacture. The Industrial Revolution in its first historical phase (England in the latter eighteenth and early nineteenth century) was marked by drastic changes in manufacture from home to factory and by dramatic shifts of population from farm and village to burgeoning cities. An agricultural revolution necessarily had to accompany this shift of population, for in simple terms: the cities had to be fed. Thus, farms had to become more efficient and more productive. New tools, scientific breeding of animals and plants had to be developed; conservation and fertilization of fields had to be learned.

In Jefferson's time, when nine of ten Americans drew all or part of their living from the soil, the farm needed to produce very little beyond subsistence to provide a surplus to feed the urban, the professional, the mercantile, and the genteel untoiling few. Today, with the ratio of man to productive acreage on a galloping increase, the necessity to wrest from the soil the utmost productivity is a matter of survival. (The other side of this particular coin, to arrest the increase of the population ratio is even more important; for as many scientific agriculturalists attest: as far as drawing on the soil more effectively, we have almost gone 'as fur as we can go').

Even at the turn of the century, though farming was far from primitive, the agricultural economy was relatively simple, the occupation was arduous but relatively uncomplicated. Farm occupations were mainly delineated as farmer, farmers' sons, farmers' wives, and hired men. All these shared in common one thing: a lot of hard work. Ancillary occupations were few, mainly: horse doctors, country preachers, blacksmiths, grain elevator and storage operators. Commission agents (representatives of marketing firms), tax collectors, and country bankers (negotiators of the all too predictable mortgage) were also part of the *dramatis personae* of the rural society. Education was in its usual historically ambivalent position in the general esteem. It was highly esteemed in the abstract, and held in some apprehension when possessed too evidently by preacher, lawyer, or teacher. Close to home, "book larnin" was held in the main to be harmless unless overindulged to waste of time, or if it caused a man 'to put on airs,' but surely beyond strictly specific purposes largely ornamental and useless.

The New England Protestant spirit continued to leaven rural America with a regard for the Scriptures and an attendent presumption of a spiritual utility in literacy. The McGuffey Readers, born in Ohio of New England gone West, show clearly the continuation of the Puritan confidence of the linkage of religious and moral fitness with material and worldly success. The state of the historical rural mind of America toward education is wrongly defined if dogmatically labeled anti-intellectual. It was ever ambivalent, of two minds, toward education. It built schools almost always early in its construction of its community; it paid its teachers stingily, but not as meanly as it did its hired men, who worked a longer if not a harder day. It enacted compulsory school laws across the land, and complied with them except when there was more important work for the boys at home. Even with respect to the connection of conscience and religion, rural America was of contradictory mind. Preaching was sufficiently linked to learning that the parson's 'book learning' was respected along with his somber black frock coat, and the denominations soon endowed in Ohio, Illinois, Iowa and points west, liberal arts colleges where some sons and daughters of the soil, like William Jennings Bryan, could get a Christian education like that in similar older colleges in New Hampshire, Massachusetts, New York, and Pennsylvania. But at the same time, from similar soil sprang a confidence in an assortment of rampant evangelical creeds, who often held, as St. Augustine had come to do, the arts and sciences of the mind highly suspect, and even came to prefer an uneducated, not to say ignorant clergy. This was, and remains, a wellspring of genuine anti-intellectualism in the American scene. Yet it is to be understood in terms which somewhat extenuate: for the rejection of the mind was a solidly expressed preference for things of the spirit—or in more modern vocabulary of affect and of emotion. For if these men and women were ignorant, their minds were abundantly challenged in the day to day assessment of pressing realities, of the chanciness of wind, rain, and weather—the dicey uncertainty of markets, and of the mortgage-holder's patience and charity. But of emotions of drama, these were lacking, or were rather present only in the pathos and struggle and frequent tragedy of their own existence in which they were too profoundly enmeshed to sense in terms other than of weariness, sickness, and agony unnamed. Willa Cather and Ole Rolvaag could later transmit the meaning of their life struggle into the American culture; but the people were the makers, not the observers, of the scene. So all across the culturally-deprived, the emotionally starved provinces, there came the circuit-riders, the ignorant high-spirited preachers, whose status gave them license to excite in ways which convention denied to others. Remember these were persons whose practice of sex was close enough to the farmyard to be nearly as perfunctory and affectiveless as the performance of bulls, stallions, and roosters: persons whose taboos and pre-Freudian 'hangups' were so intense that men and women might share a bed for decades and never view the other fully unclad. Their songs were linear, antique, stylized—uncreative, unorchestrated. Their fears of Indian, disease, death, blizzard were too real to afford pleasure in recital. And their ballads were the airs of loneliness, and unrequited sentimental love, and of train-wrecks, and dying hoboes. Thus, when Sunday morning and Sunday evening and mid-week prayer meeting came—and revival season and camp meeting too, what need could they feel for cognitive reflection? The ignorant preacher was an agent of anti-intellectualism to be sure, but he was also an agent of emotional release. If he could excite to passion, to tears, to shouting of joy, to rolling about in ecstasy, to an orgiastic one-ness of mood and feeling, to catharsis of public revelation of guilts, and doubts, and dreads of self—why, what has psychology taught us, if the need and utility of this is not understandable?

In the main rural education for the pre-technological American remained a marginal enterprise. It had yet to be turned directly to vocational purpose. Its indirect potential was at the same time strictly limited. To be able to read was useful to the extent of being able to read the paper, order from catalogs, follow the words of an occasional unfamiliar hymn, trying to grasp the extent of a lawyer's or banker's document before signing it. Arithmetic came in handy, handy enough for a man to appreciate a wife or a daughter who had gone far enough in Ray's or Barnes's series to correct his calculations. Beyond that, well, life was hard and life was busy.

of men and resources

Americans traveling in other societies often encounter exaggerated legends of the affluence they have come from. In Ecuador, for example, one of your authors encountered both from a college student and from a shoe-shine boy the report that "they knew" that in the United States men threw away their shirts and women their stockings after a single wearing. Even the sophisticated from other nations find it difficult to encompass the reality of American affluence. Russian guests at automobile plants in Detroit, for example, have been known to gaze upon the evidences of the crowded industrial parking lots with distrust. "This is how the workers come to their jobs. Yet, it is impossible. It is a Potemkin Village display—the automobiles from the entire region have been gathered here for a day to impress us." Americans too dwell amid their affluence not altogether comprehending it. They depend on it, and in a very real sense the affluence depends upon them. The power to consume is based upon purchasing power, thus high levels of broadly distributed wages and incomes are a necessity of the system. Economic demand in the market is not simply a matter of wants and needs; these require purchasing power to constitute demand.

Thus when considerable aggregates of the populace are not wielders of important purchasing power, it is damaging in two ways. They are left out of the affluence, which is especially painful because the abundance is so general and so visible, and they do not help to support the affluence because they have so little capacity to enter the market to sustain with purchasing power the flow of goods and services. This concept is especially important in helping to communicate to the relatively poor their relation to the general affluence.

An erroneous, though understandable, conceptual explanation of this relationship holds that the system, in its economic sense, rests upon the backs of the poor, that affluence exists *because* some are poor. They are the numerically many, though relatively few, who are exploited and deprived so that the many may enjoy their affluence. It is not beyond understanding that grievance against personal condition should cause a leap to such a fallacious conclusion. This fallacy is derived from primitive Marxist dogma. But its fault is not a moral one; no matter what its origin, it is bad simply because being erroneous it cannot be put to constructive use.

The poor in America are not so much exploited as left out. The system with respect to their condition is not so much punitive as it is careless. The injustice is real, but its origin lies in exclusion (which in the racial aspect has often been deliberate) rather than exploitation.

The system works moderately well, spectacularly well in comparative terms, in providing the vast majority with substantial material sustinence and a considerable ease and security of physical existence. Therefore, among the 80 percent or so who share in its benefits, the system has a general acceptance. Even if the system were supported by exploitation, though basically it is not, these percentages and conditions would not augur well for revolution. These are not the economic circumstances which nurture economic revolution.

To be sure, the underreaches of the 80 percent subsist on the frontiers of poverty. They do not share generously in the benefits, nor does their limited purchasing power do a proportionate share in sustaining the flow of goods. It is also true that dwellers within the affluent society create agencies of exploitation within the community of the poor. They hire the poor, on terms dictated by desperation, for a variety of occasional or seasonal, menial and domestic tasks. They also make economic forays into the ghettoes and impoverished neighborhoods to drain off what exists of mobile purchasing power as profitably as possible. Extortionate lending, merchandising of inferior goods at higher than going prices elsewhere, slum-lording—all these are exploitative. However, they are excursions of exploitation from bases within the affluent society. They are individual and organized unjust intrusions upon the community of the poor. But they do not constitute the system, and the system is not dependent on their loot for its support to any considerable degree.

Affluence conducts expeditions other than of exploitation into the community of the poor. It extends the reach of its institutions, such as schools and fire and police protection into this community, though usually the quality of both the education and the protection is limited and inferior to what it provides for itself. It supports agencies of private philanthropy, charitable intrusions deriving from social ethics and social theories largely of the past. Public agencies provide welfare services of many types, of which the negotiable check is the most tangible and generally welcomed.

The community of the poor, in sum, exists as a neglected area rather than as an exploited one. The community of the poor resides not under the affluent society but *beside* and *outside* of it. The game within the functioning society is the production and distribution of goods and services and the consumption and replacement of them in a more or less continual flow that is initiated, lubricated, and sustained by monies and credits awarded on more or less reasonable bases for participating in the game.

Justice, humanity, and enlightened self-interest dictate a necessity: that full participation in the game be extended to all the potential players. The objective is to get them into the system, contributing to it and sharing its benefits. Justice and humanity are the better arguments, but these have been eloquently argued and to no sufficient avail. Therefore, consider the enlightened arguments of self-interest.

Poverty is insupportable. The poor, rightly enough, regard it as unnecessary. They are pushed by necessity and by sense of injustice to vigorous protest. They are even invited to it. The media reach the public more universally than other products of affluence. Sometimes they are bought on harsh terms from exploitative foraging merchants by meagre earnings, or by allotments from welfare checks. The media encourage insatiable appetites for goods which are sufficient goad to discontent even in parts of town where purchasing power is available for some response. What of the hunger and frustration generated where wanting is created but where power to buy is negligible!

The poor then protest and organize. They even come to perceive malice where there is merely—callous neglect. Enterprising individuals sometimes conduct forays of their own to acquire socially-approved goods or power to buy them where no socially-approved methods are at hand to acquire them. The methods of going and taking, one way or another, are socially regarded as crimes. Thus crime has a large base and nurture in the community of the poor. There is a richer and more secure base of organized crime which derives from greed and gains its support from the excess of money and the human vices and weaknesses of the affluent. Its lower echelons, who are the lowest paid and run the risks of injury and arrest, are recruited mainly from the poor. But human capacity for evil, which some attribute to original sin, runs as a potential through all echelons of life, in the community of the affluent and of the poor. It is not this phenomenon which is in question. The criminal behavior at hand is sociological in origin, it is nurtured by need and frustration.

The wheels of industry grind exceedingly fast. They grind out a tremendous output of goods. These anticipate a market. When purchasing power lags, goods pile up; then the wheels slow and sometimes grind to a halt. This is trouble. This threatens affluence. Yet there are always all those people who could consume the goods, even need them. If more of them only had purchasing power. Self-interest surely dictates advantages to getting everyone in on the game. But how to achieve it?

The first step is to conceptualize the situation as it basically is, which is what we have been trying to do. Then the job is to establish the connections, and that is a two-way process. It means bringing the people into the productive and consuming network that is the system, and it means extending the reach of the system to include them. Political power is important. The poor can only affect decisions if they unite politically on issues which basically affect their condition. They must be joined to constitute majorities by others who are persuaded by a sense of justice and humanity and by the realities of self-interest to do the sensible things. This is a complex process, but it can be set into operation. In fact, it is beginning to operate. The stake in getting it fully at work is simply the continuance of the American way of life.

Institutional outreach to the poor can be greatly improved. Education and protection should be better, not worse, where the need is greatest. Educators and police alike must be attracted and trained from among the poor and taught to serve and protect them, not to work against them through either ignorance or fear. Institutional obstacles to upward mobility should be removed. Barriers to educational advance, to job access, to union membership, to social acceptance are among these.

Protections by legislation of decent wages for all work must be extended. The poor are not by any means all unemployed or on welfare. Many of them work steadily and hard and still earn not enough to bring them out of poverty. This is exploitation, but it is not essential to the system. It is in fact detrimental to it.

Education must not term *uneducability* the damage done to persons as a consequence of poverty. It must learn to teach those it has called the unteachable. Its standards must be high, and its support must be adequate to the task.

The deliberate planning of job opportunity must be conceptualized as a means of erasing the institutionalization of *welfare* in the society. Now read carefully, for this does not urge the casting adrift of the poor without even the niggardly contribution from affluence presently awarded. It says 'figure out how to get rid of the necessity of *welfare.*' Job planning may have to relate to technology in many ways. There is, of course, the necessity to up-grade skills, the better jobs of the present and the future require this. But the machine does displace workers. The farm is many times more productive with a very small labor force than it once was. Production, even of surpluses, is obviously possible at high levels, even when millions of men are kept out of productive roles to play the essentially useless war-game. The seventy millions of employed Americans work such hours, enjoy such vacations, and reap such rewards as their laboring fathers and grandfathers would have deemed Utopian. This process will have to go forward to levels as yet undreamed. The work will have to be apportioned among more participants so that all can get in on the game, and levels of compensation will have to rise so that the machinery can be kept humming. (The sense of this is one job for education to make clear; another job for education is to make the abundance of time a joy and not a drag for humanity. This is another topic.)

For the school to do its part in educating persons into the system, it will have to be financially supportive. This may include support of persons, not simply of programs. The community of poverty is too vast to be incorporated into the system by invitation alone; it must be mobilized into it. This may include paying people to get an education, which is not to be regarded as welfare but as *civic necessity*. Such a concept should not be termed "revolutionary." As a matter of fact, it has become a reality for large segments of our society. The children of the middle class and upward are well paid for going to school. We do not refer to the common patterns of extrinsic motivations which exist: dollars for As and cars for graduation. We refer to the fundamental economic fact that the middle class withholds its children from the job market while they get their education and their passports into the system. Meanwhile, they do not discipline their children, these students, to subsist in poverty. They support them well in terms of $2000 to $10,000 of personal maintenance in addition to conventional allowances, which you may be sure "child-power" insists be responsive to cost-of-living increases. The children of the poor when not paid to go to school are prone to see education, not as opportunity, but as a barrier to their aspirations, a wasting of precious time that they might better spend out hustling for the wherewithal to get the things that society awards generously to the luckier majority of children. Not to provide education because people do not have their own means is an indictment of our society. It is a sheer waste of human resources. The phrase is appealing and ordinarily well-intentioned, but we take some issue with it. Humanity must be prized and taken seriously as an end in itself not because of its uses to other men. Justice is a goal and a discipline, it is an instrument only to achieving a more perfect justice. Therefore, neglect of persons is a sufficient justification for social change, it wants no better case.

Society does, however, waste its resources, and that is a matter both for human and social concern.

waste versus conservation

America is the richest nation on earth. It is also the most wasteful. These two facts could not long coexist but for another: a prodigious endowment of all sorts of natural resources. In the midst of abundance an individual can perhaps afford to be wasteful, and perhaps a nation too. But if that abundance is threatened, what then?

This nation's development of the continent is by no means a simple tale of looting and despoiling of a great treasury of natural resources. It includes that, to be sure, but that is but one aspect of it. The history is more significantly one of application of intelligence and energy to the utilization of resources that harnessed the environment and changed it from a capacity to support a few millions at an austere standard to one that could provide a fantastically high standard of material comfort for more than two hundred million.

America does not stand alone in this achievement. The Industrial Revolution and the age of technology have meant these things in varied degree in all of the industrialized nations.

The view of resources and their uses must not be sentimentalized or simply nostalgic. The children's texts wax mournful over the passing of the buffalo. Truth to tell, the slaughter of these creatures was an epic tale of waste and plunder. But the settling and building of the West led to organized agriculture and land use that supported many millions more of much more useful and more tastily edible animals than bison and coyotes. Modern man cannot afford to take his mind off the realities of his here and now problems by indulging in pipe dreams of a romantic existence in a natural land unsullied by the scars and trademarks of society.

Historically, the American error with respect to its resources was a conceptual one. From the perspective of the early nineteenth century when the error took effect, it was a natural error. The nation simply perceived its resources to be infinite, inexhaustible.

But it was an error that toward the end of the nineteenth century began to be apparent. The limits of the resources began to be perceived. A conservation mindedness and a conservation movement began with dawning awareness to emerge. By now the evidence with respect to the depletion of our resources is alarming, and man has become increasingly aware of this. Nevertheless, instead of the strong actions that should be forthcoming we are getting only actions that are trivial and ineffective. With respect to resources, things are not getting better, even though the situation is clear that things are getting worse. What has gone wrong?

No new factors complicate the scene. Greed, stupidity, and waste were busy on the scene all along. When resources were deemed inexhaustible, these attributes seemed irrelevant. Now they have become terribly relevant. They stand stubbornly between man and the use of human intelligence to assure his future. They are not merely the names of abstractions; they are persons who direct institutions. They have great economic power and they know how to translate it into political power. They carry the names of some of the world's greatest corporations. They do many things which contribute to the common good; they manufacture steel, build roads, mine useful treasure from the earth. They also invest in a singularly noxious by-product: the despoilage of the environment. They are much appreciated for their good works; they are widely praised, even by their own well paid public relations staffs. They have been forgiven much: the nineteenth century is well forgotten. Only the historians recall such phrases as "robber barons" and "malefactors of great wealth." But productive genius does not excuse wanton, conscious spoilage. A bird may lay a tasty egg but gain a bad repute if it befouls its nest.

Greed, stupidity, and waste are not merely vestigial remnants of an unenlightened past. They are not defensive nor on the retreat. They are aggressive, alert, expansionist. Wherever the public has established a reserve of its treasures for its own uses even in pleasure, the jealousy of these three names for plunder runs high. Whether it be the little precious tract called Central Park in Manhattan or a great national forest in the West, it stands in constant peril. Connivers, plotters, plunderers are probing at the defenses of every one of these. They stand ready with persuasions, bribes, threats, and promises; they use every device from open lobbying to secret blackmail in their attempts to get the custodians of public interest to betray their trust. They have prettier words for themselves than we have used. They like to be known as "developers," but by whatever name they pass, they are dirty birds of a common feather.

The story of Lake Erie has become a national legend. The natural ecology of the inland sea has been all but ruined, say the experts. The people along it know only that the fishing has been destroyed; the use of many of its loveliest beaches has become unsafe. What would national reaction have been if one plane of a foreign power had dumped a hundred pound drum of harmful bacteria in Lake Erie? The cities dump in it tank car lots; industry spews its noxious wastes in ceaseless flow. It could all be stopped. But industry says only at a *cost*. Whose cost should be considered—the corporation's or posterity's?

For all the schools of the Lake Erie shore from Toledo to Buffalo, the study of the lake should be the center and focus of the social studies curriculum. Its study would derive from the immediate, the known, the pressing. By definition, it would be relevant. It would lead to all that needs to be considered in the most structured of curriculum—the relation of man to his environment, the effects of technology, the issues of social control, the economic system and its ramifications, the sometimes conflict of public and private interest, the concept of the common good, the decision-making process, the legal power and the real power, the role of law and of the courts, the needs of man in the modern world, the use of leisure, the city as an abode for man, conservation, the urban crisis and dilemma. What a curriculum for the children of the Erie basin! Urgent, relevant, necessitous, live, self-motivating!

Do not envy the children of northern Ohio too much. Some of their teachers will educate them where the action is; others will mourn for them the extinction of the passenger pigeon and the dodo. But wherever you live, if the school chooses, it will find a Lake Erie in its backyard. The curriculum could derive from it as fully and as well. It could be a park under attack by developers, a strip-mine operation, a polluted river, a scenic highway desecrated by billboards, an atmosphere contaminated. The odds are good that you will have a combination of inspirational sources at hand. Derive the curriculum

from these sources and you will likely encounter two forms of aston-
ishment: the excited interest of the students and the interest of
persons you have never met in what you are teaching!

The authors live in Pittsburgh. It is a cleaner city than it was
twenty years ago. It has discovered civic pride. It has built considerable monuments to that pride. You can see sunrise and sunset now
in fair weather in a variety of tones and colors instead of the murky
russet glow that was once their color. The approach to the city on a
clear day is no longer to behold it under a heavy pall of cloudy gray,
it is only tinctured a bit in a misty saffron. The city has had smoke
control for years, and all its residents have converted, at some cost,
their heating systems to conform. Many small businesses too and
larger ones at great cost have grudgingly or willingly paid the price
for being legal, for sharing in the pride of renaissance, for being decent
citizens.

But any day when the wind is right, you may get a nauseous
sulfurous whiff. Any night babies may waken coughing; old folks
gasp for breath in the heavy polluted air. Nobody likes it; everybody
knows where it comes from; organized protest comes and goes; but
the vile smoke still pours from the stacks of two great mills. How
does it happen? Will this year's legislative effort pass the council?
If so, will it be enforced? Can man's intelligence bring his environment under control when, as in this case, he knows all he needs to
know? Or will greed, and stupidity, and waste in this case cause him
to choke—and eventually to perish? These are modern man's lively
questions. If he does not have the answers, the right ones, he had
better be getting at them. Time is really running out.

Time runs out for modern man in two other decisive areas: population control and arms control.

In 1840 about 1 billion persons inhabited the earth. In 1940 it
was 2 billion. Today, 1971, it is 3 billion. By 1984, it will be 4 billion.
Observe the terrifying rate of increase.

The developed, the richer part of the world, presently holds one-
half of the productive land of the earth, but it has less than a third of
its people. By the year 2000 the developed world must feed 1.3 billion
people; but by then, the poorer nations will have 5 billion mouths to
feed. They cannot do it. They cannot begin to do it. Most demog-
raphers, economists, and agriculturists agree. Humanity is breeding
itself into imminent disaster, not eventually, but within our time.
The prospects for either divine intervention or a miracle of science
appear unlikely. The surer prospect is terrible famine, starvation,
wars of desperation, worldwide horror and fright.

The only alternative appears to be this course: recognition of the
problem; wide-spread advertising of and education in its reality and
immediacy; large investments in population control and education;
the careful and hard-boiled conservation of all natural resources.
This is an imperative for education, but it cannot do the job alone.

Education's job is to help enlighten as to the problem and the necessity, to help prepare the way for the use of the available technologies of conservation and population control.

As for arms, the situation is definitive and ultimate. The major powers possess the capacity to *overkill* the human race. This capacity is wired up; technologically, it is ready and waiting. Waiting for someone to say go, to push a button—or for something in *the system* to go wrong, for it to go without anyone saying it. Statisticians assure us that even if nations learn to discipline themselves, the unwanted will happen. The probabilities that something will happen in the system, something go wrong, increase every day. That is where we live. The only security lies in dismantling the system. Should not education assume a large responsibility for seeking that security?

educating for leisure or for living?

Modern man has time on his hands. Technology has set him free from a great burden of drudgery. For at least four decades now, the literature of education and social criticism has advanced the notion that the schools must prepare the student for the "wise use of leisure time."

Time is the dimension in which life is measured quantitatively; it is the measure of longevity. In America, whites enjoy more length of life than blacks, women more of it than men. These facts may serve to indicate in very general terms which groups are used more roughly by the demands and practices of contemporary society.

When one of your authors was a little boy, he had a well-loved grandmother, a cheerful woman with a Calvinist bent. Occasionally, when he was playing happily, that old lady would lean out the door and say, "Remember, Ryland, in the midst of life we are in death." This was not reproof; it was endorsement of his happiness. It showed a seasoned respect for the worth of time.

This is the understanding with which real education must begin. Mortal life is finally punctuated by death. Time is infinite only in the universe. For man, it is finite. Therefore, it is subject to the sense of all other limited resources. It runs short; it comes to an end. Its prudent use must be taken into account. This says in certainty that there is such a thing as wasting time, but it does not define what "wasting time" is. The schoolboy daydreaming or reading idly may be perceived by the teacher as wasting time. However, to him he is using it for something he wants. The definition of wise use of time is a very private thing. It is a matter of priorities, of choice. It is philosophical; it is a value system put to work in its most critical dimension. It is a response to the most basic of questions, "What are you to do with your life?"

Necessities define some of the uses you will make of your life: eating, sleeping, making a living. These block out a certain span of time for which choices are restricted. Modern man's time is less restricted to these necessities than human life has ever before known. A week has 168 hours of time. Most people in the nineteenth century, working at least a twelve-hour day for a six-day week, had a minor fraction of their working hours outside the dictates of necessity. The necessities were hard; hours of respite were few. Perhaps counting Sundays (which had dictates of its own) there were sixteen to eighteen hours a week to call their own. Assuming a forty-hour week (and that interspersed with coffee breaks), contemporary man, even fully employed and sleeping a full eight hours, has eighty hours of waking time approximately at his disposal. The necessity for sharing the amount of time that is needed to do the things the machines still leave him to do will lengthen his leisure.

This is a change of human condition so drastic and so rapid that it has indeed caught man culturally unready. Actually in the dimension of time he was caught short for choices of his own. The old dictates of necessity were so rigorous that in a way they governed his free hours; the best thing he could do with his extra time was easily answered: *rest*.

Carry-over from the culture of scarcity to one of abundance in respect to time produced a number of interesting cultured "hangups." Necessity was ever a hard taskmaster. One of its heaviest impositions was the habit of working. In a few hours of leisure, the conditioning of many hours of labor turned the available time into a hazard, a period of waiting to get back at it. Free time, even at rest, was an enemy, something to be "killed." "Time-killing" became a familiar phrase in the common culture. It is a hideous concept, betraying unawareness of the relationship of time itself to existence and expressing a deep revulsion against taking charge of some portion of life in which to define a meaning of self not stamped on the person by name of his occupation.

One "hangup" derives from the fact that life was so long necessitously directed to the pursuit of material sustenance. The days, the months, and the years defined life as the "pursuit of a living." In easier, more generous times this has translated itself into the pursuit of a "higher standard" of living. It has produced its satisfactions—a vast easing of living condition, a plethora of amenities and comforts and even luxuries. But all things are subject to a law of diminishing returns. There comes a point when increase of material goods simply does not bring a proportionate increase in human satisfaction. More importantly, man has a larger potential than simply to become a collector of material goods.

The work habit and the pursuit of a living, however, have a hard hold on man. Thus, when he finds eighty hours of extra time at his disposal, deep dispositions urge him to seek a lot of overtime, or to "moonlight" (take another full-time job), or to develop a hobby, an avocation, into another job—and possibly turn it to remunerative use.

The habits of the managerial classes and the extreme development of their acquisitive bent drive the middle class more specially. The institutional realms where they abide furnish inducements that are material, but that are also abstract: power, status, and prestige.

The managerial classes could work less, but they will not. They are fond of bragging in their varied trade journals that their work week runs counter to the national trend. While the work week for labor reduces to forty and even in some trades to thirty hours a week, they work fourteen-hour days, not neglecting Sundays. They take their work to lunch and dinner and to the playgrounds; they negotiate contracts on the golf course and between hands at the poker table. It is not that the work they do is so essential, or could not be done by themselves and others in a normal week. They are caught up in the acquisitive habit. They are vying for the psychic returns of power, prestige, and status.

The managerial classes take their acquired habits with them on holiday. Schedules, protocols, and efficiency mark their work behavior. No less do they characterize their leisure. The person they allowed the pursuit of goods and status to define goes to the mountain camp or beach resort. Hard, action-paced itineraries are the least of it. They are marvels at turning play into work. They are as jealous of the trademarks on their boats and fishing gear and golf equipment as of the labels in their business suits and hats and shoes. Accustomed to jockeying for position, they badger headwaiters for preferential seating, tip well to be called out loudly by name and rank. A good address means as much at the shore as in suburbia and association with the right people too. Pursuit of a living means no single roof over the head; the advertising now scorns mountain cabin or seaside shack. Nothing less than a "second home" will do.

Another hangup is also involved. The Puritanical thrust runs deep in American civilization. It involves a deep distrust of human nature and a great confidence in the discipline of imposed tasks to keep it on the straight and narrow path. Thus deep guilt inflicts the pleasure bent. The question may be raised, "What are you doing?" Perfectly sensible answers include: "Nothing at all," "Just what I please," "Relaxing," "Enjoying being alive." But to the Puritanical hangup these are threatening, self-incriminating responses. To one thus afflicted, it is a compulsive necessity to employ the work-sanctioned vocabulary to explain oneself. Note the key words in such responses as these: "I'm *organizing* a fishing trip," or "I'm *perfecting* my swing," or "I'm *planning* (budgeting) the family vacation," or "I'm getting in shape for a *hard* year's *work*."

There is no intent moralistically to prescribe the course of anybody's use of leisure. What is being emphasized is that leisure is an *opportunity for freedom* and that a great use of freedom is the defining of self on one's own terms. It is a contention that the work habit carried over into leisure, the pursuit of a living, the acquisitive drive with its concomitant hungers for power, prestige, and status, and the Puritanical distrust of self—all these infect leisure with irrelevancies and reduce the opportunity for freedom of choice.

As a matter of fact, the "unfree" are aware of their condition and complain of it. If we had to put words in their mouths, we would distrust the dialogue. Remember all Americans have lots of free time. Yet, are not comments like these thoroughly representative of the common culture? "I wish I had more time for my children." "Where do you find time to read?" "I'd really like to do something creative." The schools could easily become a force for developing the creative or meaningful use of leisure. Not by developing any specific programs thereof, but by pursuing education in a creative and meaningful manner rather than in its traditional task-minded manner.

The school, no less than the society in general, tends to perpetuate the unhappy phenomenon that we have described. Note for example the trend toward packing the curriculum of even the elementary school with more and more work-oriented practices: the diminished lunch periods that threaten to take pleasure, either social or gastronomical, out of eating and reduce it to a mere "fueling-up" for the work to be done; the massive "study halls" where the appearance of working is enforced by militarylike practices.

But it does not have to be this way with the school. School could well serve the realistic need of educating for meaningful leisure as well as for whatever "utilitarian" purposes it might have. It could well provide the means by which children could achieve some glimpses into the joys of living, a pursuit for which they are well endowed. Most important, the school could help relieve children of whatever remains of the social press of guilt for enjoying oneself.

technology and education

The job for the schools with respect to technology is to educate about it. This constitutes an obligation. There is no obligation to see how much technology can be used in the classroom. There is no sense at all in the comment attributed to the *Wall Street Journal* that ". . . new schools have to be built around the electronic gear that will cram them." In a word, what the schools need is to be intellectualized and humanized, not technologized.

The school needs to educate as to where man stands with respect to his technology. Sometimes the question is phrased as a matter of whether man will be master of his technology or be enslaved by it. This is *not* the issue at all. Such a concept invests the machine with qualities of submission or control that it does not possess. The machine does not even "serve" man. It simply operates.

No issues are at stake between men and machines. The questions of mastery and submission, exploitation and service are issues between men. The questions of human consequence have much to do with the uses of technology. Men, not machines, will decide the uses.

All sorts of technologies exist. Their uses are complex and varied. Technology makes possible the more rapid and thorough depletion of resources, if that be the sole purpose it be turned to. But technologies also exist to prevent air pollution and contamination of streams, rivers, and lakes. Vast technologies are available for the control of disease and for healing, and technologies even more vast are at hand to devastate and destroy. The choice of modern societies to invest more heavily is made by men. The hydrogen bombs did not ask to be stockpiled.

Neither does *man* make these choices. Man in the aggregate makes no choices. Men, persons, make choices. They make them in behalf of or against other men; they make them in concern for, or disdain for, or in callous disregard of, the interests of others.

When men in the aggregate rally around a good banner, we get some notion of what they really would opt for if they were real decision-makers. They have been cheered and motivated by slogans which echoed their best hopes, "life, liberty, and the pursuit of happiness," "liberty, equality, and fraternity," "social justice," "land and rights," "peace and friendship." Never mind that these slogans have been used to delude and betray the popular hopes. The aspirations of the people were clear, even when the hearts of their deluders were clouded with malice.

The people want to live. They want to be free. They want to define the good life in terms meaningful to them. The terms in which they define the good lend confidence in their judgment. They speak of brotherhood, peace, friendship, rights. They do like to have a little something to call their own, a roof, some personal belongings, a bit of land. These seem like reasonable demands on life. Most of the human bitterness, the discontent with institutions, the revolutionary zeal in history has been occasioned because so many have been denied these few, these ever so simple demands.

What causes the trouble is that there is a childish fearful grabbiness in people which goads them to seek a great deal more of basic things than they can ever need or use. When law is just, then inordinate greed is held in check. But law has not by far kept pace with greed, so vast accumulations of wealth and economic power have been built up which not only make a mockery of concepts of *fair share*, but which put men in the necessity of paying tribute to others as the price for getting some share of the benefits of organized social activity.

The Gross National Product, GNP as it is often called, is rapidly approaching a trillion dollars. That is a thousand *billions*. Goods-a-plenty and for all, you might say. Let us not dwell on the fact that some have much too much, both of goods and of power, but that many simply have much too little to satisfy the relatively limited aspirations of most men. To distribute the product a little more equitably seems like an eminently reasonable solution. Not so, say some economic theorists. If your share is too small, you must work to increase the GNP; then your same percentage share will be bigger.

But that suggestion, at any particular time and place, might be less than satisfying.

And if it is all we can offer to the poor and deprived of our nation, can we be surprised at their growing dissatisfaction and discontent; the growing numbers of their strikes and riots?

The fruits of technology are largely distributed in terms of power. Earning power and purchasing power are two exertions that the consumer places on distribution. But those who control production have another force to exert, a withholding power. They exact a share for the act of production and distribution, which is *profit*. Profit is a legitimate return for initiative, use of instruments of production, for conduct of the enterprise and exercise of distribution.

Any power to make claim upon the GNP can create imbalance, can be inflationary. If workers claim earnings which exceed their productivity, if consumers buy without regard to price or quality, if producers and distributors destroy competition in order to withhold greedily, the consequence is likely to be socially undesirable. Government, too, exerts taxing power. To the extent that the taxes go into useful social services this helps to provide a balance of benefit within society. When the government's taxing force is exerted to feed and expand a mere sprawling and unproductive bureaucratic and military force, it becomes a primary creator of inflationary tendency.

The controls within a complex economy are themselves necessarily complex. Collective bargaining serves to create some equilibrium between earning power and withholding power (profit); competition (where it exists) and enlightened consumership put restraints on withholding; public scrutiny and consent place restraints on taxing power.

With respect to the uses of technology it is important to note that profit and benefit are not the same. It may be costly to some, and profitable to none, immediately, to reclaim the cities. The benefits, however, to some would be large and immediate, and in general would be gratifying to any and all members of the society who cherished any notion of the common weal. The idea of the general welfare is profoundly rooted in American civilization; it is, indeed, a constitutionally rooted concept. The vast majority hold to the view that they do indeed live in a human community that grants to man some obligations beyond being as grabby as he can manage to be in his private sphere. Unfortunately, and education owes the children an awareness of the fact, some Americans and some who hold great power hold the great principle of the general welfare in scorn and disdain.

The confusion of profit and benefit is what educators must be wary of when technology comes to school, not as subject matter, but as a bill of goods to be sold. The "knowledge industry" includes some of the greatest names in American industry: General Dynamics, American Telephone and Telegraph, General Electric, Time, Inc., Bell and Howell, Philco, Radio Corporation of America, International Business Machines, R.C.A., Westinghouse, to name a few.

The knowledge industry comes seeking profits and claiming benefits. To seek profit is altogether legitimate and may have associated benefits. The desks, the lighting, the buildings themselves, the floors, the books, the laboratories are all necessary and serviceable; they were, in the main, sold, not given to the schools. Somebody usually made a profit on them. Without the profit motive, disciplined by competition and research and study of consumer needs they would not be nearly as good and useful as they are. This is not a diatribe against profit; it is the establishment of a distinction between profit and benefit.

It is the business of the seller to seek profit and claim benefit. It is the professional obligation of the educator to determine his own needs and to assess the benefits of goods offered for sale in relation to his needs.

Needs must be assessed in terms of priorities. An educational assessment of needs can scarcely avoid, if it be competent, a set of priorities similar to those that follow:

1. The rescue of the school from its large impersonality and dehumanization.

   The principal instruments for this would be reduced student-teacher ratios, a reduction of bureaucratic behavior within the school, the basic discipline of human concern broadly applied.
2. The rescue of specially neglected populations from educational practices that at the least fail to nurture growth and at the worst are positively destructive of children's egos and aspirations.

   Nothing other than recognition of the reality of the situation and a determination to do something about it can serve as effective instruments to this end.
3. To attend to individual differences across the whole spectrum of a child's experiences and potential.

   Nothing less than learning situations in which each child can be known in depth in terms of his own definition of self will accomplish this.
4. To give the child a chance to live and to learn what he needs to know.

   Nothing less than a vast reconstruction of curriculum and method based upon the criteria of scope, significance, effectiveness, and relevance will suffice.

Where then do the offerings of the Great Technology come in? To the thoughtful educator, insofar as they do not seem to be suggested by the foregoing, the answer will have to be "First things first. Maybe later on. We have presently more pressing things to do."

Or if tools are offered that seem relevant to the foregoing, as was earlier suggested, the educator must look to the research and not to salesmen's claims.

Can films, tape recorders, phonographs help to enrich environment, provide response to wide-ranging interests and potentials? Yes, the research has been in a long time, and classroom experience vindicates their use.

Can computer-assisted-instruction (CAI) justify its use? The answer must be "no" on the basis of the research and in proportion to its present costs. In addition, CAI has the built-in hazard of increasing depersonalization, which at present is the largest fault of the school.

Can teaching machines and programmed learnings aid in the job of relating to individual differences and in carrying the burden of the new curriculum? Not if individual difference is perceived in terms broader than rate of learning. Not in terms of gains in academic achievement, even over "conventional teaching," says the research. Not if a central objective is to nurture inquiry, choice, responsibility, or creativity.

Can a school be judged as responding to the need for change on evidence of large-scale innovation? Not if those innovations are simply instruments. Not if the content of the curriculum is not revised to the reality of the time. Not if the innovations are tied to psychological doctrines that manipulate the student rather than liberate him. Not if the instruments are strait-jacketed to the old subject matters, formalistically conceived and executed.

All in all, the school must continue to welcome the salesmen for the Great Technology. The market is a great bazaar, and the intelligent can often find useful goods among its inventories. The directive toward the school is clear, however. Only teachers can be properly responsive to the wide range of student needs, only they can develop real learning situations. The person may find machines useful, but he must never be subjected to the machine. The top priority for the school remains to intellectualize and to humanize it. To technologize, the school must at least await the achievement of that goal.

topics for inquiry

1. Examine the Curriculums of an Urban, Suburban, and Rural High School. (In what ways are they similar and dissimilar with respect to (1) vestiges of "life adjustment curriculum" and (2) use of technological innovations?)
2. Investigate the Early Research on Teaching Machines and Note the Claims that Were Being Made. (Investigate recent research to see if these claims have been substantiated.)
3. Design an Elementary School Curriculum Using as Many Technological Innovations as You Can Think of. (Devise a plan to evaluate the effectiveness of the program.)
4. Plan a Curriculum Based on the Natural Environment of a School.

subjects for discussion

1. Discuss the assumptions about the process of human learning that are implied in the new technological teaching devices.
2. Discuss the ways in which technological innovations have affected the curriculum and the operation of the schools.
3. In what ways can the schools act as a political force to influence legislation that affects the lives of its children? Discuss the pros and cons of the schools becoming an active political force.
4. Discuss the ways in which the school curriculum from grades K through 12 can bring into focus the need for conservation of our nation's natural and human resources.

selected readings

CALLAHAN, RAYMOND. *Education and the Cult of Efficiency.* Chicago: University of Chicago Press, 1962.

CALDER, RITCHIE. *Common Sense About a Starving World.* New York: Macmillan, 1962.
    A readable little book that is hard-hitting in setting forth the necessities for avoiding famine and disaster.

CARSON, RACHEL LOUISE. *The Sea Around Us.* New York: Simon and Schuster, 1959.

————. *Silent Spring.* Boston: Houghton Mifflin, 1962.
Man's destruction of his suffocating environment effectively detailed in both works.

Daedalus. Journal of the American Academy of Arts and Sciences. Two issues:
Science and Technology in Contemporary Society (Spring 1962) and *Science and Culture* (Winter 1962).

GORDON, KERMIT (ed.). *Agenda for the Nation.* Washington, D.C.: The Brookings Institution, 1968.
An excellent resource book of expert views on a wide variety of national problems.

GREEN, THOMAS F. *Work, Leisure, and the American Schools.* New York: Random House, 1968.
An intensive treatise on the ideological basis of work and leisure as they relate to education.

MAYO, ELTON. *The Social Problems of an Industrial Civilization.* Boston: Andover, 1945.
An intensely humanistic treatise by a person experienced in industrial research, the discoverer of the noted "Hawthorne effect." He speaks to educators and reminds us (p. 123), "To blame a person or persons is far easier than to study carefully, and in full detail, a situation. Yet it is only the latter study that can avail to lead us out of the chaos of misery and malice that has overtaken our once proud civilization."

NICOL, HUGH. *The Limits of Man.* London: Constable, 1967.
Shatters the illusions that suggest easy solutions to man's population and food problem.

POTTER, DAVID M. *People of Plenty: Economic Abundance and the American Character.* Chicago: University of Chicago Press, 1954.
Relevant for the 1970s even though written in the 1950s.

PYKE, MAGNUS. *The Science Myth.* New York: Macmillan, 1962.
A witty, satirical—and short—book that points up the stresses on the human biological organism from the pressures of industrial society.

VEBLEN, THORSTEIN. *The Theory of the Leisure Class.* New York: Macmillan, 1898.
Written at the turn of the century but relevant for the 1970s.

WIENER, NORBERT. *The Human Use of Human Beings.* Boston: Houghton Mifflin, 1950.
An inventive approach to communications theory in an age of technology. Profound in its implications for education. Says Wiener (p. 189),
Thus the new industrial revolution is a two-edged sword. It may be used for the benefit of humanity,

> assuming that humanity survives long enough to enter
> a period in which such a benefit is possible. If however,
> we proceed along the clear and obvious lines of our
> traditional behavior, and follow our traditional wor-
> ship of progress and the fifth freedom—the freedom to
> exploit—it is practically certain that we shall have to
> face a decade or more of ruin and despair.

Two decades seem to have borne out his prophecy.

The brief reading list on the nuclear realities that follows is only
a sample, of course, but it should suffice to convince any reader of
what all thoughtful men know: *that unless man can cease his war
game he is done for.*

CALDER, NIGEL (ed.). *Unless Peace Comes: A Scientific Forecast of
New Weapons.* New York: Viking, 1968.

COUSINS, NORMAN. *Modern Man Is Obsolete.* New York: Viking,
1945.

LAPP, RALPH E. *The Weapons Culture.* New York: Norton, 1968.

LEWIS, FLORA. *One of Our H-Bombs Is Missing.* New York: Mc-
Graw-Hill, 1967.

13
THE
SCHOOL
AND
SOCIAL
MOBILITY

One of the important tenets underlying American society is the concept of *equality of opportunity*. It is an ideal that has permeated most of the political rhetoric from the beginning of the nation. It was the ideological thrust of the common school movement. Its theme was central in a great deal of American literature, and its viability can be attested to by careers of most of the great industrialists of the late nineteenth century. However, there have been some who consider it an ideal given generous subscription in general terms but rather selective applicability in a functional sense. Obviously, it has been this view that has fired reform movements from the common school crusade to the civil rights movement. Seymour Martin Lipset and Reinhard Bendix for example, find the concept in practice has a definite bias:

> . . . the available evidence indicates that the development of both the theory and the practice of "equilatarianism" among the white majority has been aided by the continued presence of large, ethnically segregated castes. That is, one of the reasons why the belief in this system has been sustained is because opportunities to rise socially and economically have been available to "majority-Americans," and a disproportionate share of poverty, unemployment, sickness, and all forms of deprivation have fallen to the lot of minority groups, especially fifteen million Negro Americans.[1]

Thus, in a developmental sense, the concept of equality of opportunity has been defined or under-

[1] Seymour M. Lipset and Reinhard Bendix, *Social Mobility in Industrial Society*, (Berkeley: University of California Press, 1959), p. 80.

stood in a variety of ways by different people at different times. No
doubt the historical development of the concept might be best understood in its relationship to social and economic developments. It
would obviously be given a different functional meaning in an agrarian
as opposed to an industrial society or in an early period of industrialization as opposed to our modern consumption-based economy. But an
understanding of the socioeconomic relativity of the concept does not
provide us with ready-made, socially relevant definitions for our own
times. In other words, we are forced to consider what it means for us,
here and now. How do we define equality of opportunity? Do we
mean, for example, that our social arrangements allow for equal opportunity to attempt achievement of personal aspirations, that is, without any specially rigged social, political, or economic barriers? Or
perhaps more important, do our arrangements allow for equal opportunity to arrive at aspirations unencumbered by socially pressed
psychological barriers? These are the gut questions that educators
must honestly wrestle with.

To a great extent there is still a basic commitment to the concept
of equality of opportunity in this country. At least we could readily
say that it is a commitment that all but a few would accept in principle. What, then, of the reality? Is equality of opportunity in the two
previously stated dimensions a functioning reality in American society? Obviously, it is not! The social literature is overwhelmingly
supportive on this point. What then constitutes the differential between the stated commitments and the functional reality? Is the
commitment to the concept merely a practiced rhetoric? Or is the
commitment simply rendered dysfunctional by our failure to view the
concept of equality against the backdrop of contemporary society?
In other words, do we hold a romantically simple view or do we give
consideration to the complexities of contemporary social realities?

These are, in no uncertain terms, personal as well as social questions for teachers. Each of us must test our own philosophies on the
concept of equality in the process of giving it a social application. If,
hopefully, we come to a thoughtful acceptance of the concept, either
pragmatically or altruistically, then we must be willing to investigate
its meaning in today's society. This implies at least two interdependent areas. First, it implies a thoughtful appraisal of the school's
role—whether it functions to support or refute the concept of equality
of opportunity. Second, it implies an appraisal of the societal structure as it affects and is affected by the school. We shall consider one
important aspect of the latter first.

societal structure via economic stratification

By no means is economic status to be seen as a sufficient variable by
which to assign any particular meaning to any group of people in

American society. It is a most important variable, however, to consider in any discussion about equality of opportunity and its measurable variable in an industrial society, social mobility. To be sure, economic stratification does not belie the existence of social mobility; many people do move up the economic ladder, both intra- and intergenerationally. But there are some serious oversimplifications made of that fact. For the most part, such upward mobility has occurred from a particular base line, a base line set above the poverty level. In other words, the poor in America remain poor! In view of this fact, and also in view of the economic stratification in our society today, some serious implications must be considered. For example, one must carefully appraise the possible effects on the person of existing within the various economic strata. What does it mean in affective terms to be poor in America? What kind of physical and psychological deprivation can result from poverty? These questions have been worked over thoroughly in the past two decades. The social literature tells us a great deal about the effects of physical deprivation in no uncertain terms. Malnutrition and disease are measurable realities. The literature has also told us, if in less certain terms, a great deal about the psychological deprivation of poverty. Despair and hopelessness are natural attendants to hunger.

poverty amidst affluence

In 1968 the Citizens' Board of Inquiry into Hunger and Malnutrition in the United States reported that over 10 million Americans were suffering from hunger and 20 million more were not adequately fed. In both instances the terminology was based on medically defined measures. In other words, *suffering* from *hunger* means *suffering* in a physical sense. It means in many instances that children from birth onward are without the necessary nutrition for normal physical development. In some extreme cases it was found that some children weighed less at the age of one than they did at birth. In many instances the impoverished children at all age levels display irrevocable physical retardation including arrested brain development. For others, those in the 20 million poorly nourished category, it means excessive susceptibility to an all inclusive range of ailments that, if not irrevocably debilitating physically, are seriously handicapping educationally. Obviously, we are not talking in terms of social class and its relative influence via "cultural deprivation," "cultural pluralism," "class values," and so forth. We are talking about a measurable reality of our society, a shocking reality to many. The reality is this—there are literally millions of children in the United States whose most basic and limited nutritional needs are not being met. And this in a society that can boast of its affluence.

Aside from the pressing questions of basic human compassion as related to these figures, what are the questions involved in regard to equality of opportunity? A foolish question, obviously. Or do we mean to exclude those children who make up the statistics of hunger? Then, according to the figures, we can write off a sizable group. It might well be argued that the problem of hunger is one that is beyond any direct action of the school. Curricular reconstruction cannot satisfy a vitamin deficiency—but extended free-lunch programs for all children can help. Beyond this it is possible to conceive of the school becoming the most socially active institution in regard to community needs. Curricula could well be designed around real problem areas such as hunger. The schools could conceivably take responsible leadership in meeting the problem by pressing for active roles. Such a role would obviously require a near complete political metamorphosis on the part of both teachers and administrators. But if the school is vitally committed to the welfare of society and to the concept of equality of opportunity, it cannot avoid the responsibility. In this sense, the school's responsibility obviously extends beyond the problem of hunger to the broader aspects of poverty itself.

To be sure, the hungry in America are poor. Their numbers alone, however, do not define the parameters of poverty. Many who exist within what is often referred to as the "culture of poverty" in the United States are not necessarily part of the statistics of hunger. There might well be a great deal of nutritional insecurity from meal to meal or day to day, but somehow they manage to eat. However, given the base line for poverty in the United States, eating is obviously managed with great difficulty.

In 1969 the monetary definition of poverty set by the federal government was $3,553 yearly income for a family of four. The official estimate indicated that about 25.4 million people could thus be classified as poor. A more realistic figure was offered by Michael Harrington.[2] Taking into account the impact of inflation as well as the government's tendency to underestimate, Harrington would add another 12 million Americans to the poverty figure. He also pointed up the fact that arbitrary monetary definitions of poverty are dangerously misleading. Citing the fact that the government in 1967 numbered at 12 million the "near poor," those with incomes between $3,335 and $4,345 for families of four, Harrington states:

> If these numbers were underestimated in the same way as were
> the poor, there are 16 million Americans who are but one illness,
> one accident, one recession away from being poor again. If, as
> now seems so possible, America in the seventies should reduce
> its social efforts, this group will lose almost as much as the
> poor.[3]

[2] Michael Harrington, "The Betrayal of the Poor," *The Atlantic*, 225, No. 1 (Jan. 1970), 71–74.
[3] *Ibid.*, p. 72.

Harrington's statement takes on added meaning when viewed in light of his 1963 book, *The Other America.*[4] His words then, though they underestimated the extent of hunger, are still applicable:

The millions who are poor in the United States tend to become increasingly invisible. Here is a great mass of people, yet it takes an effort of the intellect and will even to see them.[5]

To be sure the other America is not impoverished in the same sense as those poor nations where millions cling to hunger as a defense against starvation. This country has escaped such extremes. That does not change the fact that tens of millions of Americans are, at this very moment, maimed in body and spirit, existing at levels beneath those necessary for human decency. If these people are not starving, they are hungry, and sometimes fat with hunger, for that is what cheap foods do. They are without adequate housing and education and medical care.[6]

To be sure, social stratification along economic lines has been an accepted reality of a modern industrial society. The pressing issues, however, are the degree of imbalance involved in that stratification and the degree to which the imbalance renders the concepts of equality of opportunity and social mobility dysfunctional. In the United States today the imbalance suggests that both have been rendered dysfunctional for about one-fifth of the population, the poor at the bottom of the scale. At the same time "opportunity" seems to be an augmented reality at the other end of the scale.

For example, in the same year of the hunger report, *Fortune* magazine (May, 1968) published a list of America's wealthiest individuals. Significant is the fact that *Fortune* assumed a base line of $150 million for their list. In their best Horatio Alger posture, and with their typical social myopia, they felt that

The United States has become so affluent that there no longer is any great prestige in being a mere millionaire. The very word "millionaire" is seldom used nowadays; indeed it has an almost quaint sound. It belongs to the era some decades back when a net worth of $1 million was considered a "fortune"; a millionaire was a member of a small class, and therefore a natural object of curiosity. To have a net worth of $1 million today is to be, much of the time indistinguishable from the omnipresent middle class.[7]

[4] Michael Harrington, *The Other America* (Baltimore: Penguin, 1963).
[5] *Ibid.*, p. 10.
[6] *Ibid.*, p. 9.
[7] Arthur M. Louis, "America's Centimillionaires," *Fortune*, 77, No. 5 (May 1968), 152.

Alongside this one must place the real figures of income distribution in the United States, in what seems to be their consistent parameters. One of the most authoritative sources is that of Herman P. Miller's *Income Distribution in the United States*. Comparing income distribution eighteen years apart, Miller presents these figures: [8]

TABLE 11

Quintile of Population	1944	1962
	Percent of Nat'l. Income	
Top fifth	46	46
Second fifth	22	23
Third fifth	16	16
Fourth fifth	11	11
Bottom fifth	5	5

Included in these figures is an inverse ratio if we contrast the top 5 percent of the population with the bottom 20 percent. It reads thusly: the upper 5 percent of the population receives 20 percent of the available income; the lower 20 percent of the population receives 5 percent of the available income; 1:4 as opposed to 4:1.

The point to be made is not simply that socioeconomic stratification exists in our society, but that the stark imbalance of that stratification holds some important implications about the functional reality of the concept of equality of opportunity. Here, of course, is where it relates to education.

Obviously, the school must take into account the possible effects of poverty on students in order to try to compensate for them. However, too often, the school, on the one hand, has generally failed to assume the responsibility to compensate for the effects of poverty on some children, while, on the other hand, it has readily accepted shallow assumptions about stereotyped social class attitudes, values, and so forth, especially about lower-class children. By basing its actions on these stereotyped class assumptions the school has consistently achieved what it has expected to achieve. In other words, the school that expects lower-class children to fail assures that failure. Again we are talking about the self-fulfilling prophecy at work. This most important concept of social dynamics is explained by Robert K. Merton thusly:

> The self-fulfilling prophecy is, in the beginning, a *false*
> definition of the situation evoking a new behavior which makes
> the original false conception come *true*. The specious validity
> of the self-fulfilling prophecy perpetuates a reign of error. For

[8] Herman P. Miller, *Income Distribution in the United States* (Washington, D.C.: Government Printing Office, 1966), p. 3.

the prophet will cite the actual course of events as proof that he was right from the very beginning.[9]

It might well be argued that the schools have been functioning under false assumptions for a long enough time to provide ample "evidence" for their tenableness. Further, by their easy acceptance of these assumptions, the schools have easily relieved themselves of any sense of failure. It is somewhat reminiscent ot the pre-Reformation practice of buying indulgences from papal emissaries for future sins. What the schools must realistically accept is their failure to provide equal educational opportunities for a sizable group of American children. Once accepting the fact of their failure, and appraising the possible causes, they might be able to bring about a greater degree of functional reality to the concept of social mobility for all.

What are these assumptions about "cultural" values by which the schools excuse their failure to serve the poor? We list just a few of the more general assumptions that have had wide acceptance for a long time:

1. Lower-class children lack aspiration.
2. Lower-class children lack motivation for learning.
3. Lower-class children have low expectations.
4. Lower-class children are not willing to "delay gratification."
5. Lower-class children have negative self-images.
6. Lower-class children are hostile and mistrustful toward the basic institutions of the society.

These particular traits may be found to exist in some lower-class youth in varying degrees. They may also exist in youth at all levels. The point is that they have been widely accepted as lower-class traits. Therefore, their existence might well be seen as a result of the expectancy itself. In other words, where they do exist, they might be seen as a result of their having been automatically imposed in stereotyped fashion on a particular class. Thus, a child, for example, a black child, from an inner-city ghetto comes to school. The school too frequently immediately assumes that the child is culturally deprived, lacks aspiration, lacks motivation, has a negative self-image, and so on, and so on. In short, the school assumes that the child is indeed poor educational material. Therefore, it feels safe in predicting his level of achievement—low, naturally. From then on the school treats the child in accordance with its expectations. By so doing the school assures the validity of its prediction. An important point to note is that it does not matter whether or not the assumptions made about the youth are accurate. The predictions and subsequent treatment function to give the assumptions seeming validity.

A 1967 study done at the National Opinion Research Center at the

[9] Robert K. Merton, *Social Theory and Social Dynamics* (New York: Free Press, 1957), p. 423.

University of Chicago attempted, among other things, to test the validity of some of the generally held assumptions about lower-class
youth. The findings of the study, reported by Ralph Underhill in
Youth in Poor Neighborhoods [10] hold up to question some of the commonly held beliefs about social class values. They should also have
important meaning for schools. Following are a few of the findings
reported:

> We found no evidence that poor youths are critical of or hostile
> toward society's basic institutions . . . no evidence that [they]
> view themselves in more negative or less positive terms than
> those who are better off . . . no evidence that [they] consider
> success to be unimportant or that they are unwilling to work
> hard for it.
>   The effect of poverty on values for youths in our sample
> seems to be limited to rather specific areas and does not appear
> to constitute a pervasive system of alienation from the values
> of society at large. . . .
>   Perhaps because of pessimism over endowments and chances
> to manipulate the environment, or perhaps because of inequality
> of opportunity, the poor have lower educational and occupational
> expectations . . . and aspirations . . . [which] may be partly a
> function of realistically low expectations. . . .
>   In sum, our general and speculative impression on the nature
> of value differences between the poor and the more well-to-do
> is that they do not indicate a lack of desire for material success
> so much as they indicate a low assessment of the chances for
> attaining material success.
>   Finally, it appears to us that the values that characterize
> middle-class culture are largely shared by the poor youths in
> our sample as well. The poor do not seem to us to have a very
> deviant subculture. If there are a few who are alienated from
> society and its values they must be a very few—fewer than
> Oscar Lewis thinks. The idea that the poor are poor because
> they want to be poor has not been empirically supported by
> this study.[11]

The implications of these findings are of vital importance for the
schools. First, they indicate that whether or not previously held assumptions about lower-class attitudes were accurate in the past, they
are not necessarily accurate today. Second, the findings supply a
viable basis from which to put into effect a direct use of the concept of
the self-fulfilling prophecy. It seems a sensible proposal then to have
the schools function on these premises: The school (and teacher, of
course) should assume that every child has an immeasurable intelli-

10 Ralph Underhill, *Youth in Poor Neighborhoods* (Chicago: National Opinion Research
Center, 1967).
11 *Ibid.*, pp. 90–91.

gence and an inestimable potential. Once relieved of the practice of placing arbitrary ceilings on a child's achievement the school will not be an added barrier to mobility but rather what it is intended to be, an equalizer, not in the sense of drawing all toward mediocrity but in the sense of affording an unlimited opportunity for all. Hopefully, this can come about through an altruistic-democratic motivation, but if not, then it must come out of a realistic appraisal of the potential threat to the society if conditions of inequality go unattended. The chaos of upheaval and revolution, or reactionary suppression, are avoidable only if such problems are realistically attended. The school's task, though never easy, is in this instance well-defined—to do the job they are supposed to do—*providing for the education of youth with a complete sense of equality.*

There has been some movement toward attending to the inequalities of educational opportunities for the poor, but in view of the needs, the movement has been minimal. In Chapter 4 we discussed one aspect of this movement, the Elementary and Secondary Education Act. There are other federal programs that have been developed as part of the war on poverty begun in the mid-1960s. The most notable of these, as related to the schools, has been Project Head Start. Developed under the auspices of the Office of Economic Opportunity, Head Start, beginning in 1965, established preschool programs for four- and five-year-olds from poverty areas in order to overcome the deficiencies imposed on them by poverty. Thus, it was felt, these children might have a better chance for success in school. The areas of concern, in general, have been health care, nutrition, language development, perceptual skills, development of wholesome self-images. The program has enjoyed the cooperative efforts of school personnel, social workers, family welfare agencies, and the clergy. There is no doubt that if Head Start, or similar projects, function in accordance with stated purposes, they hold great potential for accommodating the needs of young children. For the most part, Head Start, even though it has generally been only an eight-week program, has proven to be effective, at least in its immediate influence on the children involved. Measured results of gains made by children have given adequate support to the validity of the program. On the other hand, there has been substantial evidence that in many instances the advantages of the program tend to disappear as the child goes through the grade school.

The implication, of course, is that the school, if it functions on the same old social class biases, can work against even the positive effects of a program designed to prepare the child for school success. So, it might be argued, until the school drops its social class biases, it will continue to work against the lower-class child.

social class and the school

The discussion thus far has been directed primarily toward the school's neglect of the poor. We have, on occasion, used the term *social class*, but only as it might be defined by economic measures, and most specifically as it might be applied to the poor. To be sure, the concept of social class has never been more challenged for definition than in recent years. The writings in sociology for at least the last decade have been involved with distinctions between social differentiation and social stratification; the various positioning in power hierarchies, economic hierarchies, prestige hierarchies; relative positioning of class related values; and so forth. The concept of social class cannot be perceived in a simplistic or permanent sense. It is obviously a dynamic concept that is reciprocally related to social and economic change. For our purposes, however, we shall use the term within the simple economic parameters, for this is generally how it has been viewed by the school.

A great deal of research has attempted to draw relationships between social class and various aspects of American education. Three of the most important sociological studies, spanning some twenty-five years, are presented in very brief terms below. Their importance lies in the fact that they displayed the degree of social class bias that has so long permeated American schools.

One of the earliest sociological studies that focused on the question of social class within the American school was that of R. S. Lynd and H. M. Lynd in *Middletown*.[12] Their study, carried on in 1924–1925 in a midwestern industrial city, analyzed in detail the various attitudes, values, and behaviors of the various social strata in the population. The Lynds also studied the reaction to social class by the schools. In general, they found that the parents of all classes held high regard for and recognized the value of education. But more important to our concerns is their conclusion that the school definitely penalized lower-class children because they did not possess the symbols, attitudes, and behavior characteristics valued by the dominant class groups.

After *Middletown* the findings of the Lynds' were corroborated by numerous other studies on social class bias in education. One of the most comprehensive reports was that of W. L. Warner, R. J. Havighurst, and M. B. Loeb, *Who Shall Be Educated*.[13] Their book compiled earlier studies done by the authors on New England, midwestern, and southern localities. They concluded that the schools studied had a social class screening device that kept the upward flow of mobility at a minimum. They found it to be a pervasive functioning:

[12] R. S. Lynd and H. M. Lynd, *Middletown* (New York: Harcourt, Brace, 1929).
[13] W. L. Warner, R. J. Havighurst, and M. B. Loeb, *Who Shall Be Educated* (New York: Harper Brothers, 1944).

> This book describes how our schools, functioning in a society
> with basic inequalities, facilitate the rise of a few from lower to
> higher levels but continue to serve the social system by keeping
> down many people who try for higher places. The teacher, the
> school administrator, the school board, as well as the students,
> themselves, play their roles to hold people in their places in
> our structure.[14]

Much of their writing would be applicable to the present state of education. For example, they found that:

> one large group is almost immediately brushed off into a bin
> labeled "non-readers," "first-grade repeaters," or "opportunity
> class" where they stay for eight or ten years and are then
> released through a chute to the outside world to become
> "hewers of wood and drawers of water." [15]

The authors also pointed out that the lower-class parents definitely had educational aspirations for their children but too often any thoughts about college were compromised because of a lack of money. But that alone was not the compromising factor on aspiration. Again the school, by its practices, had a significant effect on maintaining the social status quo:

> The evidence is clear that the social class system of Yankee
> City definitely exercises a control over the pupils' choice of
> curricula. . . . The children of the two upper and the upper-
> middle classes, in overwhelming percentages, were learning and
> being taught a way of life which would fit them into higher
> statuses. On the other hand, the lower-middle and lower-class children,
> in their studies in the high school, were learning a way of life which
> would help adjust them to the rank in which they were born.[16]

A. B. Hollingshead's *Elmtown's Youth*,[17] another of the now classic sociological studies on social class and the schools, added support to the earlier findings that social class comes to school in a small midwestern city. Hollingshead clearly established that social stratification exists even within the schools. Through a great deal of direct conversation with many students with whom he had worked hard to establish confidence and rapport, he found that social class influenced school life in many ways. It was closely related to patterns of friendship, dating, election of class officers, and participation in athletics and social events. He also found, as did the others, that social class clearly had a bearing on academic motivation.

[14] *Ibid.*, p. xi.
[15] *Ibid.*, p. 15.
[16] *Ibid.*, p. 62.
[17] A. B. Hollingshead, *Elmtown's Youth* (New York: Wiley, 1949).

The general conclusion about social class bias that the preceding studies put forth has been continually supported by sociological literature. The implications of the studies are of the utmost importance to today's educators in making an honest appraisal of the school in the 1970s. What does the concept of social class imply for today's schools? There is no doubt that the findings of the cited studies, though they were local studies, can be broadly, if with modification, applied to the school in the United States in general.

Social class in the American school is an established phenomenon. It exists. Its existence poses a central problem for teachers and educators. The question is simply: What to do about it? The alternatives are basically two, each of which constitutes an active choice. To these must be added the oft chosen debilitating choice, *do nothing*. The active alternatives appear to be:

1. To accept the reality of social class structures as a guideline to education. Some sociologists have recommended this as basic realism. Its consequences would tend to perpetuate stratification.
2. To accept the fact of social class stratification as a challenge to the school. To assume its existence and to try to minimize, even to obliterate its effects.

The choice of alternatives would seem to be rather basic in determining the role of education in a free society. The nation is, indeed, given to some profound democratic commitments, which have never been officially revoked or abandoned, including (you will recall) a dedication "to the proposition that all men are created equal." The meaning of human equality, or even the reality of it, is a question much debated. Greater controversy exists, however, on the proposition that *equality of opportunity* and *social mobility* are sound operating principles for a society conceived as free, open, and democratic. The question may then be taken in terms of its bearing on these two rather generally accepted principles. Before we can consider the bearing on these principles, we must be clear on the definition of our terms.

What is social class? It is not simply another way of saying amount of wealth. True, in the United States the possession or lack of wealth is more significantly related to social position than in societies where hereditary disposition of such recognition is common. Yet this variable functions quite irregularly. Even among those whom Ferdinand Lundberg labels the superrich, social class is not surely linked to wealth of holdings. The Texas oil millionaires by and large are not distinguishable, say, from the Rockefellers and the Mellons by this variable. Yet in the matter of life style they are readily distinguished. Even more significantly in the general esteem, which is a large element in the determining of social class, the latter are held higher. Their words are taken more seriously in public counsel; their association is held to be more prestigious; their benefactions advertise them as being more socially responsible.

At the other end of the scale, it has been customary, for example, to distinguish between the "deserving" and the "undeserving" poor. The assigning of social class has a large monetary factor, but also an imputation of merit or of quality, most often assigned with little concern or thought about the social conditions that tend to obviate achievement of certain qualities.

In the middle reaches of income, where most Americans reside, social class assignments are particularly tricky. If a man is an exceptionally successful butcher, that is, comes to own a packing plant with subsidiaries in a dozen nations, his success and money alone will place him clearly in the vague reaches of the upper classes. If he then endows a university, sits among its trustees, behaves with public circumspection, he may achieve *social acceptance*, which is quite another matter.

If his butcher's business brings him in say $35,000 a year he may without doubt claim an upper-middle-class income, but this does not assure him or his children upper-middle-class acceptance. He will have, presuming he is white, no particular trouble in moving into the same suburban block with a doctor and a lawyer of approximately the same income bracket. They may speak across back lots, comparing notes on problems with crab grass or swimming pool filters, but he may not be invited to join their clubs or his children ever see the inside of his "neighbors' " recreation rooms. For especially in the broad middle class, social acceptance depends very considerably on the *prestige* of occupations. This is a prestige quite formally scaled in middle-class perceptions.

What shall the school make of this factor, whose complexities have barely been suggested? First, it must examine the essence of the term itself: *social class*. This is a concept as old as recorded history. Only lately has social class been challenged as an organizing principle for society. Ancient societies perceived worldly stratification as the logical basis for social organization even in the afterlife. Therefore, the tombs of the Egyptians and Sumerians were well stocked with the effects of refinement and luxury appropriate to the station of the dead. Yet centuries ago, the prophet Isaiah looked at the fallen Assyrian monarch and perceived with a profoundly radical insight a great existential reality: the equality of man in death. Jesus appeared to teach no awareness of class and status distinctions, except for a few direct and sometimes barbed statements to the "rich." Plato, however, was historically heeded more fully than Isaiah and Jesus in terms of the social structure of the Western world. His *Republic* was formally stratified. It was not an open society, nor was it characterized by equality of opportunity or social mobility.

The premodern Western world was feudal. In feudalism both state and church exerted their institutional weight to maintain a rigidly stratified society, although within the Catholic Church itself was one of the very few ladders of social mobility in the medieval world.

Two great revolutions of the latter eighteenth and early nineteenth centuries, one humanistic, one economic, gave impetus to a general challenge to class society. The Enlightenment spawned the philosophical undergirding of both the American and the French revolutions. "Life, liberty, and the pursuit of happiness" and "liberty, equality, and fraternity" became the rallying cry for millions convinced at least as much by oppressive conditions as by happy phrases of the intolerability of the yoke of the past. Heads rolled, old orders tottered and fell, new institutions were contrived. Yet ancient dispositions and structures persisted.

The role of the Industrial Revolution was more ambiguous with respect to its impact on social class. The nineteenth-century liberals saw the shifting of power from the old landowning titled aristocrats to the new enterprising industrialists as a profound shaking of the foundations of antique status, as indeed it was. They also saw the market as an institution where initiative and productivity would be rewarded with profit, thereby introducing a new dynamism into social structure.

Others saw the Industrial Revolution differently. The immediate effects on the lot of the workers in the new industrial cities were ugly. The factory system, in the view of Karl Marx and others, did change the power structure, but to Marx this was a change that merely pressed down on the mass of men a new serfdom, *wage* slavery. He saw a continuing struggle between owners and workers culminating in a revolution ending in a dictatorship of the proletariat that would lead to a *classless society* and *the withering away of the state*. (Where revolutions in his name have been accomplished in this century, progress toward these two conditions has not, to say the least, been conspicuous.)

In America both the political and industrial revolutions have indeed afforded some reality to the promise of equality of opportunity and social mobility. Nonetheless, in respect to both, accomplishment is considerably flawed.

Of social class, the question must be raised: Is it real or illusory? To the equalitarian, social class is largely an illusion. It presses down on the reality of human structure a false structure that makes things appear as they are not. In the extreme of stratification that is slavery, it sets up the assumption that one aggregate of men exists primarily for the use, convenience, and service of others. It places the burden of drudgery on one group, the dignity of responsibilities on the other. As to rewards, these are altogether nonnegotiable, being utterly dependent on what the slave owner's sense of the matter may be. The system of bondage also implies a basic presumption of inequality. This presumption is generalized and tends to broaden. What is acted out comes to be believed. This is the nature of self-fulfilling prophecies. It may be true of education with respect to its course on social class.

Social class functions, real or illusory. It functions in many cases to affect life styles and aspirations. It alters motivations. It divides people. It diminishes communication. It is real enough in these effects.

It is not, however, a gauge of worth or merit. Social class tells us nothing of morality or ability. To identify a man, or a student, in terms of class gives us no clue as to whether he is cruel or gentle, intelligent or stupid, responsible or careless, honest or a liar and a thief. Class bias may assert that it does, but history and research fail to sustain the assertion.

So what of the school's choice? If the school goes for the first alternative, perceived as adjusting to the reality of social class, it will do such things as these, while seeing them to be realistic:

1. It will assess its student body in terms of social class and tailor its program accordingly. If 80 percent of its student body is substantially middle class, it will stress a strong college preparatory program on the assumption that this is a realistic choice. On the other hand, if 80 percent of the students are from blue-collar workers' homes, it may stress vocational and commercial education. The guidance personnel will stand by to advise students to make "realistic" choices, in terms of keeping their aspirations within the bounds of presumed talent, employment opportunities, and economic means.
2. Among devices that reflect and perpetuate social class in the schools is academic (ability or homogeneous) grouping. On whatever base of selection, this grouping tends to mirror the social class composition of the community. Ability grouping has little research to support the hope that it is an effective device for improving academic achievement. It is, however, an excellent device for making visible the social class structure of the school.

Approaching the question of social class realistically has some bearing on the questions of equality of opportunity and social mobility. If equalizing the chance of getting a job, regardless of job description, is the standard, no doubt some kind of a case may be made for this approach. It tends to assure that students will live within their means, so to speak, as far as aspirations are concerned. In the main, it assures that students will find a place in the scheme of things not far from where their parents dwelt. It would discourage the student from "hitching his wagon to a star" and point out the impracticality of the sentiment that "a man's reach must exceed his grasp."

It is difficult, however, to escape the conclusion that this approach to education stresses primarily vocational consequence. It would also appear that bowing before the presumed reality of social class must tend to perpetuate it. Certainly, when lower-class social status means an almost automatic shunting onto a vocational track, it diminishes the school's function as a ladder of social mobility to a very stumbly stepladder indeed.

The presumed function of the school in a democratic society—*to bring the children of all the people together that they may learn about each other and from each other and get acquainted*—would surely seem to be short-circuited by this approach. Merely going in and out the same big doors together twice a day seems scarcely a profound acting out of this function.

The school that elects the other alternative—*to attempt to diminish the effect and visibility of social class*—will have its work cut out for it. It will in essence assume the obligation that it is to participate in democratizing society in terms that go beyond verbalization.

Its use of social class data, along with all its test scores, will be diagnostic rather than deterministic. Its guidance staff will be disposed to enhance rather than to diminish aspiration. This school will take from the fact of the established social class status of a student no predetermined posture: "You ought (or ought not) to go to college"; "You ought (or ought not) to enter the vocational program."

This school will work to develop a curriculum that keeps options open and enhances motivation. This means, among other things, that tracking will be minimized, the self-fulfilling prophecies of ability grouping will be abolished. No premature ceilings will be imposed on any student's hopes or on the school's hopes for him.

The social life of the school will be broad and inclusive. All clubs, activities, and programs will be continuously scrutinized for elitist tendencies, which if detected will be vigorously discouraged. No activities of the school will be accessible on an ability-to-pay only basis.

In sum, this choice directs that the school itself will endeavor to be democratic. This is realistic; as a school, it can decide to be. This choice does not compel the school to bow before the status structure of the society outside. That society has not anywhere on record asked the school to abdicate from its first responsibility: to develop democratic citizenship. Well, this is a way to do it. The choice makes no optimistic generalizations, or pessimistic ones either, about the world beyond the school. It knows something of the obstacles to equality of opportunity and the limits upon social mobility in that world. It is not sure it can do a great deal to alter conditions, but it is determined not to contribute further to the obstacles and limitations. Within the school, if it so chooses, equality of opportunity can be made real. Within the school, varied degrees of success can be assessed in terms of merit alone. Social mobility within the school can be a functioning reality. *Question*: If the schools of this nation turned their central attention to the second alternative, do you think it would take long for their efforts to make a significant impact on society? We think not. Education might then be able to become a means for achieving better living for all students. This implies a great deal more in today's society than simply education for work; it implies also educating for life in a society that promises a progressively greater proportion of time away from work. This too, should be equally shared.

topics for inquiry

1. Costs of Providing Minimal Nutritional Needs at Today's Prices
2. Compensatory Education in Your Area
3. Hidden Costs of Education in Your District
4. Effects of Malnutrition on Learning Abilities
5. Adult Education Programs in Your Area
6. Contrast of Program Emphases in "Rich" and "Poor" District High Schools
7. Head Start Programs in Your Area
8. Police and Courts' Views of Social Class
9. Educational Programs of Community Agencies
10. Leisure-time Activities of Youth and Adults in Your Area

subjects for discussion

1. The phrase "middle-class values" usually comes up in any discussion about education.
   a. What are these "values"?
   b. Are they more appropriately "behaviors"?
   c. Why are they usually thought of as class related?
2. How might the concept of the self-fulfilling prophecy be applied to the following:
   a. War?
   b. Racial attitudes?
   c. Religious prejudice?
   d. Any others?
3. Assume that the problems of poverty and its consequences, such as hunger, disease, emotional oppression, are to continue unattended by the existing agencies and programs. What then might be the new design for the school if it assumes the official responsibility for the problems? Consider these factors:
   a. Curriculum
   b. Personnel
   c. Physical plant
   d. Financing
   e. Calendar

selected readings

To this list should be added the works cited within the chapter, especially those of the Lynds and Hollingshead. Many of the suggested readings to Chapter 14 would also be useful here.

GLAZER, NONA Y., and CAROL F. CREEDON (eds.). *Children and Poverty.* Chicago: Rand McNally, 1968.
> One of the better collections of writings on poverty as it relates to education. The book scans the topic from the theoretical perspectives of sociology and psychology.

HARRINGTON, MICHAEL. *The Other America.* Baltimore: Penguin, 1963.
> The little book that reportedly shook loose the War on Poverty programs. Its importance is perhaps best seen by the fact that it has been reprinted more than once in almost every year since its publication.

LIPSET, SEYMOUR MARTIN, and REINHARD BENDIX. *Social Mobility in Industrial Society.* Berkeley: University of California Press, 1960.
> An important statement in depth on both the concept and function of social mobility in America. The authors present a comprehensive view that utilizes historical, sociological, and psychological insights.

MILLER, HERMAN P. (ed.). *Poverty American Style.* Belmont, Calif.: Wadsworth, 1968.
> A comprehensive collection of statements on poverty from the perspectives of history, economics, anthropology, sociology, and psychology plus descriptive proposals for solutions.

ORNATI, OSCAR. *Poverty Amid Affluence.* New York: Twentieth Century Fund, 1966.
> Presents some important and detailed data about the parameters of poverty.

REES, HELEN E. *Deprivation and Compensatory Education.* Boston: Houghton Mifflin, 1968.
> A comprehensive description of the educational problems as related to poverty, and especially minority groups. Discusses the major programs that have been developed and presents some evaluation of them.

RIESSMAN, FRANK. *Strategies Against Poverty.* New York: Random House, 1969.
> A collection of short essays with incisive views about many of the misconceptions about social class that must be cleared away if any strategies against poverty are to work.

UNDERHILL, RALPH. *Youth in Poor Neighborhoods.* Chicago: National Opinion Research Center, 1967.
   Well-written scholarly research on the school and social mobility.

WARDEN, SANDRA A. *The Leftouts.* New York: Holt, Rinehart and Winston, 1968.
   A broad survey of much of the relevant literature on the aspects of social class and education that work against a sizable group of children.

14
EDUCATION
AND
THE URBAN
FUTURE

Urban problems, urban crisis, urban blight, urban renewal—the dialogue about the city has apparently become locked into the vocabulary of its pathology. Thought of the city has become almost exclusively problem-centered: crime in the streets, urban education, traffic engineering, flight to the suburbs—the whole "bag." And when we speak of education, too, that is the direction we shall have to go because problems and trouble are very much the names of it, in the cities.

It is a great shame that the dominant perception of the city should have arrived at this state. It spells a sad disenchantment; this vocabulary descriptive of its city today reflects a revulsion against the metropolis. This is very sad indeed, for it must imply a disenchantment with, a revulsion against Western civilization itself. Not that it has gone that far, merely in that direction.

The names that define civilization are the names of cities far more than the names of nations. The nations have to invent and define themselves, build generalizations and legends to sustain them, to cloak themselves in a mystique to provide themselves with meaning, to draw boundaries where none exist, which only the makers of maps and treaties imagine to be real. These maps and boundaries are fluid and fleeting.

The cities are real. They require no myths to give them meaning. Their songs are not grandiose anthems about abstractions vested in boasting chauvinism. No, the songs of the cities are tunes of real stuff—sidewalks, umbrellas, bridges, towers, streets and squares, pretty girls, and urban delights. The cities are very real, very hardy; they endure.

Athens gave most of the luster to the glory that was Greece. That glory has tarnished to disrepute, but Athens persists. The empire of the Hapsburgs is shattered, not that it was ever real, but Vienna is still there, and Budapest, and Bratislava and Prague. Their citizens now rise and salute different banners to band music hailing varied abstractions, but when they sit down to eat and talk in restaurant, rathskellar, and cafe, they dine on the dishes great-great-great grandparents named, and drink the traditional brews and wines, and sing the songs no one stands for or marches to. France—there were few who could tell where France had gone in 1943. Some said that she was in England or in Africa. Only fools and knaves believed she was in Vichy. The greater fools, the invader Huns, believed she was done for. But all the time there was no question at all about Paris. Paris was real; Paris was there. No doubt about it; even the rude aliens who settled there for a while knew where they were. They were not sure of France, thinking in the hallucinatory nationalistic mood that she had become a part of the Greater Reich; yet they could not escape the reality and identity of Paris.

The cities—the big cities, the lesser cities, and the towns—are simply the places where the people are, where most people have found some good reason to be. The basic lure of the city is economic. It is a likelier place to earn a better living, a place where there is more choice, more opportunity. And then, because it is a place where more people are, it turns out to be the place where the action is. All these people drawn to the "city" have many varied tastes and appetites, and they all want to satisfy these. They want the things that make the place they live, this city, a good place to be. So they start the restaurants, build churches and temples, organize clubs, create theaters and museums. The reputation of these draws others, often lively folks with gifts of appreciation and talents to contribute to the creative processes of the city.

Let some of this be remembered when duty recalls to consideration the problem-realities of the city—the pot holes in the streets, the parks unsafe at night, the houses unfit for humans, the schools unsuitable for the nurture of children. Remember that the reason to be concerned for the city is because the city is so important for the people in it, that a blight upon the city is a blight upon civilization itself.

Never doubt the future of the cities. They are eradicable, but only by the deeds that would eradicate humanity. History well records that the cities long outlive empires and nations. The movement into suburbia and exurbia should not be mistaken as an abandoning of the city.

city and suburb

The suburbs are mainly a spillover from the city. Their breadwinners go to and from the city. The suburbs have only a local identity, and that not a very profound one. But the suburb has a profound identity as it is connected with a city. Whoever heard of Evanston, or Ladue, or Englewood, or Mt. Lebanon? These are really very nice places to live, and even to visit if you know someone nice who lives there. However, without attachment to their cities, they have no identity; in fact, they would scarcely be there at all. They only make sense when you learn that, respectively, they are really parts of Chicago, St. Louis, New York City, and Pittsburgh. Can you imagine an Evanston Museum, a Ladue baseball franchise, an Englewood art colony, or a Mt. Lebanon symphony?

Dispersal of industries is taking place, but it has no bearing on the persistence of cities. It creates a few new ones and makes big ones out of little ones. It is a process of urbanization not of de-urbanization. Its main function is to link up the cities and metropolises into vast urban nets. Already it is one large urban sprawl from Portsmouth, New Hampshire to Washington, D.C.; from Milwaukee to Gary, Indiana; from Detroit to Buffalo. Meanwhile, despite spillover, and flight, and dispersal, the cities get bigger.

There is really no escape from it. Modern man, except as he farms, or stays in town or village, or vacations, has no choice but the city. Then it follows, as far as urban problems are concerned, that their solution is *decisive*. Solve or ameliorate them somewhat, and life for modern man gets better; neglect them, let things get worse, and life gets worse, even to the point of being just about unbearable.

The suburb is not to be reviled; neither is the middle class. In respect to education, however, the suburb must cease to live with one basic illusion. The illusion that the suburb can maintain a wall of separation from the city will comfort no longer and may presently become ruinous.

Somehow the schools of the entire metropolitan area must make the concept of the *true city* come alive. At present the schools of the cities and the suburbs represent such distant views of community that they literally educate for divisiveness.

The city's view of the suburb is more than a little tinged with hostility; the suburb's view of the city more than a little infected by fear.

The city knows some of the attitude of the suburb. It knows that the daytime urban worker takes as much from the city as he can, knows that he resists contributing to the support of the city as effectively as he can. The city has some envy of the suburb, and it has resentment too. The city Sunday driver sees the signs on suburban parks, playgrounds, and swimming pools in particular, reading "For Residents of This Community Exclusively," and he knows what they

mean. He knows that beyond such signs are restrictive codes in real
estate and professional practice that are part of the effort to maintain
a wall of separation. He may or may not recall how generous, by
contrast, the city has been with its resources, including its tax-
supported ones, to its weekend visitors. The police in Central Park
are not in the habit of checking visitors' identity cards to assure themselves that they are residents of Manhattan.

The suburb knows the city well. It has free access to it. It dreads
the city in two respects—(1) that it may be forced to support it more
fully and (2) that the city will come to the suburb. The latter is a
peculiar fear, for it is a dread of the very process that created the
suburb. Nevertheless, the fear points up a fact. It was not the city
that migrated to create the suburb; it was class consciousness, ethnocentrism, and racism. Oh, that is not all of it, as we have said before.
Many suburbanites enjoy a two-way relationship with the city, work
hard for metropolitanism, fight hard on the local scene against ex-
clusiveness and racism. These may be idealists, but they are the better realists too.

They are realists because there is no escape from the city. Even
if the cities sink more deeply into the bog of their unsolved problems,
no quarantine is possible, for the suburbs are becoming urban too.
They too have, in most cases, their poor. Their schools are beginning
to bulge at the seams. Somehow the problems of housing, transportation, taxes, sanitation, and racial accommodation have grown into
their communities too. It is not really that there is no escape from
the city, but that no escape from the 1970s is possible.

If this is the central fact, and it appears to be, the division of urban
education from the rest of the educational scene is arbitrary and
senseless. It is at best a temporary expedient for drawing attention
to the particular problems of urban schools. But the problems of
the cities are not everybody's problems just because everybody is connected in some way with the fate of the cities. They are everybody's
problems because they are the unsolved dilemmas of the twentieth
century, and they are coming home to roost everywhere. The sooner
education perceives this reality, the sooner it may begin to contribute
to a solution of those problems.

new perspectives on the historic role of the black american

To move to direct attention to urban education, especially as it relates
to the "inner city," it is necessary to think about *black*. The old realities come into new focus when this concept is brought to attention.

The American of African descent will be referred to in this chapter
as black American, his chosen preferred designation. It represents a
new attitude of conscious pride in distinctiveness, in blackness itself.
"Black is beautiful" is slogan and creed of the ethnic movement to develop and strengthen black identity. The term Negro will be used in

the historical setting now and then when referring to Americans of African lineage at a time and in the context when that seemed to be the preferred respectful designation.

The candid appraisal of the degree of white racism in America by the National Advisory Commission on Civil Disorders in its report (commonly referred to as the Kerner Report) came as a shock to many. Racism, especially in the minds of many well-intentioned white Americans, was something rather regionally limited—a fault of others, in a sense of the "bad guys" who fostered prejudice, discrimination, and segregation because of historic biases, generalized ill will, psychological insecurities, economic vested interests, among other roots and causes. The facts were sound enough, but their applicability was more general than had been assumed. It took a confrontation with reality to make the majority of Americans aware of the evidence that they were living in a society that could be perceived as being profoundly and pervasively racist.

The intellectual aspect of that confrontation will have our first attention. Consider the institution of slavery in our history. No group of immigrants holds a longer claim on the American soil than those whose origins were African. Although the slave trade continued illicitly thereafter, the Constitution specifically banned it effective in 1808. Thus, this immigrant group alone can trace most of its American ancestry back to colonial and early national times, beginning in 1619.

That Constitution itself, along with the preceding Declaration of Independence, which had sonorously proclaimed that "all men are created equal," had been written and endorsed by men, many of whom were themselves slaveholders. Its Bill of Rights, the classic guarantee of the fundamental freedoms in this society, held no assurances of applicability for the black population. Its three-fifths compromise was a rough and ready statistical index of the demeaning attitude toward these people. For purposes of being counted for congressional representation, by processes in which they were unable to participate, five slaves were to be reckoned as three persons. How much a man? "A little better than half a man," this seemed to say. And in very real sense, socially, economically, culturally, psychologically, something like this appraisal has infected the attitude and the functioning of the entire nation toward its black constituency throughout our history.

Furthermore, in a terrible sense, this appraisal bore down hard upon black consciousness. Its insistence in every day and walk of life —on the job, in cautions taught at home, in schools when these became somewhat available, in all the media from minstrel show to the late, late show—gave a heavy weight of instruction in black inferiority, black inadequacy to black people themselves. The fundamental sense of self-esteem, of human worth was so broadly under attack both directly and subtly that deep and widespread psychic damage was done. Not that the slander went unchallenged, not that black men did not have the ego strength to resist and rebel against it. Nat Turner and many other strong men chose, in Camus' phrase, "resistance, rebellion, and death" as an alternative preferable to slavery. Frederick Douglass refused the partial man estimate: "Am I not a man?" he would ask his abolitionist audiences, standing in obvious vindication of self as a fine specimen of human kind. William Du Bois refused half-way houses to full acceptance and esteem. He was an outspoken critic of Booker T. Washington's educational views, seeing the acceptance of a general scheme of vocational and industrial education for Negroes, not as a stepping stone to higher status, but rather as an acceptance of admitted limitations and social and occupational ceilings, a permanent sentence to second-class status.

If American history is reckoned to begin in 1607, then in 1971 American history includes 246 years (1619–1865) of slavery out of 364: for black Americans 246 years of slavery, 106 of second-class citizenship. Chronologically, this furnishes rather convincing evidence of racism at work.

The question is often raised, and sometimes not in overt ill intent but in genuine puzzlement, "Other immigrant groups came in vast numbers, impoverished, exploited, scorned, even slandered—they made their way into the respected community, to all levels of life, including the White House, why not the Negro?"

The fact of the progress of other immigrant groups (as all Americans except Indians have been) is undeniable. The answer to the question is clear: white racism. To be so brief is not necessary. Convincing specifics can be pointed out:

1. Alone of America's ethnic groups the black man came involuntarily.
2. Alone, he spent most of his historical time in the role of slave. This fact deeply conditioned him to be traded, sold, governed, and dominated and it deeply conditioned the mind-set of the entire culture toward him.
3. In the shorter span of history since legal emancipation, the black American has suffered unique disadvantages. Four principal instruments for "making it" in the traditional American sense of achieving middle class status have been effective for all other groups. The Negro was either denied or allowed tardily very limited access to all of these, which are: (a) the labor union, (b) education, (c) the ballot box, (d) capital investment in private enterprise.
4. Alone among the ethnic minorities the black American suffered the extinction of his old-world cultural ties and origins.

Let us consider items 3 and 4. Nineteenth-century industrialism was cruelly exploitative toward labor. Indeed, part of the southern defense of slavery was the claim that the paternalistic concern for the slave gave him a better year-round life and security than that of the "wage-slaves" of New England industry. As far as physical living conditions were concerned the case was at least arguable. However, one important distinction was a reality. The worker in New England was free to try to better his wages and working conditions either by moving or more realistically by organizing to present his demands. This the workers did despite obstacles in the law, in the courts, in the press, and in economic power. Thus they improved their real wages. Immigrant citizens were large in the membership rolls and leadership of the unions. The union movement was unavailable to slaves, and as free men the Negroes found a marked inhospitality in the unions. Today, especially in the trade unions there remains one of the last major obstacles to access by black Americans.

As for education, the slave was kept almost universally unschooled and illiterate. Under legal segregation his schools were separate and unequal in the South. Under de facto segregation, his schools have been separate and unequal in the ghettoes of urban America. The black American has labored under conditions of unequal access, inferior teaching, more crowded classrooms, and a biased curriculum. He has been discouraged at the doors of college and university, and he has found the gates of the professions barred except for the slightest tokenism.

As to suffrage, in the region of his rural suffering, he was effectively deprived of it by the inventive devices of white supremacy and by outright intimidation, coercion, and murder. In the locations of his urban suffering, his ballot was long traded on by political machines who promised much and did nothing. Even possessing the ballot, he was in the city covictim of the historical imbalance of representation of rural areas over the cities with consequent unfair distribution of taxes. The northern cities from New York to Philadelphia to Chicago to St. Louis and points west are tax starved by rural-dominated legislatures. Since northern black Americans are congregated in the cities, they are primary victims of this inequity.

As to free enterprise, while the basis for the great American fortunes was being laid, both through industrial development and the rape of natural resources, the Negro was either in slavery or struggling to emerge from it. Some black Americans have acquired considerable money, but there are no great black American fortunes. Even the free lands of the West were scant resource to the black man. He was not in on the competition for them, and by the time that he had the slightest chance the good lands were all taken. As for business, that takes capital. Capital is represented by accumulated money. To accumulate money, one must inherit it, earn it, or borrow it. Fathers and grandfathers enslaved do not leave impressive estates; doors closed to education and employment do not promote large savings; and banks have historically been chary of loans to black customers.

When the black man was brought to our shores to serve the white master, his familial and cultural roots were all but obliterated. His original languages were lost to him. The European bias of Western civilization against Africa itself, "the dark continent," operated against him. He had no knowledge of the proud achievements, thriving cultures, arts and skills in his lineage. The European immigrants had continuing emotional and cultural supports. They kept in touch with relatives, and talked the old languages at family reunions and lodge meetings if not at home; on special occasions they dressed in old-world costumes. These were a part of remembering who you were and where you came from. There was a past bearable to think upon. These are not the only supports of human identity, but they are helpful. In large degree these props were rudely denied the black American.

These are the realities. And they are stated very modestly within the facts. They show conclusively that the conditions of black Americans have been most specially and uniquely disadvantageous compared with any other group.

the mind of the black community

Of course, things have changed and are changing. The confrontation has done much to make many aware. It is very much a matter first of instructing just how things have been and how they are. The confrontation also is designed to communicate exactly how these things have made the black American feel. He is telling not only his hurt, but his desperation, his anger, even his rage, and his resolve. He is explaining in very clear terms how he feels and why. And the confrontation is attempting to instruct in the reasoning back of the efforts of black Americans to construct anew an ethnic culture, to establish control of their communities, and to create black identity. Above all, the black American is committed to explaining himself, not to being explained.

The black community is not all of one mind on all particulars of its strategies to achieve justice and fundamental equality. This obvious fact should not delude educators about a fundamental reality—the black community is of a *new mind* with respect to its education.

The new mind is convinced that the schools, as much as any institution of society, have been agencies of white racism. The mind of the black community has no significant division on this point. The new mind is strongly committed to community control. The new mind is not divided over the essential quality of providing schools that enhance the identity of black students. It is not altogether united on the degree to which black studies should enter the curriculum, but it is agreed that they are a necessary part of a reconstructed school program. The new mind is not altogether united as to the roles allowable to white educators in teaching black children; it is not divided in its primary confidence that black educators are the most trustworthy custodians of the black students' destinies.

The black community is not of one mind on the possibility or even the desirability of integration as a basic social goal. Among the black nationalists, ethnocentrism goes the full route of apparently seeking a voluntary apartheid. This is the cultural counterpart of extreme white racism.

Though not committed to this extreme view, the new mind of the black community is much less interested in integration as an articulated goal than it is in achieving the specifics of justice and equality. It has much less confidence in waiting around for liberal whites to achieve integration for black people, and by integration to achieve these particulars. The new mind of black America is simply disillusioned with the pace and commitment of white America in providing full access to the American Dream. The conspiratorial murder of the last black leader to enunciate a trust in that dream, Dr. Martin Luther King, Jr., had much to do with this disillusionment. So the new mind is intent on *separation*, not necessarily in abandonment of the good hope of integration as an eventual goal.

Separatism, therefore, can be read as a new priority. It can be, but need not be, an abandonment of the integrationist goal. That issue is in abeyance and is in some dispute.

The separationist says basically that the black community must achieve justice and equality for itself. It must achieve power. It must control its own institutions. It must make good schools for its own. It must have jobs and money and influence. The separationist looks at the scene and says of integration, "What integration?"

Although the issue is not decided, it is important to note that separationism is not *necessarily* in conflict with a vision of an integrated society. The new mind of the black community points with accurate history to the course taken by other ethnic groups to give themselves self-confidence and a control of their affairs. By devices of separation they achieved the status from which they were accorded the esteem on the basis of which they were more fully integrated into the general institutional framework.

To the idealistic white integrationist, the black separationist may say (if he thinks the conversation worth his time), "OK, do your thing, but don't do it on me. You work on the white community. Get it ready for integration, if you think you can. I am tired of all this talk and no action. I am going to work for justice and equality for my people. Integration? You can't eat it."

If the new mind, whatever its divisions and range of feelings, seems to speak of deep racial divisions even of a tragic order in American life; well, you read it right. It does so speak—and there are these divisions. No amount of fine talk and pious hopes can unwrite American history. The last decade of the 1960s is with us from now on; it was a time of terrible trouble. The basic question is whether we have learned anything from it, and even more, whether we have learned the right things from it. The lessons have been in history for a long time, but many "old minds" have refused to read that history straight. History tells that tyranny means trouble and that when justice and equality are long denied to any, all will suffer from the results of that deprivation. History speaks very loudly these days, still some—stone deaf with bias and delusion—do not hear.

cultural deprivation

The very term "cultural deprivation" has been used as a weapon of implicit racism. Applied indiscriminately to masses of children from another culture, it represents, at very least, a very naïve anthropological notion. Black educators, stung by the patronizing implications of the phrase, contend that other segments of the society are explicitly culturally deprived. The point is well taken. If the phrase *cultural deprivation* is to have utility and good repute, it must be gauged by criteria constituting a common measure. It must not be an elastic yardstick, which measures long for some and short for others.

Cultural deprivation does exist. The tenacity of localism and provincialism is quite incredible. Modern man can watch an astronaut take a moonwalk; he can board a plane in Pittsburgh and arrive (by the clock) in Chicago ten minutes before he departed. The same citizen can shut off the thought of any connection between his existence and the trouble in the ghetto, a few miles and a few minutes away.

The only proper label for the inability of any citizen of the 1970s to perceive the universal and complete interdependence of humanity is *cultural deprivation*. It is very important that education penetrate the areas of cultural deprivation. To do so it must identify the primary elements of true cultural deprivation:

1. The inability to perceive the fundamental equality of man.
2. A disposition to analyze social problems in terms of their symptoms rather than their causes.
3. Unawareness of community.

The inability to perceive the fundamental equality of man is cultural deprivation of the worst order. In fact, it is not merely deprivation, for that implies simply lack of exposure to the evidence or to the facts. Inability to perceive basic human equality also amounts to a form of cultural brain damage. It means that the impressions of reality are refracted and distorted by the lenses of perception ground strangely to the curves and connections of elitist theories, of notions of ethnic and racial supremacies, of self-preferential ideas of individual differences. Cultural brain damage comes from being subjected overlong to nonsense being taught as sense. Long centuries of feudal and aristocratic teaching have "overtaught" their lessons of the fitness of hierarchical social arrangements, structures in which it is deemed fit that human persons should "know their place." The school systems that nineteenth-century nationalism built persist into the late twentieth century in inflicting this cultural brain damage. Just as all nations teach the same arithmetic, which is good sense, they also teach the same nonsense, whose universal lessons are two: (1) our nation has a peculiar excellence and its people are of a very special quality; (2) other nations are endowed with inferior institutions and ideas, and their people, except as they acknowledge the superiority of *our* way of life, are full of dangerous ideas.

The taught nonsense is only sometimes nationalistic; it is also often regional, provincial, localistic, tribal, denominational, and familial.

Cultural deprivation in its less devastating form merely derives from inexperience or illiteracy. The failure to perceive human equality can derive from being cut off from the spiritual roots of Western civilization. It can simply mean being alienated from the great Judaic-Christian heritage. Isaiah, pondering over the corpse of the fallen Assyrian monarch, saw in the leveling consequence of death the fundamental reality of equality. Jesus equated a deed to "the least of one of these" with an act toward the divine presence in man. Surely the saddest form of cultural deprivation is to be alienated from the spiritual genius of the Western world, which so deeply affirms the universal principles of human worth, of human dignity, of the equality and brotherhood of man.

The deprivation is also historical. It leaves the person unaware of the fact that most of the damage to humanity has been done under the delusions of special superiorities. The fact that progress in societal terms is only measurable in terms of gains toward equality is denied by historical illiteracy.

In contemporary terms, cultural deprivation is also marked by *a disposition to analyze social problems in terms of their symptoms rather than their causes.* For example, "student unrest" (an easy euphemism for the pervasive discontent among youth) is often perceived as a form of adolescent restlessness to be outgrown or to be suppressed by "cracking down on youth."

Simplistic concepts of law and order derive from the same disposition. At worst, the simplistic impatience to get at the symptoms is marked by a barbaric antihistoricalism. It willingly hastens to suspend the bill of rights and hard-won constitutional guarantees of personal liberties on the ignorant presumption that the primary purpose of these guarantees is to protect the criminal, when, in fact, they constitute the primary safeguards to a decent social order.

The simple-minded pursuit of law and order would extend the police power and increase the capacity of the state to incarcerate, even to jail preventively—as though to suspend civil rights were a prime device of crime prevention. Such a pursuit is doomed to defeat by its basic conceptual error: to attack the symptom rather than its cause. It is generous in budgeting for the pursuit of criminals, niggardly in its appropriations for crime prevention. A society that plays this game can never win. Its ultimate achievement is to become one vast concentration camp. Crime is the adversary, not the criminal.

To dry up the nurture and sources of criminality is the real job.

(Since the simplistic would be sure by now to raise the accusation, this is *not* an admonition to cease enforcing the laws, *not* a persuasion to cease tracking down murderers, bank robbers, rapists, and kidnappers. It is *not* an invitation to leave keys in parked cars or to fail to lock bank vaults and house doors at night. Such implications could be read into the context only by the simplistic; but since they are sure to be raised, they must be disclaimed.)

The vast increase of crime is outrunning law enforcement and overcrowding the capacities of the courts and jails. It is a symptom of unsolved social problems and of a vast alienation. The social problems are known, and they have often been enumerated. *Alienation* is the psychological aspect. Nobody can talk fundamental sense on law and order who cannot draw upon such sources as Marx, Dostoyevsky, Kafka, Durkheim, Freud, Fromm, Horney, Brecht, merely to suggest a few.

The failure to understand that profound problems must have a profound diagnosis is a common brand of *cultural deprivation*. This suggests a much more serious approach to the question of cultural deprivation than the curriculum ordinarily affords.

A third element of cultural deprivation is *unawareness of community*. Since only a few spiritual geniuses have been able to achieve a divine perspective, perhaps the school might be content to endow its students with an astronaut's point of view. Even to whip around the earth several times in the course of a day gives a lively sense of its finite character. Its oceans are traversed in minutes; its continents appear as entities; the political subdivisions are unapparent; the ecological unity is obvious. When a few men arrive at the moon, the nearest outpost in space, the earth in the new perspective looms as no more than a tennis ball in the sky. These men know better than most men where home really is. It is the earth; that is the source of all that sustains them. Even on the surface of the moon, the oxygen they breathe is borrowed from the hospitable environment of the earth, the only known fit abode for man. From that perspective, the target for return is simply earth, good old earth.

This lends added meaning to Hannah Arendt's phrase, "earth-home." Understanding this, who would befoul the environs of his home, dissipate its treasures, create contention among its members, engage in fratricide? If nothing else were learned from space adventures, man at very least might learn to appreciate his domicile.

The American nation needs also a perspective on itself that both comprehends and transcends its history. Much of its meaning lies in its use as a place of refuge, an escape from tyrannies applied and opportunities denied. Its history did truly give many men "a new birth of freedom." To comprehend America's history is to give this reality a dominant place in the perception of the nation.

Such perception provides the springboard to a transcendent view of the nation. This refuge attracted the restless and the abused from many lands; it also brought some unwillingly to its shores and lured others by guile. These people came to escape some things, but they brought their histories with them. They brought cultures, religions, prejudices, and well-remembered suspicions and grievances and hatreds. At a minimum, they brought their differences.

Yet now they share a common land and a common fate. And still they do not know one another very well. They sit in throngs side by side in stadiums across the land; at night, before their television sets they watch the same stuff in the company of millions. But if they knew the names of the persons sitting beside them at the ball game, they might be excited to vague apprehensions or very real suspicions: O'Toole, Chamberlain, Winowski, Goldberg, Schmidt, Lebois, Ivanovitch, Jones—some of these names are sometimes cues to antipathies among some of the others.

The American needs to study the essence of the many subcultures that constitute his nation. It is not enough to know Catholic, Protestant, and Jew. These are the labels for easy stereotyping. So are black, white, yellow, and red. The American needs to study *American complexity in its complexity*. What are the beliefs and customs of others? What are their relations with other subcultures? What fears do they hold, and where do they come from? How do the large labels break down within? What is the range, for example, of Catholic thought? What is the variety of Protestant denominationalism? How does Judaism vary in its orthodox, its conservative, and its reformed dimensions? What is the range in the white view of black and the black view of white?

All this suggests that a proper study for Americans is the *cultures* of America. It does not say that that is all the American need study, but it does prescribe a *must*. From a rich and varied intercultural study in depth, an awareness may begin to be derived that will furnish a cement to the mosaic of cultural pluralism. We shall call this a *transcendent Americanism*. This awareness takes nothing from the person's devotion to his faith, his origins, his family. Such awareness allows him to enter somewhat into the lives, beliefs, and aspirations of all the others. It translates "those" and "them" into "us"; it changes "their" into "our." It is the "I-Thou" relationship of which Martin Buber spoke, a transcendent view of interpersonal relations, put to work on a larger scale. Abraham Lincoln, John F. Kennedy, Louis Brandeis, Martin Luther King—they readily symbolize a transcendent view of Americans of varied origins and cultures who belong to all. The transcendent American is aware of as much of the American scene as he can comprehend, and takes it all to his heart.

Without this awareness and the capacity to transcend, he is culturally deprived.

to study justice

To suffer injustice is one of the more cruel forms of cultural deprivation. Therefore, if the school is to attack cultural deprivation, it must
study justice. The school must study justice that is not ordinarily
arrived at by hunch or intuition or impulse. In the main, a study of
justice should be a study of procedures that deep historical experience
have shown to diminish the chance of injustice being done to persons.

The school is a human institution in which people reside together,
which implies patterns of rules, regulations, and enforcements. There
is no question of the necessity for these patterns. The question is
whether the society within the school is just or unjust. It is not an
abstract or simply philosophical question. "What is justice?" remains
a question worthy of philosophical pondering, to be sure. But our
society has worked out a number of binding matter-of-fact propositions to govern the legal administration of justice. They are rooted
in the common law and the constitutional system. Among the rules
governing our society are these:

1. The presumption of innocence; a person is held to be innocent until proved guilty.
2. The right of the accused to face his accusers; anonymous accusations are not to be credited.
3. The right of the accused to be represented and to prepare a defense.
4. The banning of "star chamber proceedings," where the accused is
   tried behind locked doors with no representative in his behalf to
   defend or to overhear the proceeding.
5. No cruel or unusual punishments.
6. No person may be forced to testify against himself.
7. No deprivation of property without due process of law.
8. Every person shall be informed of his rights.

Furthermore, the totalitarian regimes have helped to define, by
common practice the procedures that democracies have learned to
hold repugnant:

1. Punishing or penalizing persons for expressing views contrary to
   those enunciated by authority.
2. The use of mass punishments when guilt cannot be ascertained on
   a personal basis.
3. Proceedings where prosecution, judgment, and punishment are
   all rested in one authority.

By and large, justice is not a central study of the school. As studied
by teachers and administrators, justice is law and has to do with
attendance requirements, length of school year, tax formulas, teacher

liability, school responsibility for student safety, and other institutional matters. Thus, not being an object of direct study, justice is not a notable pervasive quality of the typical school. Where justice is not a pervasive discipline, injustice is common. This is very true of the school. In fact, the school day is so replete with innumerable petty unfairnesses, which bespeak ignorance of justice, that no school could begin to catalog them.

Injustice is not to be defended; and within the school a multitude of little injustices abound. However, that is not the worst of the matter. Actually, the children being pretty resilient can stand a lot of injustice. The school does not execute hostages, put students on the rack, or conduct public hangings.

The worst consequence of the school's failure to study justice is that it fails, therefore, to instruct in justice. The student develops no expectations, therefore, that justice is supposed to be a normal discipline operating within society. This consideration is beyond the legislative aspect of rules and regulations. Earlier comments have indicated the relevance of a political science that involves persons in the making of rules that bind them. It has even been urged that serious thought be given to the effective sense of the codes that the school enacts and attempts to maintain. But this discussion accepts the legislative acts and concentrates on the procedures of how they are enforced upon the individual. This is a study of justice in the school.

Rather naïve assumptions often underlie the general intent of school officials to run a decent institution. Three in particular are almost universal. (1) We are "goodwilled" toward the children; we are nice people. (2) Whatever is best for the institution will be best for its members. (3) The discipline of the school must be maintained, by whatever measures are necessary. These are quite dangerous assumptions. Whatever degree of fairness in human dealing takes place in an institution governed by such assumptions is likely to be dependent solely on the human decency and goodwill among the officials. Is that not enough? Far from it. No evidence shows that people themselves are better or worse in totalitarian regimes than in constitutionally governed ones. Good procedures, not good people, assure justice. The first naïve assumption is typical of benevolent dictatorships and ordinary paternalism. The other two are standard authoritarian doctrines: the individual exists for the institution and the end justifies the means.

A survey of common school and classroom practice will recall to mind how prevalent are the infractions against basic principles of justice and how consistent the punishment. For example:

1. A teacher fails to identify the culprit who threw an eraser or put a stink bomb in a wastebasket. Her procedures included:

a. A few trial accusations against her favorite targets: *a presumption of guilt directed to the purpose of obtaining a confession.*

b. A directive to the class to leave slips of paper after class with the names of the culprits on them: *an invitation to be an anonymous accuser and an expression of willingness to credit such testimony.*

c. These failing, the imposition of an extra assignment on the whole class, or detention after school of all the children, "until somebody confesses or tells who did it," *the standard gestapo mass punishment gambit.*

2. A teacher deprives a student of an earned property, say an "A" in a course, because in her judgment, he underachieved (did not work hard enough in getting it) or because his conduct was bad; or a teacher of English prevents a student from assuming his earned place on the basketball varsity because of her inability to get him to achieve well in his subject. *Are these procedures not indicative of flouting basic principles of due process?*

3. The school finds missing school property in a student's locker. The student is taken into the principal's office, together with his homeroom teacher and the custodian. They tell him that he has stolen school property, and hold him under questioning for two hours. His failure to admit guilt is met by a threat to call in juvenile authorities. The whole thrust of the two hours "in star chamber" is based on an assumption of his guilt and an attempt to convince him that a confession will be to his advantage. (The *injustice* in this type of proceeding is *exactly the same* if the student were *guilty,* as if he were *innocent.*)

the school of the inner city

So . . . to the point where the problems of modern America come educationally into their sharpest focus—the schools of the inner city. The key to the situation is that the *school of the inner city expects to fail and lives up to its expectation.* The children have an expectation and a knowledge; they expect to fail and they know they are expected to fail. This is a hard combination to beat.

Nevertheless, sometimes the children do beat it. In that case the student has something special going for him. It may be a parent or parents who support him, drive him, push him, and reward him in what resembles a typical middle-class way. Or this student may have a special talent in music, or art, or athletics that is exploitable capital for the school. Such talents can change potential dropouts to favorite sons and daughters of academia.

In the main, however, self-fulfilling prophecies, as you have seen, get fulfilled.

Somehow the child of the inner city, who is so often a black child, must get a decent self-image. The new black leadership has become convinced that this will come only from the black community. The beginning of re-creation of identity is the accepting of blackness with pride. Thus, *black is beautiful*. The re-created view asserts an identity and a separateness of culture: black culture. It puts its arts, its songs, its dances, its literature at the center of its own culture. The meaning of its culture is self-fulfillment and cultural identification; it is its own end. The black American no longer sings and dances to win the favor and largesse of *the man*, the masterful white man.

The black American then comes on hard. He asserts things that the school finds hard to hear. "Urban education is black education." "White teachers can't teach black students." "The school practices genocide against black children." "The entire curriculum must be made black relevant." "Integration is a fraud; the black community must be separate."

Never mind that not all black people support all these contentions. Never mind that some of the assertions are confident overgeneralizations. It is, nonetheless, a significant rhetoric. It has passion and conviction to sustain it, as well as a lot of evidence. In fact, an eagerness to deny the evidence that supports this rhetoric may itself be an evidence of the pervasive white racism.

It is exasperating for white parents and teachers to hear urban education claimed as a black domain. But the claim is an appeal to the forgotten evidence. In many inner cities most of the students are black. The problems reside most heavily in the schools accommodating the black students. The black community has no viable educational alternative to the city public school. In many real senses, urban education *is* black education.

Many black spokesmen speak conviction when they say "White teachers can't teach black children." They have seen enough abuse of children by racially biased teachers to think so. It is patently true that teachers can scarcely perform as true teachers among students whom they fear, distrust, or perceive as unlikely learners. It is obvious that in the American culture these attitudes are often a function of racist bias. Furthermore, teachers are not usually very effective in working in another culture until they have learned many things, including respect for it, about the culture from which the student comes. The nonresident white teacher in the black community is not the likeliest candidate to be a real teacher. Suppose he is not so much racist as unknowing. How well will he function if he perceives every dimension of *cultural difference* as *cultural deprivation*? What can the white teacher do to make this general indictment untrue at least with respect to himself? These things at least:

1. He can seek for awareness of vestigial racist attitudes and postures in himself, and with awareness prepare to end them.
2. He can begin his homework: the study of black history, black literature, black culture.
3. He can begin his fieldwork: the observation of the realities of the black community, the listening to its voices, the learning of the identity of its artists and its folk heroes.
4. He can learn the language. If one is to learn by listening, it is only the most absurd of schoolteacherish postures to insist that others learn your tongue in order that they may instruct you.

When certain conditions are met, then certain adjectives become irrelevant. *Teachers càn teach children.* Meanwhile, for black children the track record indicates that the conditions often have not been met. Then black teachers, who may not be perfect teachers, but have a much better likelihood of knowing *black*, seem to offer the much better prospect. The sentence "White teachers can't teach black children" sounds like a weapon. Sometimes it may be. Yet Rhody McCoy of Ocean Hill–Brownsville, in Brooklyn, New York, did retain more white teachers than he sought to have transferred. In the main, it would seem that the best response the urban schools might make to rhetorical overstatement would be to diminish the evidences that make the overstatements so nearly true.

obstacles to improvement

Though the schools have often created failure by default, they do not need to persist in it. They have misnamed cultural difference as cultural deprivation; they have been laggard in attacking the real cultural deprivation. The prospect for urban education need not be hopeless, for a good deal is known that has bearing on improving urban education. The previous chapters, for example, contain much that would improve not only urban education, but all education. The problem is that *too little* of what is known has been brought to bear upon the problem. Numerous factors already established plus others share the responsibility. Certain of these stand out for their adverse affect on education. In the remainder of this section we shall examine them.

flight of the middle class from the urban schools

We have already noted in some detail the exodus to the suburbs. A large percentage of the middle class who have moved out of the city give as their prime reason the desire to have their children attend the "better" suburban schools. The reputation of a suburb's school system is often the determining factor in the purchase of a house. Frequently, too, the racial composition is important. Those of the middle class who elect to remain in the city in growing numbers figure the cost of sending their children to private school as the price that they pay for having the conveniences and advantages of the city at their doorsteps.

tax bind of the cities

The cities lack sufficient monies adequately to run their plants and provide the necessary services. Thus, all services suffer, including the schools. The monies collected in taxes in the cities that go to the state treasury are not reapportioned to the urban areas equitably. The cities do not receive a fair share of the state's income because of rural control of state legislatures, archaic tax systems, and a failure to develop a metropolitan political science that incorporates all of the population aggregate that constitutes the *true city* so that it may identify its real problems and mobilize all its resources to meet them.

institutional mindedness of the administration of urban schools

The leadership of urban schools attends to the system in institutional rather than educational terms. This fact is a central obstacle to improvement of the schools, for it makes doubtful whether a great new access of funds would significantly improve the schools. Without "educational-mindedness," increased support can easily mean running the same mediocre, and bad, schools more expensively. It is simply not true that money solves educational problems. Intelligence solves problems; money then makes it possible to put the solutions to work.

emphasis of teacher power

Understandably in view of the past, teacher power has been directed toward getting better material rewards and institutional status for teachers. Teacher power has as yet been only marginally directed toward improved professionalization. Solidarity is a means often mistaken for an end by organizations. The teaching profession, if such it be, needs to exert its power toward drastic improvement of curriculum and teaching practice. It needs to concern itself directly with getting incompetence out of the classroom. Actually, its drive for such goals is barely discernible. It is altogether possible that teacher power may become institutional rather than intellectual and educational. The consequence of this would be to render it sophisticated and aggressive in seeking its status and salary goals and, at the same time, conservative and standpattish with respect to curriculum, defensive and formalistic with respect to instructional practice.

racism and damaging social class assumptions

Neglect and abuse of children must be the end result of racism and damaging social class assumptions. Easy devices are invented for

getting the responsibility for educational failure off the back of the
school, where it surely belongs. The school speaks of uneducability,
cultural deprivation, socioeconomic factors in terms of an alibi rather
than of diagnosis.

inattention to curriculum change

Curriculum change often parades itself as deep involvement in curriculum development. On examination, much so-called curriculum development turns out to be concerned with everything but curriculum:
revision of courses of study (old wine in new bottles); devices of
scheduling, modular and otherwise; new instruments of instruction;
new arrangements of teachers; new testing programs. Such innovations may deserve serious experimental attention, but they are only
marginally connected with curriculum; these matters are not the stuff
of curriculum.

Curriculum is what is taught. A better way to say it is curriculum
is the substance of the experience to which learning is invited and directed. The summary that follows does not wrap it all up, of course,
but you can take these four points as a reliable check list as to whether
any real action is taking place with respect to curriculum change.

1. Is there a drastic meddling with "subject-matter integrity," thus
scrapping the antique notion of academic disciplines? If so, you begin to see new functional content arrangements, mergers, and partner-
ships (or in educational terms—core curricula, common learnings, integrated courses). History, literature, and the arts tend to merge into
"civilization" courses and area studies. World history incorporates
the methods and findings of the social sciences and becomes "world
cultures." Subjects for inquiry furnish the names of studies: conservation, atomic energy, population, for example. Such subjects are
nobody's academic property; they name broad human problems. To
study them well demands an incorporation of knowledge from many
sources: history, political science, biology, physics, chemistry, economics, sociology, diplomacy, literature, photography, drama—to name
a few.

2. Does the curriculum include more than just a passing reference
to the last two decades and the contemporary scene? This does not
imply, nor has it been the contention of this book, that this is all of
it. It does say that if you do not find the seventies, or even the sixties,
let alone the twentieth century, getting a large and central play in the
curriculum, *you have a dead school*. That is what it says.

3. Are controversial issues an integral part of the learning situation? This, as was established earlier, simply relates the curriculum
to reality. Fundamentally, education is rooted in one great controversy, the controversy as to which shall decide man's fate—enlightenment or ignorance. Thus, because ignorance has many voices, the

school that shuns controversy refuses to educate. This does not say that everything worth teaching excites controversy—not quite. It does say that if you do not find day by day all over the school classrooms alive to issues, vibrant with controversy, *you have a dead school.* It does say that.

4. Are voices of objection raised to what the school teaches? Are they allowed to be heard? This simply proves that the school is performing educationally. Education challenges ignorance, which is excitable. And education also seeks its evidences on behalf of humanity. The corrupt, the manipulators, the exploiters, the vested interests, the deluders, the fanatic, the extremists, the prejudiced—all these have special reasons for wanting the evidences hid, for not allowing the voices of dissent to articulate their views, for preferring that the school direct its study to the not too recently dead persons and issues. These are not the majority, but the *dead school* serves them well. If the voices of objection are raised, it is an encouraging sign. Then the schools are educating, and they are serving the community well. They are becoming a good place to send the children, for they are taking humanity and man's fate seriously.

the private school alternative

Severe problems cry for solutions. Not all responses to need are constructive; sincere men may utter false prophecies. Desperate situations invite despair, but despair solves no problems. The literature of critical discontent with American education these days is pregnant with antipathy toward the public school. From the New Left and the Old Right a coalition of strange bedfellows urges an active extension of the private school alternative. This is too bad, for if the American school system is ever distracted from its main course, which is to provide education for all the children of all the people at public expense, the best hopes of American civilization will go down the drain.

In the main, the American school system is comprised of public education. There is no intention to minimize the contribution of or to contend with the extensive Roman Catholic school system. It is an established part of the American school system carrying about ten percent of the total burden, sharing many educational purposes with the public school, and adding to its curriculum special aspects of instruction in denominational faith.

The public and the parochial school have worked out a more or less harmonious working partnership. Issues, of course, exist. They are primarily with respect to varied views on separation of church and state and issues relating to assorted questions of public support. Except when a specific issue momentarily flares up, an increasing concord between public and parochial school has characterized American educational history since the Oregon decision of the mid-1920s.

Students transfer from one to the other without undue prejudice. Teachers are trained in the same or in similar institutions. Educational leaders attend many of the same conferences, and teachers read the same or similar journals. Athletic teams schedule one another and compete in the same tournaments. The election of John F. Kennedy to the presidency in 1960 symbolized the advance of accord on the national level.

Furthermore, public and parochial school share together the big job of educating the whole public in an undismayed confidence that it can be done. Most educational problems are encountered in common —social class range, cultural variations, student motivation, institutional depersonalization, antiintellectualism, inadequate buildings, mortal limitations, budgets. Both possess the good and the bad in ample measure.

The private school alternative runs a gamut from social class escapism to evangelical utopianism. The old-line private school was rooted in social class snobbery. Its patronage was largely by those who could afford to pay for special privilege or held to the fearful conviction that their children were somehow too precious and frangible to be subjected to the contamination of contact with the common herd. These schools, in the aggregate, were inconsequential on the scene, enrolling only about 1 percent of the American student body. They had one primary asset: nobody took them seriously except those who attended them.

The old motivations, both entrepreneurial and social, that supported the private schools, have been enhanced by the Supreme Court decision of 1954 seeking to end racially segregated schools and the decision of 1969 that puts teeth to it. Wherever desegration advances significantly, a new rash of private schools breaks out. Often the purpose is simple: to provide a refuge of bias for those who just do not want their children to go to school with black students. Ordinarily, this motivation is advertised plainly and flagrantly. Occasionally, it is camouflaged by admission of a few "middle-class" blacks, preferably of foreign birth, on a token basis. In some affluent districts, where race may not be the issue, private schools have also shown some increase in enrollment. In particular instances the motivation may be a dissatisfaction with the public schools, but more often it seems to come from elitist attitudes about education.

However, a new source of support for the private school alternative has appeared on the scene. Its proponents are best to be characterized as *the deluded high-minded.* They are profoundly aware of and articulate with respect to all the sorry consequences of bureaucratization and institutionalism and depersonalization of the school system. With respect to these, they are no more aware or no more articulate than many authorities, but they have lost faith, and are wallowing in their despair among self-defeating alternatives.

Moreover, they are terribly vulnerable to corruption. The original hippie enclaves in Greenwich Village in New York and Haight-Ashbury in San Francisco were for a little time refuges for the considerably pure in heart. Droves of innocents, the "flower-people," congregated to do their thing, to dissociate from the ugliness of striving and contention, to speak of love and peace. But the opportunists and exploiters moved in. The wolves descended on the lambs. Entrepreneurs moved in to sell costumes and souvenirs, to establish tourist traps. The original innocents were corrupted or victimized, or forced to flee.

A parallel can be drawn for the new innocents waving the banners of the new private school alternative. They are initially the idealists, enthralled with A. S. Neill and Paul Goodman, sick at heart at the callousness of the system and the big school. They set up shop in store-front schools, warehouses, and church basements. That they move into a vacuum in some respects is the sad, undeniable truth; but that they join in an escapist thrust is likewise true.

The opportunists, the cultists, and the entrepreneurs have moved in on them. Among the cultists are the anarchists. The anarchist can see (no one more clearly) the defects and the human wastage of "the system." *But the anarchist is not the democrat.* The democrat can see as clearly, but he knows better alternatives to running or to destroying. He knows how to rebuild. These little ventures trading on disillusion and escapism attract the charlatan, the amateur, and the entrepreneur.

The protagonists of the new educational privatism do argue a plausible case. The school system will benefit from *competition* (a new word in the mouths of these reformers), and these schools can experimentally show the way to broad reform.

Examine this contention. Competition is at work in the schools. Formalism competes with progressivism; mechanization competes with humanization; bureaucratization competes with personalization. These take place where the action is: within the system. And that is where the action will be won or lost. Competition takes place from classroom to classroom, from school to school, between parochial and public models, in the minds of the public. The alternative of the new "experimental" private school distracts from the true competition. It spells retreat, not combat.

As for experimental practice, they set out to demonstrate what is already known. The things they build on need no proof—that children neglected can be restored by attention, that better learning takes place in small classes, that the person gains no self-esteem from residing in great edifices, that the student must be known as an individual and so set to learn, that informality and communication go hand in hand, that students and teachers must share a part of life together, that the school must be part of the community, and knowing of it, that human concern is the big "medicine."

The private school delusion can be a tragic mistake—not because the good is bought expensively in them, or that the quality sought is often elusive and usually transient. The tragedy lies in diverting good energies and civic interest from the battle that must be won: the battle to turn the American school into an educational institution. The competition against that goal is adequate. What is needed is known. The big job, which needs an undiverted energy to achieve, is to realize four goals for the schools of the public:

1. To educate the public so that it is aware of what good education is all about.
2. To get the schools closer to the people and the decision-making power closer to the communities.
3. To professionalize education so that the schools will be conducted by persons, a new breed if you will, who really know what they are doing.
4. To place the student at the center of a profound educational concern for his own sake; to rescue the schools from institutionalization and to restore them to human learning.

To achieve these goals is no easy matter. Let us consider speculatively what could be done to create a lively school that would put new life into the system. It will take the major American school— the public school—to do it. The children are being short-changed; they are getting a poorer education than we know how to give and those in the cities are getting the worst of the system. We agree with the high-minded that the children do deserve a full measure of devotion and human concern, but they deserve a setting for it and a resource far better than a store front, warehouse, or church basement.

toward a good urban school

This book has invested much thought and space to an analysis of forces and factors that stand in the way of having good schools. Do not let that obscure the fact that good schools *do exist*. The characteristics of good schools are known; good schools are well within the reach of man.

The good urban school described here is a composite of going practices, used here and there, which are research-vindicated. It is not a perfect school, just a very good one. The model is set forth as an elementary school, partly because that is the most neglected dimension in most cities, but even more because it is the most crucial aspect of the learning continuum. To be stressed is that it is a school accessible to *all* children.

The cost factor is not ignored—neither is it worried about. The principal factor in this good school is the *soundness* of *educational practice* exercised within it, not the money lavished upon it. We do not intend to argue the historically proved point that good schools are excellent investments. *Only bad schools are costly.* Any *one* of three alternatives will handily cover whatever added costs of good schools are involved:

1. The channeling of all present and potential federal and foundation funds into the central areas of educational needs. This means moving away from grandiose projects that are public-relations-oriented, and all the waste and exploitation and amateurish careerism that *projectitis* spells. These funds will then be available to get at the essence of education. The question remains: Will they produce better schools or only a plentiful supply of glossy, well-illustrated reports of marginal successes?

2. Or, the acceptance of a broader concept of societal bookkeeping. This means the acceptance of the fact that the costs of failing to educate well far exceed the costs of good schools. This is practical sense, which some who regard themselves as "hard-headed realists" scoff at. Good schools have no dropouts; they develop productive citizens. They do not produce social charges.

3. Or, develop an improved set of municipal priorities. This means that spending what is already spent more sensibly would also pay the added costs of good schools. Pittsburgh, for example, has built a new stadium for the advantage of professional baseball and football. Even granting the obvious cultural necessity of such civic adornments, is it an evidence of an advanced state of civilization which puts the building of stadia ahead of schools for its children?

Any one of the above would foot the bill for the good school that can be created. Sound economics are involved. Charge up to the account of bad education a good part of the costs of crime and delinquency, the maintenance of institutions of detention and punishment, the mental health programs for the alienated and despairing, the unemployment and welfare rolls, drug addiction, and the loss of taxes from those who take but do not have the capacity to earn. Do this, and the economy of creating good schools will be self-evident.

Even if good schools were expensive, would not wisdom and love of children dictate their creation? Our affluent culture indulges itself richly in luxury. Its tourists' dollars provide major items in the budgets of many nations. Good schools are no luxury, but if they were, who could deny that America—which lavishes so much that is junk upon its children—can well and easily afford them? The more imponderable factor is whether those who have the fate of the schools in their hands—the boards, the administrators, and the teachers—can put it together, can conduct the good schools that available evidence and research demonstrate to be possible.

The good school would be a relatively small unit housing a student body from K through 5 (which accepts the going logic of the 6 through 8 middle school). Each unit would attempt to accommodate no more than 300 to 500 students.

The classroom would be self-contained, but not in a walled-off or defensive sense. Twenty students would be the maximum for the learning group. Each group would work with two adults—a teacher and a well-trained, well-selected paraprofessional. Flexible and adaptable structures and free time for cooperative planning would invite and encourage unstructured *teaming* among professional peers.

The school would be colorful and inviting. Its floors would be variously carpeted. It would have no ornamental and foot-forbidden lawns but extensive play spaces around the school—and on the roof and inside the building. The *childhood* of the student would be held in deepest respect. The school would be responsible to his need for play and fully aware of the developmental potential in playful activity. The sense that allows an eight-hour work day for adults to be punctuated by coffee breaks even in the name of efficiency will not be less generous in allowing recesses to the eight-year old from the strictures of his six-hour work day. The play spaces will be open to him the day round; the school will be community property and ungrudged to its community uses. Community control and *closeness to the school* will be reciprocals in the development of its ethos.

This school will conduct no *open-house* ceremonies. It will be an open school. It will welcome its parents, whom it will reach out to and induct into responsible roles in the learning process. It will spend some time in phasing visits purposefully and to schedule parental participation so that it will not overload the capacity of the school. It will diminish nagging and intrusive parental calls by turning parental concern into a guided and constructive study of the learning process as it is taking place. Visitors will be in the classroom in flesh-and-blood presence. They will also observe learning in special facilities under professional guidance by means of closed-circuit television. This school will undertake to educate the community about education as one of its fundamental obligations. It will develop community support, not by public-relations devices or by putting on shows for the public, but by showing them what education is all about.

The adult force of the school will be active in its study of the community. Not all of the staff, but much of it, will be drawn from the community, and resident within. This school will regard community involvement as a necessary qualification for its staff, for one definition of this school is that it is *community-involved*.

It will be a school that refuses to fail to educate. It will not use the name of *failure* in its dialogue or in its records. It will create the conditions for successful learning. When it has done that, it can put the responsibility upon teachers to see to it that learning takes place. On the whole, teachers will respond to these conditions. Those who do not must be first invited into programs of essential reeducation; if they are unresponsive and uneducable, a just and due process for "selecting out" must be established.

Our good school will reverse the common process in two particu-

lars. It will enhance intelligence, not diminish it. It will create enthusiasm for learning, not destroy it.

It will accomplish this by enhancing opportunity for freedom and
responsibility as the years go by, not by cutting back on it. It will
teach the children to read. Then it will make reading a constant
invitation. Each classroom will have its library of good books to
read; a child's choice of what to read will always be respected. Reading improves spelling, improves language use, is builder of writing
skills, is correlated with success in all manner of subjects, improves
measurable intelligence. Even more, reading is an essentially civilized
use of time, and it makes accessible the most valid and reliable source
of the answers humanity needs—*the book*. So there will be the library
and the little reading rooms along all the corridors. The library will
have an outside access so that it may be open and available after
school, during evenings, and on weekends.

The adults will be carefully taught. They will learn the delights of
teaching, and they will be instructed in the self-defeating quality of
the schoolteacherish. Each teacher will have a full hour of privacy a
day, an essential respite from the taxing obligation to be open and
responsive to the children all the other hours. The necessity of
learning to smile and to listen and to speak kindly will be impressed
upon those to whom these graces do not come naturally.

The evidence of grace will distinguish this school. Persons will
not be regimented into lines, shouted at, jarred by raucous bells and
intrusive announcements. Fire drills will be laughing matters because
the firetraps that now infest the scene will be demolished. A child
who skips through the corridors will be cherished not reproved.
Music will be taught, but not inflicted. The children will bring their
songs to school, not merely have the songs of the school put onto them.

Individual differences will be attended to, respected, and used.
But they will not be measured in precise terms and channeled into the
speedy pursuit of programmed learning or individually prescribed
instruction. Individual differences will be seen as being too important
and personal to be met by sterile exercises of somebody else's purposes.

This school will live with number and quantification. It will pursue mathematical system systematically, and it will extend its reach.
It will make the use and fun in arithmetic a constant. The meaning
of number and process involving quantification will be related to the
realities that the child encounters. It will not lack for problems to be
solved if it searches the child's experience for his needs.

Our "model" will have learned from the travails of high school and
college the consequences and roots of student discontent. Therefore,
it will consciously forestall alienation and rebellion. To do this, it
will build student participation in planning and deciding upon learning
activities into its everyday process. The student's presence will be
acknowledged every minute of the day.

This school will be sophisticated enough to realize that man's greatest need is to communicate. Therefore, it will reverse the purpose of its customary vigilance. The ordinary school, the bad one, watches its students closely. When it finds them talking to one another, it reproves them and "keeps" them after school. When this school catches students just talking with one another, it recognizes that the students are behaving in a civilized way. It stands aside to let the conversation proceed, and, if invited, modestly joins in. It will stop a fight, but not a dialogue. No matter what it is about? Yes, no matter what it is about! People talk about what is important to them; thus, let what is important to students come to school. The school must become the arena for the open forum. Then the students will trust it to listen without eavesdropping. Thus, the school can get the cues by which to make its education relevant.

This good urban school (which would be a good one in suburb or small town, too) would be a place of doing and good living. As such, it would delight the spirits of John Dewey and the old progressives, for it would indicate that they had not appeared on the scene for naught. The doing would include studying, which these students would have been taught to do. The counterfeit of study, the going through the motions of imposed meaningless tasks, would not be allowed in this environment for learning. To study is to inquire meaningfully upon a subject worthy of personal time and effort. Environments for study would be maintained and held sacrosanct. Such environments usually require quiet and comfort and privacy and freedom from interruption.

A great ingenuity and respect for study might teach the school to mend its ways with regard to study. Imagine a school so excellent that if a student had a "study-thing" going, it would not interrupt him for a day or for weeks at a time while he studied. Not to call him away from his books, or his experiments, or his practice for class, or assemblies, or games all that time, not even to remind him of lunchtime? Exactly that. That would be a school so excellent in its respect for *study* and in its regard for individual differences that it would verge on Utopia.

This school would keep itself. The children would learn to work by working, not by turning good learning into drudgery. The students would work. This will be an institutional adjustment to reality, not a throwback to Puritanism. Work, real work, is good to grow up on. When it improves and maintains the place you live in, it is especially fulfilling.

So the children will learn to sweep and to scrub floors, to wash windows, to dust and to tidy up. They will get a good feeling about school by finding that it is a place where you can get your hands dirty by necessity. They will arrange the books and furniture. They will sweep the sidewalks and mow the lawns. And for that matter, since somebody will have to do it, they can keep the bathrooms clean too.

It will not hurt them. It will be theirs to clean the tables and wash the dishes in the cafeteria. And they will learn to operate and maintain the audiovisual equipment around the place. Work will be central in the curriculum, for this school takes human competence seriously. And it will produce eleven- and twelve-year-olds that a pioneer community might have been proud of.

The adults around this school will have to possess more than schoolteacherish competence too. In teaching to work it is necessary to develop job analysis, and skill, and teamwork, and system. Work is not just blundering through tasks to get them done.

Teachers will have to acquire competencies to keep ahead of their students. This school is going to find out how things work by taking them apart and putting them back together again: toasters, clocks, carburetors, toys, lamps, radios, vacuum cleaners, washing machines. The children who attend this school will be able to do things which pioneer children never dreamed of. But even a pioneer kid could come to the twentieth century and learn to turn on switches and yell "fix it" to somebody if it didn't work. What we want are persons who are not basically helpless in the modern environment, as most persons are.

Take it from there. The good schools are going to be yours to make, not the products of paragraphs by textbook writers. They will be better schools if you are unconstrained by tradition and the limitations of institutional practice as now defined. They will be good to the degree that you liberate and nurture the complete human potential. If they are good enough for you to be well-satisfied, to take pride in your handiwork, you will know it by this sign: your school will be the happiest place in town.

topics for inquiry

1. The Ocean Hill-Brownsville Dispute
2. Conflicting Theories on Cultural Deprivation
3. Outcomes of the Head Start Program
4. The Teacher Corps Program
5. The Concept of Black Culture
6. Black Studies: Varied Viewpoints
7. Profile of an Existing Urban School
8. The White Teacher in the Inner-City School
9. City and Suburb: Contrasts in Life Style
10. Cultural Deprivation in the Suburban School

subjects for discussion

1. On separate days invite to class a panel of urban teachers and a panel of urban students, each to discuss the broad topic "Urban School Problems."

   How do the perceptions of problems differ between these groups? On what points are they in agreement? How do you account for any differences in viewpoint that may have appeared?
2. Should special programs of sensitivity training and black history and culture be required for all white teachers working in schools with large populations of black students? Explain your answer.
3. What bearing does the previous chapter on Social Class have on the question of urban education?
4. Read and discuss the recommendations of the Kerner Report with respect to education.
5. In *Humanizing the School* it is said:

   > The school will be humanized, the city remade by a
   > population that has discovered and asserted its own
   > worth. The educator will play a man's role in this
   > future, will be identified with the student with whom
   > he enters the school as psychic peer. Either will be
   > fit company when he finds himself alone with the other;
   > both will be capable of community; neither will need
   > to push the other; and both will be very difficult to
   > push. They will plan solid constructions, dream good
   > dreams, and love life together.

   What are the implications of this comment for education? What changes in institutional practice would be necessary to make such a condition a reality?
6. How would you describe a good urban school?
7. Was the school as you knew it a student and practitioner of justice? In what respects, yes and no?

selected readings

BERNSTEIN, ABRAHAM. *The Education of Urban Populations.* New York: Knopf, 1968.

   A very readable and erudite text on the subject. It is loaded with imaginative suggestions, practical and otherwise, for attacking the problem.

MALCOLM X and ALEX HALEY. *The Autobiography of Malcolm X.* New York: Grove, 1965.

BROWN, CLAUDE. *Manchild in the Promised Land*. New York: Macmillan, 1965.
> A pair of books that serve a special function in helping the white reader to cross the culture barrier to see something of what the life of the street means to the black person who grows up there. Both are shattering and illuminating experiences for many readers.

COX, HARVEY. *The Secular City*. New York: Macmillan, 1965.
> The best effort to date to attempt to mobilize the religious conscience for effective involvement in meeting the problems of the cities.

CRARY, RYLAND W. *Humanizing the School*. New York: Knopf, 1969.
> Chapter XIII, "Education for Urban America," and Chapter XIV, "Since 1967—The Urban Effort Reconsidered," particularly pertinent.

Daedalus. Journal of the American Academy of Arts and Sciences. *The Conscience of the City* (Fall 1968).

GREENE, MARVIN L. *Something Else*. Glenview, Ill.: Scott, Foresman, 1970.
> A fine example of a book for school use that can help the curriculum "get with it" and reach the children "where they really live." It is illustrative of possibilities for closing the relevance gap.

HOLT, JOHN. *The Underachieving School*. New York: Pitman, 1969.
> As in his earlier books *How Children Fail* and *How Children Learn*, the burden for educating and the responsibility for failure placed exactly where it belongs—on the school. Holt's point of view is compatible with the central thrust of this text.

KEACH, EVERETT T., ROBERT FULTON, and WILLIAM E. GARDNER (eds.). *Education and Social Crisis*. New York: Wiley, 1967.
> A useful anthology rich in anthropological and sociological data on backgrounds of urban educational problems.

PASSOW, A. HARRY, MIRIAM GOLDBERG, and ABRAHAM J. TANNENBAUM (eds.). *Education of the Disadvantaged*. New York: Holt, Rinehart and Winston, 1967.
> Another anthology with much sociological and anthropological data on backgrounds of urban educational problems.

Report of the National Advisory Commission on Civil Disorders. New York: Bantam, 1968.
> The famous Kerner Report, which every serious educator should know.

ROGERS, CARL R. *Freedom to Learn*. Columbus, Ohio: Charles Merrill, 1969.
> A prime resource for those who want practical instruction in developing a classroom based on trust, freedom, and open human relations. Very likely this volume will be a revelation to many readers.

The four books listed below give cross-sectional insights as to the human problems within the urban school. They are portraits of effort and frustration—the live stuff of teaching in difficult situations. The conflict of the person versus the system are vividly revealed.

HERNDON, JAMES. *The Way It Spozed to Be*. New York: Simon and Schuster, 1969.

KOHL, HERBERT. *36 Children*. New York: New American Library, 1967.

KOZOL, JONATHAN. *Death at an Early Age*. Boston: Houghton Mifflin, 1967.

SCHRAG, PETER. *Village School Downtown*. Boston: Beacon Press, 1967.

In addition to works by Claude Brown, a reading program on the "new" black American could include the titles that follow:

BALDWIN, JAMES. *The Fire Next Time*.
———. *Go Tell It on the Mountain*.

BRINK, WILLIAM, and LOUIS HARRIS. *Black and White*. New York: Simon and Schuster, 1966.

CARMICHAEL, STOKELY, and CHARLES V. HAMILTON. *Black Power*. New York: Vintage Books, 1967.

CLARK, KENNETH B. *Dark Ghetto*. New York: Harper & Row, 1965.

GRIER, WILLIAM H., *and* PRICE M. GIBBS. *Black Rage*. New York: Bantam, 1968.

15

OPPOR-
TUNITY
AND THE
FUTURE

In our concluding chapter we shall look at the future in two dimensions. The discussion will relate to your future by examining career opportunities—a real and legitimate personal concern for every professional. In conclusion, it will in broad terms attempt to look ahead, sensibly if not prophetically, to assess the prospects for man and the role of the schools in affecting those prospects.

The teacher's education is quite a different matter from *teacher education*. Teacher education is institutional; this book is a part of it. Teacher education is an attempt to give the student the rudiments of professionalism that allow him to enter the school with a competence that begins to match his certification. The teacher's education, of course, has to do with the teacher's life effort to keep himself a learning and developing person. That is a curriculum that each person must develop for himself. This book has suggested some of the potential content. One aspect of a teacher's education that is often neglected is the career possibilities. Teaching as a profession does not have tight encircling career limitations. Far from being a narrow blind alley profession, teaching offers high career ceilings, a broad variety of professional choices, and chances for excitement and even adventure. Therefore, a concluding overview of a selection of extended careers in education.

extended careers in education

No career in education is as important as teaching itself. Teaching is the conducting of learning experiences, which is what the school

is all about. The other jobs in education are supportive and supplementary to the teaching function; they exist so that more effective
teaching-learning situations may occur. However, this fact does not
diminish the other jobs. On the contrary, they enhance the teaching
function and are enhanced by their relationship to it. The other jobs
within the educational profession include administration, teacher education, supervision, school librarian, research, coaching, special education, curriculum specialist, audiovisual specialist, guidance and
counseling, organizational activities, and international education.

A lifetime in teaching is no blind alley. The oft-repeated intangible
rewards are not hokum. The tangible rewards today are not so bad
either. Improved salary schedules, fringe benefits, tenure, teacher
retirement plans plus social security—altogether these assure a reasonable participation in the American affluence, not too near the top
but well above the median income.

In the course of time new members of the educational profession
discover special competencies and interests that they wish to develop
and practice. Legitimate ambitions for other responsibilities, increased mobility, more decision-making power, even greater pay occur
to some. Among those who enter the schools as teachers are some
who find teaching less attractive than they have anticipated. Some
find themselves lacking the temperament or the necessary skills to
function happily and effectively in the classroom. To discover these
things, after a fair trial and thoughtful appraisal, does not constitute
failure or defeat. Many career decisions are made this way. Such a
decision does not even necessitate leaving the schools; not all educational careers take place in the classroom.

Thus it is important to career development and decision-making to
learn early something of the range and diversity of occupation within
the educational profession.

Whatever the career in education eventually chosen, it should stem
from an initial experience of from two to five years in the classroom.
Since the other jobs are supportive to teaching, this experience is
essential education. Most certification requirements support this
contention. Most of the other professional branches, including administration and supervision, accept the sense of it. The guidance
and counseling people, who are sometimes quite isolated in their
view of their work, are in continuing dispute as to the merits of the
case. However, the extended classroom is the place where education
takes place. This is where the student lives most of his school days.
The classroom is the place where the educator, whatever his role,
learns what school is all about.

In surveying the range of educational opportunities, it is essential
to take note of special qualifications, advanced educational requirements, and the duties and responsibilities of these fields of endeavor.

administration

Managing and making things go is the central function of administration. Administration begins with the responsibility or subresponsibility for a single unit of a school system, a building principal or vice-principal. At the summit, in a manner of speaking, is the superintendent of a large school system.

Administrators are the best paid of educational workers. In a sense, they carry the heaviest responsibilities. Ordinarily, they work the longest hours. Theirs, too, is usually a year-round job, not relieved by the long summer vacation teachers enjoy. The pay of the lowest level of administration customarily begins where the best paid teaching ends. The superintendent's salary is seldom less than twice that of senior teachers, often three times as much.

Within administration are numerous specializations, including budget and finance, school law, school management, personnel, building and planning—to name a few. Although these are the designations of special jobs, they are also some of the things that every administrator needs to know something about. Certification for administrators frequently goes well beyond the Master's degree in requirements. Because of the complexity of the job, and also because of the increased qualification of the competition, teachers aspiring to become administrators are well advised to consider embarking upon the pursuit of a doctor's degree in school administration. But before this, a more basic consideration should take place: a realistic appraisal of the special demands of the job.

These demands may be summed up in one explicit phrase: *the ability to take it.* The administrator, whether building principal or city superintendent, catches it from every direction. Students, teachers, parents, public, press—all direct their problems and their complaints in his direction. He is in the public eye; he is responsible. To be sure, that is what he gets paid for. But it is a telling demand. The administrator does not enjoy tenure: he can be fired, and, like baseball managers, he often is. In fact, the big city superintendency has become so demanding—to a degree approximating that of the mayoralty—that it is almost mortally impossible, a man-killer. Look at troubles and tensions that zero in on this office: racial issues, often accompanied by the politics of confrontation; salary negotiations, accompanied often by strike or threat of strike; tax dilemmas, compounded by advancing program and building needs accompanied by increased competition for the tax dollar; a public press, not ordinarily hostile to education but ever alert to exploit the news value of criticism of the schools, from any quarter, and of every indication of trouble and contention. Small wonder strong men have been known to leave this arena for the relative tranquillity of a post at an institution for teacher education.

First and foremost, the prospective administrator should ponder his ability to take it. Without attempting to summarize the abundant literature on the subject, other qualifications for this role may be stated:

1. *A sense of justice.* This is crucial to the conduct of a good institution. In addition, it is a tremendous asset for survival in the atmosphere of contention in which administration resides. Nothing succeeds in holding a man somewhat immune from personal abuse from contending forces like an earned reputation for being a fair man.
2. *A sense of humor.*
3. *A developed skill in human relations,* based on a genuine liking for others. He is fortunate, too, if he has rid himself of clinging biases. If these linger, they will render his best efforts hypocritical. They will become visible, and they will destroy his effectiveness.
4. *A trust in self* and, therefore, in others. The first rule of good administration is the ability to delegate responsibility and authority. The small ego may force itself by rule to do this, but it cannot live well with doing it. It will lose sleep over the work of trustworthy and competent associates; it will nag and irritate and be generally destructive of morale by constant checking and intrusion on delegated chores; it will be eager to find scapegoats and jealous of credit for work done.
5. *A sense of system.* To have such a sense one must have a profound understanding of education and a foundational conception of the nature and function of the school. Since form has congealed around antique functions so generally in the school, the new administrator must have the ability to create new forms to suit changing functions. Thus, a sense of system does not say an addiction to neat patterns and tables of organization and established structures. On the contrary, a sense of system is essential to the *creative* exercise of the managerial function.

There is more, much more, but these are some of what it takes. When you begin as a teacher, count yourself fortunate if your administrators have these qualities in discernible amount, but do not expect all in one person.

One necessary footnote to the foregoing must be admitted. Administration reflects a general antifeminine bias. It must be so, or there would be many more women in the ranks. Except at building principal level in the elementary school, there are hardly any women in school administration. No good reason exists beyond a very effective working cultural bias. This should encourage rather than discourage young women from declaring their intent to go this direction. Study the attributes required for the job; not one of them has a research-vindicated relation to sex. This condition is rooted in injustice; and there is an obligation to challenge injustice. Are we suggesting a new brand of militancy within the educational scene? Yes.

teacher education

One vocation in education should be specially reserved for those who liked classroom teaching particularly well and who more than ordinarily succeeded at it. Teacher educators should never be recruited from those who opted out of the classroom either from lack of enthusiasm or want of competence. The familiar canard "Those who can, do; those who can't, teach" is often extended to say "and those who can do neither, teach teachers." This does not need to be true, but when it is, it is terrible. Of course, teacher educators should come to the job via the classroom. Those who have not are usually "bad news."

Teacher education assumes qualification beyond successful teaching, however. Education is a complex process with a vast literature, a large body of research, and a great many unanswered questions. To be a teacher educator on the basis of passing on a certain number of practical tricks of the trade derived from one person's experience, however successful, is like being a cracker-barrel philosopher.

The teacher educator must be a scholar in education. He must know his way around in the literature of history and philosophy of education and relevant aspects of psychology, anthropology, and sociology. He needs to be aware of significant research. In addition, he must build his own specialization: methodological, administrative, theoretical, or curricular. He can never discontinue his studies.

Since teacher education takes place in a college or university setting, the educator who chooses this role must accept further institutional obligations. He will reside in halls devoted, as no others are, to the nurture of intellect. He must cultivate a life of the mind that is aware of intellectual domains beyond the purely professional. Furthermore, he must extend his educational concerns to include a study of higher education itself. He must do so if he is to be a responsible member of the institution, which is like no other, and he must do it because higher education is so "fast-grown" that it badly needs the inquiry and analysis of professional minds to make sense of it. In addition, the teacher educator, being a part of higher education, must not hitchhike through his career on the knowns established by others. He must, in a word, be himself a "puller of a good oar" in experimentation and research, which does not imply that he succumb to the pressure of "publish or perish." It is recognition of an obligation entailed within his role. The teacher attempts to communicate the *knowns* in usable form; the scholar attacks the *unknowns* and seeks to push the frontiers of enlightenment a little further outward.

The qualifications bespeak in academic terms the necessity for an earned doctorate. But they by no means speak of efforts that can well be suspended with the receipt of the degree. To the person content to admit these qualifications as obligations, teacher education is rewarding.

It also has its rewards. College teachers work hard enough but, in general, less hard than elementary and secondary school teachers. Certainly they lead lives less structured by school bells. Usually they are paid better than school teachers. Their career life is extended; their retirement programs superior. They have opportunities to travel, to write and publish, to speak, and to consult.

Teacher education is the teaching of teachers. It is a rapidly changing and demanding field. Its curriculum is affected by every contest and controversy reported in this work. It is a growing field. In fact, it is expanding in sophistication as well as in size. A "Triple T" program is now reported, perhaps apocryphally, to exist. Training Teachers of Teachers!

guidance and counseling

Often in both training and practice the dissimilar functions of guidance and counseling are merged. The guidance function is usually a matter of student personnel activities. It involves giving tests (rather too many of them), keeping student records, scheduling students, assigning to programs, and pursuing college and vocational placement for graduating students. Guidance is closely tied to the institutional role of the school. The talents required are somewhat scattered—a considerable talent for detail, capacity for systematization of a conventional order, a great tolerance for paper work, a willingness to spend a great deal of time on the telephone and in conducting correspondence, and a selfless commitment to helping students attain tangible goals.

Counseling, on the other hand, is based upon a highly personalized, noninstitutional, relationship with students. It is closely related to teaching of the highly existential variety. Its primary instrument is the one-to-one relationship. Like teaching, counseling is torn by dispute over the merits of many theoretical modes. These range from flagrant manipulation by behavioristic approaches to extremely liberative techniques in the nondirective manner of Carl Rogers.

The merged function of guidance and counseling contributes to the fact that the workers in this field are among the most overworked and frustrated employees of the school. The Conant Report recommended a ratio of one guidance worker to 250 students. Much more common ratios are in the neighborhood of 1 to 500 or 1 to 600. In practice, 400 students for each professional constitutes a pretty favorable working condition. In the merged function, this means that the bread-and-butter aspects, which are guidance, tend to dominate the actual job description. The typical professional in this field is one who spends most of his time on guidance and yearns for a little time to do some real counseling.

Actually, if the functions were separated, as they probably should be, the guidance worker should perhaps legitimately claim exemption from the requirement that he serve for a time in the classroom. He needs to know his tests, his college catalogues, and his employment-opportunities data. A large acquaintance among college admissions officers, personnel officers, and employment agents will serve him and the practical interests of students well.

The counselor, on the other hand, must know the classroom. It is only in the classroom that he will get the sense of the milieu in which the student lives. There he will learn how students in a particular school relate to one another and how students relate to teachers. He will discover the dynamics of social class and cultural pluralism as they operate from day to day. These learnings will help him to understand the students who come to him seeking counsel. He will better comprehend their frustrations, tensions, conflicts, and their cross-purposes because he has lived among their sources. Beyond this, a very practical necessity exists relating to the student caseload that he carries. If the counselor is to develop an effective program that reaches all the students, he cannot carry it all on his own back. Thus he will have to make a sizable fraction of the faculty counseling conscious. To do this in the face of other legitimate preoccupations of the teaching force requires that he have the confidence of the teachers and a well-established rapport with them. At best, it is not easy, but a colleague relationship is a necessary and useful instrument. When the counselor understands the goals and purposes of teachers and knows other than hearsay of the demands on their time, he is closer to that relationship. He will perceive both the common ground and the distinctions between counseling and teaching more clearly. In the atmosphere of a developed rapport, he can create a cadre of teachers who will work with him in homeroom, in class, and in other activities toward common goals in humanizing the school.

The counselor needs a strong professionalized education. He needs time with individual students to be reckoned in hour-long open conversations. The records of the guidance function are official property of the school. The less official, the more private and confidential the knowledge of the student acquired by the counselor, the more effective his contribution to the school. The institution and the individual are not in complete harmony; they never can be. The function of the counselor is not to institutionalize the student. The school has plenty of agents for that purpose. His job is to be found by or subtly to seek out those students who are lost in the lonely crowd, or are alienated, or in whom conflict with the institution is doing large damage. His job is to authenticate the person, to extend his perception of himself and his relationships, to help the person to develop the ego strength that will enable him to survive, to learn, and to communicate. He does this, it must be remembered, on behalf of the person, not the institution. However, the healthy institution will not be jealous of this function. It will respect its necessity and cherish it.

coaching

No disrespect is intended in listing coaching as a function separate from teaching. Coaching is teaching and teaching active in all dimensions of learning. It relates itself to groups and to individuals. It is rich in both the cognitive and the affective. It is evaluated in sterner tests than is most teaching. Academic achievement in this realm is advertised inexorably and publicly upon the scoreboard.

Yet coaching as a career does separate into channels of development away from the classroom. Success in coaching leads to more coaching, or to athletic directorships, or to upward mobility from junior high to senior high, or from senior high to college, and now and then to professional ranks. The fantasy life of every coach takes him at least now and then to the big leagues.

The coach is in the public eye at all times. Like the administrator, he must be able to take it. He is a vulnerable target of public abuse; coaching knows no tenure. Coaches, better than most, know that the public's favor is fickle. Consider a true incident. A few years ago a coach in a small town took his basketball team farther than it had ever gone before. The boys won the first tournament in the state series and went to the finals of the next tournament. In that game they met and lost a close contest to a high school with an enrollment twenty times their own. *Whereupon*, the school board (none of whom was known ever to have visited the school), who were all in attendance at the game, assembled in the balcony of the gymnasium at the sound of the final gun. They declared themselves in official session *and fired the coach!*

Such is fame. And thus, the desirability, if not the necessity, that coaches be philosophers.

The rewards of coaching? Coaches are paid better than the (other) teachers. In winning years they give talks for varying fees, and sometimes on nights off they officiate. A coach's life, though, is a taxing existence emotionally.

As most coaches know, coaching is not enough for coaches. Sooner or later it must occur to an adult male that a lifetime of teaching games to boys is not necessarily a complete fulfillment of manhood. It quite possibly, indeed, contains the hazard of arrested development. This does not disparage coaching or suggest departing from it. It suggests the advisability of exploiting the connections of the job with the total life of the school. The coach often becomes the principal object of trust for many boys. He becomes a father figure plus. There are hazards in this, but opportunity also. If the coach is to counsel, he ought not be content to do it as a rank amateur. In his field, he is a professional. It will extend his life-reaches if he will visit the counselor, talk with him, borrow his books, and invest himself with some professional competence. The coach too should study the whole life of the school and give much thought to how his work relates to the total educational purpose of the school. The most mature and manly coaches do these things.

Sometimes coaching serves as a good end run into administration. This is true because coaches are men, they become public figures, and the common culture is much taken with games. If the coach possesses the real qualities that a good coach or administrator requires, then he does well. However, when the coach acquires the title of principal or superintendent but retains the mind and concerns of an athletic director, it is a disaster.

research

Educational research is an important and growing field. Major school systems now have Divisions of Research; often these are limited in their activities to the primary function of collecting statistics about the going operation of the schools. Schools of education and independent research institutes also furnish employment opportunities in this field.

Research competence is acquirable from many sources. Training in the discipline and methodology of one of the social sciences is likely to be most productive in its applicability to education. In addition, since much research is of an empirical order, competence in research design, statistical methods, and computer usage is also desirable. A basic knowledge of the language of research and statistics is essential for general literacy, for the communication level of research reporting presumes such competence.

Though much resistance to the idea exists, educational researchers in any aspect of the field of education should be required to produce evidence of classroom experience. Relevant research depends on knowing what the real questions are, and it is from the classroom that the real questions come. Educational research presently enjoys a good deal of prestige and a large funding from federal and foundation sources. Unfortunately, a great amount of time and money have been spent seeking answers that were already recorded or pursuing questions of marginal importance.

Researchers in education at the moment tend to be of three basic types: (1) enthusiasts for a special process or device so that their researches tend to be contaminated by special interest and even enthusiasm, and results in studies that tend *to demonstrate* rather than to evaluate devices; (2) "money-jumpers" who find an immediate interest in whatever is known to be the present bandwagon of foundation or federal funds; (3) the "cool" men who are neutral to all

questions and devoid of all commitments except to the esthetics of research design and computer games. The prevalence of these types
is responsible for the fact that the only splash on the educational pond
stemming from research takes place when the size of the grant is
announced, the findings themselves producing merely the tiniest rip-
ples of significance.

Two illustrations will point up the uneconomical consequence of
researches that pursue wrong questions for lack of knowledge of the
full professional context.

Many millions of dollars of the Ford Foundation and the United
States Office of Education have been spent on so-called research on
the instructional uses of television. (Sometimes, of course, research
was simply the guise under which these installations were introduced
into the classroom.) The research found out *nothing* simply because
the question had already been answered. The essential research had
to do with developing television, a medium that would effectively
transmit in one direction a sight-and-sound projection of reality. All
educational implications and uses were present in the completion of
that research. Television could carry any part of a learning situation
dependent on the one-way transmission of sight and sound. Unless
the technology failed briefly, it could be counted on for that—and for
not one thing more. All of the expensive subsequent exercises, often
miscalled research, added not one iota to this basic finding, which was
a technological, not an educational, finding. The subsequent research
on uses consisted of incessant repeated testing out in varied classes at
varied levels in varied subjects whether what was known was known.
The application of television to classroom uses was not served by
redundant and repetitive demonstrations of the fact that television
really was television. Its uses had to be determined by persons who
knew what a full-dimensioned learning situation amounted to: what
part of it consisted of a one-way audiovisual transmission. When that
was determined, to varied extent from situation to situation, an intelligent disposition of the medium could be made. This would entail
a great range from instructional model to instructional model and
from one educational purpose to another. The sensible utilization
was not dependent on further research once the signal question was
answered and television was there. It depended on choices derived
from learning purposes and educational theory. So, educational researchers must know about these things to save themselves time and
money—and embarrassment.

Next, consider the research fate of teaching machines and programmed learning. Over and over the researches, even conducted by
ardent protagonists of the instruments, reveal the same dreary tale—
when compared to academic achievement of "conventional classrooms," no statistically significant differences. What was the problem? Not knowing, in an educational sense, what they were doing.
Had the researchers been better students of the conventional class-

room, it would have become quite apparent that they were setting out to do the same things, with only a different instrumentation. Both the conventional classroom and the instructional program run the same course. Both pursue a linear course through a predigested subject matter; both leave the student out of the planning and exploration of learning; both extinguish creativity; both turn inquiry into a blind-alley travel into established pathways; both reinforce immediately by cries of "right" and "wrong"; both motivate with extrinsic briberies; both perceive individual differences simplistically in terms of rate and quantity of learning. And, of course, both lead to similar outcomes—as much, or as little academic learning, and the reduction of learners to utter boredom.

Protagonist researchers, frustrated in their zeal and literally not knowing what they are doing, often seek refuge from the indeterminate findings. Sometimes they simply brush the research under the rug and increase the decibel count of their claims. In a manner that we choose to designate the "cry-baby posture," they often fall back on two defenses: (1) they protest the measuring instruments as being loaded against their instrument, and (2) they state that their products are in their infancy, that it is too early to expect a breakthrough. These are unpersuasive statements. One of your authors might once have broken the then world's record for the broad jump had his best effort been measured at ten inches to the foot; the other author could have been the world's fastest human if his hundred-yard dash had been timed by a slower clock. As for breakthroughs, these apologists forget the nature of true science. Science is reticent as to its claims until the evidence is in. Then the outcome is clear and apparent. The airplane is not invented until it flies; when it flies, it is an airplane. Jonas Salk and Albert Sabin broke through on polio prevention. They did not approach the public with a product that proved out to make "no statistically significant difference" and a rhetoric of hopeful apology for its future.

Research is a great frontier in education. It will need many recruits driven by passion to get at real answers to real questions. They must be dispassionate in inquiry and disciplined by science and objectivity. They must understand that many profound questions cannot be quantified. Among them must be persons schooled in other methods of inquiry: historical, philosophical, conceptual. They must have among them theoreticians competent enough in educational practice to do "action research."

The educational researcher must have his technical skills, and these of a high order. However, he must first be an educator. Then he will know what is already known and what the real questions are. He will have the capacity to systematize his efforts, not to tailor them to the demands of the grant market. He will be able to discipline himself to budget his efforts and his resources to a reliable guideline: a sophisticated set of educational priorities.

international education

The professional educator can, with sensible planning, enrich his career or life experience by seeking assignments in international education. He may elect to work in this sphere on a now-and-then basis, or he may actually build a full-time career within it. To avail oneself of opportunity in international education requires something of initiative and a spirit of adventure. Opportunity is, of course, enhanced and made more rewarding if one prepares for it.

Educational institutions now frequently offer solid instructional programs for direct specialization in the field of international education. Sometimes these are geared to rather general programs in comparative education; however, the more modern emphasis is directed toward professionalization in education as an institutional force in the developing nations.

Preparation for either occasional ventures or career development in overseas programs can be advanced by building such elements as these into the teacher's undergraduate and graduate education: language competence to a high level of proficiency; area studies concentrated on a field intended for special qualification, such as Latin America, Far East, Middle East, East Africa, West Africa; studies in history and politics, especially international relations; courses in the social sciences, especially anthropology and sociology. Such is the beginning of preparation for effective work in this field. If it seems demanding, that is exactly the case. No educational assignment puts more demands on the breadth and quality of educational preparation as does international education. In addition, work in this specialization requires unusual exercises of such personal attributes as adaptability, open-mindedness, sociability, and resilience.

One other area of competence is also essential. Whether he would choose so to regard himself or not, every American who works in a foreign location becomes an expert on American civilization. He will be increasingly, in direct proportion to the extension of his acquaintance, used as such. He will be constantly questioned on a broad range of subjects, such as American customs, public affairs, books and literature, cinema and drama, politics and economics, race relations, and the educational system. He might prefer to avoid many subjects, to stay close to exercising his "expertise" in the comfortable confines of his specialization, but the situation seldom allows him this luxury. Like it or not, he educates about America. What he teaches carries a sobering degree of authority. If his responses are notional and "half-baked," provincial and biased, superficial and misleading, that will be the sad limitation upon the way he serves his nation. Therefore, the international educator carries a dual burden of preparation. He must work to ready himself for effective effort within another culture, and he must labor to render himself capable of somewhat adequately representing his own.

The occasional participant in international education has such options as these to inquire among: teacher exchange programs, the Peace Corps, summer study tours (a rather limited and passive option); Fulbright teaching and research fellowships, teaching at American dependents' schools at overseas military installations. These options may be built into the apprenticeship for a career in international education as well. Long-range planning for such a career is best conducted under the advice and guidance of specialists in programs of international education. Most of the opportunities for career development lie in programs connected with governmental technical assistance efforts. These are accessible by direct employment in governmental agencies which conduct such programs, or by working under the auspices of a university that has contracted to conduct a project related to such programs. Narrower ranges of opportunity exist in programs supported by private foundations and international agencies, especially the United Nations Educational, Scientific, and Cultural Organization (UNESCO).

other choices

The exploration of career options has been intended to sample, not to create, a comprehensive survey. Other vocational branches within education offer different but equally challenging opportunities for persons of varied interests and talents.

The *school librarian* attends to the very heart of the school. Her job is to bring minds to the books, books to the minds. Axiomatically, she should know and love books. Yet in the school setting, it is more crucial perhaps for her than for any other teacher also to know and love children. Her act of love in this profession is simply to lead the children to learn to love to read.

The *supervisor* has very often been an agent of sterile institutionalization. The job of supervisor reconstructed can be for the teacher what humane proficient counseling is to the students. Educated as "change agents," supervisors can actually help the school to move from institutionalism to education. Success in the classroom and special professional education can lead to this responsible role.

The *curriculum specialist* needs to be the most widely read and most serious student of education on hand. The job is too often misconstrued as a maker of syllabuses and courses of study. Reconstructed, this position will provide educational leadership and make certain that the parts of the program fit into a coherent mosaic rather than pile up in a senseless hodgepodge.

The *audiovisual specialist* needs to be ready for a dual role: resource person to educate the school as to the variety and utility of available technical aids, and keeper and mobilizer of these tools within the school. Far from being an ardent salesman to push technology indiscriminately, he should be the most responsible student of the research on all these instruments and the most reliable source of cost-wise judgment on sound investment in them.

Government agencies, foundations, charitable organizations, industrial training programs, and publishing firms also have a wide range of educational, quasi-educational, and education-related vocations. Religious education is a special field requiring special motivations, but it is becoming increasingly professionalized in ways which establish common denominators with secular education. Special education, a field of broad variety and technically sophisticated varied subprofessions is rooted in two directions: (1) in the world of social services and health professions and (2) in the realm of institutional education as well. Like counseling, it is more basically dependent on one-to-one relationships than most teaching. No other dimension of education is more profoundly rooted in an activist concept of human concern.

The opportunities reviewed and touched upon do not cover the complete gamut of opportunities in education. Thus it is evident that education is far from a narrow-channeled field of vocation. Its opportunities are diverse, far-reaching, demanding, and exciting. Rich futures, well-rewarded, invite the individual. Yet, the future for any of us is increasingly dependent upon the future for all of us. To these prospects final attention is invited.

the schools of the year 2000

To wax Utopian is not the purpose of this discourse. The "impossible dream" is well worth holding. It is merely that it seems more appropriate to try to envision an achievable reality. Even our view of an achievable reality is conditional. The achievable reality is simply this: *America can have very good schools by the year 2000.*

If.

IF?

IF!

If the institutional paranoia among the nations is reduced to a contest in disarmament *so that* the institutions of world order may be translated into effective agencies for reduction of all disputes, *so that* the budgets of the developed nations shall be directed not to building the instruments of their fears, but may be directed toward what is truly fearful—the famine and ignorance of the underdeveloped nations.

If the school is given a true community in which to dwell—a community that sends its students to school, not as agents of its fears and hostilities and class prejudices and racial biases, but already instructed in goodwill and appreciation of cultural pluralism. Thus school will not be torn apart by cultural divisiveness nor so preoccupied with correcting and combatting home and tribal jealousies.

If poverty has disappeared as a mass phenomenon in the land *so that* education will not have to labor so hard to compensate for un-necessary damage, not of its own making, to persons who come to it; so *that* the prospects for a proper vocational emphasis shall not be so disparate among its students—so promising for some, so discouraging for others.

If some constraints of decency and ethics and legal controls are placed upon the other agencies of society that deliver messages to the mind *so that* the school will not have to contend with expensively financed campaigns that tell lies for profit, *so that* confusion among messages ceases to persuade the youth that there is no reality to de-pend on and no sense beyond getting something for yourself.

If the deeply ingrained and dominant value system of self-seeking materialism is brought into the perspective of a larger and better value structure *so that* a student may take some confidence that an ordinary man may have a decent regard for the common good, *so that* a concern for fellow man may be regarded as an achievable discipline upon all good citizens and not as a qualification for a saint.

If the effects of the present universality of education turn out to have been educational after all *so that* this and the next generation, which by the year 2,000 will have been graduated, are much more profoundly humanized, have lost some of the common vulgarity and childish preoccupation with games, have their identities more firmly established, have interests that endow and support the finer arts half as well as they now endow and support the absurd and vulgar.

Really it is all one IF. If the nation in its world has turned its intelligence and vital energies, and its budgets, toward the solution of its real problems, the prospects for education will be good. If not? If not, you speculate upon the prospects. They are too unbearable to set down here.

An achievable reality arising from these conditions adequately attended to could be very good to live and teach in.

Think of it. The children could come to school without dread of one another's skin color or family origins. The little children would not have to learn that each and all lived under the threat of a nuclear sword of Damocles. The teachers would not be indoctrinated in the myths that make failure a self-fulfilling prophecy for so many stu-dents.

The curriculum for each child could become inner-directed. His free explorations could discover his life purposes, even his vocation. He would achieve a secure self-identity. He would no longer be the pawn of the persuasions of the salesmen, of the "child-buyers" of college and corporations, of the manipulators of the curriculum that school has decided will be good for him.

The adolescent will have time to live a day at a time and still plan a long future. He will not reside in fear of conscription or in plans to avoid it. He will have a better use for his better qualities than to revile the absurd, shout bitterness at betrayal, inveigh against hypocrisy. The conditions of these "ifs" when contended with rip away the abundant source and nurture of the absurd, and the betrayal, and the hypocrisy that so offend the most serious and most sensitive today.

To achieve such a reality! Think of an achievement that would mean that the more serious and sensitive the person, the greater would be his satisfaction with his community and his school.

Think of what parents could be if they could greet the growing awareness of the child without guilt and without apology. The hypocrisy and the anger that create the generation gap would not be generated. The parents could stand without comment, knowing that the legacy of peace and freedom and friendly regard spoke its own worth. "Look what I've done for you" in pointing at a new car or wedding check would be antique behavior. It would no longer be said, or, if said, in smiling generosity, it would no longer carry the sting of subliminal reminders—"Yeah, look at how you still take your payment for it."

American civilization has tremendous achievements, noble commitments, and great resources. The future remains to be made, though it is in the making everyday. With wise choices, some of them hard ones, the future may be better than present prospects indicate. Though it draws on optimism and courage to say it, the future for man could be made very good. Humanity might emerge triumphant. A good future will not just happen. The course of happenstance is leading to disaster. It takes no large gift of prophesy to see that. Man must accept responsibility for his fate, decide to survive and to triumph, take matters into his hands to create the world he wants. He cannot do much bare-handed, and in ignorance his hardest labors will be self-defeating. His building of a future will require tools and skills, vision and enlightenment. The burden upon the schools is real and clear. *But* the schools that we do *know* how to conduct, if only we would, would be equal to the task. Then, *if* the effort were made, the remaining decades of the twentieth century might create a hopeful prospect for the twenty-first so that it might be the best, and not the last, century for man on earth.

INDEX

A NOTE ON THE TYPE

The text of this book was set on the Linotype in Aster, a typeface designed by Francesco Simoncini for Ludwig and Mayer, the German type foundry. Starting out with the basic old-face letterforms that can be traced back to Francesco Griffo in 1495, Simoncini emphasized the diagonal stress by the simple device of extending diagonals to the full height of the letterforms and squaring off. By modifying the weights of the individual letters to combat this stress, he has produced a type of rare balance and vigor.